The System 7 Book

The System 7 Book
Second Edition for System 7.0 & 7.1

Craig Danuloff

VENTANA PRESS

The System 7 Book, Second Edition for System 7.0 & 7.1
Copyright © 1993 by Craig Danuloff

All rights reserved. This book may not be duplicated in any way without the expressed written consent of the publisher, except in the form of brief excerpts or quotations for the purposes of review. The information contained herein is for the personal use of the reader, and may not be incorporated in any commercial programs, other books, databases or any kind of software without written consent of the publisher or author. Making copies of this book, or any portion for any purpose other than your own, is a violation of United States copyright laws.

Library of Congress Cataloging-in-Publication Data

Danuloff, Craig, 1963-
    The System 7 book : 2nd edition for System 7.0 &
7.1 / Craig Danuloff. - 2nd ed.
        p.   cm.
    ISBN 1-56604-027-2
    1. Operating systems (Computers) 2. System 7. 3. Macintosh (Computer)--Programming. I. Title.
QA76.76.063D348 1993
005.4'469–dc20   93-3111
                                                      CIP

Book design: Karen Wysocki
Cover design: Nancy Frame, Nancy Frame Design
Second Edition cover revisions: Spring Davis-Charles, One-of-a-Kind Design
Cover illustration: Katherine Mahoney
Proofreader: Diana Cooper
Editorial staff: Ruffin Prevost, Pam Richardson
Production staff: Rhonda Angel, Brian Little, Karen Wysocki

Second Edition 9 8 7 6 5 4 3 2 1
Printed in the United States of America

Ventana Press, Inc.
PO Box 2468
Chapel Hill, NC 27515
919/942-0220
FAX 919/942-1140

Limits of Liability and Disclaimer of Warranty
The author and publisher of this book have used their best efforts in preparing the book and the programs contained in it. These efforts include the development, research and testing of the theories and programs to determine their effectiveness. The author and publisher make no warranty of any kind, expressed or implied, with regard to these programs or the documentation contained in this book.

    The author and publisher shall not be liable in the event of incidental or consequential damages in connection with, or arising out of, the furnishing, performance or use of the programs, associated instructions and/or claims of productivity gains.

Dedication

Charles and Lillian Danuloff
Louis and Lillian Reisman

Trademarks

Trademarked names appear throughout this book. Rather than list the names and entities that own the trademarks or insert a trademark symbol with each mention of the trademarked name, the publisher states that it is using the names only for editorial purposes and to the benefit of the trademark owner with no intention of infringing upon that trademark.

Colophon

This book was created on Macintosh computers using various versions of System 7, ranging from pre-release versions to System 7 Version 7.1. It was written and edited using Microsoft Word 5.0 and produced in Aldus PageMaker 4.2 on a Macintosh Quadra 700. Screen shots were taken with Capture and Image Grabber, and edited using DeskPaint. Adobe Photoshop and Aldus FreeHand were also used for creating and editing some illustrations.

Digital Typeface Corporation's Garamond family was used throughout the book, with display type set in Garamond Condensed and body type set in Garamond.

Other Books by Craig Danuloff

*Encyclopedia Macintosh**
*Encyclopedia Macintosh Instant Software Reference**
Up & Running with PageMaker on the Macintosh
*The PageMaker Companion**
*Mastering Aldus Freehand**
Expert Advisor: Harvard Graphics
*Desktop Publishing Type & Graphics**

* Co-Author Deke McClelland

Table of Contents

Introduction   xvii

Chapter 1: System Software Basics   1
    What Does System Software Do? 2
    Parts of the System Software 4
    Using System Software 7
    Basic Macintosh Operations 9
       The Graphical User Interface 9
       Files & Folders 17
       Floppy Disks 18
       Macintosh Utilities 19
       The Clipboard and the Scrapbook 23

Chapter 2: The Finder   27
    New Finder Menus 29
    Finder Windows 34

    The Views Control Panel 36
    The View Menu 44
    Hierarchical Views 48
    Navigating From the Keyboard 51
    Dragging Files Between Windows 54
    Working With Multiple Files 55
    Title Bar Pop-Up Menu 57
    Improved Zooming 59
    Cleaning Up Windows and Icons 59
The Help Menu & Balloon Help 61
    Balloon Help Limitations 63
    Additional Help 64
Trash & Empty Trash 64
    Trash Tips 66
The Get Info Dialog Box 67
    Get Info for the Trash 71
    Get Info for Alias Icons 72

Chapter 3: Managing Your Hard Drive   75

Aliasing 76
    Basic Aliasing Concepts
    (or "How I came home from work with a tan") 76
    Creating & Using Aliases 81
    Advanced Aliasing Concepts 84
    Aliasing Folders or Volumes 88
    Using Aliases 90
    Aliasing Summary 95
The Find Command 96
    Using the Find Command 97
    The Find Dialog Box 98
    The Find Item Dialog Box 100
    Find Command Tips 105

Table of Contents

Labels 107
    Configuring the Label Menu 107
Comments 110

Chapter 4: **The System Folder**   **113**

System 7's System Folder 115
    The Apple Menu Folder 116
    The Control Panels Folder 119
    The Extensions Folder 121
    The Fonts Folder 123
    The Preferences Folder 124
    The Startup Items Folder 125
The System File 126
    System File Access 126
    Modifying the System Folder 128
    Adding Files to the System Folder 129
    Deleting Files From the System Folder 132

Chapter 5: **System 7 & Your Software**   **135**

System 7 Compatibility 136
    What Is Compatibility? 137
Launching 139
    Launching Methods 143
Stationery Pads 144
    Creating a Stationery Pad 145
    Using Stationery 147
    Stationery Pad Tips 150
The Desktop Level 152
    Dialog Box Keyboard Equivalents 154
Desk Accessories 156

Chapter 6: Working With Multiple Applications — 161

- What Is Multitasking? 162
- MultiFinder in System 6.0x 165
- Working With Multiple Applications 167
    - Foreground & Background Applications 168
    - Background Processing 171
    - Using the PrintMonitor for Background Printing 172
    - Copying Files in the Background 175
    - Hiding Applications 176
- Multitasking Tips 179
- The Memory Implications of Multitasking 180

Chapter 7: The Edition Manager & IAC — 185

- The Edition Manager 186
    - How Publish/Subscribe Works 187
- Publish/Subscribe Commands 191
    - The Create Publisher Command 191
    - The Subscribe To Command 193
    - The Publisher Options Command 194
    - The Subscriber Options Command 197
    - The Show Borders Command 200
- Editing Subscribers 201
- Edition Files at the Finder 202
    - Edition File Links 203
    - Unavailable Edition Files 205
    - Edition Files & Your Network 206
- Edition Manager Tips 207
- Inter-Application Communication 211
    - Understanding Apple Events 212
    - Apple Events & Program Linking 214

Chapter 8: **Fonts in System 7** — 217

- Fonts on the Macintosh 218
    - PostScript Fonts 219
    - PostScript Font Challenges 222
    - Printing PostScript Fonts 227
- Installing Fonts 228
    - Font Changes in System 7.1 231
    - Printer Fonts in System 7.0 233
    - Removing Fonts 234
- TrueType 234
    - TrueType & PostScript 235
    - TrueType Technology 238
- A Mixed World 240
    - Picking Your Font Standard 240

Chapter 9: **Introduction to File Sharing** — 245

- What Is File Sharing? 246
    - The Limits of File Sharing 249
    - A File Sharing Quick Tour 250
- Preparing for File Sharing 251
- Starting File Sharing 253
- Registering Users & Groups 258
    - Creating New Users 261
    - Configuring User Preferences 262
    - Creating & Working With Groups 264
    - Configuring Guest Preferences 265
    - Configuring Owner Preferences 267
- Sharing Folders or Volumes 268
    - Icons of Shared Items 273
    - Unsharing 274

Access Privileges 275
    Access Privilege Strategies 280
Monitoring File Sharing 283

Chapter 10: Working on a Network   285

Accessing Network Volumes 286
    Connecting With the Chooser 286
    Selecting Specific Volumes 289
    Remote Volumes & Access Privileges 290
    A Volume Access Shortcut 292
    Disconnecting From Remote Volumes 293
    Accessing Your Hard Drive Remotely 294
Program Linking 295
Networks With Macs Running System 6.0x 297
    Updating LaserWriter Drivers 297
    Accessing File Sharing Volumes From System 6.0x 299

Chapter 11: Memory Management   301

Memory vs. Storage 302
    RAM & You 303
The Memory Control Panel 303
    Disk Cache 305
    Virtual Memory 306
    Enabling Virtual Memory 308
    Virtual Memory Performance 309
    Disabling Virtual Memory 310
    32-Bit Addressing 310
    Memory Control Panel Tips 312
Controlling Memory 313
    About This Macintosh 314
    An About This Macintosh Tip 317

The Get Info Dialog Box 317
    Get Info in Version 7.0 318
    Get Info in Version 7.1 320
    Setting Memory Options 323

Chapter 12: **Apple's System 7 Extensions**   327
MODE 32 328
PC Exchange 328
Adobe Type Manager 329
    Using ATM 330
At Ease 332
QuickTime 333
    QuickTime Movies 335
    QuickTime & Data Compression 337
    Using QuickTime 339
ColorSync 340

Chapter 13: **Third Party Utilities**   345
Apple Menu Utilities 346
Trash Utilities 349
Alias Utilities 351
Font Managers 354
System Software Selectors 357
File Sharing Utilities 359
Extension Managers 360
Finder Performance Boosters 363
Utility Collections 366

Appendix A: **Installing or Updating System 7** 377

    Hardware Requirements 378
    Replacing System 6.x With System 7 378
        Back Up Your Hard Drive 379
        Prepare Your Hard Drive 380
        Run Apple's Compatibility Checker 381
        Delete Existing System Software 385
        Run the Installer 386
        Configure the System 7 System Folder 389
    Updating System 7 392

Appendix B: **A Brief History of System 7** 393

    The Many Faces of System 7 393
        System 7.0 394
        System 7.0.1 394
        System 7 Tune-Up 394
        System 7.1 395
        System 7.1 Hardware System Update 1.0 398
        System 7.0.1P, System 7.1P 398
        Which Version Should I Use ? 399
        Enablers 402

Glossary 405

Index 409

Introduction

Once upon a time, there was a computer that was incredibly easy to use: Macintosh. It was full of youthful innocence, simple elegance and a kind of conservation of motion that made it impossible to describe any of its operations as complex.

Today, the Macintosh is grown up. It has traded innocence for experience, simplicity for sophistication, and singularity for an incredible flexibility. Not surprisingly, the software at the core of the Macintosh has grown up, too.

System 7 provides powerful new features, extensive additional hardware and network support, and an expanded array of core technologies for software applications. Overall, it redefines the way the Macintosh is used, but it does so within the same intuitive framework of previous system software versions.

In the *System 7 Book*, you'll explore every aspect of System 7, learning how you can use each feature to be more efficient and productive.

Who Should Read This Book?

The System 7 Book was written for both the experienced Macintosh user who is upgrading to System 7 and the new Macintosh user who is learning the Mac and System 7 at the same time. The information provided in this book will suit users of every Macintosh model (since System 7 is compatible with every Mac) and applies equally to the casual and the habitual user. In summary, this book is for everyone who uses the Mac.

Experienced System 6 Users

If you have experience with System 6 and have recently upgraded to System 7, this book will

- **Describe each new feature in System 7.** You won't have to play the trial-and-error guessing game in order to fully understand the system software upgrade.

- **Provide specific tips on using System 7.** We'll go beyond the basics and look at ways you can take advantage of the new System 7 abilities to improve your productivity and enhance your computing power.

- **Explain ways that System 7 will alter the way you use the Mac.** There are a number of areas where System 7's new abilities will alter the way you do things. To help you make the most of these changes, I'll give you real-world situations that show the results of these features in your work.

New Macintosh Users

If you're new to the Macintosh, you'll want to pay special attention to Chapter 1, "System Software Basics." Much of the information in this chapter describes general Macintosh operations, setting the stage for System 7 features covered in later chapters. You could also consult other resources focused more on introductory topics, including the reference manuals that came with your Macintosh and *The Little Mac Book*, by Robin Williams (published by Peachpit Press).

System 6 Users Who Aren't Upgrading

If you're a Macintosh user who has not yet upgraded to System 7, this book will

- **Explain all the new System 7 features.** I'll discuss what's new in a way you can understand even without hands-on System 7 experience.

- **Give you a clear picture of System 7's benefits.** And you'll also look at a few drawbacks. You'll be able to make an informed decision about whether you should upgrade now.

- **Clarify System 7's hardware requirements.** A few System 7 features are supported only by specific Macintosh hardware configurations. I'll identify those that may require you to upgrade your hardware.

- **Wait patiently on your bookshelf for the day you do upgrade.** At that time, *The System 7 Book* will provide all the details you need in order to quickly set up and operate your Mac using System 7.

What's New in System 7?

Any great product improvement keeps the existing product's solid familiar features, adds exciting new breakthrough features and throws in subtle enhancements for good measure. System 7 is no exception. As a result, booting up with System 7 will give even the most sophisticated Macintosh user a renewed sense of power and possibility.

Broadly speaking, the new System 7 features fall into three categories:

- **Enhanced ease-of-use.** The basic metaphors that make the Mac so friendly, such as point-and-click operation of mouse and icons, have been extended, so that even more complex tasks—like moving fonts and changing control panels—are now more intuitive. The result is a Macintosh environment that is easier to use and customize.

- **Support for recent hardware advances.** Almost every aspect of Macintosh hardware and peripherals has evolved and improved by several orders of magnitude since the January 1984 introduction of the 128k Macintosh; but until now, the system software has never received the overhaul it needed to fully support this equipment. System 7 is a completely new system software, designed for the technology of the '90s.

- **Inter-application communication.** The Macintosh has always allowed data to be shared between separate applications, using the Clipboard or the Scrapbook. In System 7, the interaction between applications moves forward light years, not only improving data-sharing between programs, but also making it possible for applications to communicate with and control one another.

It would take a whole book to describe everything new in System 7 (hey, there's an idea); but just to whet your appetite, here's a brief listing of specific new ways System 7 improves the Macintosh:

- Allows file sharing between AppleTalk-connected Macs.
- Displays hierarchical outline-format views of nested files and folders.
- Replaces the Control Panel.
- Eliminates the Font/DA Mover.
- Enhances MultiFinder and Background Printing functions.
- Expands application launching options.
- Expands file-finding capabilities.
- Improves font display and typographic support with TrueType.
- Introduces the ability to store files in more than one place.
- Introduces live copy-and-paste of data between applications.
- Provides additional file information in Finder windows.
- Supports full-color icons.
- Supports virtual memory for increased RAM availability.

System 7 continues in the Macintosh tradition of providing intuitive features. But despite the range and depth of these improvements, a deliberate effort has been made to retain the Macintosh spirit, in commands and design elements. You may not even notice the improvements when you first use System 7—everything seems like the familiar Macintosh environment you're used to. But closer inspection will show you signs of change almost everywhere. We're not in Kansas anymore!

A Word About Versions

Since its initial release, System 7 has been enhanced, extended and updated several times. At the time of this writing, there are three main System 7 versions (7.0, 7.01 and 7.1), three different bug-fix/performance improvement extensions (Tune Up 1.0, 1.11 and Macintosh Hardware System Update 1.0), two special versions (7.01P and 7.1P, for the Macintosh Performa line), and a slew of system enablers.

This book covers all these versions of System 7. Any time the reference "System 7" is used, the features being described are common to all versions listed above. Whenever a feature unique to one version of System 7 is being described, the software is referred to by its specific version name, such as "Version 7.01" or "Version 7.1P."

A detailed description of the differences between the various System 7 versions, explanations of the tune-ups and enablers, and information on selecting the correct version for you is presented in Appendix B.

What's Inside?

The System 7 Book is made up of 13 chapters, two appendixes, plus the usual glossary and index.

Chapter 1: System Software Basics

In order to provide a context for discussing System 7's enhancements and additions, Chapter 1 summarizes basic concepts about the system software and the way it functions on the Macintosh. This information can be used as a review for those who need it and an introduction for first-time Mac users.

Chapter 2: The Finder

The Finder gives you tools for organizing and manipulating your disks and files. System 7's Finder greatly expands these capabilities with new menu commands, more ways to view and manipulate files in Finder windows, additional on-screen help, improved Get Info dialog boxes and more.

Chapter 3: Managing Your Hard Drive

Several new System 7 features can help you organize your hard drive more efficiently and access your stored data quicker and more conveniently. These features include "aliases," the new Find command, the Label menu and improved support for comments. This chapter shows you how all these features help you control your hard drive and other storage media.

Chapter 4: The System Folder

The System Folder remains a unique and important part of your Macintosh in System 7, but many changes have been made to the way you use the System Folder and its files. You'll learn about the new System Folder organization and many of the files and folders found there. You'll also learn how to modify and customize the System file.

Chapter 5: System 7 & Your Software

The introduction of System 7 will have a direct impact on every software application you use on your Macintosh; this chapter shows you how and why. First, the important issue of System 7 compatibility and the requirements for the new "System 7-Savvy" status are discussed. Then we look at some new features System 7 provides to all applications, including ways to launch applications, using Stationery Pads, the Desktop level and the new status of desk accessories.

Chapter 6: Working With Multiple Applications

System 7 allows you to open and use as many different programs as your Macintosh's available memory can accommodate. This chapter introduces the concepts and capabilities of multitasking, providing examples of how multitasking helps you work more efficiently. Included are discussions of the Hiding commands and the memory implications of using multiple applications.

Chapter 7: The Edition Manager & IAC

The Edition Manager and Inter-Application Communication (IAC) are two brand-new System 7 features that make a significant contribution to data-sharing between applications. The Edition Manager provides the much-talked-about "live copy and paste" that makes it possible to share data between applications and update that shared data at any time. Inter-Application Communication provides a framework that software developers will use to facilitate automatic data-sharing and communication between programs.

Chapter 8: Fonts in System 7

One area where System 7 presents dramatic changes from past system software is font management. The Font/DA Mover is no longer used in System 7, and fonts reside instead directly in the System file (version 7.0) or in the new Fonts folder (version 7.1). This chapter examines all aspects of font management, reviewing bitmapped fonts, PostScript fonts and introducing the new TrueType font technology provided by System 7.

Chapter 9: Introduction to File Sharing

When you're running System 7, you can share any folder or volume from your hard drive with any other computer on your Macintosh network. This chapter looks at the many advantages of the File Sharing feature, including granting others access to your shared files, controlling access privileges to those files and folders, and monitoring the use of your shared data by other network users.

Chapter 10: Working on a Network

This chapter looks at the other side of the File Sharing coin—ways you can access data from other Macintoshes on your network. Included is information on using AppleShare file servers and logging onto your own Mac hard drive from another network computer. The IAC feature of Program Linking is reviewed, and issues involved in working on a network that includes Macintoshes still using system software 6.0x are also covered.

Chapter 11: Memory Management

Additional system software features, together with today's more sophisticated Macintosh hardware and software, put more demands than ever on your Macintosh's memory. This chapter documents two new System 7 features that expand the amount of memory you can make available to your Mac, and focuses on overall concepts of memory management that relate to System 7's built-in multitasking.

Chapter 12: Apple's System 7 Extensions

Another important change that has arrived with System 7 is Apple's ability to update the system software without waiting for the next major upgrade release. Bug fixes, new features and other modifications can all be released in the form of extensions, and users who don't want to take advantage of the new features don't have to. This chapter examines some of Apple's special extensions—like QuickTime and ColorSync—that add significant power and performance to your Mac.

Chapter 13: Third-Party Utilities

While Apple has eventually provided—in the form of extensions—some of the features System 7 was lacking, there are still dozens of little things about the Mac and the way it works that most people would like to see improved upon. Fortunately, an army of third-party software developers and shareware authors are working to provide Mac users with the features and capabilities that System 7 lacks. This chapter looks at some of the best third-party System 7 utilities and helps you find software that picks up where System 7 leaves off.

Appendix A: Installing or Updating System 7

Unless you were fortunate enough to have Apple or your computer dealer install System 7 on your hard drive, the first thing you must do to get running is use the System 7 Installer. Appendix A explains how to use Apple's Compatibility Checker utility, and helps you understand the options and intricacies of the System 7 Installer. Also included is information on using the Installer on an AppleTalk network to install System 7 from a remote Macintosh.

Appendix B: A Brief History of System 7

Apple has exploited a major strength of System 7 in releasing special customized versions of it to different groups of specialized users. This allows Performa owners to have system software tailored to their machines and Quadra owners to have system software that addresses their particular needs. Appendix B examines the release histories and different versions of System 7 that have evolved since its initial introduction.

Other Sources of System 7 Information

There are many other sources of Macintosh information you may want to use as well:

- **Other books.** For the widest possible range of Mac tips, tricks and information for intermediate to advanced users, *Encyclopedia Macintosh*, by Craig Danuloff and Deke McClelland (published by Sybex), is selfishly recommended.

- **Magazines.** Popular informative periodicals, such as *Macworld, MacUser* and *MacWEEK*, provide the latest news on Macintosh hardware and software, including issues that relate to using System 7 on your Mac.

- **User groups.** It's a great idea to visit your local Macintosh user group. User groups provide local support on virtually every Macintosh topic. The introduction of System 7 will undoubtedly be the topic of many user group meetings. You can find a group near you by calling the Apple User Group Connection at 800-538-9696, extension 500.

- **Bulletin board systems.** If you have a modem, check out the many Macintosh-related areas on America Online or the CompuServe Information Service. They provide you and your Mac direct access to thousands of other Mac users and to many software and hardware developers. Spending a little time online is often the best way to get a Macintosh-related question answered; you can also browse through detailed information on almost any Macintosh topic and even download useful software utilities or upgrades.

The Ventana Mac Update

System 7 is the last word in Macintosh system software—for now. And *The System 7 Book* is the last word in System 7 information—for now.

In the coming months, Apple is sure to introduce updates to System 7, and new information and tips about using System 7 will be discovered as users accumulate more experience. To keep you informed of these developments, your purchase of *The System 7 Book* includes a free two-copy subscription to *The Ventana Mac Update*, a newsletter that provides up-to-date information about the features and use of System 7, as well as a wealth of other news, tips and tricks about everything Macintosh: online services, games, shareware, product reviews and more.

To get your free copies of *The Ventana Mac Update*, all you have to do is return the registration form you'll find in the back of this book.

Comments, Ideas, Suggestions?

We would like to hear what you think of *The System 7 Book*, and what you think of System 7 in general. Are there any aspects of System 7 you wish were covered more completely? Do you think our explanations and examples are clear? Did you find a typo? Please let us know!

Also, we'd love to hear any tips on additional ways to use specific System 7 features that you've discovered. We'll pass them on to our other readers in future editions, or in *The Ventana Mac Update*. And any questions you have about System 7 features are always welcome too.

You can send us your messages electronically or by letter at the addresses below. Thanks in advance for your comments and assistance.

Craig Danuloff
CompuServe: 76566,1722
AppleLink: PubRes
Fax: 206/524-4935

Ventana Press
PO Box 2468
Chapel Hill, NC 27515
America Online: Ventana500
Internet: Ventana500@aol.com
CompuServe: 70524,3216
919/942-0220
Fax: 919/942-1140

Chapter 1: System Software Basics

Why is the Macintosh so popular? Is it the "graphic user interface?" Maybe it's that all Macintosh applications use similar menus and commands. Or is it because configuring hardware and peripherals on the Mac is so easy?

The answer, as everyone knows, is "all of the above." But while you probably know how easy a Macintosh is to use—it's friendly, consistent and expandable—you may not know *why*. The reason is because the system software that controls the computer also gives it all of these qualities.

The release of System 7 has given Macintosh system software new prominence; the topic was rarely discussed in the past. And though this emphasis is largely due to Apple's marketing agenda, anyone who uses a Macintosh ought to understand the role of the system software and its capabilities, including how to use it most effectively.

This chapter introduces and defines the functions of the Macintosh system software. It also offers a quick tour of Macintosh basics, using some of the more common commands and features the system software provides.

This tour is designed for those who are using a Macintosh for the first time, and people who'd like a little review before diving into the details of System 7's features. If you're comfortable using your Macintosh, you can probably skip the "Basic Macintosh Operations" section of this chapter and skim "What Does System Software Do?" and "Using System Software" before moving on to Chapter 2, "The Finder."

What Does System Software Do?

What makes the Macintosh smile when you turn it on? Why does the disk icon appear on the desktop when you insert a floppy disk? How are fonts shared among all your applications? The answer to each of these questions is the same: the system software does it.

System software (or an *operating system* as it is known on other computer platforms) has three main responsibilities: it controls the hardware built into your Macintosh (and any peripherals you have connected), it provides common elements and features to all your software applications, and it lets you manage your disks, files and directories. Let's briefly look at each of these areas.

- **Hardware control.** In order for your Mac to work, its RAM, disk drives, video monitor, keyboard, mouse, printer and scanner (or other peripherals), must be individually controlled and collectively managed. Saving files to disk, drawing images on the screen and printing are examples of hardware control managed by the system software.

- **Common software elements.** Every Macintosh software application has common elements, such as menus, dialog boxes and support for fonts. These common elements are delivered to software applications from a "software toolbox" in the system software. Apple assures consistency among applications and spares software developers the difficult task of programming these elements by centrally providing these elements and including conventions for their use as part of the system software.

- **Disk and file management.** The Finder, which is a part of the system software, provides the ability to format disks, lets you find, copy, move, rename and delete files, and displays icon and text-based information about disks and files. The Finder also allows you to launch other applications, and acts as a "home base" when you start up or after you quit other programs.

Without system software, each application would have to provide its own self-contained operating features for running the hardware and managing your disks and files. There would be no continuity from one application to the next, and software programs would be far more complex, as well as time-consuming and costly to develop.

Fortunately, Apple's system software performs all these tasks well, allowing developers to focus on unique and sophisticated programs, while leaving the rest to Apple.

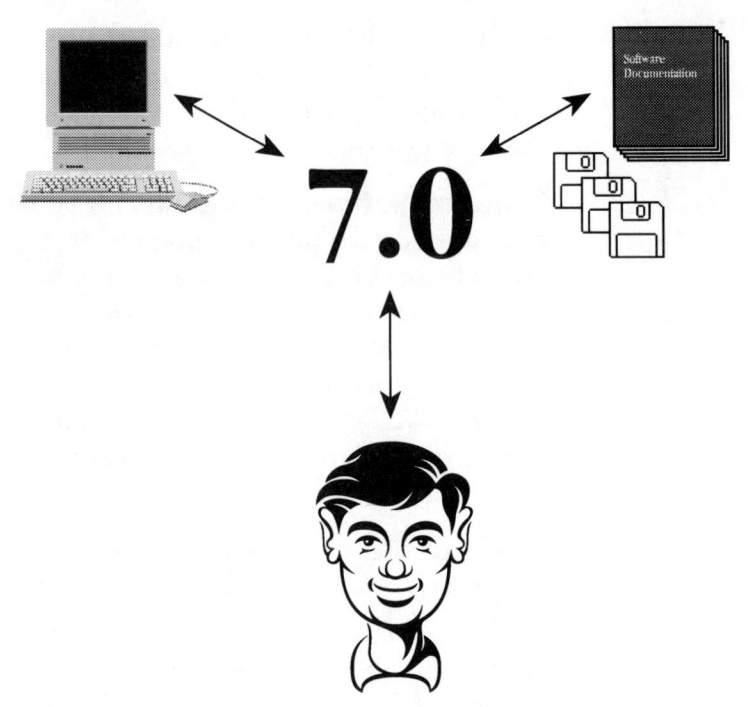

Figure 1-1: System software provides the link between you, your Macintosh and your software.

Parts of the System Software

The most prominent files that make up the Macintosh system software are the System file and the Finder, but printer and network drivers, control panel devices, extensions and resources (fonts, desk accessories, sounds, function keys) are also part of the system software. The list below summarizes the functions of these components:

- **System file.** The System file is involved in the most important and most frequently used aspects of the system software. It also acts as a framework that other parts of the system software can connect to. The System file helps the Mac start up, and provides many of the dialog boxes and menu bars, commonly used icons and code that help applications manage memory and other hardware resources.

- **Finder.** The Finder is a program designed to help you control your disks, drives and files. It provides many utility features such as formatting disks, printing disk catalogs and deleting files; it's also a "home base" for sorting and working with files and launching other applications.

- **ROM.** Portions of the Macintosh operating system are stored in Read-Only Memory (ROM) chips on the computer's logic board. These are not technically considered part of the system software, but they're vital to its operation. ROM-based software handles startup and many basic aspects of Mac hardware control.

- **Printer drivers.** Printer drivers are small conversion programs that change data from its original format into a format the printer can digest and output. Printer drivers are selected in the Chooser and "run" with the Print command.

    Apple provides printer drivers for most Macintosh printers and output devices, but other vendors offer printer drivers that allow the Macintosh to be used with output devices that Apple drivers don't necessarily support.

- **Network drivers.** Network drivers are also accessed using the Chooser control panel. They help your Macintosh communicate with network file servers, print service, remote modems and other network devices. Apple provides network drivers for AppleTalk, Ethernet and Token Ring network communications. Many other network drivers are provided along with third-party Macintosh network hardware.

- **Extensions.** Because Macintosh system software is modular, it can be enhanced, modified or extended by small files that temporarily become part of the system software when loaded at startup. These files are called extensions. (They were called INITs in previous versions of the system software.)

    Several extensions are provided with the system software, but most are created independently by third parties. Most extensions add some new feature or capabilities to the system software. Examples include Super-Clock!, which displays the current time on your menu bar; DiskDoubler, which lets you compress your files to save drive space; and Suitcase II, which makes using fonts, sounds and FKEYs more convenient.

- **Resources.** Resource files also add capabilities to the Macintosh. Resources, including fonts and sounds, can exist as stand-alone files or can be placed into the System file itself.

- **Control panels.** These are mini-applications that provide preference or general control over some aspect of the system software, an extension utility or a hardware peripheral. Control panels, provided along with the system software, control your Mac's memory, its internal clock, colors, File Sharing and many other system attributes. At the system level, control panels work much like extensions, but they feature an interface which offers the user control over certain variables in the device's function.

- **Desk accessories.** These are also independent files, and in System 7 they operate just like normal applications. (In previous versions of the system software, desk accessories were special files accessed only from the Apple Menu.) Desk accessories (DAs) provide utility functions not built into the system software. DAs provided as part of the system software include the Chooser, Alarm clock, Calculator and Key Caps.

Using System Software

System software is used almost constantly from the moment you turn on your Macintosh. To further help you understand its role, let's take a look at a few of the tasks it controls or assists:

- **Startup.** From just a moment after the power is turned on, your Macintosh's system software controls the startup process, running any available extensions, verifying that your hardware is functioning properly and loading the Finder.

- **File management.** When you work on the Finder desktop, manipulating windows and icons, your actions are translated from the on-screen graphic display into actual changes to the files on disk. But files aren't stored on disk as cute little icons; they're simply strings of magnetic 1's and 0's. It's the system software that turns them into meaningful text, graphics, sounds and moving images.

- **Application launching.** When you run a software program, the system software accesses the computer and sees to it that the correct portions of the file are read from disk, that the available memory is properly managed and that data files (and sometimes temporary work files) are created and maintained on disk.

- **Font usage.** Every time a font is used on the Macintosh, whether it's a bitmapped, PostScript or TrueType font, character information, including the way it should look in any particular size and style, is provided by the system software.

- **Dialog boxes.** System software provides the basic format of almost every dialog box used on the Macintosh. For Open... and Save As... dialogs, the system software also supports the scrolling file listing and reading or writing files.

- **Printing.** An application must pass its data through one of the system software's printer drivers so it can be converted into a format the printer can understand. After this, the system software communicates the file to the printer, and in some cases receives feedback from the printer during output.

- **Screen display.** System software is responsible for producing the display that appears on your Macintosh screen. Applications communicate the display information to the system software in a format called QuickDraw; then the ROM-based portions of the system software convert this information and use it to draw the screen.

- **Networking.** Nearly every aspect of communication between the Mac and its peripherals is controlled by the system software. This includes data transfer from the disk to the AppleTalk port (and other ports); the timing of operating network communications while other software is being run on-screen; cabling; and two-way communications with sophisticated printers, modems and storage drives.

So as you can see, almost any task you perform on your Macintosh—from the smallest mouse click to the largest data transfer—relies on the system software. Fortunately, you don't need to understand the technical intricacies of how system software does its tasks in order to use your Macintosh. But it is useful to have an appreciation for the range and depth of the system software's functions.

Basic Macintosh Operations

From the technical descriptions of the system software provided above, we'll now turn to the easiest and most fundamental aspects of using the Macintosh. This section looks at the things you do need to know in order to use the Macintosh efficiently. It also defines terms you'll encounter throughout the book.

This information is intended primarily for those who are using System 7 in their first experience on the Macintosh. If you've been working with the Macintosh under system software 6.0x, you'll probably want to skip this section and move ahead to Chapter 2, "The Finder."

The Graphical User Interface

The first and most fundamental requirement for using the Mac is understanding its graphical user interface. Instead of communicating your commands in words, you select pictures—or icons—that represent words. These icons, along with windows and menus, represent Macintosh hardware and software functions and features. And you use the mouse cursor to communicate with the Macintosh. (Yes, you'll use the keyboard too, but we'll assume you've already mastered that device.)

Let's look at each of these elements individually:

- **Icons.** These are small graphics (drawings) of things that appear on the Macintosh screen and represent items such as disks and folders (the icon actually looks like a disk or folder, as shown in Figure 1-2).

Figure 1-2: Disk and folder icons.

Various versions of icons are used to represent files stored on your disks. The particular version of a file's icon tells you what kind of file it is. The standard application file icon and the standard document file icon are shown in Figure 1-3. But many application and document files use custom icons. A collection of custom application and document file icons appears in Figure 1-4.

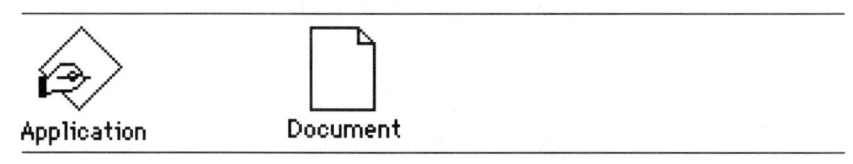

Figure 1-3: Standard application and document file icons.

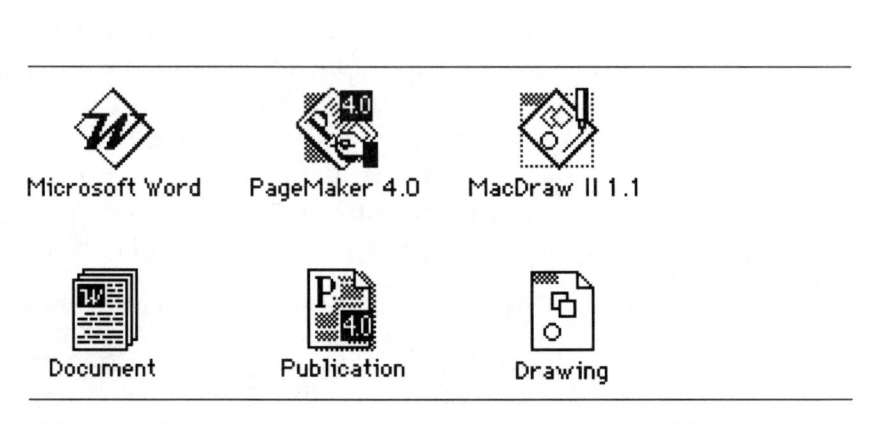

Figure 1-4: Custom application and document file icons.

- **Windows.** When a Macintosh file is opened, its contents are displayed in a window. The most common type of window looks like the one shown in Figure 1-5: it includes a *title bar* at the top and scroll bars on its right and bottom edges. You can move a window around (by dragging its title bar), close a window (by clicking the close box in its upper left corner), and change the size of a window (by dragging the size box in its lower right corner).

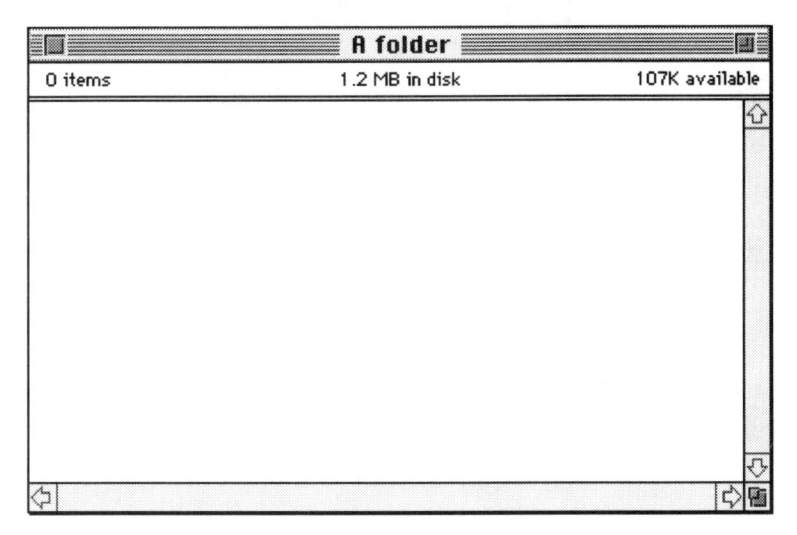

Figure 1-5: A sample Finder window.

However, there are other types of windows, including *dialog boxes*. A sample dialog box is shown in Figure 1-6. These small specialized windows usually present a set of options that allow you to customize a command or activity.

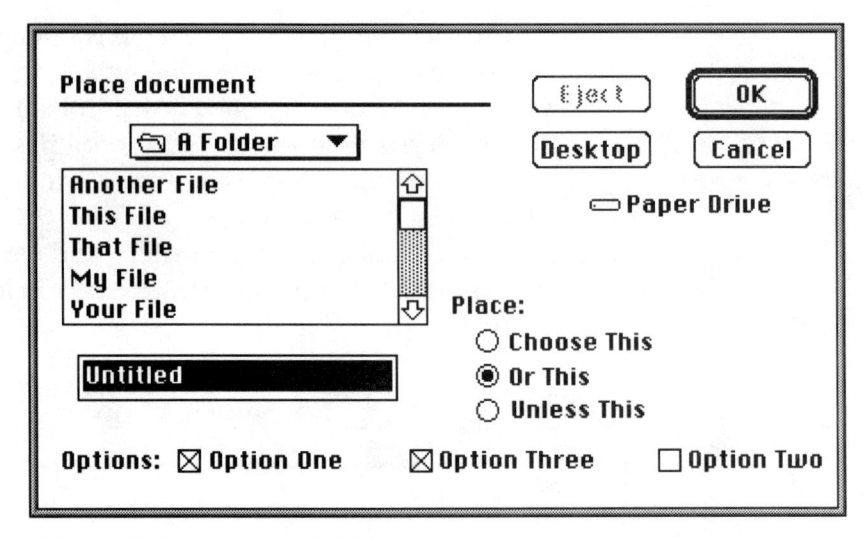

Figure 1-6: A sample dialog box.

There are four common kinds of dialog box options. Small round *radio buttons* present a set of mutually exclusive choices. Small square *check boxes* present a set of choices you can select in any combination. An *option box* is a small area where you type in your choice. Some options provide a set of alternatives in a *pop-up menu*; you can click on the one you want with the mouse.

Some dialog boxes don't present options but simply provide information. Usually this information is feedback concerning a command or action you're engaged in, or a message from one of your hardware devices. These are called *Alert dialogs*; a sample is displayed in Figure 1-7.

Chapter 1: System Software Basics 13

Figure 1-7: An Alert dialog box.

Another type of window, used in some software applications, is called a palette. A palette is a small "floating" window, so called because you can move it around easily. Unlike an ordinary dialog box, which disappears after you've selected options or dismissed it, palettes may remain open for the duration of a work session. A palette presents a set of icons that represent tools you can work with; or sometimes it presents a text list of commands or options you can choose from.

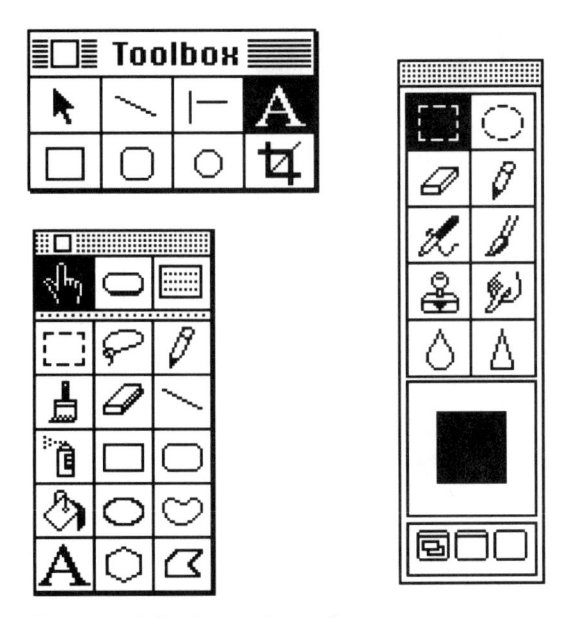

Figure 1-8: Sample palettes.

- **Menus.** Most commands in Macintosh applications are presented in menus displayed along the menu bar at the top of the screen. Commands are usually grouped logically, with logical names that provide clues about what they're used for.

    Menus drop down when the mouse is clicked on the menu name; they remain visible for as long as the mouse button is pressed. As you drag the mouse down, each command highlights as it's selected. Releasing the mouse while the command is selected executes that command. (More about using the mouse later in this chapter.)

    There are four basic types of menu commands. Some commands execute as soon as they're selected. Others toggle the status of some features on and off. Command names that end with an ellipsis points (...) bring up a dialog box of related options.

    And the fourth type presents a hierarchical display of subcommands. Holding the mouse button down lets you select one of these normal, toggling or ellipsis subcommands. Examples of all four command types are shown in Figure 1-9.

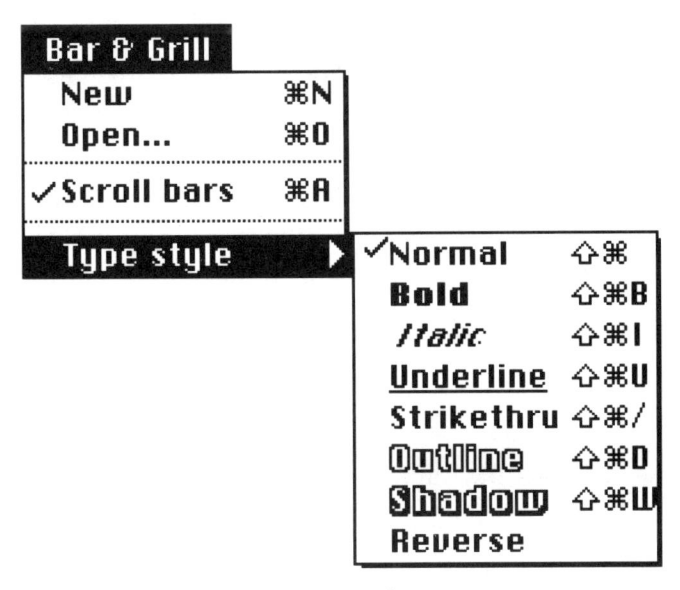

Figure 1-9: Four command types.

All these graphic elements interact with your Macintosh via mouse manipulation. Operating the mouse is simple enough: you move the mouse on your desk and the mouse cursor moves on-screen accordingly. The type of cursor that appears at any given time depends on the item being pointed to, the software being used, the commands chosen and the keys pressed on the keyboard. When working in the Finder, the mouse cursor will be the arrow.

Arrow cursors appear whenever you're pointing to the menu bar, regardless of the application being used. Macintosh applications also use the arrow cursor to select and manipulate objects. Other common cursors are shown in Figure 1-10.

Figure 1-10: Common cursors.

There are five common actions you can make with the cursor. These actions manipulate icons, invoke Macintosh commands and control application tools:

- **Pointing.** Positioning the cursor over a particular icon or other object or window element. If the cursor is an arrow, the arrow's tip marks the specific point. Other cursors have their own "hot spots."

- **Clicking.** Quickly pressing and releasing the mouse button. In most cases, the click executes when the button is fully released, not while it's depressed. Mouse clicks select objects, including icons, buttons and dialog box options.

- **Double-clicking.** Pressing and releasing the mouse button twice in rapid succession. Most beginners don't double-click fast enough to prevent the Macintosh from interpreting them as two single clicks instead of one double-click. Double-clicking controls many Macintosh actions, like opening icons to display their windows.

- **Pressing.** Holding down the mouse button while a command or action is completed. For example, the mouse button must be held down for menus—they're visible on-screen only while the mouse button is down.

- **Dragging.** Moving the mouse—and therefore the cursor—while the mouse button is pressed (held down). This action usually moves an item or causes the current cursor tool to be used while the mouse button is down (such as drawing a line with a pencil tool).

Files & Folders

Once you understand icons and windows, and you're comfortable working your mouse, you're ready to put all that knowledge and skill to work. One of the most important tasks will be manipulating files on the desktop.

There are many different types of files—including applications, data documents, system software files, utilities, fonts and dictionaries. To keep all these files organized, you'll put them into *folders*. You can create new folders to hold any type of file whenever you like, using the File Menu's New Folder command. You can also create folders inside other folders, establishing a hierarchical arrangement of files and folders, as shown in Figure 1-11.

To reposition files or folders—adding them to a folder, or copying them to another disk or hard drive—point to the icon of the file or folder you want to manipulate, click and hold the mouse button, drag the file onto the destination icon and release the mouse button. If you drag files to a different folder on the same disk, the files are *moved* (they now appear only in the new location, not in the old location). If you drag files to a different disk, or to a folder on a different disk, they're *copied* (they appear—and exist—in their new location and the old location).

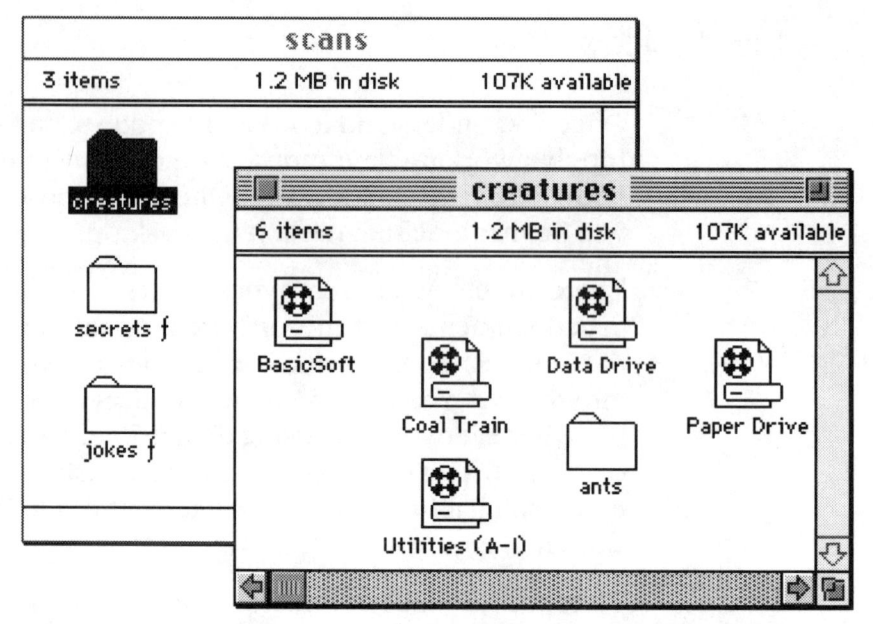

Figure 1-11: In this example, the "ants" folder is inside the "creatures" folder which is inside the "scans" folder.

Floppy Disks

Two types of floppy disk are supported by the Macintosh: *800k* floppies, (sometimes known as "regular" or "double-density") and *1.44 Mb* floppies (sometimes called "high-density.") Most Macs can use either disk type, but some (Mac Plus, Classic, Mac II and older Macintosh SEs) can use 800k disks only.

Before using a floppy disk for the first time, it must be *formatted*. This erases the disk and prepares it for use. (If the disk has been used before, formatting erases whatever is on it.) When you insert a new floppy disk, the Macintosh can tell that the disk has never been used, and asks you if you want to format it. You can reformat a disk at any time, deleting all its

Chapter 1: System Software Basics   19

files, by inserting the disk, selecting its icon and choosing the Erase Disk... command from the Special Menu.

Macintosh Utilities

There are several built-in utilities you use frequently when you're working on the Macintosh:

- **The Chooser** This desk accessory is an electronic switchbox that lets you select from printers, networks and file servers your Macintosh is connected to. The Chooser appears, as shown in Figure 1-12, when its name is chosen from the Apple Menu. On the left side of the Chooser are icons representing the devices that may be available. Selecting an icon brings up a list, in the right side of the dialog box, of available devices. Selecting the name of the device you want connects your Macintosh to that device.

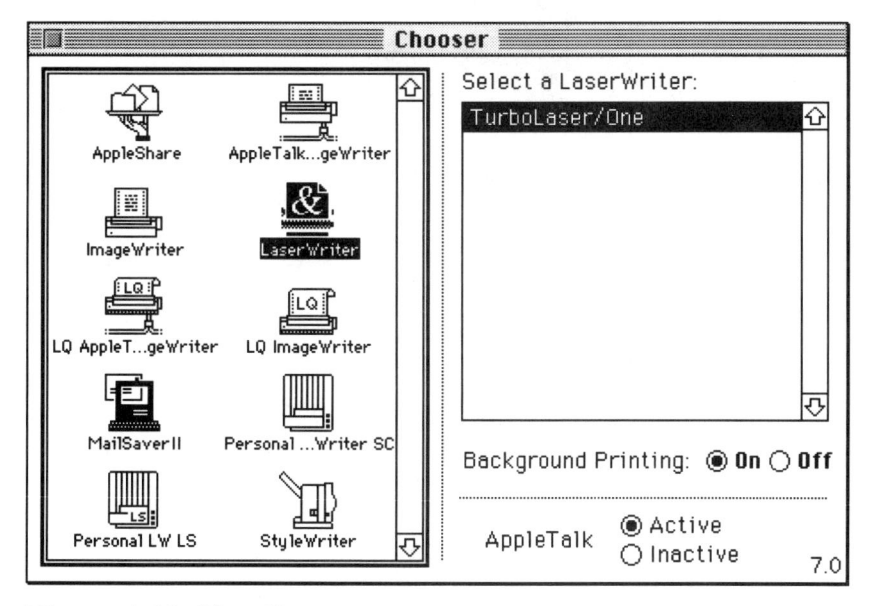

Figure 1-12: The Chooser.

- **Control Panels** Several of the control panels in the Control Panels folder, accessed in the Apple Menu, are used to specify basic settings and preferences for your Macintosh.

    The *General control panel* is used to set the color and pattern that appears on the desktop, as well as other aspects of how the Finder functions. The General control panel is shown in Figure 1-13.

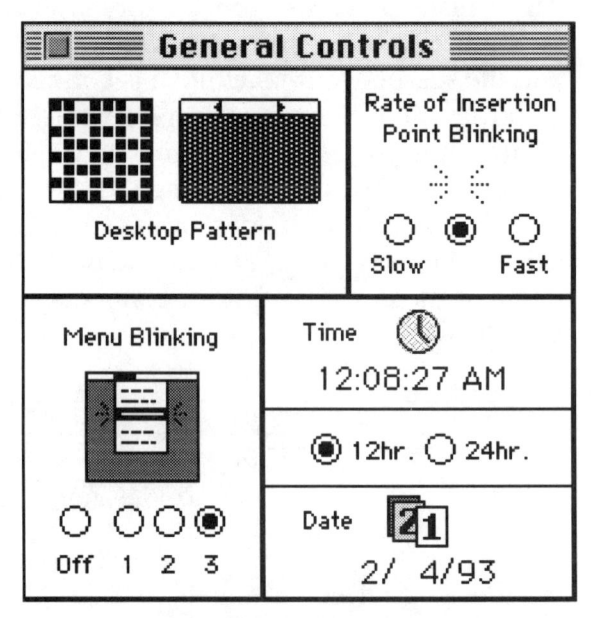

Figure 1-13: The General control panel.

The *Monitors control panel* is used to define your monitor's display of colors or gray values. It also lets you set the relative position of each monitor, if you have more than one connected to your Macintosh. The Monitors control panel is shown in Figure 1-14.

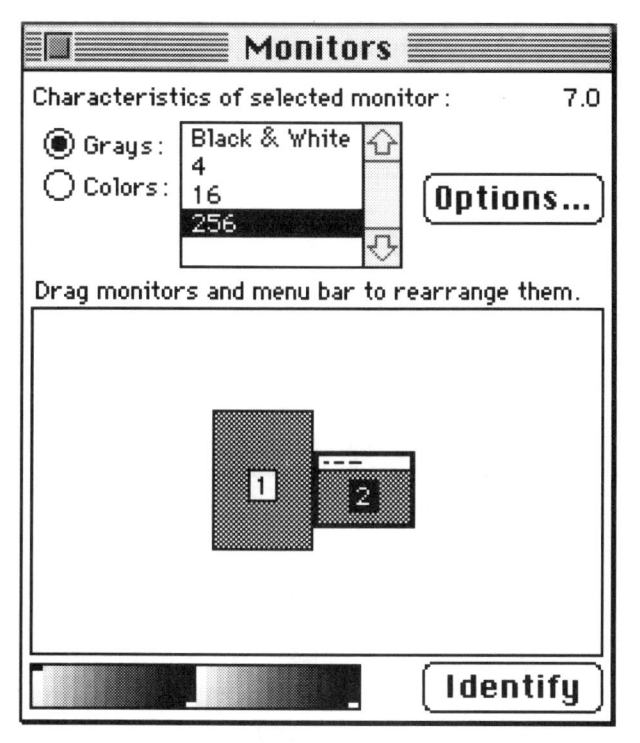

Figure 1-14: The Monitors control panel.

The *Mouse control panel* is used to define the speed of your on-screen cursor relative to how fast you move the mouse, and the amount of delay between clicks which will be interpreted as two separate mouse clicks instead of one double-click. The Mouse control panel is shown in Figure 1-15.

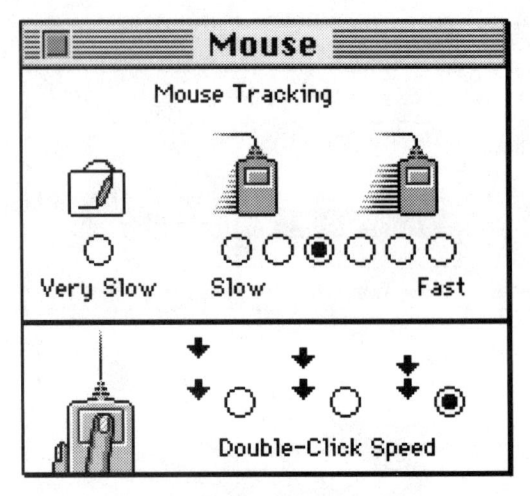

Figure 1-15: The Mouse control panel.

The *Sound control panel* lets you specify the volume and type of sound used as the system beep. Several sound options are provided, and many more are available from bulletin boards and user groups. If your Mac has a built-in microphone, you can even create your own sound. The Sound control panel is shown in Figure 1-16.

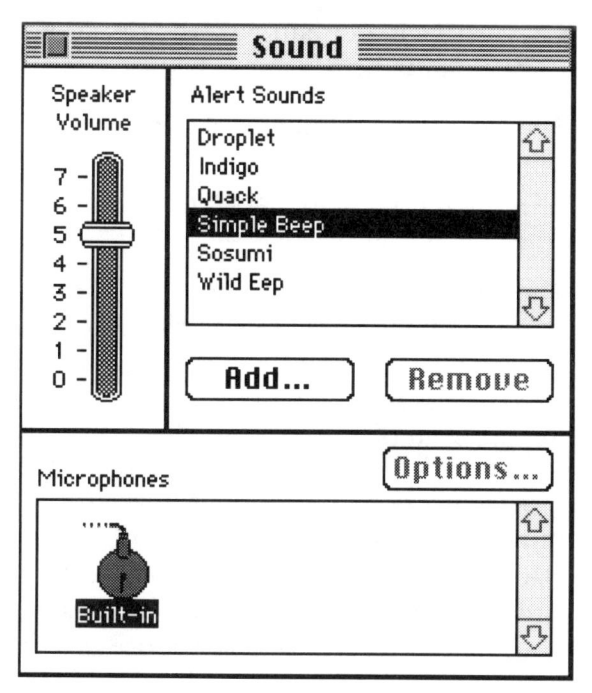

Figure 1-16: The Sound control panel.

The Clipboard and the Scrapbook

The Macintosh system software provides a simple built-in method for transferring text, sounds, graphic elements, and even movies from one location to another—the Clipboard. You can use the Clipboard to move items within a document or from one document to another—even if the documents were created by different software applications.

You never access the Clipboard directly; instead, you manipulate the contents of the Clipboard using the Cut, Copy and Paste commands.

- The Cut command removes the selected objects from their current location and places them on the Clipboard, replacing the previous Clipboard contents. (The

Clipboard can contain only the result of the last Cut or Copy command.)

- The Copy command places the selected objects on the Clipboard, but leaves them in their current location as well. The objects that are copied replace the previous contents of the Clipboard.

- The Paste command places a copy of the objects currently on the Clipboard into the current document at the cursor location. Using the Paste command does not remove items from the Clipboard; you can paste the same item repeatedly.

There are many ways to use the Clipboard. The most common is to move an element—like a paragraph or graphic item—from one place to another in the same document. To do this, you select the element, choose the Cut command, position the cursor at the new location, and choose the Paste command.

The Clipboard is also used to move elements between different documents, even ones created by different applications. For example, to move a chart from a file you created with your spreadsheet into a word processor file:

- Open the spreadsheet and choose the chart. Use the Copy command, since you want to leave the chart in the spreadsheet even after it has been moved to the word processor.

- Open the word processor, or switch to it if it's already open. Open the document that will receive the copied chart. You can quit the spreadsheet, but it's not necessary. (Details on opening and switching between several applications are presented in Chapter 6, "Working With Multiple Applications.")

- Position the cursor in the word processor file where you want the chart placed. Choose the Paste command.

Another related Macintosh tool is the Scrapbook, a desk accessory that can hold a catalog of text and graphic elements you use frequently or need to move from one document to another. Elements are moved into or out of the Scrapbook via the Clipboard and the Cut, Copy and Paste commands previously described. A Scrapbook displaying a single element is shown in Figure 1-17.

Figure 1-17: The Scrapbook.

For example, if you needed to use a set of icons throughout a magazine layout you were creating, you could transfer them all into the Scrapbook and access them from there as needed. To do this, you would:

- Open the file containing the icons. Select one icon, and choose the Copy command to move it to the Clipboard.

- Open the Scrapbook, and choose the Paste command to move the icon on the Clipboard into the Scrapbook. The Scrapbook automatically creates a new page each time you paste in a new element.

- Go back to the file containing the icons, select another icon, and again use the Copy command to move it to the Clipboard. Access the Scrapbook again, and paste in the new icon. Repeat this process until the Scrapbook contains all the needed icons.

- Open your page layout program, and as each icon is needed, open the Scrapbook, locate the icon, and use the Copy command to transfer it from the Scrapbook onto the Clipboard. Set the cursor at the location where the icon is needed, and choose the Paste command to transfer the icon into your layout. Repeat this procedure until all icons are in place.

Moving On

System software is the core of what we think of as the Macintosh. System software makes it possible for the computer to interact with other programs. It also helps in controlling Mac hardware and peripherals. System software standardizes the Macintosh, and allows software developers to produce high-quality applications.

Some of the features the Mac's system software provides to the user include

- Icons, Windows and Dialog Boxes
- Mouse controls and Menus
- Windows and palettes
- The Clipboard and Scrapbook

In Chapter 2 we'll examine another important aspect of system software, the Finder, which provides tools that help you to control the disks and files you use on the Macintosh.

Chapter 2: The Finder

Most people don't think of the Finder as a software application, but it really is—just like your word processor, spreadsheet or graphics program. But while each of those other applications is dedicated to the creation and manipulation of one specific type of data, the unfortunately named Finder focuses on helping you manage your disks and files.

It does this by providing you with the well-known Macintosh desktop, with icons for each disk, drive, folder and file—plus the Finder menus and the Trash. The Finder lets you view and modify the contents of your disks and drives in many different ways, and allows you to launch other applications or control panels.

System 7 introduces many enhancements to the Finder, providing more information about your disks and files, more consistency in commands and features and additional customizing capabilities. Fortunately, these benefits come without a change in the Finder's familiar interface—if you're comfortable working in Finder 6.0 you'll have no problem adjusting to the new Finder and taking advantage of its expanded capabilities.

This chapter starts by examining the Finder's menu commands, and then looks at the important topic of Finder windows. Other changes in System 7's Finder such as Balloon Help, the Trash and the Get Info dialog box are also covered.

This chapter is not, however, the only place in this book where you'll read about new Finder capabilities. Many Finder features are introduced in this chapter and then elaborated on in later chapters in more appropriate contexts. For example, aliasing, the Find command and the Label menu are the subjects of Chapter 3, "Managing Your Hard Drive," the Sharing command is explained in Chapter 9, "Introduction to File Sharing," and the About This Macintosh... command is described in detail in "Chapter 11, Memory Management."

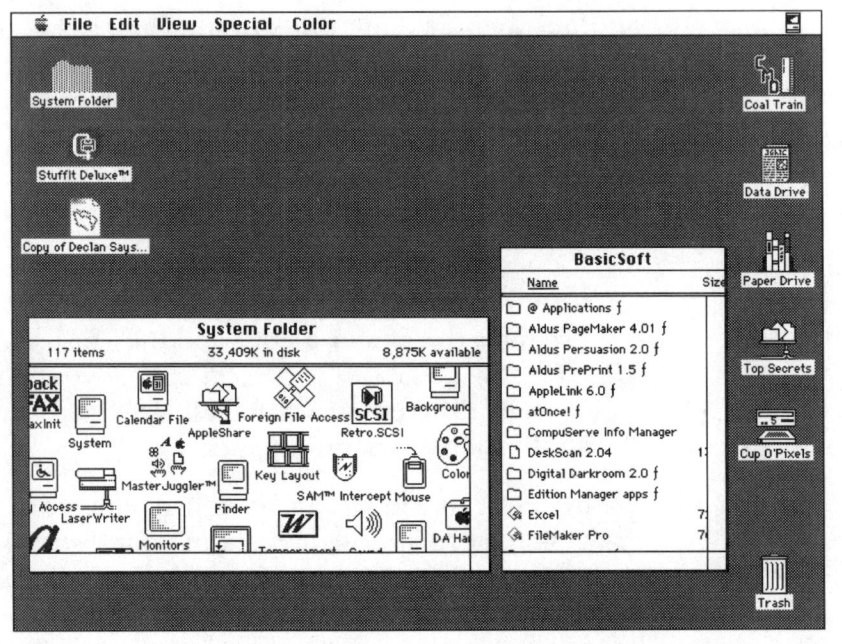

Figure 2-1: The Finder desktop in system software 6.0.x.

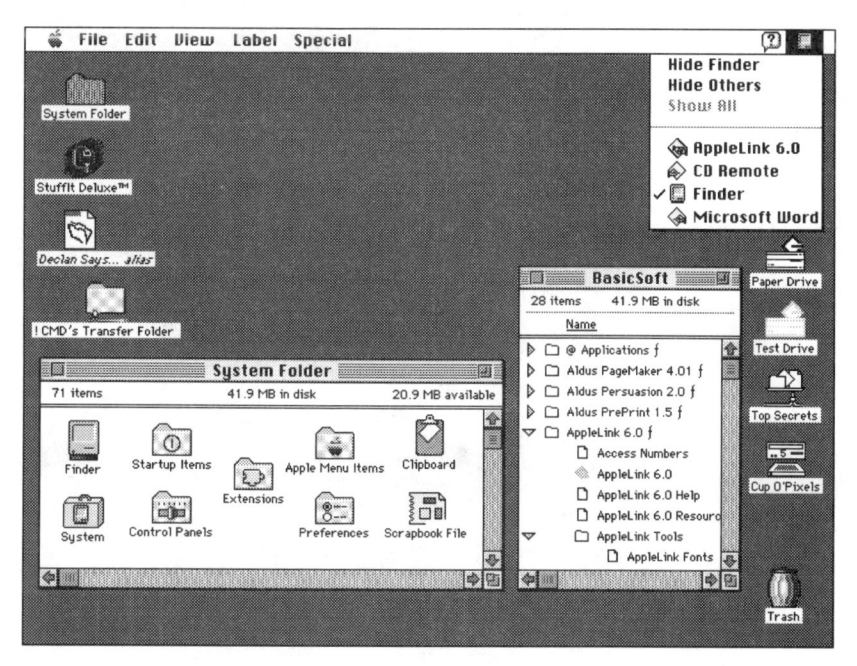

Figure 2-2: The Finder desktop in system software 7.

New Finder Menus

A good way to become familiar with any new or upgraded application is by taking a quick tour through its menu bar and menu commands. We'll use this approach to start learning about the Finder.

Figure 2-3 shows the Finder menus and commands as they appear on most Macintosh systems when System 7 is first installed. Your menus may vary slightly, depending on your hardware configuration and option settings.

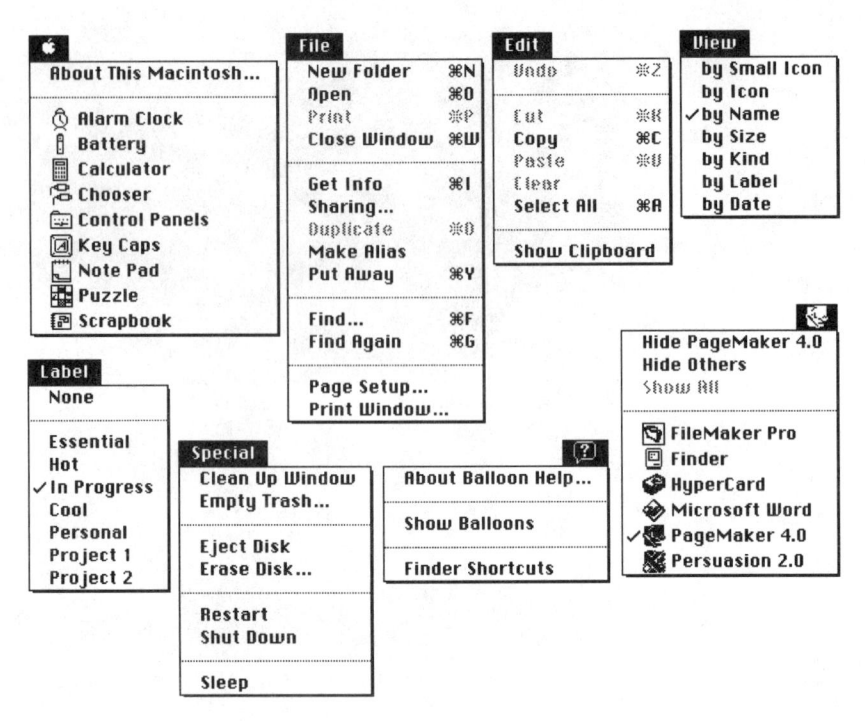

```
 ───────────────┬──────────────────┬──────────────┬──────────────
  ⬢             │ File             │ Edit         │ View
 ───────────────┼──────────────────┼──────────────┼──────────────
  About This    │ New Folder   ⌘N  │ Undo    ⌘Z   │ by Small Icon
  Macintosh...  │ Open         ⌘O  │              │ by Icon
                │ Print        ⌘P  │ Cut     ⌘K   │ ✓by Name
  ⏰ Alarm Clock│ Close Window ⌘W  │ Copy    ⌘C   │ by Size
  🔋 Battery    │                  │ Paste   ⌘V   │ by Kind
  🖩 Calculator │ Get Info     ⌘I  │ Clear        │ by Label
  ☎ Chooser     │ Sharing...       │ Select All ⌘A│ by Date
  📁 Control    │ Duplicate    ⌘D  │              │
     Panels     │ Make Alias       │ Show Clipboard│
  🅺 Key Caps   │ Put Away     ⌘Y  │              │
  📝 Note Pad   │                  │              │
  🧩 Puzzle     │ Find...      ⌘F  │              │
  📘 Scrapbook  │ Find Again   ⌘G  │              │
                │                  │              │
                │ Page Setup...    │              │
                │ Print Window...  │              │
```

Figure 2-3: The default Finder menus in System 7.

More than half the Finder commands are unchanged in name or position from previous versions, and most work the same today as they did previously. To save space (and avoid boring you), this section discusses only commands new to System 7's Finder or previous ones that have been improved or upgraded.

The new commands are listed on the following pages in the order they appear in the menus, from left to right on the menu bar.

- **About This Macintosh...** (Apple Menu). The dialog box this command brings up now displays more information about your Macintosh, such as available memory and open applications. (More information about this dialog box is in Chapter 11.)

- **Sharing...** (File menu). This command controls access privileges you grant other users on your AppleTalk network. You can allow or disallow sharing of your Macintosh files, and determine which users can read and write particular folders and volumes of shared files.

  The Sharing command does not appear unless File Sharing has been installed; it remains dimmed until File Sharing is turned on. (A complete discussion of File Sharing and other System 7 networking features is in Chapter 9.)

- **Make Alias** (File menu). Make Alias, found in the File menu, creates a duplicate icon for a file or folder without duplicating the file or folder itself. This duplicate icon, called an alias, can be freely positioned on any volume or folder and used as if it were the original file or folder. The benfit of creating and using an alias rather than a copy is that an alias takes up almost no space on your hard drive, the alias remains linked to the original file and any changes made to the alias are reflected in the original and vice versa.

  The Make Alias command lets you store a file or folders in two places at once—in fact, in any number of places at once, since you can create many aliases for a single file or folder. (More about aliasing is in Chapter 3.)

- **Find...** (File menu). The Find command, located in the File menu, replaces the Find File desk accessory of previous system software versions. This new Find command can search for files by file name, size, creation date, label, etc., and when files matching your search criteria are located, the Finder opens the window containing the file (or files) and selects the file's icon. Using the Find Again command, (Command-G) you can repeat the last search, locating and displaying the next file matching the current search criteria. (A complete discussion of the Find and Find Again commands is in Chapter 3.

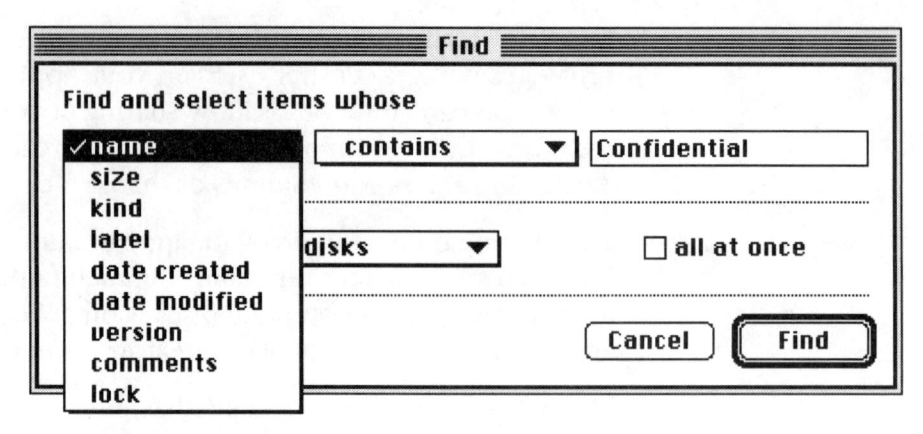

Figure 2-4: The Find items dialog box.

- **Label menu.** The new Label menu is in some ways similar to the Colors menu used in system software 6.0x: it allows you to specify colors for file and folder icons. A few important improvements have been added to this colorization process: you can now color-code your files by specifying a classification title for each color (see Figure 2-5). In addition, color labels are supported by the View menu and Find command, so you can use label categorizations as part of your hard-disk organization and management strategy. (You'll find more on the Label menu in Chapter 3.)

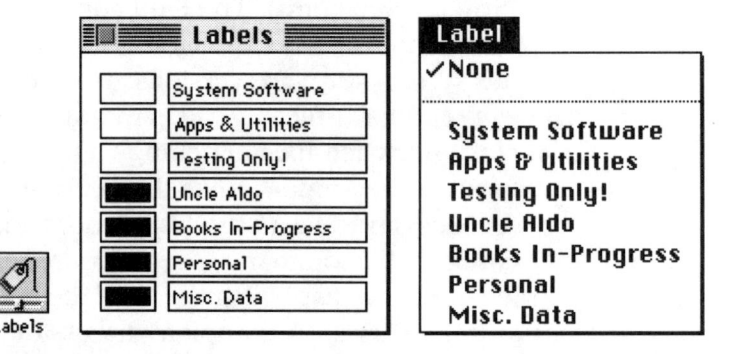

Figure 2-5: The Label control panel icon (left), Label control panel (center) and customized Label menu (right).

- **Clean Up** (Special menu). The new Clean Up command is an enhanced version of its old counterpart used to rearrange icons on the desktop or in Finder windows. (You'll find more information on this command later in this chapter.)

- **Empty Trash** (Special menu). This is an improved version of the Empty Trash command from previous versions. In System 7's Finder, files and folders remain in the trash until the Empty Trash command is selected; they're not deleted when applications are run, when your Macintosh is shut down or at any other time. (More information on this command is presented later in this chapter.)

- **Balloon Help menu.** Near the right edge of the menu bar, under the question-mark icon, is the new Help menu, which is available at all times, not just in the Finder. The most important command in this menu is Show Balloons, which turns on context-sensitive help balloons that pop up as you point to menu commands, dialog box options, icons and other Macintosh screen elements. (More on the Help menu is presented later in this chapter.)

- **Applications menu.** This is the last addition to the menu bar; it's located in the upper-right corner. This new feature lets System 7 open multiple applications simultaneously, so you can quickly switch from one open application to another. It's available at all times, not just when you're using the Finder.

The name of every open application will automatically appear in this menu. To switch from one application to another, select the name you want from the Application menu, and that application and its windows immediately appear.

```
Hide PageMaker 4.0
Hide Others
Show All
..............................
    🗊 FileMaker Pro
    🖥 Finder
    💼 HyperCard
    ◆ Microsoft Word
  ✓ 📄 PageMaker 4.0
    📄 Persuasion 2.0
```

Figure 2-6: The Applications menu.

The Applications menu also lets you temporarily hide all windows from the current application or all windows except those of the current application, thus reducing the on-screen clutter that can result from running multiple applications at once. (See Chapter 5, "System 7 & Your Software.")

Finder Windows

As a disk and file management tool, the Finder's menu commands play only a small part. Most of the time, you move, copy, delete, arrange and open files by using the mouse to directly manipulate icons on the desktop and in Finder windows. In System 7, your ability to see and manipulate files and folders in windows has been dramatically improved.

The basic attributes of Finder windows, however, have not changed:

- Windows are created each time a volume or folder is opened.
- Each window has a title bar, zoom box and close box.
- Windows can be freely positioned by dragging their title bars.
- Windows can be resized by dragging on the resize box.
- Windows display the files and folders contained in a single volume or folder.
- The window display is controlled via the View menu.

The improvements to the Finder in System 7, however, give you more control over windows, a more consistent user interface and a wider range of display options:

- The font, icon size and information displayed in Finder windows is customizable.
- Keyboard commands let you navigate windows and select files without using the mouse.
- Smart zooming opens windows only enough to display their content.
- The contents of any folder or subfolder can be displayed in hierarchical format in any window.
- Hierarchical levels allow files in different folders to be manipulated simultaneously.

These and other new features and improvements to the operation of Finder windows are discussed in detail later in this chapter.

The Views Control Panel

In previous Finder versions, the presentation of text and icons in Finder windows was preset and could not be modified. Text was always listed in Geneva 9 point, and icons appeared in preset sizes in each icon view. In System 7, the Views control panel provides a variety of options that let you control the information and the way it's displayed in Finder windows.

It should be noted that control panels are the System 7 evolution of the cdevs (control devices) that appeared in the System 6.0x Control Panel desk accessory. In System 7, a control panel is a small independent application launched by double-clicking on its icon, just like other applications. The only distinction between a control panel and a regular application is that the control panel is implemented in a single window and provides no menus. Control panels are stored in the Control Panels folder, which is stored inside the System Folder.

To access the Views control panel, you can either open the System Folder and the Control Panels folder, or you can select the Control Panel command from the Apple Menu. (Although the Control Panel command initially appears in the Apple Menu, it may not appear there if your system has been customized.) Once the Control Panels folder is open, double-click on the Views icon to open the Views control panel (shown in Figure 2-7).

Changes in Finder windows register instantly as you modify the options in the Views control panel. You don't need to close the Views dialog box to see the effect of your selections. When you're satisfied, close the Views control panel by clicking the close box in the upper-left corner of its title bar.

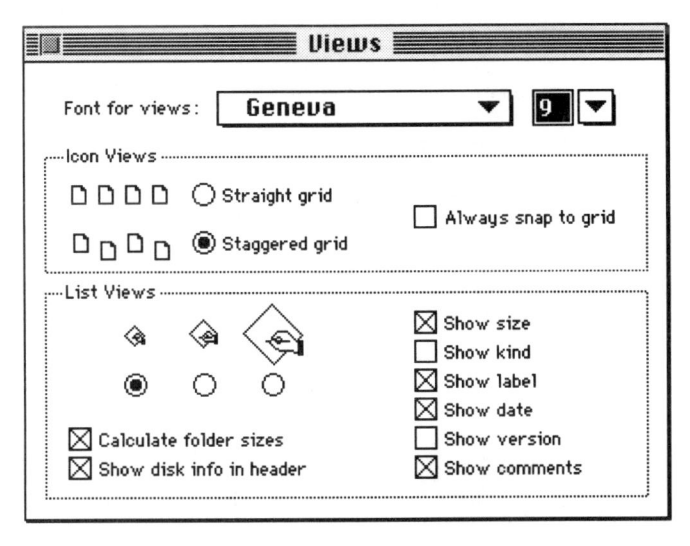

Figure 2-7: The Views control panel.

The Views control panel options are grouped in three sets. The first is Font for views, a typeface and type size option that controls the display of text in all Finder windows. A font pop-up menu presents the names of all installed fonts; you may select the one you want for all Finder windows. Use the size pop-up menu to select the point size for the text display. If you want to use a point size not available in the pop-up menu, type the size you want directly into the Size option box.

A word of warning: Although it's appealing to be able to choose from such a wide range of fonts and sizes, you may find that the default, Geneva 9-point, provides the most legible text display. Geneva is optimized for on-screen display, and while it doesn't look very good in print, it remains an excellent font for display purposes.

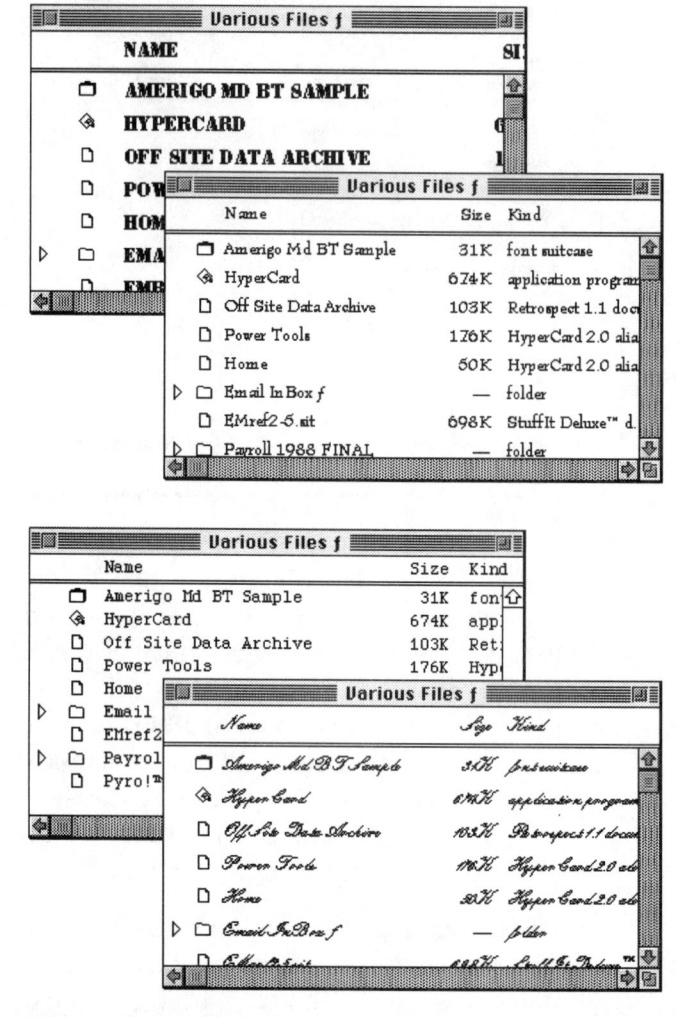

Figure 2-8: Finder windows in various fonts.

The second set of Views dialog box options is grouped under Icon Views. These options affect the way icons are positioned when the By Icon and By Small Icon commands from the View menu are selected. The Straight grid and Staggered grid options determine whether icons are arranged on a common or an irregular baseline. All versions before System 7 have arranged icons on a straight grid, which can sometimes force file names to overlap, leaving them illegible, as shown in Figure 2-9. The Staggered option positions icons so their names cannot overlap.

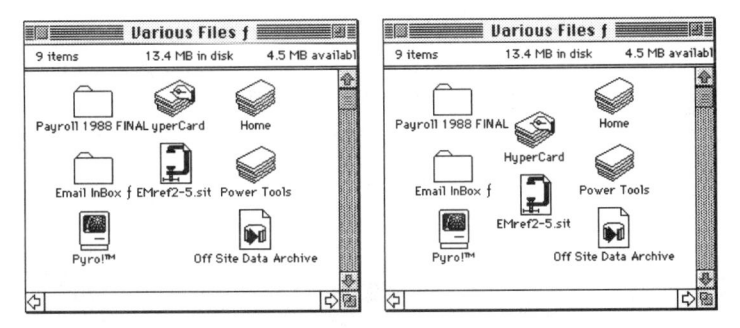

Figure 2-9: Examples of Finder windows using the Straight grid and Staggered grid options.

The Always snap to grid option forces any repositioned icons to automatically snap to the nearest point on an invisible grid. This is the same invisible grid used by the Clean Up command, and will result in either normal or staggered baseline alignment, depending on whether the Straight grid or the Staggered grid option is chosen. The concept of keeping files always grid-aligned in this way may sound appealing, but it can be disconcerting when the Finder grabs and relocates files while you're trying to position them. In most cases, it's probably better to leave this option off and use the Clean Up command to correct any icon alignment problems in Finder windows.

List Views is the final set of Views dialog box options. These options apply to the display for all windows except those using the By Icon or Small Icon commands from the View menu (by Name, Date, Size, etc.). This set of options includes three groups: one specifying icon size, one offering additional information in Finder windows and the last controlling the window columns and View menu commands.

The icon display size is chosen by using the three different icon size radio buttons. The result of each option is shown in Figure 2-10. As with the Font for views option discussed earlier, icon sizes are probably best left unchanged.

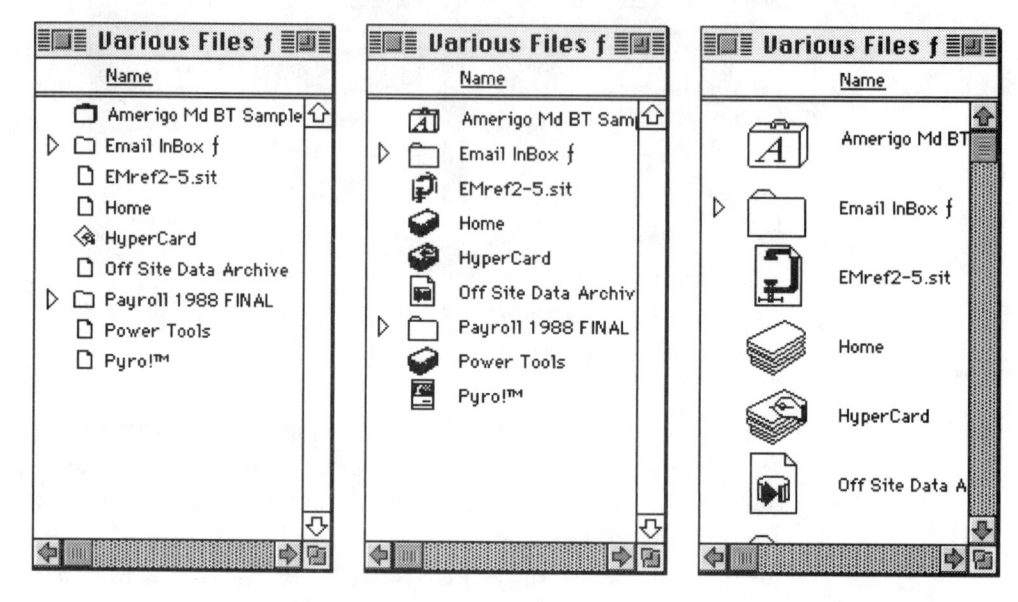

Figure 2-10: Finder windows using the small, medium and large icons corresponding to the Views control panel options.

Below the icon size radio buttons are two check-box options: Calculate folder sizes and Show disk info in header. These options add additional information to that already provided in Finder windows.

- **Calculate folder sizes.** It would be difficult to determine the "one little thing" that most bothered users in previous Finder versions, but the fact that folder sizes were not displayed in Finder windows was high on many users' pet-peeves list. The Calculate folder sizes option lets you add the size of a folder's contents to all text view displays.

This option, unfortunately, causes a perceptible slowdown in the display of some windows, particularly when the windows contain numerous large folders. You'll have to decide whether the slower display speed is a fair price to pay for the additional information, and turn this option off or on accordingly. When it's turned off, an alternate way to determine the size of a folder is by selecting the folder and choosing the Get Info command from the Finder's File menu.

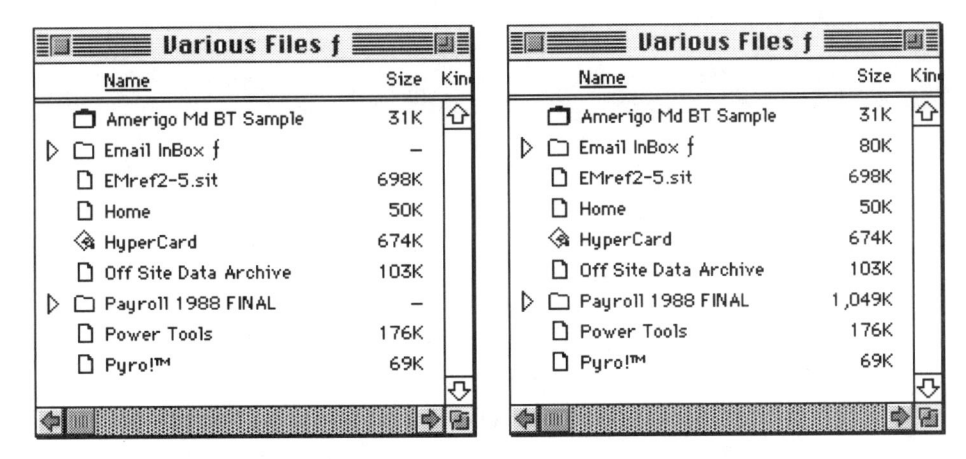

Various Files ƒ			Various Files ƒ	
Name	Size		Name	Size
Amerigo Md BT Sample	31K		Amerigo Md BT Sample	31K
▷ Email InBox ƒ	—		▷ Email InBox ƒ	80K
EMref2-5.sit	698K		EMref2-5.sit	698K
Home	50K		Home	50K
HyperCard	674K		HyperCard	674K
Off Site Data Archive	103K		Off Site Data Archive	103K
▷ Payroll 1988 FINAL	—		▷ Payroll 1988 FINAL	1,049K
Power Tools	176K		Power Tools	176K
Pyro!™	69K		Pyro!™	69K

Figure 2-11: The same Finder window with and without folder sizes displayed.

- **Show disk info in header.** Selecting this option adds three pieces of information to the upper section of each window: the number of items contained, the total space consumed by files on the disk, and the amount of free space on the current volume. This information fits discreetly in the window header, as shown in Figure 2-12.

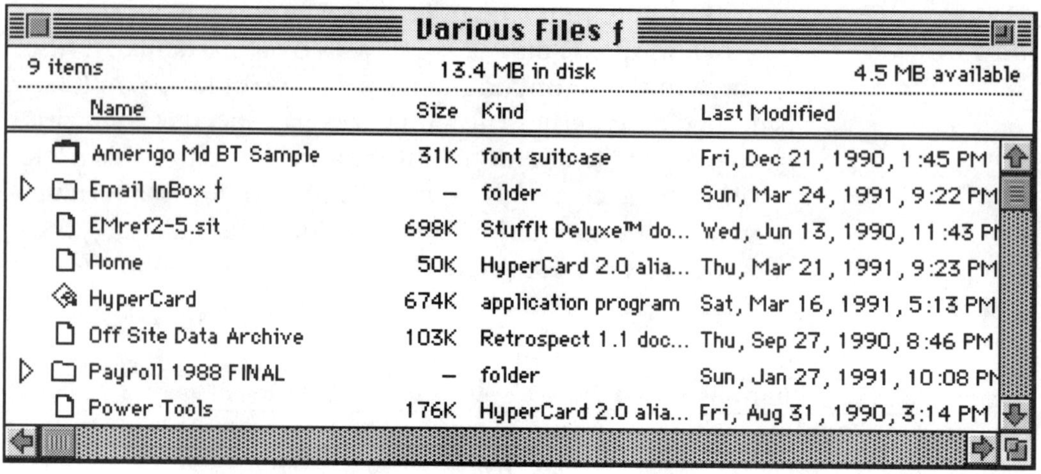

Various Files ƒ				
9 items	13.4 MB in disk		4.5 MB available
Name	Size	Kind	Last Modified
Amerigo Md BT Sample	31K	font suitcase	Fri, Dec 21, 1990, 1:45 PM
▷ Email InBox ƒ	—	folder	Sun, Mar 24, 1991, 9:22 PM
EMref2-5.sit	698K	StuffIt Deluxe™ do...	Wed, Jun 13, 1990, 11:43 P
Home	50K	HyperCard 2.0 alia...	Thu, Mar 21, 1991, 9:23 PM
HyperCard	674K	application program	Sat, Mar 16, 1991, 5:13 PM
Off Site Data Archive	103K	Retrospect 1.1 doc...	Thu, Sep 27, 1990, 8:46 PM
▷ Payroll 1988 FINAL	—	folder	Sun, Jan 27, 1991, 10:08 P
Power Tools	176K	HyperCard 2.0 alia...	Fri, Aug 31, 1990, 3:14 PM

Figure 2-12: A Finder window including the information added by the Show disk info in header option.

The last set of options, listed on the right side of the List Views box, toggles the display of commands in the Finder's View menu and the display of columns in Finder windows. If you deselect the Show date option, for example, the By Date command is removed from the View menu, and the Date column is removed from all Finder windows.

These commands can customize your Finder windows to suit the way you work with files and organize your hard drive, eliminating the display of information you don't find useful and reducing the on-screen clutter of windows with too much information. For example, if you're not using the Label menu to apply meaningful labels to your files, then the Show label option should be deselected. Similarly, if you won't be entering extensive comments into the Get Info dialog boxes of your files, the Show comments option can be deselected. (The Get Info dialog box and comments are discussed more thoroughly later in this chapter.)

Figures 2-13 and 2-14 show the Finder window resulting from two different option settings.

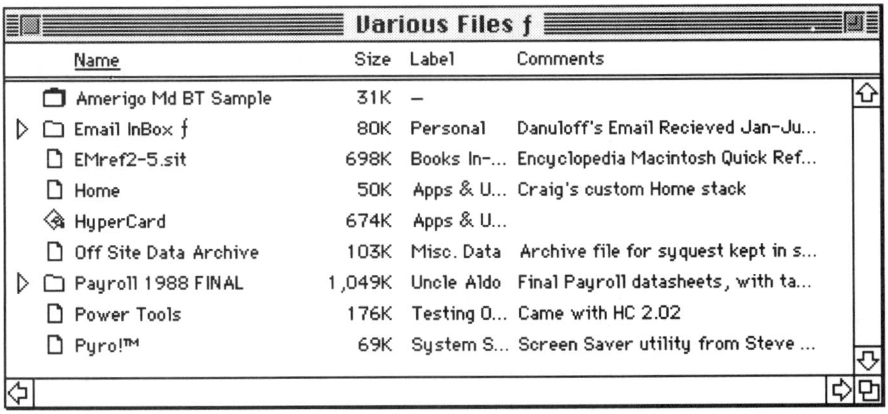

Name	Size	Label	Comments
📁 Amerigo Md BT Sample	31K	—	
▷ 📁 Email InBox ƒ	80K	Personal	Danuloff's Email Recieved Jan-Ju...
📄 EMref2-5.sit	698K	Books In-...	Encyclopedia Macintosh Quick Ref...
📄 Home	50K	Apps & U...	Craig's custom Home stack
📄 HyperCard	674K	Apps & U...	
📄 Off Site Data Archive	103K	Misc. Data	Archive file for syquest kept in s...
▷ 📁 Payroll 1988 FINAL	1,049K	Uncle Aldo	Final Payroll datasheets, with ta...
📄 Power Tools	176K	Testing O...	Came with HC 2.02
📄 Pyro!™	69K	System S...	Screen Saver utility from Steve ...

Figure 2-13: A Finder window as it appears when the Show kind, Show date and Show version options are deselected in the Views control panel.

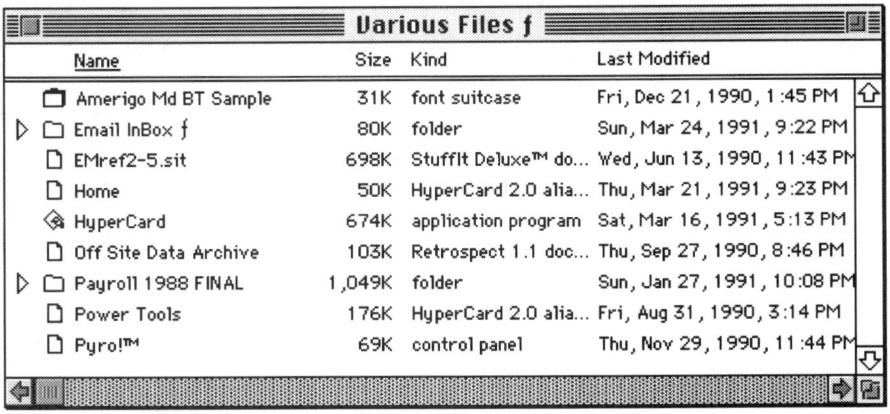

Name	Size	Kind	Last Modified
📁 Amerigo Md BT Sample	31K	font suitcase	Fri, Dec 21, 1990, 1:45 PM
▷ 📁 Email InBox ƒ	80K	folder	Sun, Mar 24, 1991, 9:22 PM
📄 EMref2-5.sit	698K	StuffIt Deluxe™ do...	Wed, Jun 13, 1990, 11:43 PM
📄 Home	50K	HyperCard 2.0 alia...	Thu, Mar 21, 1991, 9:23 PM
📄 HyperCard	674K	application program	Sat, Mar 16, 1991, 5:13 PM
📄 Off Site Data Archive	103K	Retrospect 1.1 doc...	Thu, Sep 27, 1990, 8:46 PM
▷ 📁 Payroll 1988 FINAL	1,049K	folder	Sun, Jan 27, 1991, 10:08 PM
📄 Power Tools	176K	HyperCard 2.0 alia...	Fri, Aug 31, 1990, 3:14 PM
📄 Pyro!™	69K	control panel	Thu, Nov 29, 1990, 11:44 PM

Figure 2-14: A Finder window without label, version or comments.

The View Menu

The Finder's View menu, like View menus in past Finder versions, determines how information is displayed in the current active window. Previous versions of the View menu let you display files and folders by icon, small icon, name, date, size, kind and color. In System 7, the View menu provides all these view methods except for color, but adds view by label, version and comment.

Each time you apply a View menu command to a particular window, that window's display is arranged according to the selected format (by icon, by small icon, etc.) and it retains that view format until a different View menu command is applied to it. When a window is closed and later reopened, it always appears in the same display view as before it was closed. There's no way, unfortunately, to change the view option for all open or closed windows, since the View menu controls each window independently.

Choosing the By Icon or By Small Icon commands cause only the file icon and file name to be displayed. The other view commands display a small icon, the file name and additional columns of data as specified in the Views control panel described above. The particular view command that's selected determines the order in which files in the window are sorted:

- **By Size.** This command sorts files in descending size order. If you've selected the Show folder sizes option in the Views control panel, folders are also sorted in this list according to their size. Otherwise, folders are grouped alphabetically at the end of the list.

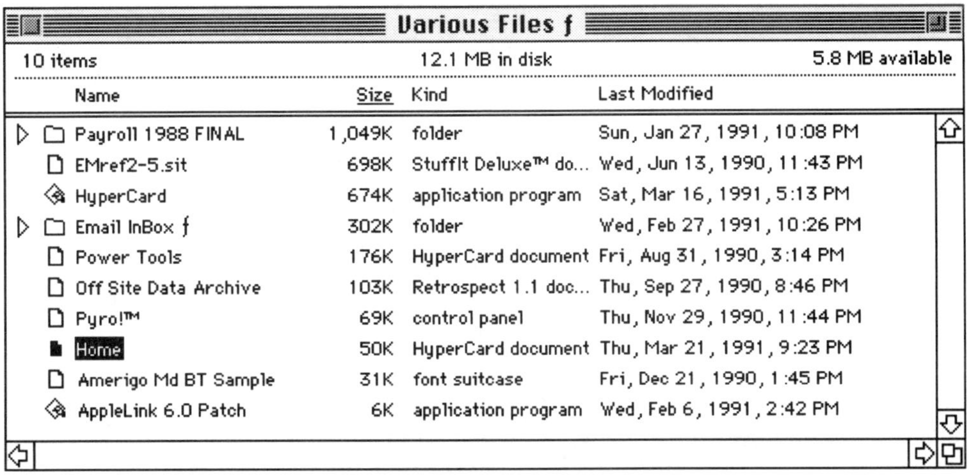

```
╔═══════════════ Various Files f ═══════════════╗
  10 items              12.1 MB in disk          5.8 MB available
      Name              Size  Kind              Last Modified
  ▷ 📁 Payroll 1988 FINAL  1,049K folder             Sun, Jan 27, 1991, 10:08 PM
    📄 EMref2-5.sit         698K  StuffIt Deluxe™ do... Wed, Jun 13, 1990, 11:43 PM
    📄 HyperCard            674K  application program  Sat, Mar 16, 1991, 5:13 PM
  ▷ 📁 Email InBox f        302K  folder               Wed, Feb 27, 1991, 10:26 PM
    📄 Power Tools          176K  HyperCard document   Fri, Aug 31, 1990, 3:14 PM
    📄 Off Site Data Archive 103K Retrospect 1.1 doc... Thu, Sep 27, 1990, 8:46 PM
    📄 Pyro!™                69K  control panel        Thu, Nov 29, 1990, 11:44 PM
    ■ Home                   50K  HyperCard document   Thu, Mar 21, 1991, 9:23 PM
    📄 Amerigo Md BT Sample  31K  font suitcase        Fri, Dec 21, 1990, 1:45 PM
    📄 AppleLink 6.0 Patch    6K  application program  Wed, Feb 6, 1991, 2:42 PM
```

Figure 2-15: A Finder window viewed by size.

Commonly, the By Size command is used to find files known to be either very large or very small, or to locate large files that could be deleted to free up space.

- **By Kind.** This command sorts files alphabetically by a short description based on the file type, a four-letter code assigned by the developer or application creator. Document files associated with a particular application program include the name of their application, using "Word 4.0 document" or "HyperCard 2.0 document," for example, as the kind.

  Common file kinds include Alias, Application Program, Chooser Extension, Database Extension, Desk Accessory, Document file, Folder and System Extension. Viewing files by kind is useful if you know the kind of file you're looking for and if the window containing that file has many different files in it. Figure 2-16 shows a System folder using the By Kind view.

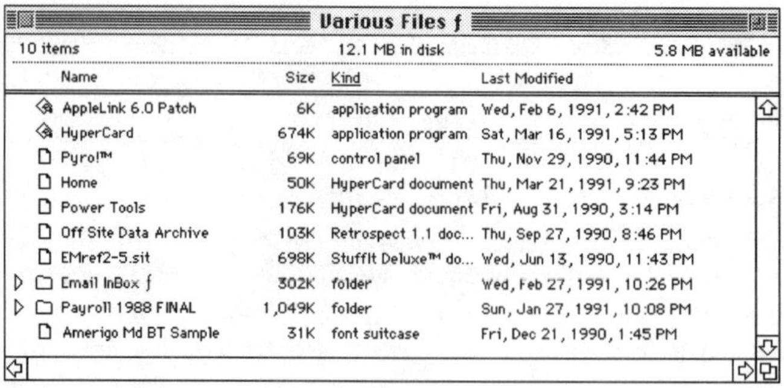

```
┌─────────────────────────────────────────────────────────┐
│ ▤▤▤▤▤▤▤▤▤▤▤▤▤  Various Files ƒ  ▤▤▤▤▤▤▤▤▤▤▤▤▤         │
│ 10 items              12.1 MB in disk      5.8 MB available│
│         Name              Size  Kind       Last Modified │
│    ◈ AppleLink 6.0 Patch    6K  application program  Wed, Feb 6, 1991, 2:42 PM │
│    ◈ HyperCard            674K  application program  Sat, Mar 16, 1991, 5:13 PM │
│    ▯ Pyro!™                69K  control panel       Thu, Nov 29, 1990, 11:44 PM │
│    ▯ Home                  50K  HyperCard document  Thu, Mar 21, 1991, 9:23 PM │
│    ▯ Power Tools          176K  HyperCard document  Fri, Aug 31, 1990, 3:14 PM │
│    ▯ Off Site Data Archive 103K  Retrospect 1.1 doc... Thu, Sep 27, 1990, 8:46 PM │
│    ▯ EMref2-5.sit         698K  StuffIt Deluxe™ do... Wed, Jun 13, 1990, 11:43 PM │
│  ▷ ▭ Email InBox ƒ        302K  folder              Wed, Feb 27, 1991, 10:26 PM │
│  ▷ ▭ Payroll 1988 FINAL 1,049K  folder              Sun, Jan 27, 1991, 10:08 PM │
│    ▯ Amerigo Md BT Sample  31K  font suitcase       Fri, Dec 21, 1990, 1:45 PM │
└─────────────────────────────────────────────────────────┘
```

Figure 2-16: A Finder window as it appears using the View menu's By Kind command.

> ▪ **By Label.** This command sorts by the label name given to the file with the Label command. Labels, as discussed in Chapter 3, group files according to some user-defined scheme. For example, you might have a group of files that all relate to personal (non-business) issues, a group relating to one project you're working on, etc.
>
> In any case, this command lets you sort the files in the current window according to labels previously applied. Files are arranged as they appear in the Label menu. Unlabeled files appear at the bottom of the listing.

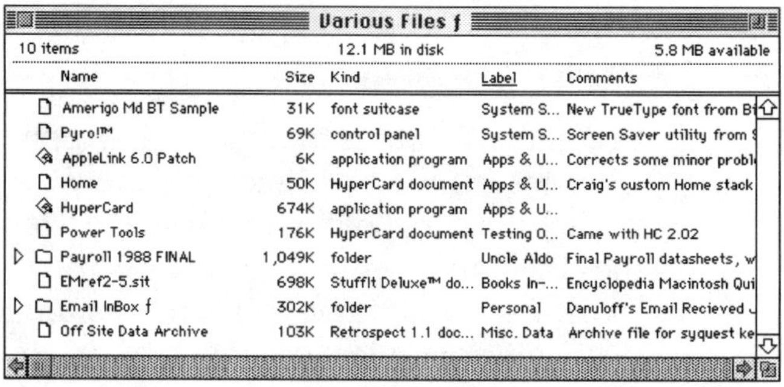

```
┌─────────────────────────────────────────────────────────┐
│ ▤▤▤▤▤▤▤▤▤▤▤▤▤  Various Files ƒ  ▤▤▤▤▤▤▤▤▤▤▤▤▤         │
│ 10 items              12.1 MB in disk      5.8 MB available│
│         Name              Size  Kind       Label      Comments │
│    ▯ Amerigo Md BT Sample  31K  font suitcase    System S... New TrueType font from B │
│    ▯ Pyro!™                69K  control panel    System S... Screen Saver utility from  │
│    ◈ AppleLink 6.0 Patch    6K  application program Apps & U... Corrects some minor probl │
│    ▯ Home                  50K  HyperCard document Apps & U... Craig's custom Home stack │
│    ◈ HyperCard            674K  application program Apps & U... │
│    ▯ Power Tools          176K  HyperCard document Testing O... Came with HC 2.02 │
│  ▷ ▭ Payroll 1988 FINAL 1,049K  folder            Uncle Aldo Final Payroll datasheets, w │
│    ▯ EMref2-5.sit         698K  StuffIt Deluxe™ do... Books In-... Encyclopedia Macintosh Qui │
│  ▷ ▭ Email InBox ƒ        302K  folder            Personal   Danuloff's Email Recieved │
│    ▯ Off Site Data Archive 103K  Retrospect 1.1 doc... Misc. Data Archive file for syquest ke │
└─────────────────────────────────────────────────────────┘
```

Figure 2-17: A Finder window as it appears using the View menu's By Label command.

- **By Date.** This command sorts files by the date they were modified, with the most recently updated files at the top of the list. This view is useful when you're looking for files that are much older or much newer than most of the other files in a certain folder.

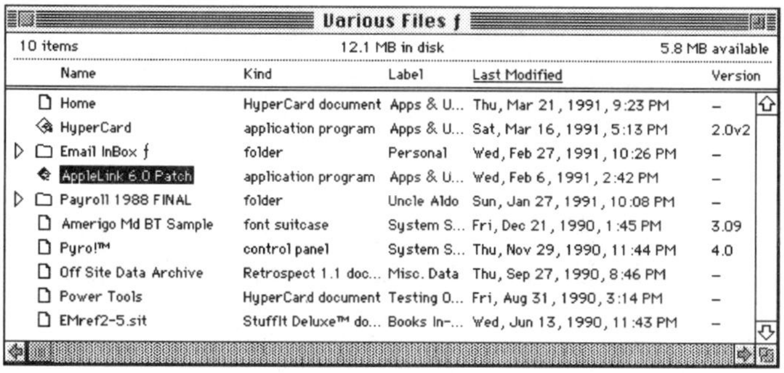

Figure 2-18: A Finder window as it appears using the View menu's By Date command.

- **By Version.** Useful only for application files, this command sorts by the software developer's assigned version number. Ancillary application files (e.g., dictionaries and references) and data files you create do not have this type of version number.

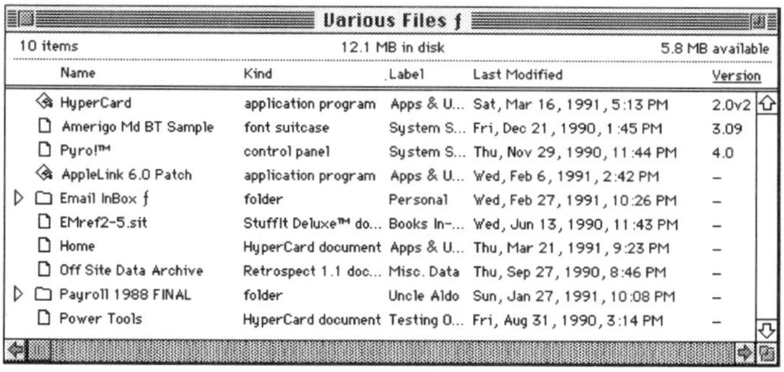

Figure 2-19: A Finder window as it appears using the View menu's By Version command.

- **By Comment.** This command sorts files alphabetically by the text contained in their Get Info dialog box comment fields. Displaying comment text in Finder windows is a major new file management feature, but it's useful only if the first characters of the comment are significant, or if you just want to separate all files that have comments from those that don't. Files without comments are placed at the top of any windows using the View menu's By Comment command.

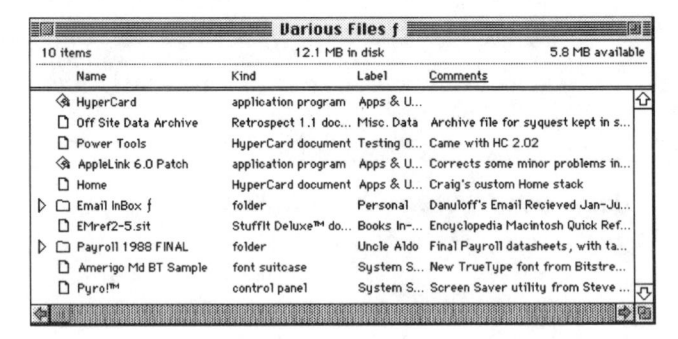

Figure 2-20: A Finder window viewed by using the By Comment command.

Hierarchical Views

This important feature displays the contents of any folder without opening a new folder window. In previous versions, the only way to view and manipulate folder contents was to open the folder, thereby creating a new window. In System 7, you can display any folder contents by clicking on the small triangle that appears to the left of the folder icon. The contents then appear, indented slightly under the folder icon, as shown in Figure 2-21.

```
┌─────────────────────────────────────────────────┐
│≣≣≣≣≣≣≣≣≣≣≣≣≣≣≣≣≣ Coal Train ≣≣≣≣≣≣≣≣≣≣≣≣≣≣≣≣│
│ 47 items           47.1 MB in disk    15.8 MB available │
│   Name                          Size  Kind              Version │
│ ▽  □ Aldus PrePrint 1.5 ƒ        —    folder              —  │
│      ◈ Aldus PrePrint           430K  application program Version 1 │
│      □ Calibrate.sep             47K  Aldus PrePrint doc... — │
│      □ Calibration Editor        51K  HyperCard document  1.0p │
│ ▽  □ Color Files ƒ               —    folder              —  │
│      □ Color.Tif                447K  Aldus PrePrint doc... — │
│ ▽  □ PNT files ƒ                 —    folder              —  │
│      □ Apple.Pnt                  7K  document             —  │
│      □ Job Jacket                36K  PageMaker 4.01 do... — │
│    □ Registration Card.sep       56K  Aldus PrePrint doc... — │
│ ▷ □ AppleLink 6.0 ƒ              —    folder              —  │
│ ▽ □ atOnce! ƒ                    —    folder              —  │
│      ◈ atOnce!                  908K  application program 1.01 │
│      □ atOnce! Help             550K  atOnce! document    1.00 │
│ ▷ □ CompuServe Info Manager      —    folder              —  │
└─────────────────────────────────────────────────┘
```

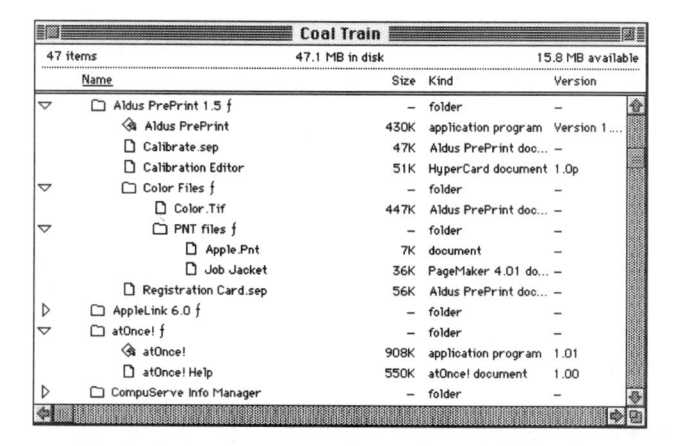

Figure: 2-21: A Finder window with hierarchical display.

This display is a hierarchical view because it allows you to see the contents of several levels of nested folders (folders inside of folders) at one time simply by clicking on the triangle next to the appropriate folder. (Alias folder icons, which you'll examine in Chapter 3, appear without a triangle and cannot be displayed hierarchically.) Figure 2-22 shows a window in which aliased folders are not displayed hierarchically.

```
┌─────────────────────────────────────────────────┐
│≣≣≣≣≣≣≣≣≣≣≣≣≣≣≣≣≣ Coal Train ≣≣≣≣≣≣≣≣≣≣≣≣≣≣≣≣│
│ 21 items          191.9 MB in disk     8.8 MB available │
│   Name                          Size  Kind              Version │
│    □ DiskFit Pro ƒ alias          4K  alias               —  │
│ ▽ □ MHS Folder                   —    folder              —  │
│      □ Garrison.pict             11K  Adobe Photoshop...  —  │
│ ▽    □ invest.ƒ                  —    folder              —  │
│        □ Ferrie.pict             11K  Adobe Photoshop...  —  │
│        □ Hidell.pict             11K  Adobe Photoshop...  —  │
│        □ Marcello.pict           11K  Adobe Photoshop...  —  │
│        □ Shaw.pict               11K  Adobe Photoshop...  —  │
│    □ Miscellaneous alias          4K  alias               —  │
│ ▽ □ Pete's Figures               —    folder              —  │
│      □ fig8.1                   189K  Now Scrapbook doc.. — │
│      □ fig8.2                   200K  Now Scrapbook doc.. — │
│      □ fig8.7                   144K  Now Scrapbook doc.. — │
│    □ Rhonda's Stuff               4K  alias               —  │
│ ▽ □ TypeSpec 1.1 Folder          —    folder              —  │
│      ◈ TypeSpec 1.1              25K  application program 1.1 │
└─────────────────────────────────────────────────┘
```

Figure 2-22 Finder window with hierarchical folders open.

You can drag hierarchically displayed files and folders from one location to another just as if they appeared in separate windows. In the example above, you could move the file "Job Jacket" to the "AppleLink 6.0 ƒ" folder by dragging its file icon into that folder. You can also drag files or folders to other volumes (copying the files); to other open Finder windows (moving the files); to the desktop; or to the Trash. In short, you can take advantage of the new hierarchical view to do everything you need to.

The primary benefit of hierarchical views is the elimination of desktop clutter, since there's no need to open a new Finder window for every folder you want to open. In addition, hierarchical views allow you to select and manipulate files and folders from different hierarchical levels at the same time, which was not possible in previous Finder versions because each time you clicked the mouse in a new window the selection in the previous window was released.

Figure 2-23 displays this ability, showing four different files and a folder, each on a different hierarchical level. The files and folder in this selection can now be copied, moved, trashed or manipulated like any single file. To select files and folders at multiple levels of the hierarchy at the same time, hold the Shift key while selecting the file names.

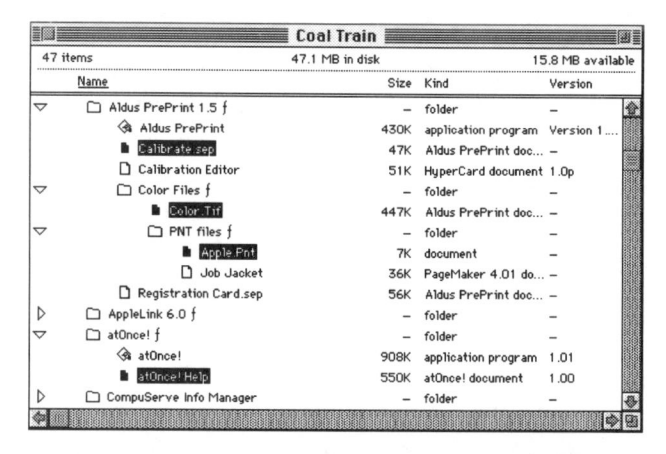

	Coal Train			
47 items		47.1 MB in disk		15.8 MB available
Name		Size	Kind	Version
▽ 📁 Aldus PrePrint 1.5 f		—	folder	—
Aldus PrePrint		430K	application program	Version 1....
Calibrate.sep		47K	Aldus PrePrint doc...	—
Calibration Editor		51K	HyperCard document	1.0p
▽ 📁 Color Files f		—	folder	—
Color.Tif		447K	Aldus PrePrint doc...	—
▽ 📁 PNT files f		—	folder	—
Apple Pnt		7K	document	—
Job Jacket		36K	PageMaker 4.01 do...	—
Registration Card.sep		56K	Aldus PrePrint doc...	—
▷ 📁 AppleLink 6.0 f		—	folder	—
▽ 📁 atOnce! f		—	folder	—
atOnce!		908K	application program	1.01
atOnce! Help		550K	atOnce! document	1.00
▷ 📁 CompuServe Info Manager		—	folder	—

Figure 2-23 Finder window with multiple open nested folders with four files selected.

To collapse a folder's hierarchical display, click the downward pointing triangle next to the folder icon again; the enclosed files and folder listing disappear. When you close a window, the hierarchical display settings are remembered and will reappear the next time the window is opened.

Of course, you can still open a new window for any folder, rather than display its contents hierarchically. Simply double-click on the folder icon rather than the triangle. Or select the folder icon, then the Open command from the File menu.

Navigating From the Keyboard

Even though the Macintosh relies primarily on its graphic interface and the mouse, there are many times when you need keyboard control. A variety of keyboard shortcuts can now be used to select files, move between file windows and manipulate icons. The keyboard commands that follow are available in all Finder windows and on the desktop:

- **Jump to file name.** Typing the first few letters in a file name selects that file. For example, if you want to select a file named "Budget," when you type "B," the first file name starting with a "B" is selected. When the "u" is typed, the selection will be the first file name starting with "Bu," etc. You must not pause between letters or the Mac will interpret each additional letter as the first letter of a new search.

  If you don't know an exact file name, type an "A" to cause the display to scroll to the top of the list, an "L" to scroll to the middle or a "Z" to scroll to the end.

- **Select next alphabetical file name.** This is done by pressing the Tab key. All files visible in the current window, including those displayed in hierarchically open folders, are included in this selection.

- **Select previous alphabetical file name.** Press Shift-Tab. This is useful when you press the Tab key one time too many and need to back up one step in reverse alphabetical order.

- **Select next file.** Down, Left and Right Arrow keys select the next file or folder icon in the respective direction.

- **Open selected folder.** Command-Down Arrow opens the selected file or folder, unless the selected file or folder is already open, in which case this key combination brings its window to the front.

- **Open selected file or folder and close current window.** Press Command-Option-Down Arrow. If the selected file or folder is already open, this key combination brings its window to the front and closes the current folder or volume window.

- **Open parent folder window.** Press Command-Up Arrow. If the selected file or folder is already open, this key combination brings its window to the front.

- **Open parent folder window, close current window.** Pressing Command-Option-Up Arrow closes the current window.

- **Edit file name.** Press Enter or Return. (File names can also be opened for editing by clicking the cursor on the text of the file name.) You can tell the name has been selected for editing when its display is inverted and a box is drawn around the file name.

  Once open for editing, the backspace key deletes characters, the Right and Left Arrow keys position the cursor. To complete the renaming, pressing Enter or Return again saves the file-name changes and returns the name to an inverted display.

- **Make desktop active.** Command-Shift-Up Arrow makes the current window inactive and the Finder desktop active.

The following keyboard commands are available only when working in Finder windows using text views (By Name, Size, Kind, Version, Label or Comment):

- **Expand hierarchical display.** Command-Right Arrow hierarchically displays the folder contents.

- **Expand all hierarchical display.** Command-Option-Right Arrow hierarchically displays the contents of the current folder and all enclosed folders.

- **Collapse hierarchical display.** Command-Left Arrow collapses the hierarchical display of the current folder.

- **Collapse all hierarchical display.** Command-Option-Left Arrow collapses the hierarchical display of the current folder and all enclosed folders.

Dragging Files Between Windows

Another new feature lets you select and move a file from an inactive window. In previous Finder versions, as soon as an icon was selected, the window containing that icon became the active window and brought the window forward. This created a problem when that window overlapped and obscured other folder icons. In the Finder, any visible icon in any window can be selected and dragged to a new location without the source-file window becoming active.

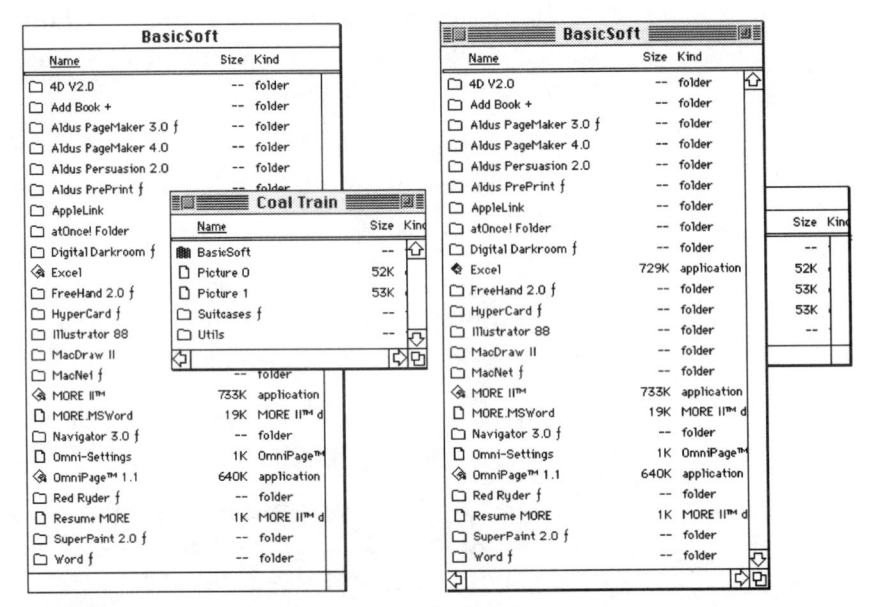

Figure 2-24: Dragging files between overlapping windows is made possible in the Finder under System 7.

This is more clearly described by an example. Suppose we want to drag a file or folder from the "BasicSoft" window into a folder on the "Coal Train" drive. This would be impossible in previous Finder versions without repositioning the Coal Train window; as soon as the BasicSoft file was selected the

BasicSoft window covered the Coal Train window, as shown at the right of Figure 2-24.

In System 7's Finder, however, we can simply point the mouse to the item to be moved from the BasicSoft window and hold the mouse button down while dragging the icon into the Coal Train window. As long as the mouse button is not released, the BasicSoft window won't be selected and therefore won't overlap the Coal Train window.

However, this method cannot be used to move more than one file. To move multiple files from BasicSoft to Coal Train, the Coal Train window would have to be repositioned. To move a Finder window without making it active, hold down the Command key while dragging the inactive window's title bar.

Working With Multiple Files

To perform any operation on one or more files, first select that file or group of files. Most aspects of selecting files in System 7 is the same as in System 6.x, but there are some changes and new features:

- **Immediate marquee selection.** The marquee (selection rectangle), created by clicking the mouse button and dragging with the button pressed, now selects files as soon as any part of the file name or icon is inside the selection rectangle. In previous versions, files were not selected until the mouse button was released, and only files completely contained in the selection rectangle were selected.

- **Marquee selection in text views.** Previously, the marquee could be used only in By Icon or By Small Icon views or on the desktop. In System 7, the selection rectangle is supported in all Finder windows; you can drag-select in the By Name or By Date views, for example.

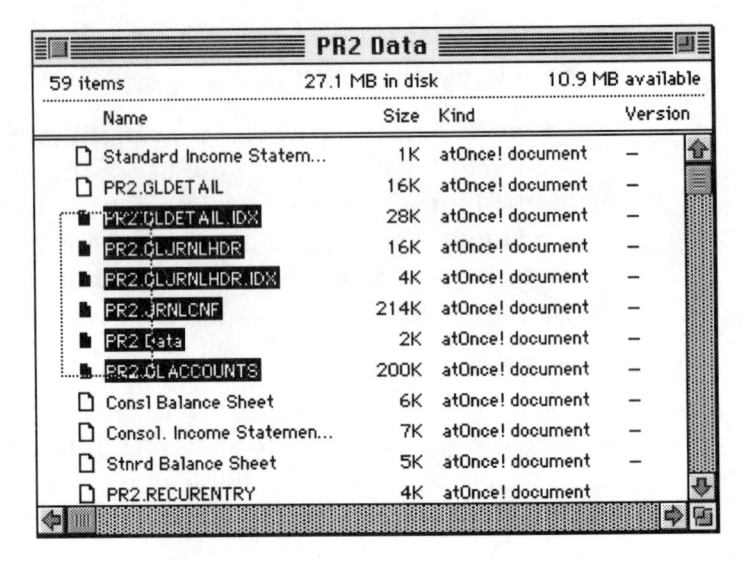

```
┌─────────────────────────────────────────────────┐
│≡≡≡≡≡≡≡≡≡≡≡≡≡≡≡≡≡ PR2 Data ≡≡≡≡≡≡≡≡≡≡≡≡≡≡≡≡≡≡≡│
│ 59 items          27.1 MB in disk     10.9 MB available│
│   Name                      Size   Kind        Version│
│   D Standard Income Statem...  1K   atOnce! document  —│
│   D PR2.GLDETAIL              16K   atOnce! document  —│
│   ▪ PR2.GLDETAIL.IDX          28K   atOnce! document  —│
│   ▪ PR2.GLJRNLHDR             16K   atOnce! document  —│
│   ▪ PR2.GLJRNLHDR.IDX          4K   atOnce! document  —│
│   ▪ PR2.JRNLCNF              214K   atOnce! document  —│
│   ▪ PR2 Data                   2K   atOnce! document  —│
│   ▪ PR2.GL ACCOUNTS          200K   atOnce! document  —│
│   D Cons1 Balance Sheet        6K   atOnce! document  —│
│   D Consol. Income Statemen... 7K   atOnce! document  —│
│   D Stnrd Balance Sheet        5K   atOnce! document  —│
│   D PR2.RECURENTRY             4K   atOnce! document  —│
└─────────────────────────────────────────────────┘
```

Figure 2-25: Multiple files can be selected using the marquee, even when files are listed by name.

- **Shift select.** Using the Shift key, the marquee can select discontiguous sections of any Finder window.

- **File dragging.** It's still possible to drag tiles by clicking on their names. To open a file name for editing, click on a file name and wait a few seconds for a box to appear around the file name.

- **Finder scrolling.** When dragging with a marquee, the Finder window scrolls automatically as soon as the cursor hits one of its edges, as shown in Figure 2-26. This is very useful when selecting in Finder windows displaying icons.

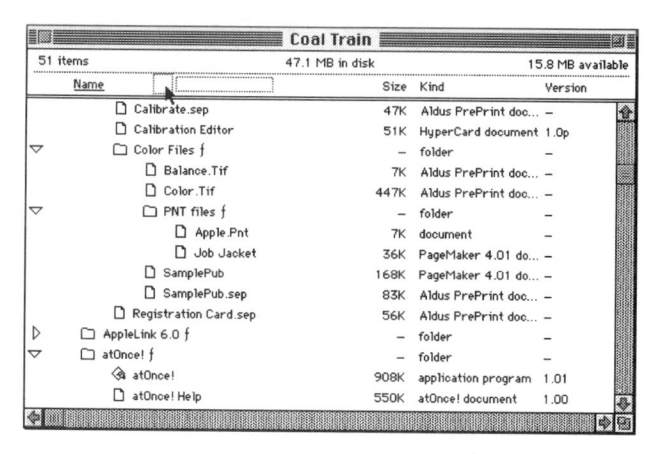

Figure 2-26: Finder windows scroll automatically when items are dragged past their edges.

Title Bar Pop-Up Menu

While hierarchical window views make it easy to move down the folder hierarchy, there's also a new way to move up the folder hierarchy—via a pop-up menu that appears in the title bar of any window when you hold down the Command key and click on the folder's name.

Figure 2-27 shows the pop-up menu for a folder named "System 7 Letters *f*", which is inside the "Technology Topics *f*" folder, which is inside the "Email Inbox *f*" folder, on the "Data Drive" disk. This pop-up displays the current folder's parent folder names and the volume on which the current folder is located. (In this case, since the "System 7 Letters *f*" folder is inside the "Technology Topics *f*" folder, "Technology Topics *f*" is the parent folder and "System 7 Letters *f*" is the child.)

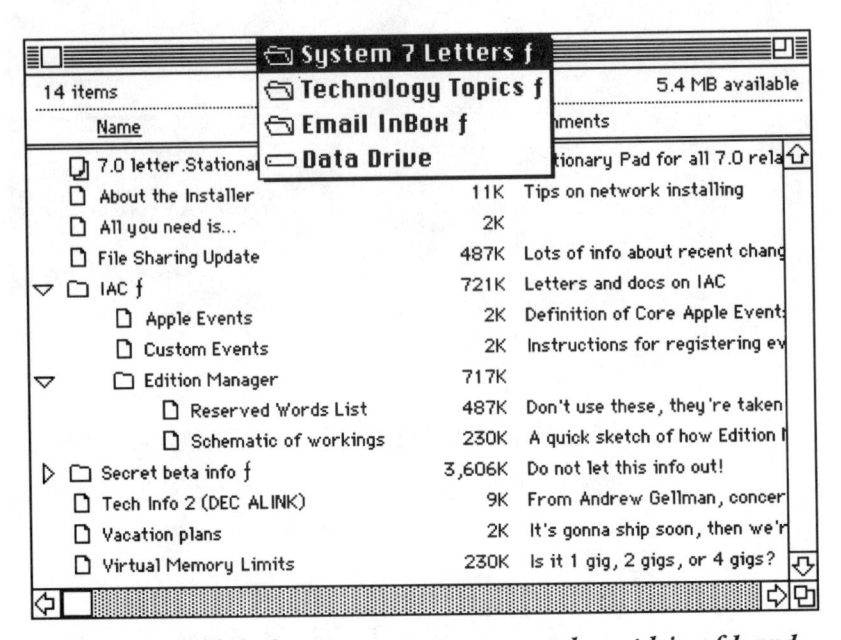

```
┌─────────────────────────────────────────────────────────┐
│ ▤  ▭▭▭▭▭    📁 System 7 Letters f        ▭▭▭▭▭      □▤ │
│ 14 items       📁 Technology Topics f      5.4 MB available │
│    Name        📁 Email InBox f           ments          │
│                💾 Data Drive                             │
│    📄 7.0 letter.Stationa              tionary Pad for all 7.0 rela │
│    📄 About the Installer        11K   Tips on network installing │
│    📄 All you need is...          2K                     │
│    📄 File Sharing Update       487K   Lots of info about recent chang │
│  ▽ 📁 IAC f                     721K   Letters and docs on IAC │
│       📄 Apple Events             2K   Definition of Core Apple Event │
│       📄 Custom Events            2K   Instructions for registering ev │
│  ▽    📁 Edition Manager        717K                     │
│          📄 Reserved Words List 487K   Don't use these, they're taken │
│          📄 Schematic of workings 230K  A quick sketch of how Edition │
│  ▷ 📁 Secret beta info f      3,606K   Do not let this info out! │
│    📄 Tech Info 2 (DEC ALINK)     9K   From Andrew Gellman, concer │
│    📄 Vacation plans              2K   It's gonna ship soon, then we'r │
│    📄 Virtual Memory Limits     230K   Is it 1 gig, 2 gigs, or 4 gigs? │
└─────────────────────────────────────────────────────────┘
```

Figure 2-27: Title bar pop-up menu, and graphic of hard drive arrangement producing this menu.

Selecting a folder or volume name from this pop-up menu opens a new Finder window that displays the folder or volume contents. If a window for the selected folder or volume was already open, that window is brought forward and made active. This feature is a real time-saver when hunting files down in the Finder.

Holding down the Option and Command keys while selecting a folder or volume name from the Title bar pop-up menu causes the current window to be closed as the new folder or volume is opened, helping you to avoid a cluttered desktop by automating the process of closing windows that aren't being used.

Holding down the Option key also closes windows in several other situations:

- **Folders.** While opening a folder by double-clicking on its icon at the Finder, the current folder will close as the new one is opened.

- **Windows.** While clicking the close box in any Finder window, all Finder windows close.

- **Applications.** While launching an application, the window in which the application appears closes.

Improved Zooming

To resize an open window, you can either drag the size box in the lower-right corner or click in the zoom box in the upper-right corner of the window title bar. The zoom box operation is improved in System 7: it now expands the window size just enough to display the complete file list or all file and folder icons; it no longer opens the window to the full size of the current monitor unless that size is necessary.

Cleaning Up Windows and Icons

As in previous system software versions, the Clean Up command rearranges icons in Finder windows or on the desktop to make them more orderly and visible. Several new Clean Up options have been added in System 7, however, to help arrange icons in specific situations, or to create custom icon arrangements. These options appear in place of the standard Clean Up command, depending on the current selection and whether you're using the Shift, Option or Command key:

- **Clean Up Desktop.** When you're working with icons on the desktop (not in a Finder window), the Clean Up command normally reads Clean Up Desktop, and will align icons to the nearest grid position.

- **Clean Up All.** Holding down the Option key, however, changes the command to Clean Up All, which returns all disks, folders and volume icons to neat rows at the right edge of your primary monitor. (Again, this command is available only on the desktop, not in Finder windows.)

- **Clean Up Window.** When you're working in a Finder window, the Clean Up command is dimmed when the View command is set to anything other than By Icon or By Small Icon. When By Icon or By Small Icon is selected, the Clean Up Window command appears and arranges all icons in the current window into either aligned or staggered rows, depending on the settings in the Views control panel (as discussed earlier).

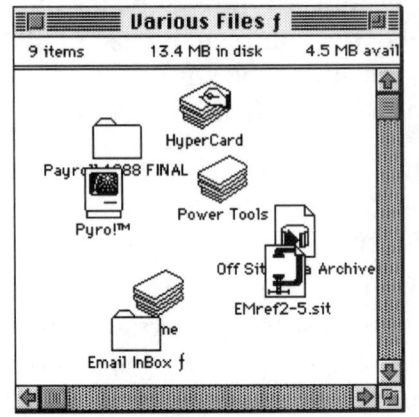

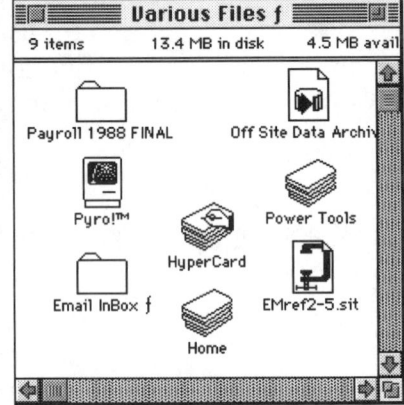

Figure 2-28: A Finder window before and after using Clean Up Window.

- **Clean Up By Name (By Size, etc.).** Holding down the Option key while selecting a Finder window lets you arrange icons by file name, size, date, comment, label or version. The specific option presented is the one selected in the View menu before the By Icon or By Small Icon command was chosen.

To arrange icons by size, select the respective windows for the icons you want to affect, choose By Size from the

View menu, choose By Icon (or By Small Icon) from the View menu, then hold down the Option key while choosing Clean Up By Size.

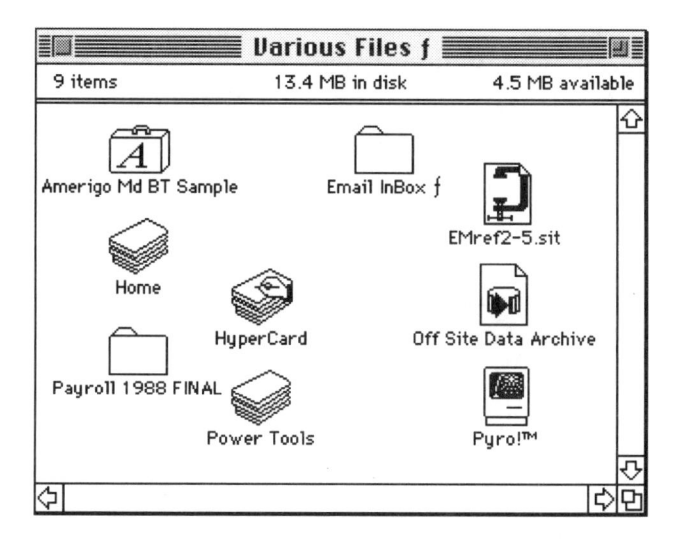

Figure 2-29: A Finder window with icons arranged alphabetically.

- **Clean Up Selection.** While a specific file or group of files is selected, holding down the Shift key presents Clean Up Selection, which will reposition only the selected files.

The Help Menu & Balloon Help

System 7 includes several features which were often touted by Apple as primary benefits of their new system software, but which have in fact turned out to be either impractical, poorly implemented, or just plain useless. The Help menu and Balloon Help is one example.

The Help menu and Balloon Help give Macintosh software applications the ability to provide on-screen context-sensitive information. It works by providing the Show Balloons command, which, when selected, causes a help balloon to be displayed when the arrow cursor is positioned over any menu command, window element, dialog box option, tool or icon. This help balloon provides a brief description of that command, element or icon function.

The System 7 Finder and control panels supply extensive help balloons, some of which are shown in Figure 2-30.

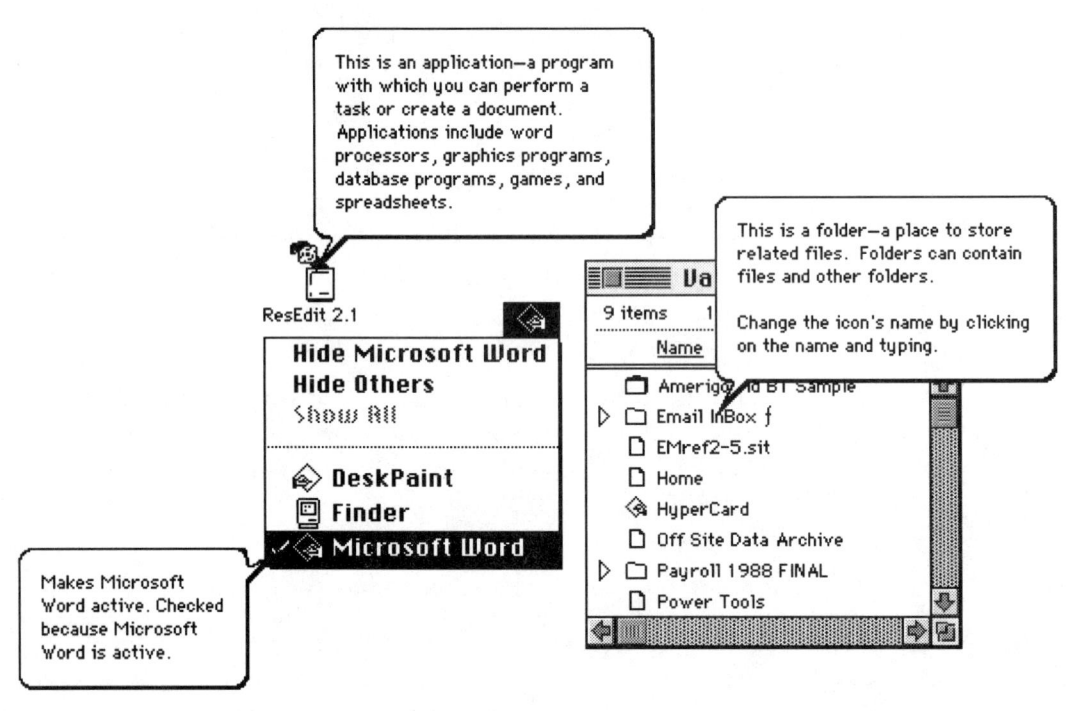

Figure 2-30: A sampling of the Finder's help balloons.

After the Show Balloons command has been chosen, it changes to the Hide Balloons command, which can be used to turn off the display of help balloons.

Balloon Help Limitations

In theory, Balloon Help makes it easier to learn new applications and refresh your memory when accessing infrequently used commands or dialog box options. However, these balloons can appear only in applications that have been written or upgraded specifically for System 7 and in which Balloon Help has been specifically implemented. More than two years after the introduction of System 7, only a limited number of programs fully support Balloon Help.

In those programs that do offer Balloon Help, the information provided is usually too limited or too generic to be truly helpful. This appears to be caused by the limited amount of space available for balloon text, and limited efforts from developers in balloon text development.

A bigger problem is the annoying way that help balloons pop up from every element your cursor points to once the Show Balloons command has been chosen. Someone wishing to take advantage of Balloon Help is unlikely to need assistance on every single object, command and element—but instead would like to read the one or two help balloons relevant to a single, specific problem. Unfortunately, Apple's current "all-or-nothing" implementation of Balloon Help leads to a very distracting display that tends to encourage many users who might occasionally benefit from Balloon Help to instead stay away from it completely.

A better implementation would display help balloons only when the cursor has pointed to a specific item for more than a few seconds, or only if a modifier key was held down. Several third party developers offer extensions that modify the way Balloon Help works, making it more pleasant and practical. These are described in Chapter 13, "Third-Party Utilities for System 7."

Additional Help

Optionally, in addition to Balloon Help, applications may add additional commands to the Help menu, usually to provide access to more in-depth online Help systems. The Finder provides an example of this additional help with the Finder Shortcuts command and dialog box. This dialog box is shown in Figure 2-31. In each application, check the Help menu for additional commands and online Help systems.

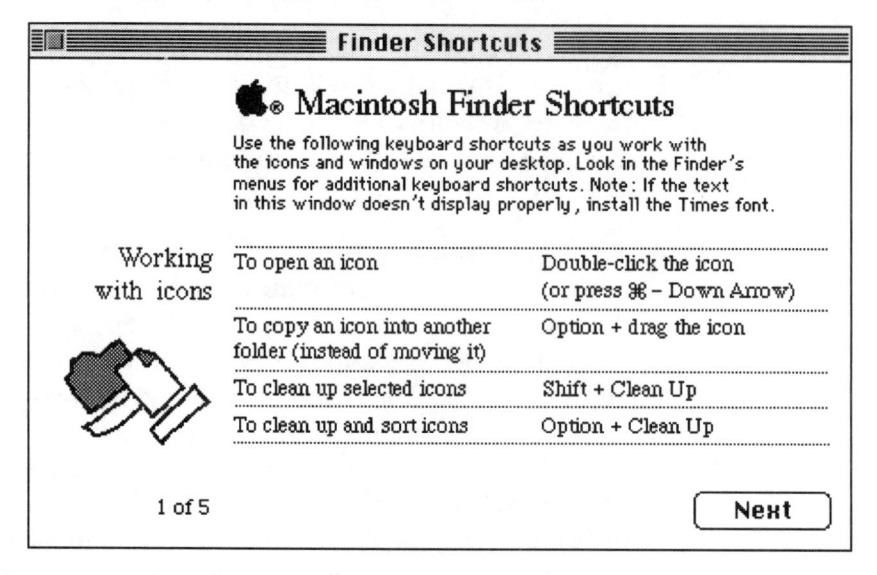

Figure 2-31: The Finder Shortcuts dialog box.

Trash & Empty Trash

The big news in System 7 trash is that the garbage collector no longer comes without being invited—the Trash is emptied only when the Empty Trash command is chosen from the Special menu. In previous versions of the system software, the Trash was automatically emptied when any application was launched, or when the Macintosh Restart or Shut Down commands were selected. Now, items remain in the Trash until Empty Trash is selected, even if the Mac is shut down.

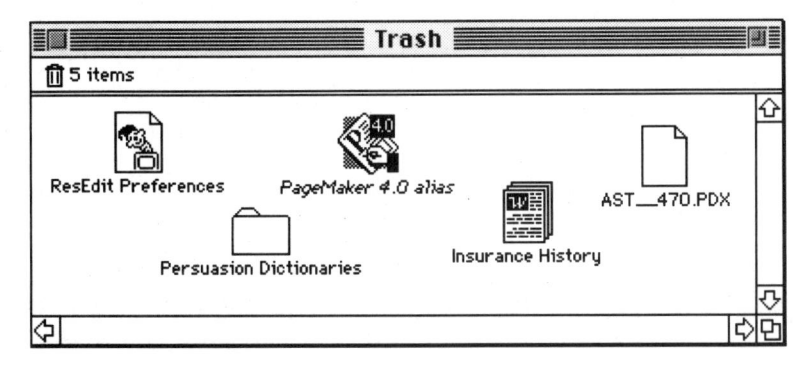

Figure 2-32: The Trash window displays files currently in the trash.

When the Empty Trash command is accessed, a dialog box appears asking you to confirm that you want to delete the current Trash files. This dialog box appears regardless of what files the Trash contains, and informs you how much disk space will be freed by emptying the trash.

Figure 2-33: The Empty Trash? dialog box.

Trash Tips

While the basic use of the Trash is straightforward, there are several less-obvious aspects you'll want to know about:

- **Avoid Trash warnings.** If you hold down the Option key while choosing Empty Trash, the confirmation dialog box will not appear and the Trash will be emptied immediately.

- **Disable Trash Warnings.** You can also disable the warning dialog by selecting the Trash, choosing the Get Info command and deselecting the Warn before emptying option. Of course, this will make it easier to delete application and system software files accidentally, so this option should be deselected with caution.

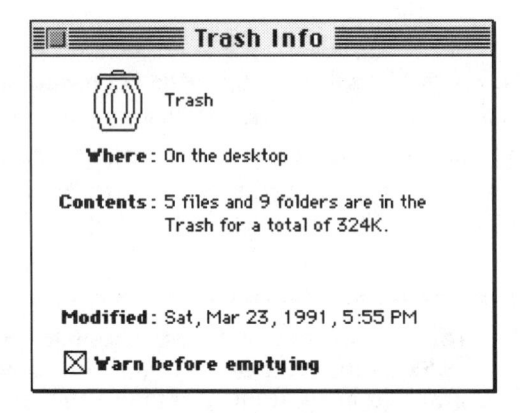

Figure 2-34: The Trash Get Info dialog box.

- **Retrieving Trashed Items.** Any time before the Empty Trash command is chosen, items inside the Trash may be recovered and saved from deletion. This is done by double-clicking on the Trash icon and dragging the file icons you want to recover out of the Trash window and back onto the desktop, or onto any volume or folder icon.

- **Freeing disk space.** Only when the trash has been emptied and this command is chosen is disk space released. In previous systems, dragging items to the Trash alone was sufficient to cause disk space to be freed—although not always immediately.

- **Repositioning the Trash.** In System 7, you can reposition the Trash on your desktop and it will stay there even if you reboot. It's no longer automatically returned to the lower right desktop corner each time you reboot. This is helpful if you use a large monitor or multiple monitors.

The Get Info Dialog Box

As in previous Finder versions, selecting any file, folder or drive icon and choosing the Get Info command from the File menu brings up an Info dialog box (usually called a Get Info dialog box) that displays basic information and related options. The basic System 7 Get Info dialog box, as shown in Figure 2-35, is only slightly different from those in previous Finder versions.

```
┌─────────────────────────────────────────┐
│ ▤ ▤▤ ═ FileMaker Tips V.1 Info ═ ▤▤ ▤   │
├─────────────────────────────────────────┤
│   ┌──┐                                   │
│   │W │  FileMaker Tips V.1               │
│   └──┘                                   │
│      Kind: Microsoft Word document      │
│      Size: 63K on disk (64,512 bytes used) │
│                                          │
│     Where: Data Drive : Magazine Writing: │
│            MacUser ƒ : FileMaker Tips    │
│            (MacUser) :                   │
│   Created: Tue, Dec 4, 1990, 12:57 AM    │
│  Modified: Wed, Dec 12, 1990, 10:24 PM   │
│   Version: not available                 │
│                                          │
│  Comments:                               │
│  ┌────────────────────────────────────┐ │
│  │ A collection of tips for FileMaker Pro.│ │
│  │                                    │ │
│  │                                    │ │
│  └────────────────────────────────────┘ │
│                                          │
│  ☐ Locked              ☐ Stationery pad │
└─────────────────────────────────────────┘
```

Figure 2-35: The Get Info dialog box for files.

There are now five different versions of the Get Info dialog box—one each for files, folders, applications, volumes and alias icons. Options may differ among versions, but the basic information each provides is the same:

- **File name.** The exact file name that appears on the desktop, which cannot be changed from within this dialog box.

- **Icon.** This appears to the left of the file name, providing a visual reference for the file.

  You can customize the icon of almost any data file, application or volume by pasting a new icon on top of the existing icon here in the Get Info dialog box. To change an icon, copy any MacPaint or PICT graphic onto the Clipboard, select the icon you want to replace in the Get Info dialog box (a box will appear around the icon, indicating its selection) and choose the Paste command from the Edit menu. Close the Get Info dialog box and the new icon will appear in the Finder window or on the desktop. Likewise, you can copy and paste any icons from between Get Info boxes.

- **Kind.** Provides a brief description of the selected file. For data files, this usually includes the name of the application that created the file.

- **Size.** The amount of disk space that the file consumes.

- **Where.** The location of the selected file, including all folders enclosing it and the volume it's on.

- **Created.** The date and time when the file was created. This date is reset when a file is copied from one volume to another or if a new copy is created by holding down the Option key while moving a file into a new folder.

- **Modified.** The date and time the contents of the file last changed.

- **Version.** Lists the software application's version number. No information on data files, folders or volumes is provided.

- **Comments.** Although it isn't obvious here, System 7 vastly improves its support for adding comments to this Get Info dialog box field. This is possible because comments can be displayed in Finder windows and you can use the new Find command to locate files by the comment text. Unfortunately, comments are still erased whenever the Finder's invisible Desktop file is recreated. A complete discussion of comments is provided in Chapter 3.

Several other options appear in some Get Info dialog boxes:

- **Locked.** Makes it impossible to change or delete the selected file. The Locked option appears for data files, applications and aliases. Locking ensures that unwanted changes are not accidentally made to data files that should not be altered. Locked data files can be opened, in most applications; but changes cannot be saved unless you use Save As... to create a new file.

Locked files are also spared accidental deletion, since they must be unlocked before they can be emptied from the Trash. If you try to delete a locked file, the dialog box shown in Figure 2-36 appears. It's important to note, however, that locked files will be deleted from the Trash without notice or warning if you hold down the Option key while you choose Empty Trash from the Finder's Special menu.

Figure 2-36: The warning that appears when locked items are in the Trash.

- **Memory.** These options appear only for application files and include Suggested size and Current size. Suggested size specifies the application developer's recommendations for the amount of memory to be allocated to the program when it's opened. The Current size option specifies how much memory will actually be allocated to the program when it's opened. (A discussion of these options is presented in Chapter 11.)

- **Stationery Pad.** Available for data files only, this turns the selected document into a template. (A template is a master document on which new documents are based.) With this option, each time the selected document is opened, a copy of the file is created, and any changes or customizations are made to this copy, leaving the original Stationery Pad document available as a master at all times. (A complete discussion of Stationery Pads is provided in Chapter 5.)

Get Info for the Trash

The Trash's Get Info dialog box, shown in Figure 2-37, contains two important pieces of information and one useful option. The dialog box lists the number of files and the amount of disk space they consume, which lets you know how much space will be freed by the Empty Trash command. It also lists the date when the most recent item was placed in the Trash.

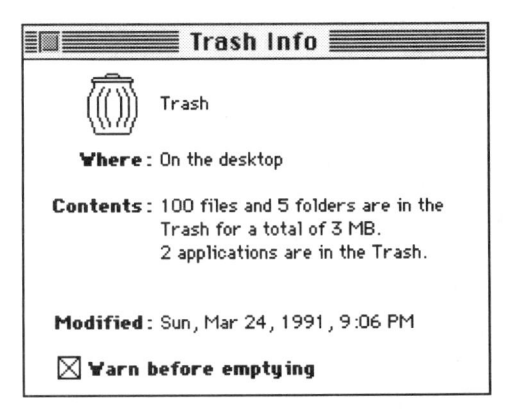

Figure 2-37: The Trash's Get Info dialog box.

The Warn before emptying option, which is a default, causes the dialog box to display when the Empty Trash command is selected (shown in Figure 2-38). If you don't want the dialog box to display each time the Empty Trash command is chosen, deselect the Warn before emptying option. But without this warning dialog box, you increase the risk of permanently deleting files you may want later.

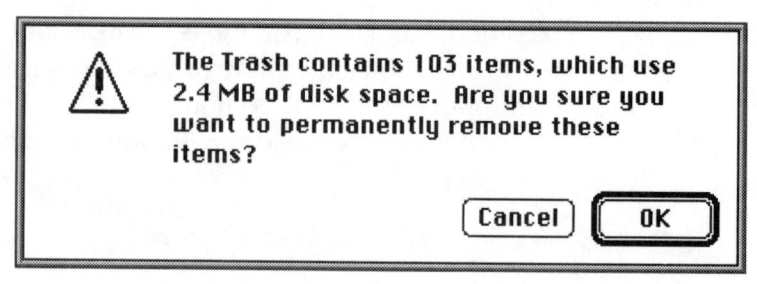

Figure 2-38: The Empty Trash confirmation dialog.

Get Info for Alias Icons

The Get Info dialog box for alias icons is different in several ways from the one used by standard files. First, the version information normally displayed beneath the dates is replaced with the path and file name of the original file.

Figure 2-39: The Get Info dialog box for an alias icon.

Also, the Get Info dialog box includes the Find Original button that locates the disk or folder containing the original file (from which the alias was made). It can open the disk or folder window and select the original file icon. If the disk or volume containing the original file is not available, a dialog asks you to insert the disk containing the original file, or in the case of a network volume, the volume will be mounted.

Comments and Locked are available for aliases, behaving exactly as they do for any other files. The "Stationery Pad" option, however, is not available for alias icons.

Moving On

The Finder is the most visible part of the Macintosh system software; as we've seen in this chapter, it gives you powerful and intuitive tools to manage the disks and files you're using with your Macintosh:

- The new Finder menus.
- The many ways you can see and manipulate data in Finder windows.
- The Help menu and Balloon Help.
- The Trash and Empty Trash command.
- The Get Info dialog box, in its many forms.

From general disk and file management tools, we move into Chapter 3, "Managing Your Hard Drive," where four new System 7 features will be documented in detail. Aliasing, the Find... command, labels and comments—all used at the Finder—are vital to control and productivity on your Macintosh.

Chapter 3: Managing Your Hard Drive

As we've seen already, the Finder provides a comprehensive set of commands and features that help you manage disks and files. The new Finder does not, however, require you to organize your electronic files in any particular way; it's still up to you to decide the best way to arrange your files.

File management is an interesting challenge; you must balance your available storage space with the quantity and size of files you need to keep available, and you must design a logical arrangement that will allow you to quickly locate the files you need.

Fortunately, System 7 provides several file-management tools, including the Make Alias command, the Find command and the Label menu. These commands will affect the way you store files on your hard disk—and on floppy disks, removable cartridges, network file servers or any other storage devices. In this chapter, we'll take a look at these new features and how they can help you organize your hard drive.

Aliasing

Wouldn't it be nice to be in several places at one time? Imagine, for example, that while you were hard at work earning your paycheck, you could also be lying on a beach enjoying the sun. And if being in two places at once sounds appealing, how would you like to be in any number of places at one time? For example, you could be at work earning a living, at the beach getting a tan, at the library reading a book and on a plane bound for an exotic destination—all at the same time.

System 7 extends this convenience to your electronic files through a feature called *aliasing*. Aliasing is perhaps the most significant improvement System 7 offers the average Macintosh user, because it removes the single largest constraint—space limitation—from the task of organizing files and thereby makes it easier to take full advantage of your software applications and data files.

Basic Aliasing Concepts
(or "How I came home from work with a tan")

In simple terms, an *alias* is a special kind of copy of a file, folder or volume. Unlike copies you might create with the Duplicate command or other traditional methods, an alias is only a copy of the file, folder or volume *icon*.

To understand this distinction, think of a file icon as a door; the file that the icon represents is the room behind the door. As you would expect, each room normally has just one door (each file has one icon), and opening that door (the icon) is the only way to enter the room.

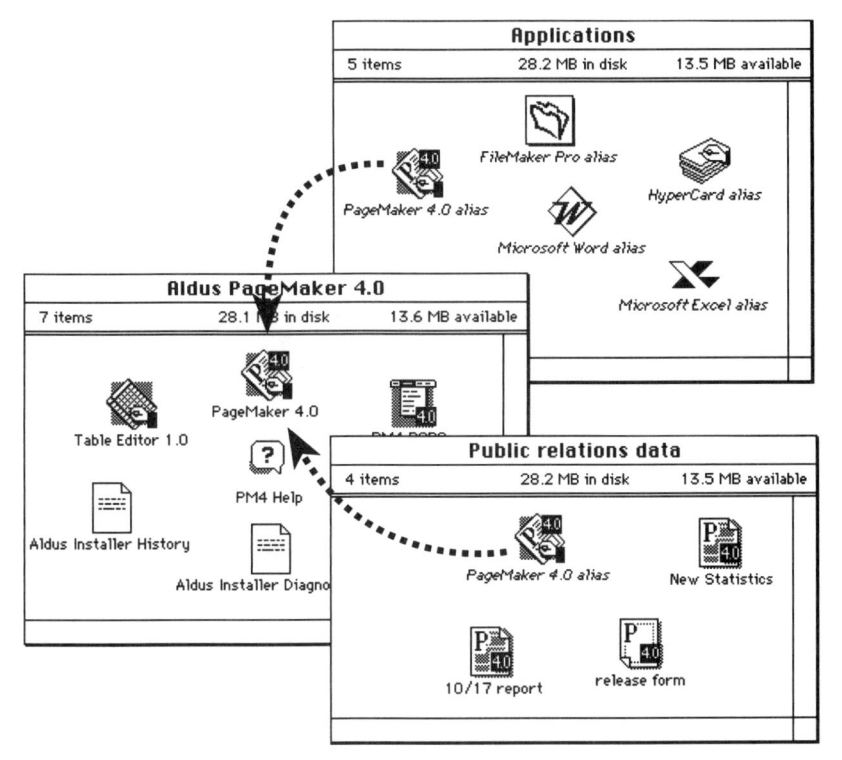

Figure 3-1: Each alias points to the original file that was used to create it.

Creating an alias is like adding an additional door to a room; it presents another entrance, usually in a location different from the existing entrance. Just as you wouldn't have two doors to the same room right next to each other, you won't usually have two icons for the same file (the original and an alias) in the same location. This is the first important feature of an alias: it can be moved to any folder on any volume without affecting the relationship between the alias and its original file. In fact, the link between an alias and its original file is maintained even if both files are moved.

Another key feature of an alias is that it requires only about 1k or 2k of disk space, regardless of the size of the original file. That's because the alias is a copy of the icon, not a copy of the file itself. The alias's small size is an important attribute, since it consumes very little storage space.

Details about these and other aspects of aliases are provided later in this chapter, but before getting too far into the technical aspects, let's take a quick look at a few practical ways to use aliases:

- **To make applications easier to launch.** Since double-clicking on an application's alias launches that application, aliases make applications easily accessible.

    For example, you can keep one alias of your word processor on the desktop, another in a folder full of word processing data files and yet another alias in the Apple Menu Items Folder. You could then launch this application using the icon most convenient at the moment.

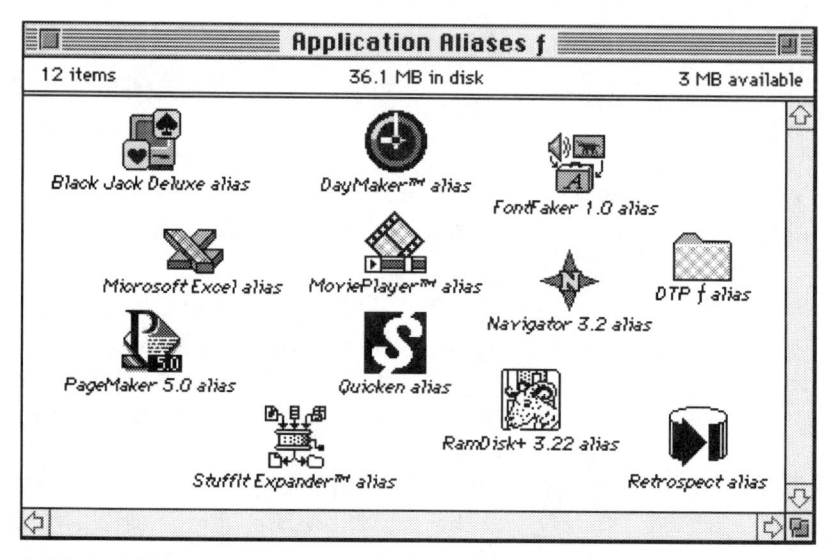

Figure 3-2: Aliasing an application makes it more convenient to launch.

- **To organize data files more logically.** You can keep alias copies of data files in as many folders as they logically belong in.

If you keep a spreadsheet file with information on your income taxes, for example, in a folder along with all the spreadsheets you've created during that year, you could also keep an alias copy of that same spreadsheet in a personal-finances folder, in another tax-file folder and in a general-accounting folder.

Storing alias copies in multiple locations has several benefits. First, it lets you quickly locate the file you're looking for, because there are several places to find it. It's also easier to find files because they can be stored along with other files they're logically connected with. Finally, archival storage lets you move the originals off the hard drive, saving disk space while still allowing access to the file via aliases.

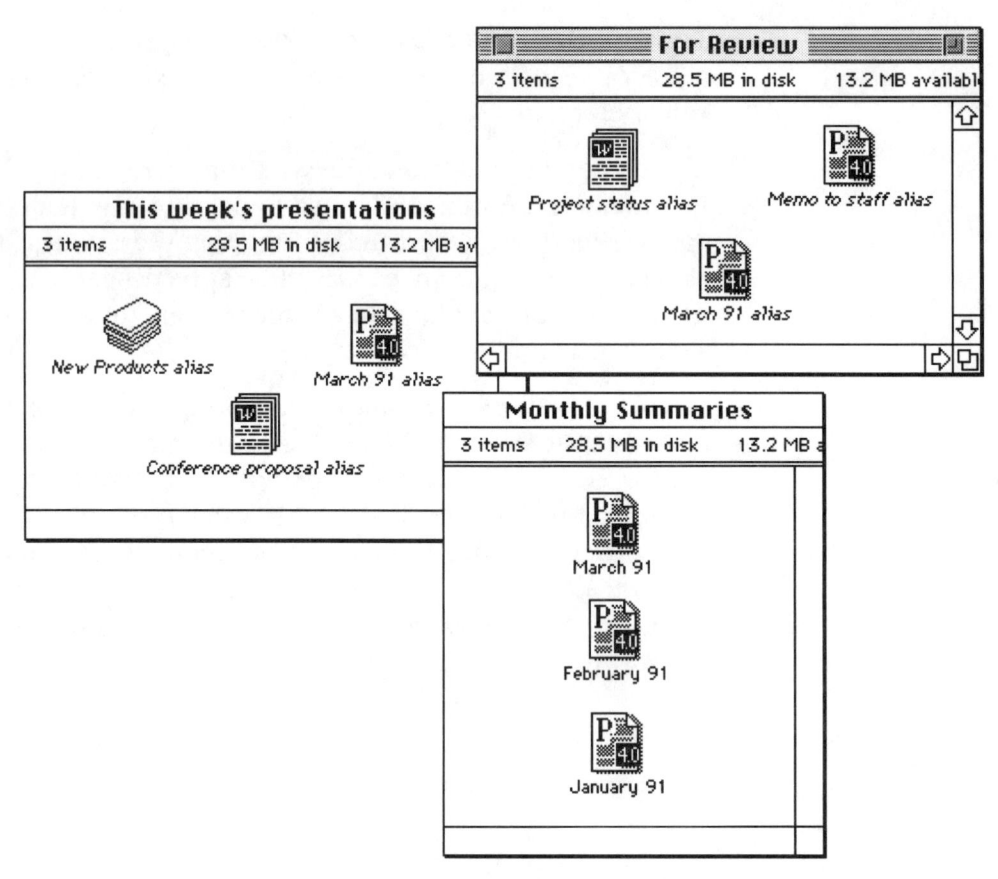

Figure 3-3: Aliasing data files allows them to be stored in multiple logical locations.

- **To simplify access to files stored on removable media.** Keeping aliases from floppy disks, removable hard drives, CD-ROMs and other removable storage media on your local hard drive lets you locate those files quickly and easily.

    When an alias of a file stored on removable media is opened, the Macintosh prompts you to insert the disk (or cartridge) that contains the original file.

■ **To simplify access to files stored on network servers.** Placing aliases of files from network file servers on your local hard drive is another way to quickly and easily locate the files no matter where they're stored.

When an alias of a file stored on the network server is opened, the Macintosh automatically connects to the server, prompting you for necessary passwords.

Creating & Using Aliases

To create an alias, select the file, folder or volume icon and choose the Make Alias command from the File menu. An alias icon will then appear, with the same name and icon as the original, followed by the word "alias," as shown in Figure 3-4.

Figure 3-4: An original file and an alias of that file.

For the most part, alias icons look and act just like other files, folders or volumes. You can change the file name of an alias at any time; changing the file name doesn't break the link between the alias and its original file. Changing a file name is like changing the sign on a door; it doesn't change the contents of the room behind the door.

Figure 3-5: An original file and an alias of the file that's been renamed.

You've probably noticed that alias file names appear in italic type. This is always true, even when they're listed in dialog boxes (*except* when aliases are listed under the Apple Menu). The italic type helps you distinguish alias files from original files.

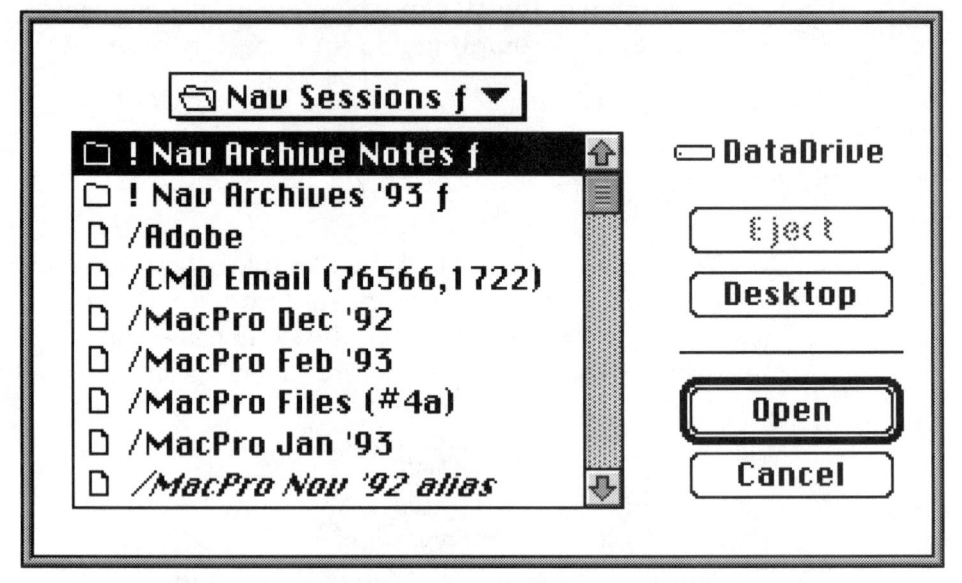

Figure 3-6: Alias file names appear in italics in dialog boxes.

As mentioned earlier, alias icons can be moved to any available folder or volume without losing the link they maintain to the original file. This is the magic of aliases and the key to their utility. No matter how files are moved, the links are maintained.

Original files can also be moved, as long as they remain on the same volume; and they can be renamed without breaking the link with their aliases. When the alias icon is opened, the Macintosh finds and opens the original file.

To illustrate how this automatic linkage is maintained, assume you have a file called "1991 Commission Schedule," which is stored in a folder named "Corporate Spreadsheets." You created an alias of this file, moved the alias into a folder called "1991 Personal Accounting" and renamed the alias "1991 Commissions" (see Figure 3-7).

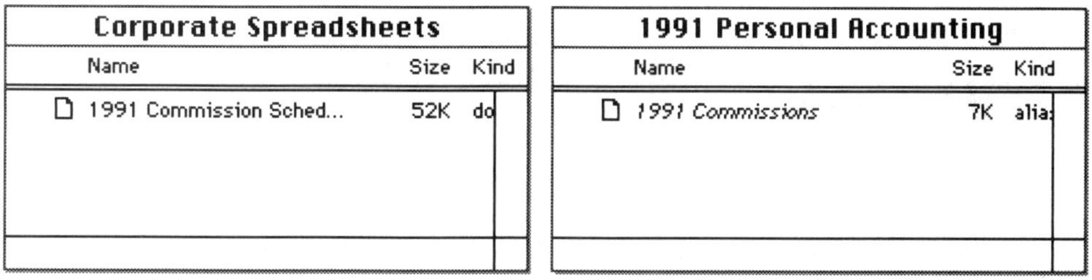

Corporate Spreadsheets		
Name	Size	Kind
1991 Commission Sched…	52K	do

1991 Personal Accounting		
Name	Size	Kind
1991 Commissions	7K	alias

Figure 3-7: Files and aliases as originally named and positioned.

Later, you decide that this file will contain only data for the first six months of 1991, so you rename the original file "1991 Pt1 Comm Sched," and put it in a new folder inside the "Corporate Spreadsheets" folder named "Jan-June Stuff" (see Figure 3-8).

Even though both the original file and the alias have been moved and renamed since they were created, double-clicking on the "1991 Commissions" file (the alias) will open the "1991 Pt1 Comm. Sched" file.

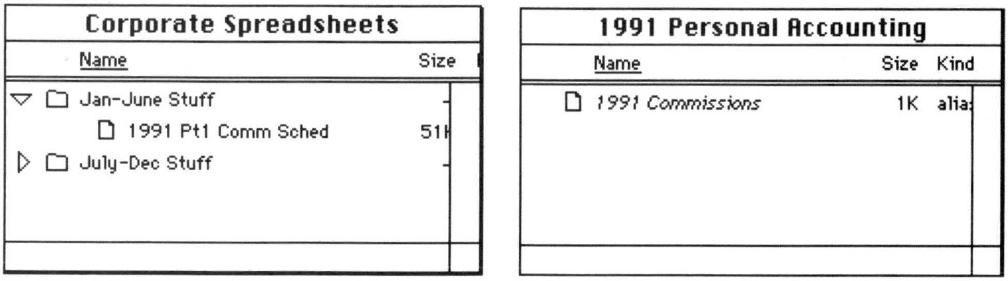

Corporate Spreadsheets	
Name	Size
▽ 🗀 Jan-June Stuff	
1991 Pt1 Comm Sched	51K
▷ 🗀 July-Dec Stuff	

1991 Personal Accounting		
Name	Size	Kind
1991 Commissions	1K	alias

Figure 3-8: Files and aliases after being moved and renamed.

Advanced Aliasing Concepts

Once you understand the basic concepts of aliases and begin using them, you may have questions, such as: How many aliases can one file have? Is it possible to alias an alias? What happens when an alias's original file is deleted? The answers to these and other questions follow.

- **Multiple aliases.** There is no limit to the number of aliases you can create from a single file, folder or volume.

  When creating multiple aliases, alias names are designated by numbers, to distinguish them from existing alias names. The first alias of a file named "Rejection Letter" is named "Rejection Letter Alias"; the second, "Rejection Letter Alias 1"; and the third, "Rejection Letter Alias 2"—and so on until the earlier aliases are renamed or moved to different locations. These alias numbers have no significance beyond serving to avoid file-name duplication.

- **Aliasing aliases.** You can create an alias of an alias, but this causes a chain of pointing references: the second alias points to the first, which points to the original. In most cases, it's better to create an alias directly from the original file.

  If you do create a chain and any one of the aliases in the chain is deleted, all subsequent aliases will no longer be linked to the original file. To illustrate this problem, assume an alias named "New Specs Alias" was created from an original file named "New Specs," then "New Specs Alias 2" was created from "New Specs Alias" (see Figure 3-9).

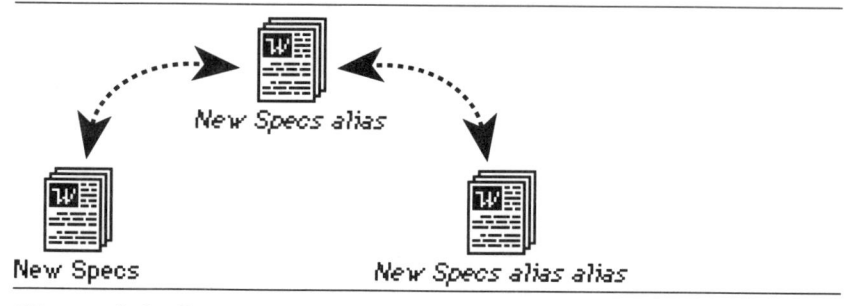

Figure 3-9: Creating an alias of an alias causes a chain that can be broken if one alias is deleted.

At that point, each of these files can be repositioned and renamed and the alias links will be automatically maintained. However, if the "New Specs alias" file is deleted, "New Specs alias alias" will no longer be linked to "New Specs." There's no way to reestablish the link should a break occur.

- **Deleting aliases.** Deleting an alias has no effect on the original file, folder or volume. It simply means that in order to access the item that the alias represented, you'll have to access the original item or another alias.

  You can delete aliases in any of the ways you delete normal files: drag the alias to the Trash, then choose the Empty Trash command, or delete the alias using some other file deletion utility.

- **Moving original files.** The link between an alias and its original file is maintained regardless of how the original is moved on one volume; but links are not maintained when you copy the original file to a new volume and then delete the original file. In other words, there's no way to transfer the alias link from an original file to a copy of that original file.

  If you're going to move a file from which aliases have been created from one volume to another, and you must delete the original file, all existing aliases will be unlinked and therefore useless. You could create new aliases from the original file in its new location and replace the existing aliases with the new ones, but you'd have to perform this process manually.

- **Deleting original files.** Deleting a file from which aliases have been made has no immediate effect; no warning is posted when the file is deleted. But when an attempt is made to open an alias of a file that's been deleted, a dialog box appears informing you that the original file cannot be found. There's no way to salvage a deleted file to relink with this alias, so in most cases you'll want to delete the orphaned alias.

  The exception to this rule is when the original file is still in the Trash. In this case, if you try to open an alias, a dialog box will inform you that the file cannot be opened because it's in the Trash. If you drag the original from the Trash, it's again available to the alias.

- **Finding original files.** Although an alias is in many ways a perfect proxy for a file, there are times when you'll need to locate the alias's original file—for example, if you want to delete the original file or copy the original onto a floppy disk.

  To locate the original file for any alias, simply select the alias icon in the Finder and choose Get Info (Command-I) from the Finder's File menu. This brings up a special Get Info dialog box (shown in Figure 3-10) that displays basic information about the alias icon, the path information for the original file, and the Find Original button.

  When the Find Original button is clicked, the original file, folder or volume is selected and displayed on the desktop. If the original file is located on a removable volume that's not currently available, a dialog box appears prompting you to insert the disk or cartridge containing that file. If the original file is located on a network file server, the Macintosh attempts to log onto the server to locate the file, prompting for any required passwords.

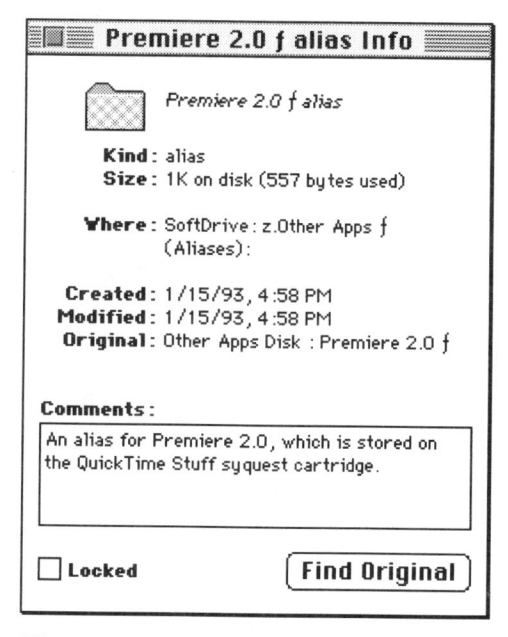

Figure 3-10: The Get Info dialog box for an alias.

If the current alias is an alias of an alias, clicking the Find Original button will find the *original* file, not the alias used to create the current alias. If the alias file has been accessed via File Sharing, the Find Original button will usually be unable to locate the original file, although its location is accurately documented in the original text of the Get Info dialog box.

- **Replacing alias icons.** As introduced in Chapter 2, "The Finder," new icons can be pasted into the Get Info dialog box for any file. This is also true of alias icons. Replacing the icon of any alias has no effect on the icon of the original file.

Aliasing Folders or Volumes

So far, most of this section has focused on aliasing in relation to application and data files. But almost without exception, aliasing works the same way for folders and volumes. Folder aliases are created, renamed, repositioned, deleted and linked to their originals in exactly the same way as the file aliases previously described:

- Aliasing a folder creates a new folder icon with the same name as the original, plus the word "alias."

- The name of an alias folder appears in italics on the desktop or in dialog box listings.

- Folder aliases can be renamed at any time. Of course, an alias cannot have the same name as an original or another alias while in the same location.

- Folder aliases can be moved inside any other folder or folder alias or to any volume.

- When an alias folder is opened, the window of the original folder is opened. Aliasing a folder does not alias the folder's content. For this reason, the original folder must be available anytime the folder alias is opened. If the original folder is on a volume that's not currently mounted, you'll be prompted to insert the volume or the Macintosh will attempt to mount the volume if it's on the network.

- Deleting a folder alias does not delete the original folder or any of its contents.

But there are some unique aspects of folder aliases:

- When a folder alias is displayed hierarchically in a Finder window, it cannot be opened hierarchically (no triangle appears to its left) because the folder alias has no contents, strictly speaking. You can open the folder alias by double-clicking on it to open a new Finder window.

- Folder aliases appear in standard file dialog boxes, and the contents of the original folder can be revealed from within these dialog boxes.

- Anything put into a folder alias is actually placed into the original folder, including files, folders and other aliases. The folder alias has no real contents; it's just another "door" to the original folder.

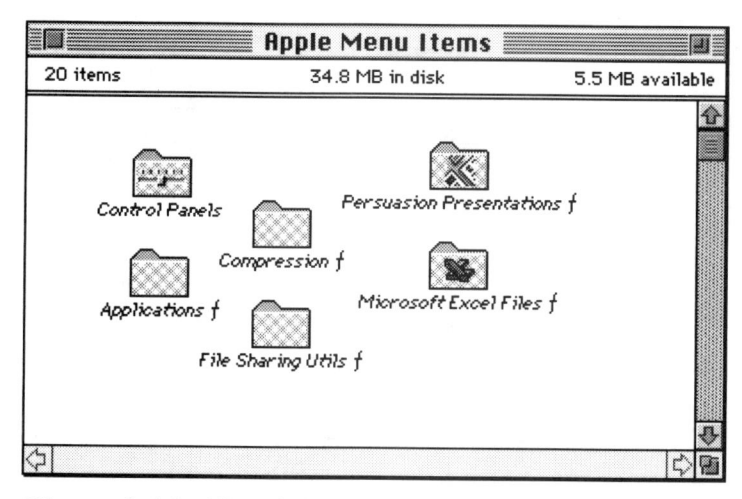

Figure 3-11: Alias folders are commonly used in the Apple Menu.

Volume aliases are similar to file aliases but have some of the same characteristics as folder aliases:

- Opening a volume alias mounts the original volume if it's not already available. If the original volume is not currently mounted, you'll be prompted to insert the volume, or the Macintosh will attempt to mount the volume if it's on the network.

- Opening a volume alias displays the Finder window of the actual volume and the contents of this window.

- Aliasing a volume does not alias the volume contents, just the icon of the volume itself.

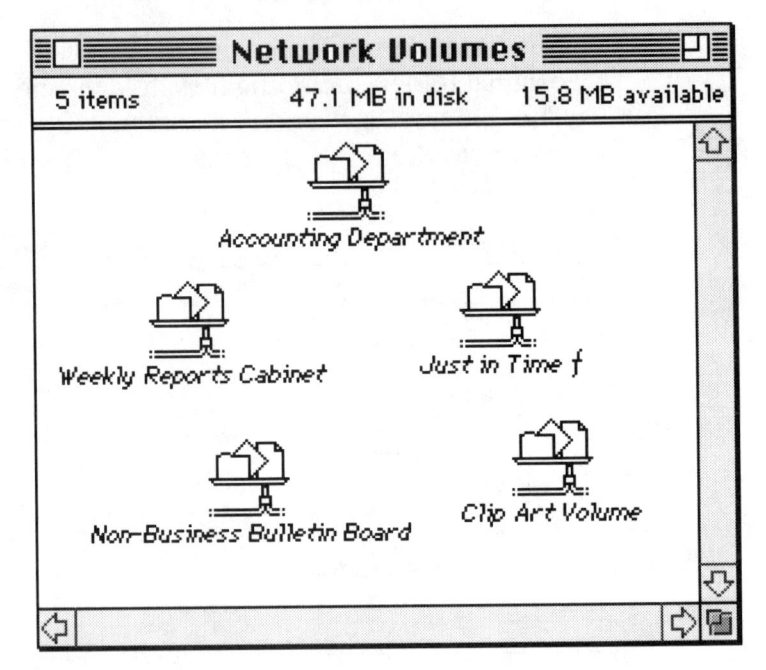

Figure 3-12: Alias volumes, stored in a folder.

Using Aliases

Aliases have a multitude of uses. Following are some of the more interesting possibilities:

- **Alias applications.** The easiest way to launch an application is to double-click on its icon. But many of today's applications are stored in folders containing a morass of ancillary files—dictionaries, color palettes, Help files, printer descriptions and so on. Amid all this clutter, it's hard to locate the application icon in order to launch it. Aliasing allows easier access.

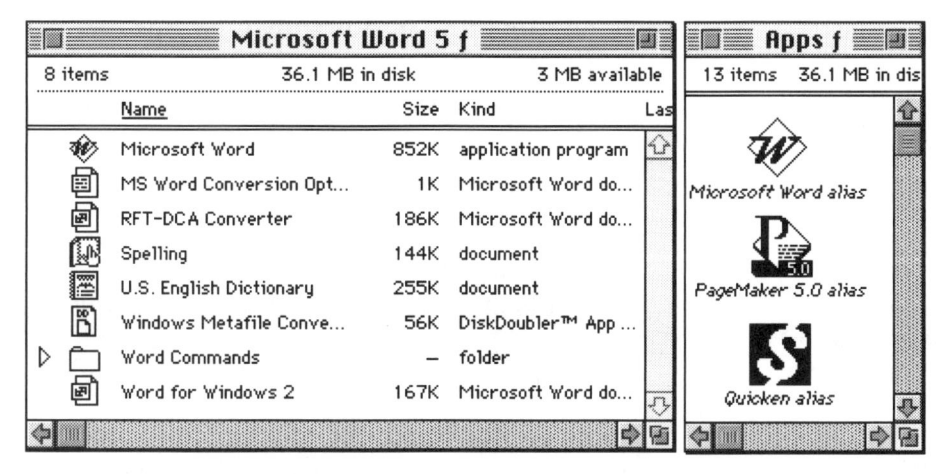

Figure 3-13: Microsoft Word, along with its ancillary files (left), and an alias of Word in a folder with other application aliases (right).

The most straightforward way to simplify application launching is to alias each of your applications and place these aliases in the Apple Menu Items Folder of your System Folder. You can then launch the applications by simply choosing their names from the Apple Menu.

Or, instead, you might group your application aliases into folders, then alias these folders and place them in the Apple Menu. Doing it this way takes two steps instead of one, but this method leaves room in your Apple Menu for other folder, volume and file aliases. Of course, you could leave a few applications that you use extensively directly in the Apple Menu.

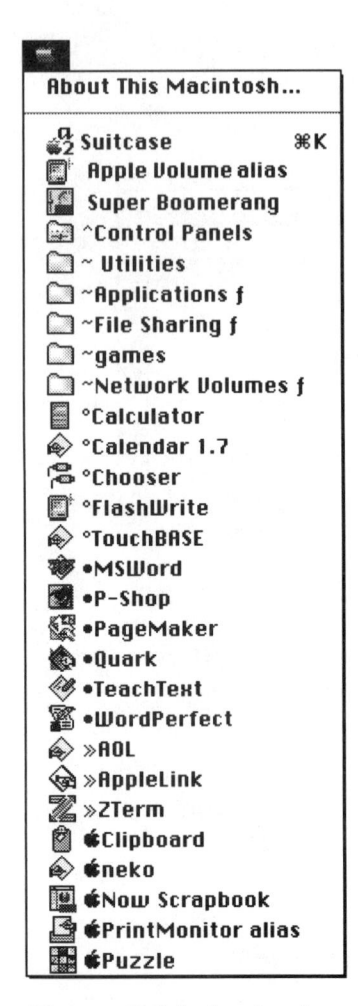

```
About This Macintosh...
  Suitcase                ⌘K
  Apple Volume alias
  Super Boomerang
  ^Control Panels
  ~Utilities
  ~Applications ƒ
  ~File Sharing ƒ
  ~games
  ~Network Volumes ƒ
  °Calculator
  °Calendar 1.7
  °Chooser
  °FlashWrite
  °TouchBASE
  •MSWord
  •P-Shop
  •PageMaker
  •Quark
  •TeachText
  •WordPerfect
  »AOL
  »AppleLink
  »ZTerm
   Clipboard
   neko
   Now Scrapbook
   PrintMonitor alias
   Puzzle
```

Figure 3-14: An Apple Menu customized with folders and applications.

Figure 3-14 shows an Apple Menu configured with application-group folders. Note that a tilde (~) has been added to the start of each folder name. This not only makes it easy to identify folders from other elements in the Apple Menu, but more importantly it groups them all together in one section of the Apple Menu listing. (See Chapter 4, "The System Folder," for more tips on working with the Apple Menu.)

You can also put application aliases, along with groups of documents created with the application, on your desktop. But since double-clicking on any document will launch the application anyway, this is not really very useful.

- **Multiple data-file aliases.** To avoid having to remember all the places where a frequently used file is stored every time you want to use it, you can use aliases to store each data file in as many places as it logically fits—anywhere you might look for the file when you need it later.

Suppose, for example, that you write a letter to your boss about a new idea for serving your company's big client, Clampdown, Inc. Depending on your personal scheme, you might store this letter, along with other general business correspondence, in a folder pertaining to Clampdown, Inc., or you might even have a file where you keep everything that has to do with your boss. Using aliases, you can store the file in all these locations and in a folder of all work you've done in the current week.

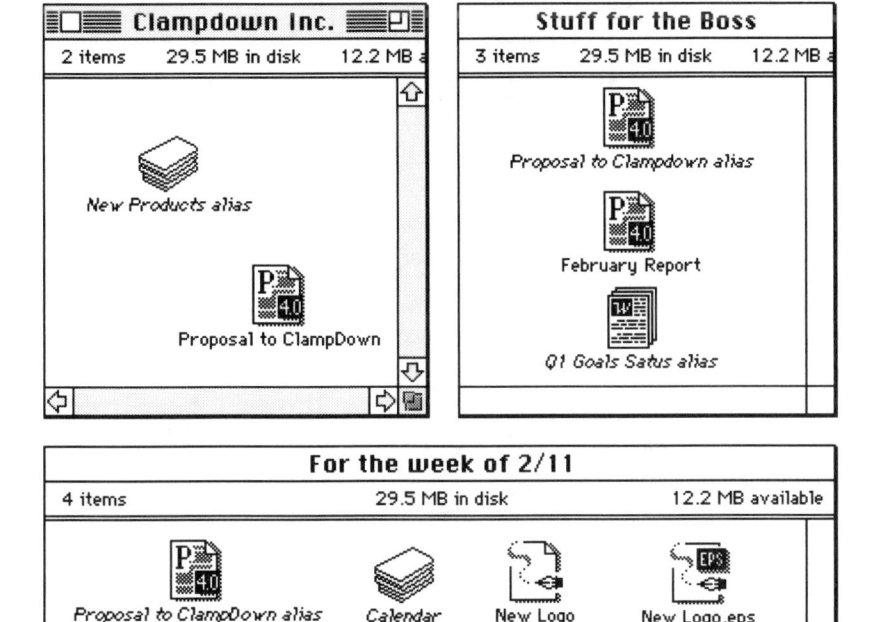

Figure 3-15: Aliasing a file into multiple locations.

- **Aliases of data files from remote or removable volumes.** You can store hundreds of megabytes worth of files on your hard drive, regardless of how big it is, by using aliases. Keeping aliases of all the files you normally store on removable disks or drives and all the files from network file servers that you occasionally need to utilize lets you locate and open the files by simply searching your hard drive (at the Finder, in dialog boxes or using a search utility) without the cost of hard-drive space.

  This is perfect for storing libraries of clip-art files, downloadable fonts, corporate templates or other infrequently used file groups. Storing these aliased files on your hard drive lets you browse through them whenever necessary. The hard drive will automatically mount the required volumes or prompt you for them when they're needed.

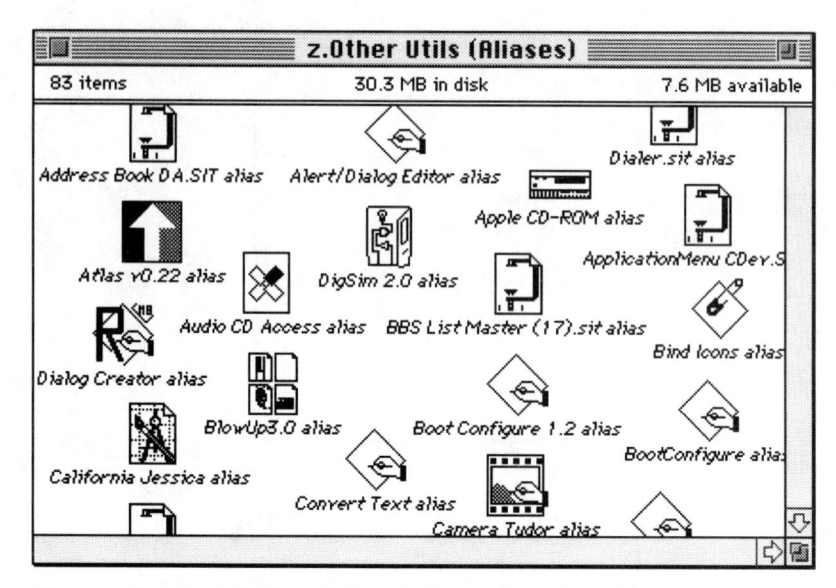

Figure 3-16: A folder full of aliased utility files stored on a removable volume.

- **Trash alias.** You can alias the Finder's Trash and store copies of it in any folder. Dragging folder files to the Trash alias is the same as dragging them to the actual Trash. Files trashed in this way will not be removed until you choose Empty Trash from the Special menu, and they can be retrieved by simply opening the Trash (or an alias of it) and dragging the file back onto a volume or folder.

- **Removable cartridge maps.** Create a folder for each removable cartridge, drive or floppy disk. Alias the entire contents of these volumes and store the aliases in the volume's folder. Then you can "browse" these volumes without mounting them. You may also want to keep other aliases of files from these volumes in other locations on your drive.

- **Network file-server volume maps.** Create a folder called "Network" and place an alias of each remote volume inside that folder. You can then log onto any remote volume by simply double-clicking on the volume alias. This eliminates the need to access the Chooser, locate the file server, and locate the volume every time you want to use the volume. Of course, you'll be prompted for any required passwords.

- **Hard-drive alias.** If you work on a large AppleTalk network, put an alias icon of your hard drive on a floppy disk and carry it with you. If you need to access your hard drive from another location, all you have to do is insert the floppy disk containing your hard drive alias into any Macintosh on the network, double-click on the alias icon and your hard drive will be mounted via AppleTalk.

Aliasing Summary

- You can alias any file, folder, volume icon or the Trash.
- To create an alias, select the desired icon and choose Make Alias from the Finder's Special menu.
- An alias initially takes the same name as its original file with the word "alias" appended.
- Alias names always appear in italics, except in the Apple Menu.
- Aliases can be renamed at any time. The standard Macintosh 32-character name limit applies.
- Aliases can be moved to any location on the current volume or any other volume.
- An alias is initially given the same icon as its original. The icon can be changed in the Get Info dialog box.
- Most alias icons require only 2k or 3k of storage space.

- The link between an alias and its original is maintained even when the files are renamed or repositioned.

- Deleting an alias icon has no effect on its original file, folder or volume.

- Copying an alias to a new location on the current drive (hold down Option key while dragging) is the same as creating a new alias of the original file—it does not create an alias of an alias.

- Use the Get Info command to locate an alias's original.

- Opening a folder alias opens the window of the original.

- Opening a volume alias opens the window of the original volume.

The Find Command

Regardless of how well organized your electronic filing system is, it's impossible to always remember where specific files are located.

To solve this problem in the past, Apple provided the Find File desk accessory to let you search for files—by file name—on any currently mounted volume. Find File locates the files and lists them in a section of its window. Once a file is found, selecting the file name reveals the path of the located file, along with other basic file information, as shown in Figure 3-17. Using this information, you can then quit the Find File DA and locate the file yourself, or Find File can move the file to the desktop where it's easy to access.

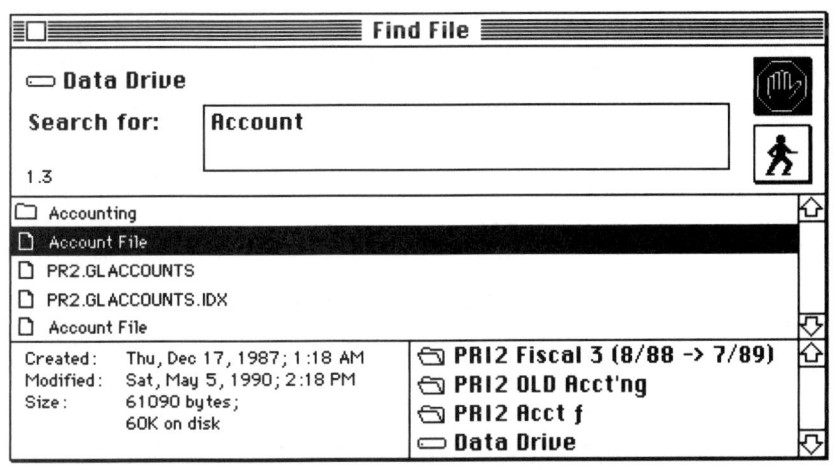

Figure 3-17: The Find File desk accessory.

Beyond Find File, other file-finding utilities have also been available. Most of them let you search for files not only by file name but also by creation date, file type, creator, date modified, file size and other file attributes and combinations of attributes. Like Find File, most of these utilities locate matching files, display the path information, and let you return to the Finder and use or modify the file as required.

In System 7, a new Find... command has been added to the Finder. This command and its companion, Find Again, significantly improve on the Find File desk accessory. Because these new commands are built into the Finder, they offer important advantages over other file-finding utilities.

Using the Find Command

The new Find command is located in the Finder's File menu, while desk accessory-based utilities put it in the Apple Menu. Having the Find command in the Finder is not really a disadvantage, since the Finder is always available in System 7. (To access the Find command while using another application, you use the Applications menu in the upper-right corner of the menu bar to bring the Finder to the foreground. After using the Find command, you use the Applications menu again to return to your application.)

When the Find command (Command-F) is selected, the Find dialog box appears. This dialog box, shown in Figure 3-18, can search files only by name, much like Find File. Additional search criteria are accessed by clicking the More Choices button, which brings up the Find Item dialog box (shown in Figure 3-19).

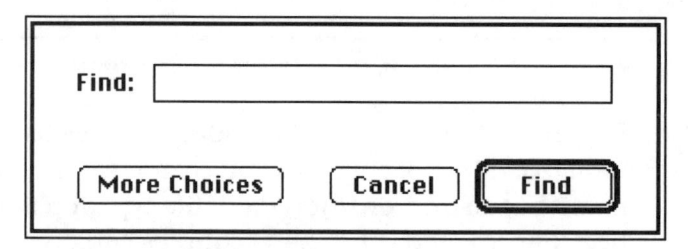

Figure 3-18: The Find dialog box.

Let's start with the simple Find dialog box; later in this section, you'll look at the other options available with the Find Item dialog box. In both sections, you'll evaluate the Find command's capabilities in finding files, but it should be noted that the Find command will also locate folders matching the selected search criteria.

The Find Dialog Box

Using the basic Find dialog box to locate files by name, you can enter the complete file name or only the first portion of the file name.

- **Enter a complete file name.** If you know the complete file name you're looking for, enter it into the Find option box. In most cases, only the correct file will be found, but if you make even a slight error in spelling the file name, the correct file will not be found. This is not the most efficient way to execute a file search.

- **Enter only the first portion of a file name.** Entering the first few characters of the file name is the most commonly used and usually the most efficient file-name search method. This locates all file names that begin with the characters you've specified. The exact number of characters you should enter will depend on the circumstances; the goal is to enter enough characters to narrow the search down but not so many that you risk a spelling mistake and therefore a chance of missing the file.

  As an example, if the file you wanted to locate was "Archaeology Report," specifying only the letter "A" would yield a huge number of files to sort through. On the other hand, entering six or seven characters could allow files with spelling errors, such as "Archio" or "Arhcae," to escape the search. Decide on the number of characters according to how common the first few characters are among your files and how well you remember the file name. In this example, searching for files starting with "Arc" would probably be the best strategy.

After specifying the search criteria, click the Find button to start the search. The search starts at the startup drive and proceeds to all mounted volumes. If the search will take more than a few seconds, a Progress dialog box appears. When a file matching the search criteria is located, a window is opened, and the file is displayed.

At this point, you can use or modify the file as required. If the selected file is not the one you wanted, or if after modifying the selected file you want to continue searching for the next file that matches the search criteria, choose the Find Again command from the File menu or press Command-G. As each matching file is located, you can use or modify it (or simply ignore it), then repeat the process to proceed to the next matching file.

The Find Item Dialog Box

Clicking the More Choices button in the Find dialog box brings up the Find Item dialog box (see Figure 3-19), which has several advantages over the standard Find dialog box:

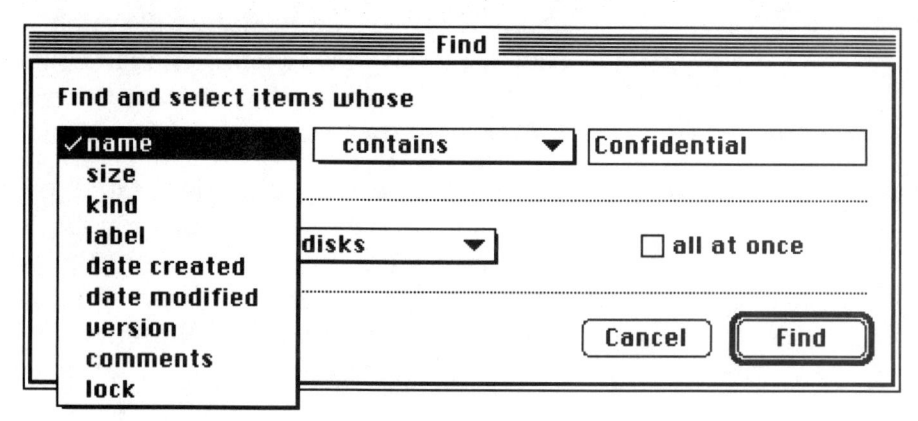

Figure 3-19: The Find Item dialog box.

- **More search criteria.** While the basic Find dialog can search only for file names, the Find Item dialog can search with the additional criteria shown in Figure 3-19. You can also limit your search location to specific volumes or selections.

- **More range control.** For each search parameter, the Find Item dialog lists specific search constraints (see Figure 3-20).

- **More result control.** The all at once option lets you look at a group of files matching the specified criteria all together.

Search by	Constraint	Range
Comments	contains/does not contain	any text
Date created	is/is before/is after/is not	any date
Date modified	is/is before/is after/is not	any date
Label	is/is not	any label/none
Lock	is	locked/unlocked
Name	contains/starts with ends with/doesn't contain	any text
Size	is less than/is greater than	any # k
Version	is/is before/is after/is not	any number

Figure 3-20: The available search criteria and their respective constraints and ranges.

To specify your criteria, select an option from the first pop-up menu. Depending on the option you select, the second or third part of the Find specification will become either a pop-up menu, an option box or a date. Enter your search specification. (To change a date, click on the month, year or day and then use the arrows to reset that portion of the date.) Several sample criteria are shown in Figure 3-21.

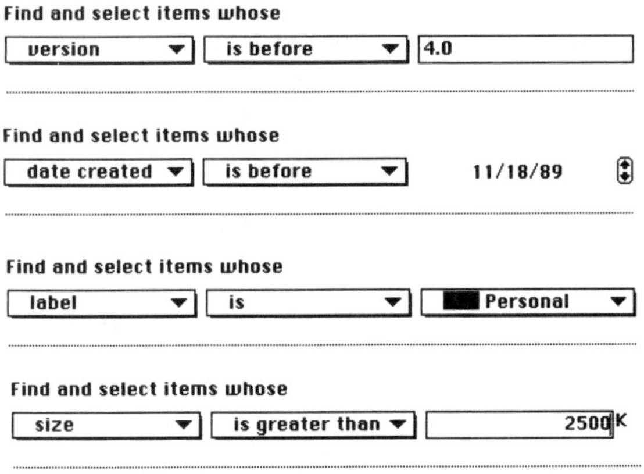

Figure 3-21: Several different search criteria as specified in the Find Item dialog box.

You can also specify the search range using the Search pop-up menu, shown in Figure 3-22.

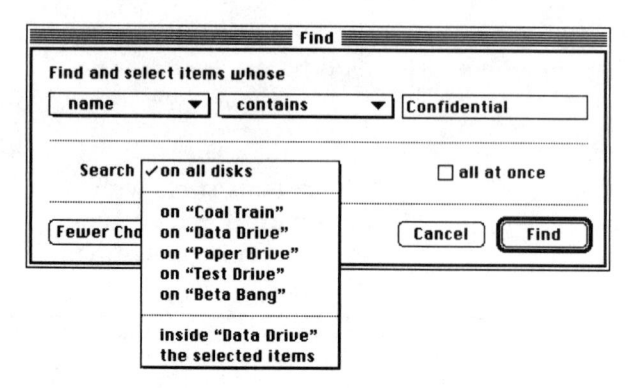

Figure 3-22: The Search pop-up menu.

The Search options are:

- **On all disks.** This will search all mounted volumes, including all folders and items appearing on the Finder desktop. With this option, the all at once option isn't available.

- **On ‹any one currently mounted volume›.** Limits the search to one particular volume.

- **Inside ‹the current selection›/on the desktop.** Limits the search to the currently selected volume or folder. If no volume or folder is selected, the option becomes on the desktop, which searches all mounted volumes.

- **The selected items.** Confines the search to those items currently selected. This is often used to further limit the results from a previous search yielding a multiple-criteria search.

For example, suppose you need to free some space on your hard drive, so you search for all files larger than 250k, using the all at once option, which will give you an open Finder window with all 250k or larger files selected. To locate only those larger than 250k that have not been changed in more than one month, choose the Find command again and search the selected items for all files modified prior to 30 days ago. You can now back up and delete these files.

The all at once option determines whether files matching your search criteria are presented individually or all together. A single window for the volume or window being searched is displayed, and all files matching the search criteria are selected in that window. Files located in subfolders are displayed hierarchically. This option cannot be used when the on all disks search-range option is selected.

If the all at once option is not selected, clicking the Find button locates the first file in the specified search range that matches the search criteria; the file window is opened and the file is selected. If the selected file is not the one you want, or if you want to find the next matching file after modifying the selected file, choose the Find Again command from the File Menu (Command-G) and the search will continue, using the same search criteria and range. Again, you can continue using the Find Again command as required.

After completing all the required options in the Find Item dialog box, click the Find button to execute the search. If the search is going to be prolonged, a progress dialog box will appear indicating the percentage of range already searched.

When a matching file is located,

- The progress dialog box, if visible, disappears.

- A window opens for the folder or volume containing the matching file.

- If the all at once option was selected, a window listing all files matching the specified criteria appears, as shown in Figure 3-23.

- If the all at once option was not selected, the matching file's icon is selected, as shown in Figure 3-24.

Any time you're working in the Find Item dialog box, you can click the Fewer Choices button to return to the Find dialog box, described above.

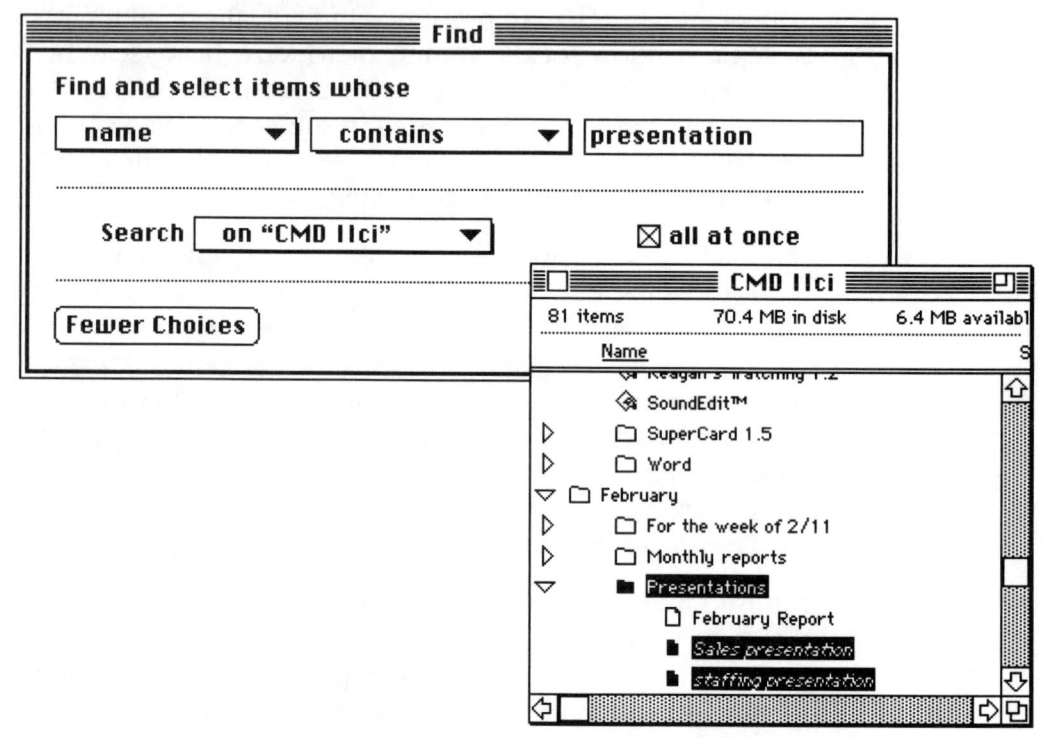

Figure 3-23: A group of files located by the Find command.

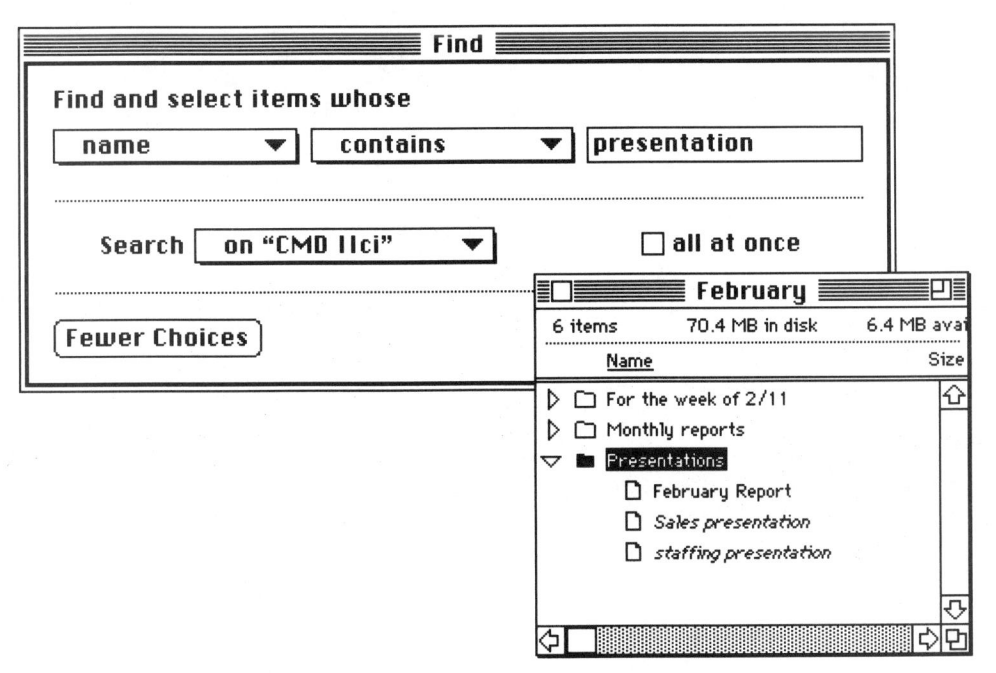

Figure 3-24: A single file located by the Find command.

Find Command Tips

- **Find does not look inside the System file.** Items like fonts or sounds that have been placed inside the System file will not be located by the Find command.

- **Find locates aliases as well.** Any alias that matches the specified search criteria can be found just like regular files.

- **The Find Again command (Command-G) can be used at any time.** The search parameters entered in the Find or Find Item dialog box remain until the Mac is restarted or the parameters are changed. You can always repeat the last search using the Find Again command.

- **Find also locates folders and volumes.** Any folder or volume matching the specified search criteria will be found, just like any other file.

- **Search By Kind to locate all data files created by one specific application.** To use the by kind search criterion, specify the file kind (for example, all spreadsheet files) that the application assigns to its data files. (See the sample file kinds in Figure 3-25.)

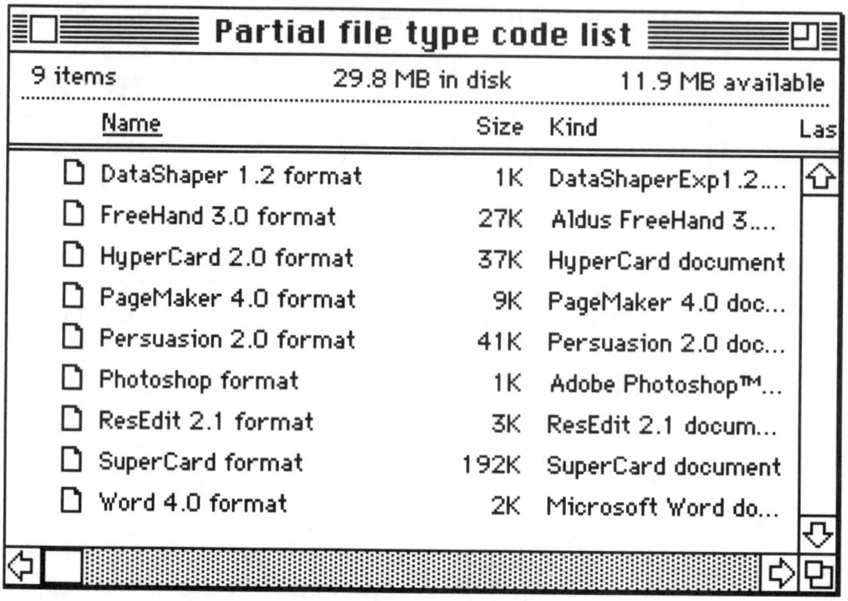

Name	Size	Kind
DataShaper 1.2 format	1K	DataShaperExp1.2....
FreeHand 3.0 format	27K	Aldus FreeHand 3....
HyperCard 2.0 format	37K	HyperCard document
PageMaker 4.0 format	9K	PageMaker 4.0 doc...
Persuasion 2.0 format	41K	Persuasion 2.0 doc...
Photoshop format	1K	Adobe Photoshop™...
ResEdit 2.1 format	3K	ResEdit 2.1 docum...
SuperCard format	192K	SuperCard document
Word 4.0 format	2K	Microsoft Word do...

Partial file type code list — 9 items, 29.8 MB in disk, 11.9 MB available

Figure 3-25: The Kind column displays the name of the application that created the file.

- **Use Find to do quick backups.** After you've used the Find command to locate all files on a volume modified after a certain date, you can drag those files to a removable volume for a "quick and dirty" backup. Of course, this procedure shouldn't replace a good backup utility—but you can never have too many backups.

- **Use the selected items search range to perform multiple-criteria searches.** For example, the Find command will locate all file names beginning with S that are less than 32k in size and have the word "medicated" in their comments (or any other set of multiple criteria). The first criterion is searched for using the on <any one volume> range; then you search for each additional criterion using the selected items range.

Labels

The Label menu is a great new System 7 tool that helps you categorize your files, identify certain types of files, locate these files and, in some cases, manipulate them as a group.

Configuring the Label Menu

The Label menu is in the Finder menu bar; it's configured using the Labels control panel. Figure 3-26 displays the open Labels control panel. The text and color of your labels are configured in this control panel.

To set label text, click in each label text block and enter the name of the label category you want to define. In label assignments, form must follow function; there's no advantage in having label assignments that don't help you use and manipulate your data more efficiently.

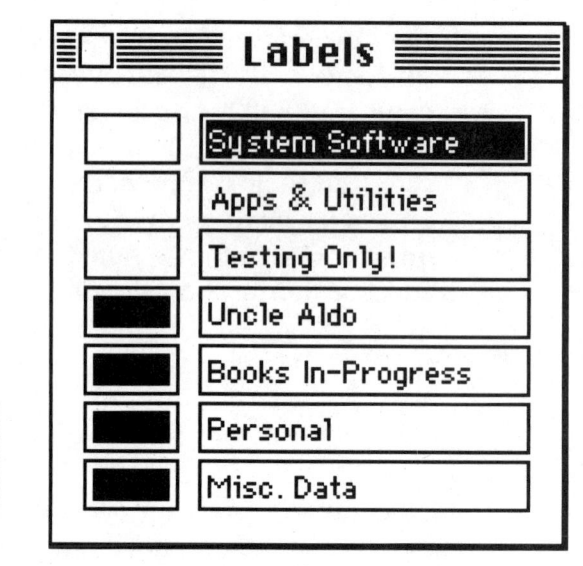

Figure 3-26: The Labels control panel.

There are several ways to use labels:

- **To categorize files.** Labels provide an additional level of categorization for files. Files are already categorized by type, creation and modification dates and related folders, but—using aliases—you can also classify them by topic, importance or any other way you choose.

- **For visual distinction.** Color-coding icons helps you quickly distinguish one type of file from another on a color monitor. For example, all applications can be red, making them easier to spot in a folder full of dictionaries, Help instructions and other files. You can also use the Labels column in Finder windows, which lists label names next to file names.

- **To facilitate data backup.** You can find all files assigned to a specific label, then copy them to another disk or volume for backup purposes.

- **To indicate security requirements.** When using File Sharing, you can create labels that remind you of the security level of specific folders, files and volumes.

There are many ways to use the available label categories:

- **Categories for logical subdivisions of data files.** If your work is project-based, you can specify large projects by individual lables and use one miscellaneous label for smaller projects. You could also have Long-Term Projects, Short-Term Projects and Permanent Projects labels.

- **Categories for software applications.** You can differentiate launchable applications or label both applications and their ancillary files. You might want a separate label for utility programs, including third-party extensions, control panels, desk accessories and utilities that are launchable applications.

- **Specify security levels.** If special security is required in your work environment, label one or two folders to identify them as secure. You can then use encryption utilities to safeguard these files, use them carefully with File Sharing or apply third-party security utilities to protect them.

Once labels are defined, you can alter label colors (available only on color Macs). To do this, click on any color in the Labels control panel to bring up the color wheel dialog box, shown in Figure 3-27. Specify the color you want for the label. Because label colors are applied over existing icon colors, weaker colors with lower hue and saturation values (found toward the middle of the wheel) work best.

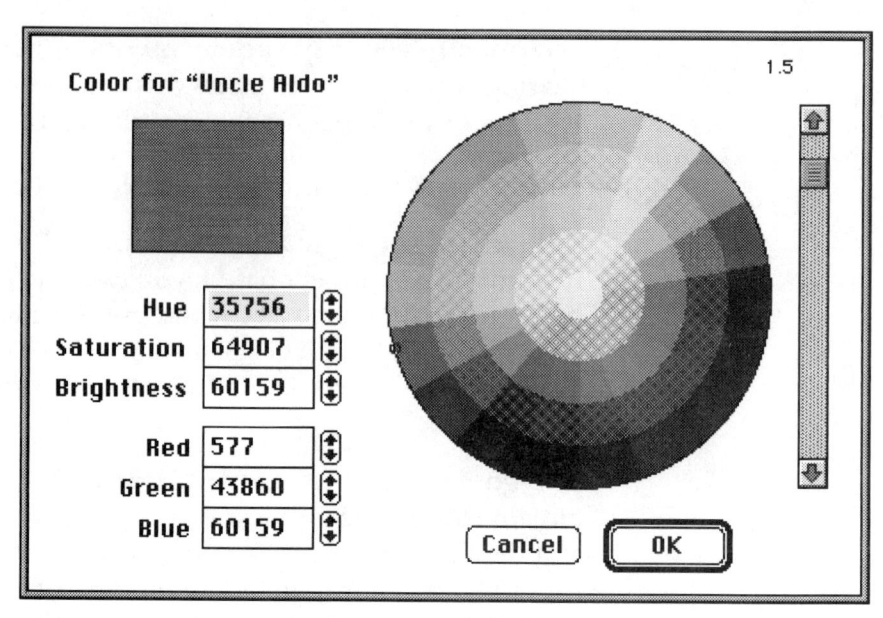

Figure 3-27: The Apple color wheel.

After you've modified the label names and colors, close the Labels control panel. The Label menu and any files or folders affected are then updated. You can reopen the Labels control panel any time you need to reset the text or colors.

Comments

In the past, adding lengthy comments to Macintosh files has been unsatisfactory, to say the least. The main problem was that the comments were likely to disappear every time the invisible desktop file was replaced or rebuilt (unfortunately, this problem still persists under System 7). Most people stopped using comments when they discovered that they could never be sure how long they'd last. Plus, comments could only be seen by opening the Get Info dialog box, so they were inconvenient to use.

System 7 attempts to breathe new life into file comments, correcting some of their former shortcomings and adding some interesting possibilities that could make comments an important part of working with your Macintosh files.

In the Finder, comments have been improved in two important ways:

- **Visibility.** You can now see comments in Finder windows. When the show comments option in the Views control panel is selected (as detailed in the previous chapter), comments will display in Finder windows. This makes them practical to use.

- **Searchability.** The new Find command lets you search for text in file comments, making it possible to locate files by comment entries.

People will find other productive ways to use these new comment features. One idea is to use comments as cues: key words or phrases can provide information not already included in the file name, date, kind or other file information. Client names, project titles, related and document names are a few examples. This additional information would be displayed in Finder windows via the Find command.

Unfortunately, as mentioned earlier, Finder comments are still lost when the desktop file is rebuilt. (The "desktop file" is actually a pair of invisible files that the Finder maintains on each disk or drive you use with your Mac.) The desktop file is sometimes automatically rebuilt by the system software when minor disk problems are detected. Or, you can force the desktop to be rebuilt by holding down the Command and Option keys during startup.

Figure 3-28 shows some files with comments added. Complete comments make it easy to see at a glance what these files contain when browsing Finder windows; it also makes the files easy to retrieve with the Find command.

	System 7 Letters f		
9 items	32.5 MB in disk		5.4 MB available
Name	Size	Last Modified	Comments
7.0 letter.Stationary	231K	Tue, Dec 4, 1990, 11:58 PM	Stationary Pad for all 7.0
About the Installer	11K	Mon, Jan 29, 1990, 8:09 PM	Tips on network installing
All you need is...	2K	Wed, Feb 21, 1990, 11:04 PM	
File Sharing Update	487K	Sat, Feb 23, 1991, 11:18 AM	Lots of info about recent
IAC f	719K	Wed, Feb 27, 1991, 9:40 PM	Letters and docs on IAC
Secret beta info f	3,606K	Tue, Feb 26, 1991, 11:38 PM	Do not let this info out!
Tech Info 2 (DEC ALINK)	9K	Mon, Jan 29, 1990, 8:10 PM	From Andrew Gellman, co
Vacation plans	2K	Wed, Feb 28, 1990, 7:59 PM	It's gonna ship soon, then
Virtual Memory Limits	230K	Fri, Dec 28, 1990, 4:49 PM	Is it 1 gig, 2 gigs, or 4 gi

Figure 3-28: A Finder window as it appears when using the Show Comments option.

Moving On

The power and importance of the capabilities introduced in this chapter cannot be overestimated. As you become more familiar with System 7, you'll use these features frequently:

- Aliases help you locate and launch files and access network data quickly and easily.
- The Find command will solve your "where is that file?" problem.
- Labels make it easier to keep important files organized.
- Comments remind you of details about particular file or folder content.

Next, in Chapter 4, we'll examine the most important folder on your hard drive, the System Folder. In System 7 the System Folder is still the home of your system software, but it's organized a little differently. Innovations include automatic file placement, and a new way of working with fonts and other resources used by the System file.

Chapter 4: The System Folder

There's one folder on every Macintosh hard drive that's distinct from all others—the System Folder, home of the Macintosh system software and many other important files. The System Folder is given special treatment by the system software, by other software applications and by you as a Macintosh user.

While you can arrange files on your hard drive (and all other volumes) to suit your personal needs, you can only change the organization of the System Folder in certain ways. That's because of the fundamental role software in the System Folder plays in the operation of your Macintosh.

In January 1984, when Version 1.0 of the system software was released with the Macintosh 128k, the System Folder contained 22 items that consumed only 225k of disk space. Using System 6 on a Mac with a normal assortment of applications and utilities could easily result in a System Folder containing 100 files or more, and the total size of the System Folder can easily soar above one megabyte.

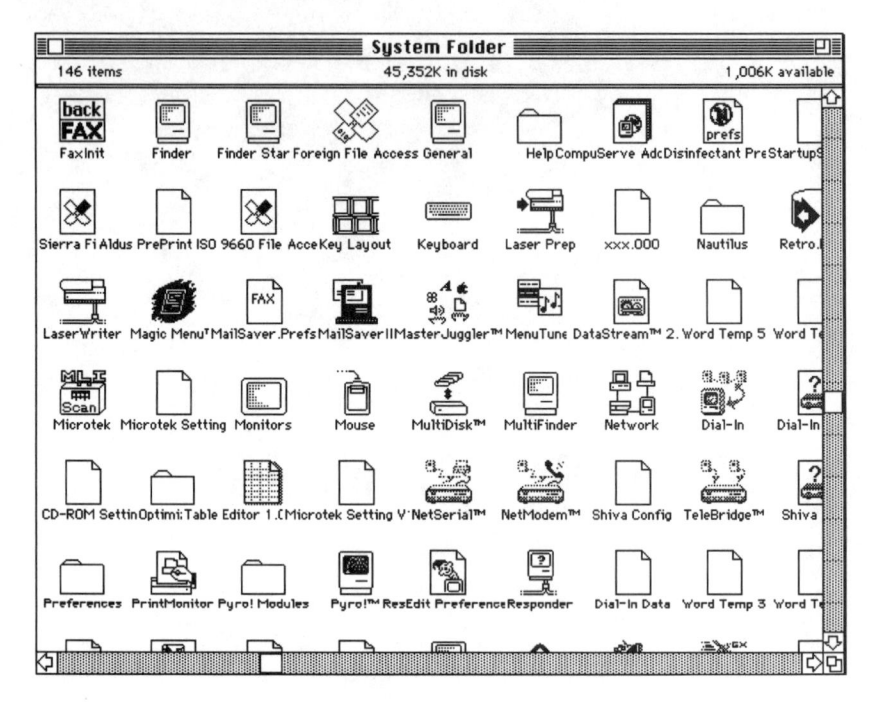

Figure 4-1: The author's large, messy System 6.0x System Folder.

The main problem with such a large System Folder is the resulting lack of organization, as shown in Figure 4-1. A crowded System Folder is slow to open at the desktop, and finding what you want in the maze of files is a slow and tedious process.

Increasing complexity has been partially responsible for the growth of the system software, but a more direct cause has been the growing number of non-system software files that reside in the System Folder. These include third-party fonts, sounds, desk accessories, FKEYs, control panels and extensions. Adding these files place obvious demands on disk space, and has also resulted in chaotic System Folder organization and some measure of system instability.

System 7 does little to reduce the pace of System Folder growth, but it does provide new methods of maintaining System Folder organization. It also introduces a few basic means of avoiding the instability caused by the old System Folder organization.

In this chapter, we'll look at the new System Folder organization, and offer some suggestions to help you effectively manage this important resource.

System 7's System Folder

In System 7, the System Folder includes a number of predefined subfolders, each of which is designed to hold a specific type of file. This new organizational system is created by the System 7 Installer when System 7 is installed, and greatly reduces the potential for clutter.

This new organization uses folder designations and file arrangement based on the same logic you use in organizing your hard drive. Subfolders include the Apple Menu Items folder, Control Panels folder, Extensions folder, Preferences folder, Fonts folder, and Startup folder. A display of this new System Folder organization is shown in Figure 4-2.

In some ways, the new System Folder is more complex than the old. Fortunately, as we'll see, Apple has built in an "invisible hand" to help make sure that System Folder files are always located correctly.

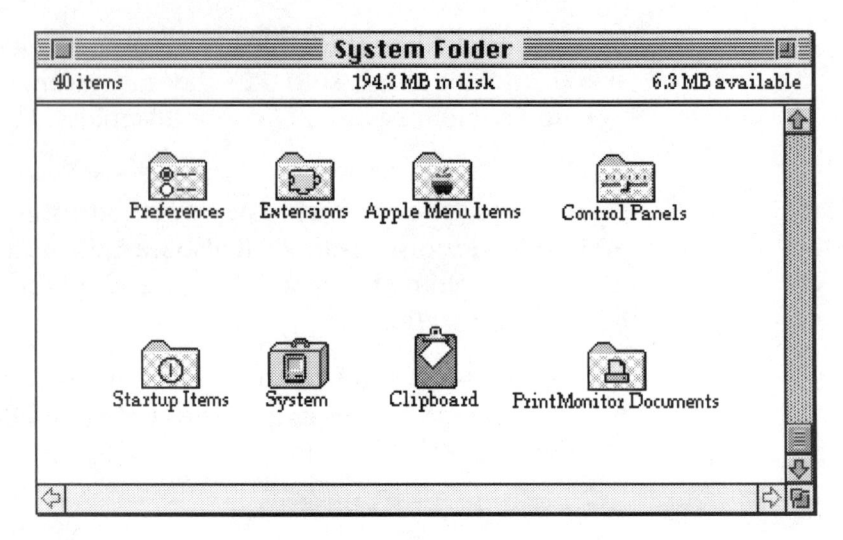

Figure 4-2: A standard System 7 System Folder.

Because the new System Folder and subfolders are so important to the operation of your Macintosh, it's important to understand what type of files should be placed in each folder. This section describes the folders and provides some basic tips for organizing and using them.

The Apple Menu Folder

One of the best things about desk accessories was their accessibility, via the Apple Menu, from inside any application. In System 7, the convenience of the Apple Menu has been extended beyond desk accessories to include applications, documents, folders and even volumes. And best of all, this powerful new Apple Menu is completely customizable.

When System 7 is installed, the Alarm Clock, Calculator, Chooser, Key Caps, Scrapbook desk accessories and a Control Panels folder alias appear in the Apple Menu. If you open the Apple Menu Items folder inside the System Folder, these are exactly the files you find inside, as shown in Figure 4-3.

To modify the contents of the Apple Menu, add or remove files and aliases. The Apple Menu is updated immediately and displays the first 50 items (alphabetically) contained in the Apple Menu Items folder.

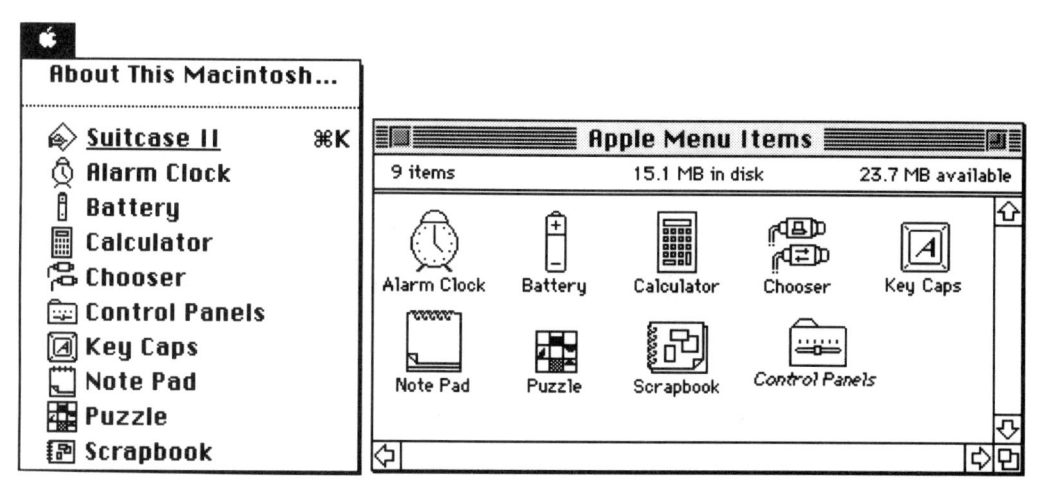

Figure 4-3: The System 7 Apple Menu and Apple Menu Items folder (as configured by the Installer).

The four types of files you'll probably want to place in the Apple Menu Items folder are applications, documents, folders and volumes. Each is much easier to access in the Apple Menu than by using traditional double-click methods. Choosing an item from the Apple Menu is equivalent to double-clicking on the item's icon: the selected DA or control panel is run, or the selected folder or volume is opened.

Most of the files added to the Apple Menu Items folder should be alias icons rather than original files, to avoid moving the file, folder or volume icon from its original location. In the Apple Menu Items folder, the file name remains displayed in italics but the file name appears in standard roman font in the Apple Menu—you can't tell by looking at the Apple Menu that the file in the Apple Menu Items folder is an alias.

🗋 (space bar)	🗋 . (.)	🗋 œ (Op-Q)	🗋 ¶ (Op-7)	🗋 º (Op-9)
🗋 ! (Sh-1)	🗋 / (/)	🗋 w (w)	🗋 ß (Op-S)	🗋 º (Op-0)
🗋 " (Op-[)	🗋 = (=)	🗋 z (z)	🗋 ® (Op-R)	🗋 Ω (Op-Z)
🗋 " (Op-])	🗋 ? (Sh-/)	🗋 [([)	🗋 © (Op-C)	🗋 ¿ (Sh-Op-/)
🗋 # (Sh-3)	🗋 @ (Sh-2)	🗋] (])	🗋 ™ (Op-2)	🗋 i (Op-1)
🗋 $ (Sh-4)	🗋 å (Op-A)	🗋 ^ (Sh-6)	🗋 ≠ (Op-=)	🗋 ¬ (Op-L)
🗋 % (Sh-5)	🗋 A (Sh-A)	🗋 ` (`)	🗋 ∞ (Op-5)	🗋 √ (Op-V)
🗋 & (Sh-7)	🗋 æ (Op-')	🗋 { (Sh-[)	🗋 ≤ (Op-,)	🗋 ƒ (Op-F)
🗋 ' (Op-])	🗋 B (Sh-B)	🗋 } (Sh-])	🗋 ≥ (Op-x)	🗋 ≠ (Op-X)
🗋 ' (Sh-Op-])	🗋 c (c)	🗋 ~ (Sh-`)	🗋 ¥ (Op-Y)	🗋 Δ (Op-J)
🗋 ((Sh-9)	🗋 ç (Op-c)	🗋 † (Op-T)	🗋 µ (Op-M)	🗋 … (Op-;)
🗋) (Sh-0)	🗋 E (Sh-E)	🗋 ¢ (Op-4)	🗋 ∂ (Op-D)	🗋 - (0--)
🗋 * (Sh-8)	🗋 f (f)	🗋 £ (Op-3)	🗋 Σ (Op-W)	🗋 — (Sh-Op--)
🗋 + (Sh-=)	🗋 G (SH-G)	🗋 § (Op-6)	🗋 π (Op-P)	🗋 ÷ (Op-/)
🗋 - (-)	🗋 ø (Op-O)	🗋 • (Op-8)	🗋 ∫ (Op-B)	

Figure 4-4: The list above demonstrates, from top to bottom, left to right, the special characters that can be used to alphabetize files in the Apple Menu, and the keys you press to access them.

Because the Apple Menu displays files alphabetically, you can reorder the menu items by modifying their names with numerical or alphabetical prefixes. A list of the prefixes available appears in Figure 4-4. The result of using some of these is shown in the Apple Menu pictured in Figure 4-5, in which applications, folders, desk accessories, control panels, documents and volumes are ordered separately.

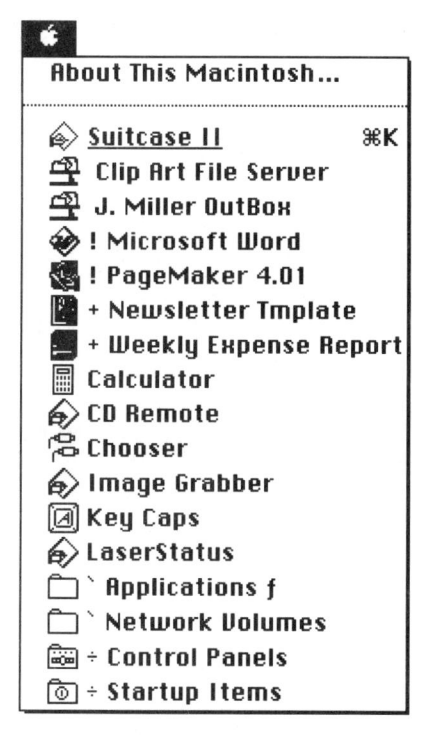

```
             _____
            |  🍎                             |
            | About This Macintosh...         |
            |.................................|
            | 🔷 Suitcase II            ⌘K   |
            | 🖥  Clip Art File Server       |
            | 🖥  J. Miller OutBox           |
            | ◆  ! Microsoft Word            |
            | 🔶 ! PageMaker 4.01            |
            | 📄 + Newsletter Tmplate        |
            | 📄 + Weekly Expense Report     |
            | 🔢 Calculator                  |
            | 🔷 CD Remote                   |
            | 🗂  Chooser                    |
            | 🔷 Image Grabber               |
            | 🅰  Key Caps                   |
            | 🔷 LaserStatus                 |
            | 📁 ` Applications ƒ            |
            | 📁 ` Network Volumes           |
            | 📷 ÷ Control Panels            |
            | ⏱  ÷ Startup Items            |
            |_____|
```

Figure 4-5: Files are arranged in this Apple Menu using file name prefixes.

The Control Panels Folder

Control panels are the evolution of control devices (cdevs) that used to appear in the System 6.0x Control Panel desk accessory. In System 7, a control panel is a small, independent application launched by double-clicking on its icon. The only difference between a control panel and a regular application is that the control panel is implemented in a single window and provides no menus.

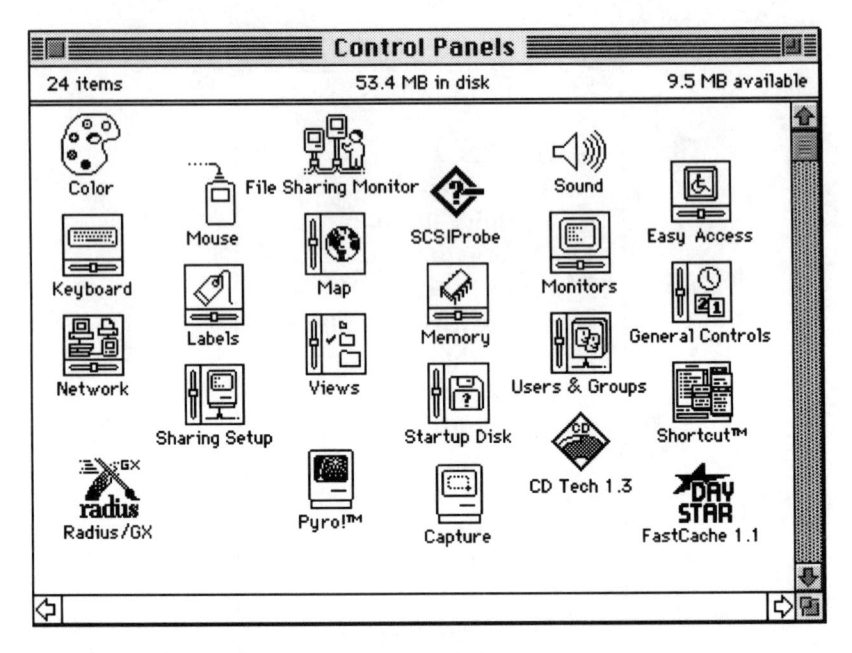

Figure 4-6: The Control Panels folder.

Control panels are stored in the Control Panels folder, which itself is stored inside the System Folder—mainly because control panels often contain special resources (like extensions) that must be run during startup. If the extension portion of the control panel isn't loaded at startup, the control panel may not function properly.

If you want to keep a copy of any control panel in another location, create an alias and move the alias to your preferred location. You could, for example, store aliases of frequently used control panels in the Apple Menu Items folder or in a folder containing other utility applications.

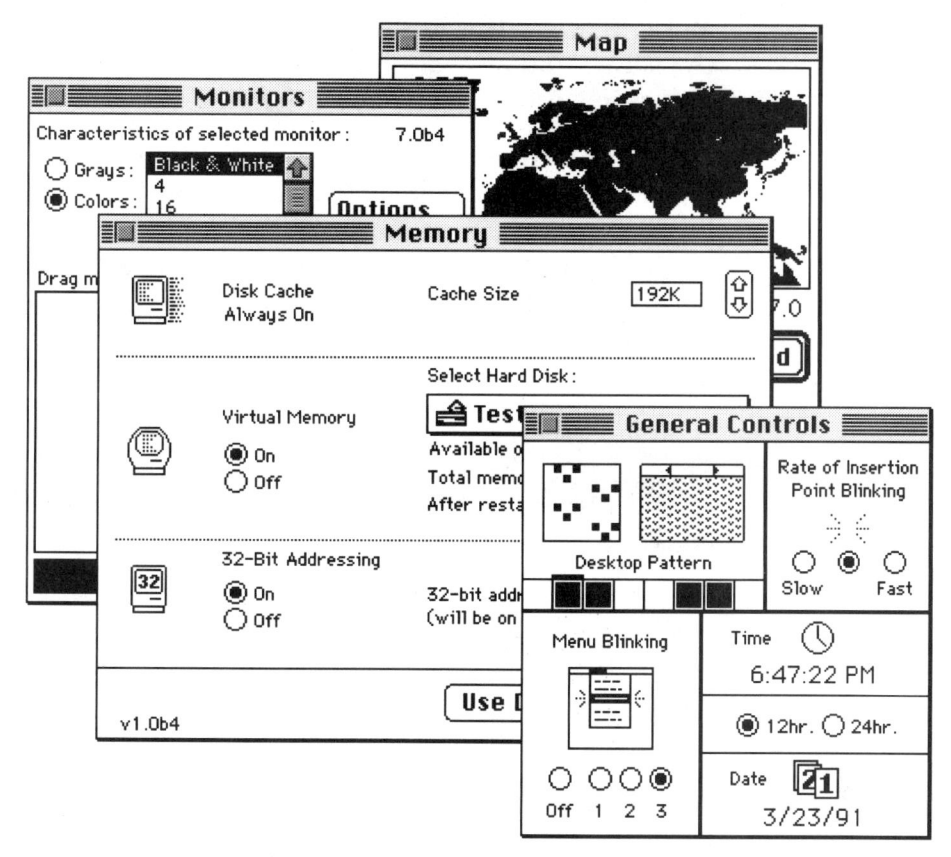

Figure 4-7: Control Panels appear in independent windows.

The Extensions Folder

As mentioned previously, INITs (now called extensions), printer drivers and network drivers are major contributors to System Folder overcrowding. In System 7, these files, which have invaded System Folders in epidemic proportions since the introduction of System 6.0, now have a new home in the Extensions folder.

Most INITs add features to the Mac's system software, hence the name "extensions." Drivers extend system software capabilities in a less dramatic but important way.

During startup, the system software looks in the Extensions folder and executes the code found there. These files can also be accessed during startup from the Control Panels folder, but separation of files between these two folders should be maintained. Extensions and control panels that aren't stored in the Extensions or Control Panels folders won't execute at startup and won't operate properly until they're correctly positioned and the Macintosh is restarted.

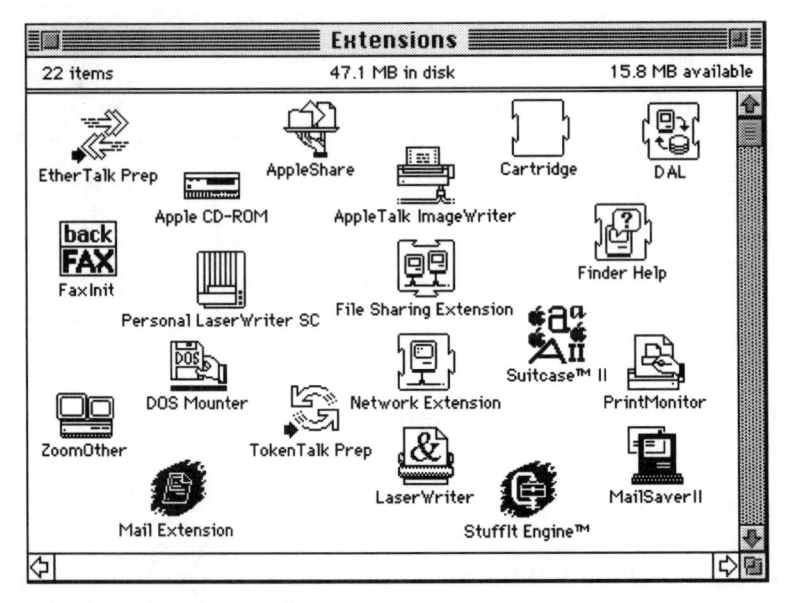

Figure 4-8: The Extensions folder holds extensions, printer drivers and network drivers.

Because extensions and control panels modify or enhance the system software at startup, a new extension or control panel may cause your Macintosh to crash if the item is incompatible with the system software, some other extension, another control panel or a certain combination of extensions and control panels. If you experience a compatibility problem, hold down the Shift key while restarting your Macintosh. This will disable all extensions and allow you to remove the incompatible file from the System Folder.

When you restart or start up with the Shift key held down, the words "Extensions Off" will appear under the "Welcome to Macintosh" message, as shown in Figure 4-9. As soon as these words appear, you can release the Shift key, and the Macintosh will start up without executing any of the items in the Extensions folder or the Control Panels folder.

> Welcome to Macintosh.
> Extensions off.

Figure 4-9: The Welcome to Macintosh dialog box as it appears when the Shift key is pressed at startup.

A final word about positioning extensions: Although System 7 is designed to house startup items in the Extensions folder or in the Control Panels folder, extensions located directly in the System Folder *will* execute during startup. This is necessary because some older INITs and cdevs don't operate properly when nested in System Folder subfolders. New versions of these items have since been made compatible with the new System Folder structure; but if you find and item that doesn't load properly from the appropriate subfolder, try placing it directly in the System Folder.

The Fonts Folder

Support for a wide range of typefaces has always been an important characteristic of the Macintosh, but it's surprising that eight years after the first Macintosh, Apple is still trying to figure out an elegant way of handling fonts in its system software. But it's true. System 7.0 brought major changes to the way fonts were handled, and System 7.1 brings additional changes.

The Fonts folder, introduced in System 7.1, holds PostScript screen fonts and printer fonts, as well as TrueType fonts. After screen fonts or TrueType fonts are added to the Fonts folder, they become available in all subsequently launched applications. Fonts moved out of the Fonts folder, or into subfolders of the Fonts folder, are no longer available to applications.

All aspects of working with Fonts in System 7.0 and 7.1, including the Fonts folder, are described in detail in Chapter 8, "Fonts in System 7."

The Preferences Folder

Preferences files created by application programs and utilities also became important contributors to System Folder growth under System 6.0x. In System 7, these files are stored in the Preferences folder.

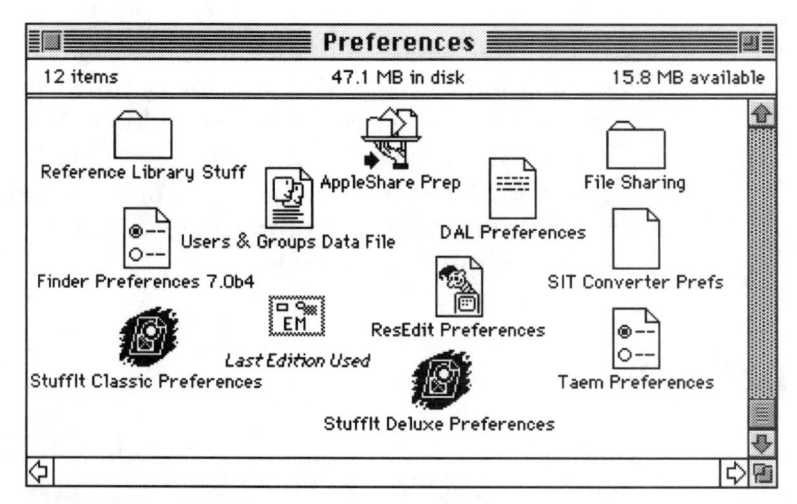

Figure 4-10: The Preferences folder.

As a user, you shouldn't have to do anything to the Preferences folder or its files. Your application programs should create and maintain these files automatically. However, you might want to check this folder occasionally and delete the preferences files of unwanted applications or utilities that you've deleted from your drives.

The Startup Items Folder

Applications, documents, folders and volumes in the Startup Items folder automatically run (or open) each time your Macintosh is started or restarted. This folder takes the place of the Set Startup... command found in the Special menu of previous system software versions. As with the Apple Menu Items folder, most of the icons in the Startup Items folder will probably be aliases.

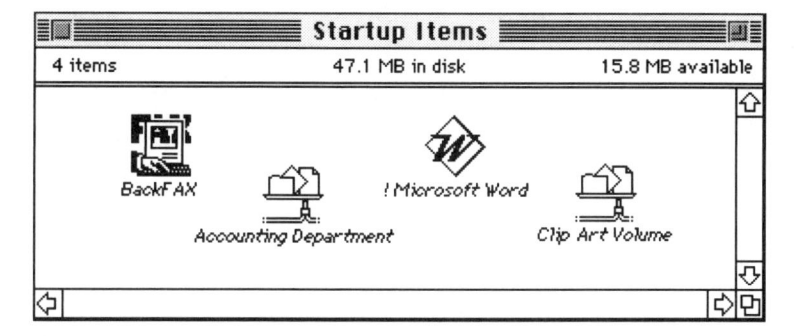

Figure 4-11: The Startup Items folder with alias icons that will be launched or mounted at startup.

While the Startup Items folder's main purpose is to open applications and documents, it's also a good place to put folder and volume icon aliases. These aliases will be opened, or mounted, at startup—a simple but useful function. (Of course, before mounting any networked volumes, any required passwords will be requested.)

The System File

The System file remains the centerpiece of Macintosh system software, overseeing all basic Macintosh activities and assisting every application and utility that runs on the Macintosh. As a user, you can remain blissfully ignorant of most of the work performed by the System file. You should understand, however, the System file's traditional role as home to fonts, desk accessories, FKEYs, sounds and keyboard resources.

When stuffed with these items, a single System file in the days before System 7 could grow to 600k or larger—often much larger. This overload often resulted in an unstable System file that would easily and frequently become corrupt, making the annoying and time-consuming effort of deleting and rebuilding the System file necessary.

The release of System 7 provided some relief to bulging System files by providing the Apple Menu Items folder (described earlier in this chapter) as the new default home for desk accessories, and by allowing DAs to be converted into stand alone applications that can be stored anywhere on your hard disk (as described in Chapter 5, "System 7 & Your Software"). As a result of these two changes, DAs are no longer stored inside the System file.

Fonts, on the other hand, remain in the System file in System 7.0, although in System 7.1 they have moved instead to the new Fonts folder, as described above. (For more information about fonts, see Chapter 8.)

System File Access

Before System 7, the only way to add or remove fonts, desk accessories, FKEYs or sounds was to use specialized utilities such as the Font/DA Mover or ResEdit. In System 7, the

System file's contents can be manipulated directly: you can open the System file by double-clicking on it as if it were a folder. A window opens, displaying icons for all fonts, sounds and keyboard configurations it currently contains.

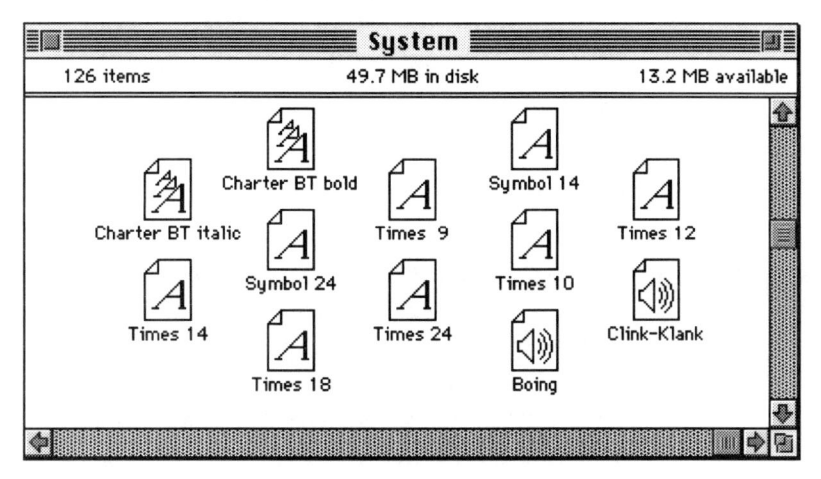

Figure 4-12: An open System file window.

While the System file is open, any font, sound and keyboard files will appear with unique individual icons. Double-clicking on any of these icons will open the resource file, displaying a font sample or playing the sound. (See Figure 4-13.)

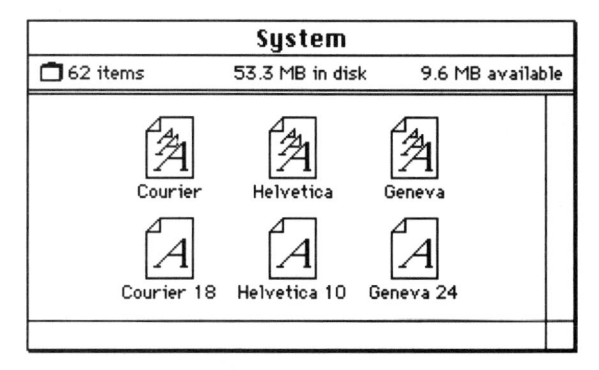

Figure 4-13: Both bitmapped and TrueType fonts can be installed in the System file in System 7.

Fonts, sounds, and keyboard files can be added to the System file by simply dragging their icons into the System file window, the same way files are dragged in or out of any normal Mac folder. (All other applications must be closed before adding to the System file.) To remove fonts or sounds, drag their icons out of the open System Folder window and into another folder or volume, or directly into the Trash.

Modifying the System Folder

The System Folder and its subfolders are created by the Installer when you first install System 7, and at that time, all system software files are placed into their proper locations. The System Folder is constantly modified, however, as you install other software applications or perform other common tasks on your Macintosh.

There are several types of files added to the System Folder after the initial installation: fonts and sounds, system extensions (which add functions to the system software), and miscellaneous files that enable other software applications to function properly.

System extensions modify the way the system software works or extend the options provided by system software features. They include extensions, control panels and printer or network drivers. There are hundreds of examples of extensions and drivers that modify your system software. SuperClock, Pyro, Vaccine, AppleShare, DOS Mounter, NetModem, MailSaver, Autographix, PageSaver and SuperGlue are a few of the most popular. You've probably added files of this type to your System Folder.

Many applications store miscellaneous files in the System Folder which don't interact directly with the system software. They're placed in the System Folder for other reasons:

- **Safety.** The System Folder is the only "common ground" on a Mac hard drive that applications can rely on in every configuration.

- **Simplicity.** The Macintosh operating system can easily find the System Folder, regardless of what it's called and where it's located. This allows applications quick access to files stored in the System Folder.

- **Security.** The System Folder is a safe place for applications to add files because most users are not likely to disturb files in their System Folder.

Some of the many application-related files (or folders) that use your System Folder as a safe storage place are Microsoft Word's Word Temp files, the PageMaker Aldus folder, and StuffIt's Encryptors, Translators and Viewers.

Printer font files are also in this category. Printer fonts are placed in the System Folder so they are available when needed for automatic downloading to a PostScript printer, and so they can be found by Adobe Type Manager. Usually, these are the most space-consuming files in the System Folder—30k to 50k each. Although utilities like Suitcase II and MasterJuggler make it possible to store printer and screen fonts in other locations, many people choose to keep them in the System Folder anyway.

Adding Files to the System Folder

There are several ways that files may be added to the System Folder after its initial creation:

- **By the Apple Installer.** To add additional printer drivers, network drivers or keyboards, you can rerun the Apple Installer application at any time. The Installer adds the selected files to your System Folder, placing them into the proper subfolders.

You don't have to use the Installer to add drivers or files from the system software disks; you can drag-copy files directly from these disks into your System Folder.

- **By application software installers.** Many software applications use installation programs that copy the software and its associated files to your hard drive. Installers that have been specifically written or updated for compatibility with System 7 can place files correctly into the System 7 System Folder or subfolders.

   Older installer applications often place all files directly in the System Folder, ignoring the subfolder structure. In these cases, the application may require that the files remain as positioned by the installer. However, most extensions should be moved to the Extensions folder, and control panels should be moved to the Control Panels folder—regardless of how they were originally positioned. (Although all extensions should be placed in the Extensions folder or Control Panels folder, most items of this nature located directly in the System Folder will be executed at startup.)

- **By software applications.** Historically, many software applications read and write temporary and preferences files to the System Folder. Others use the System Folder for dictionaries and other ancillary files. Applications updated for System 7 should properly read and write files in the System Folder and its subfiles.

   Older applications not rewritten for System 7 may not use the subfolders, but files placed directly in the System Folder will be accessed properly and won't cause any problems for your system software or other programs. New program releases will address subfolder location, in the interest of further System Folder simplification.

- **By you—the Macintosh user.** Since some programs and utilities don't use installer applications, many files must be placed into the System Folder manually. These files can be dragged onto the System Folder icon or dragged into an open System Folder window.

  When files are dragged onto the System Folder icon, the Macintosh automatically positions them in the correct System Folder or subfolder. This Helping Hand helps you manually add files to the System Folder correctly, even if you know nothing about the System Folder structure.

  Before positioning files, the Helping Hand informs you it's at work and tells you how it's positioning your files, as shown in Figure 4-14. The Helping Hand works only when files are dragged onto the System Folder icon.

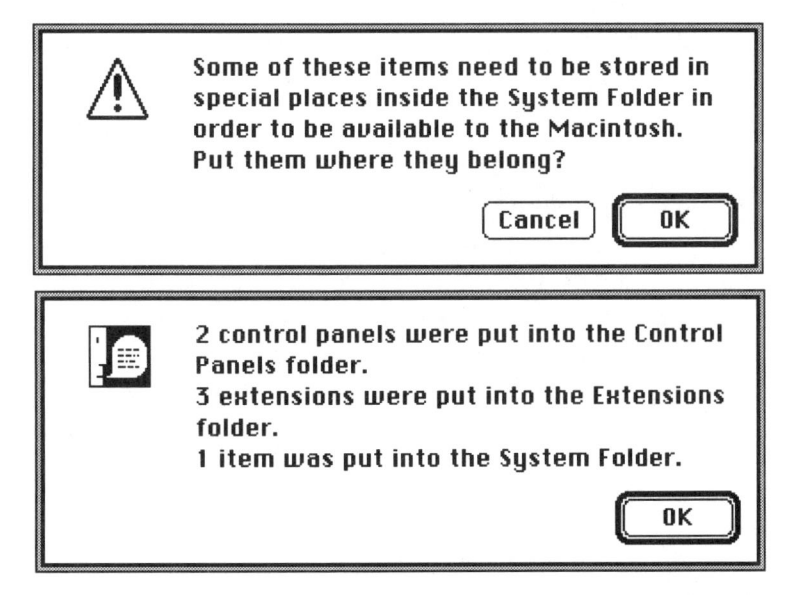

Figure 4-14: The System Folder's Helping Hand makes sure files are positioned properly.

Of course, once files are in the System Folder, you can reposition them freely. The Helping Hand will not affect the movement of files within the System Folder.

You can also avoid the action of the Helping Hand by dragging files directly into an open System Folder window. When you drag files this way, you can place files into any System Folder subfolder, or into the System Folder itself, without interference.

Deleting Files From the System Folder

For the most part, files in the System Folder can be deleted just like any other file, by dragging them into the Trash. However, some files cannot be deleted because they're "in use." "In use" files include the System file; the Finder; any extensions or control panels with code that ran at startup; open control panels and any temporary or preferences files used by open applications.

To delete the System file or Finder, you must restart the Macintosh using another boot disk. To delete an "in use" extension or control panel, move the file out of the Extensions or Control Panels folders, restart the Mac, then delete the file. To delete open control panels or temporary or preferences files of open applications, simply close the control panel or open application and drag the file to the Trash.

Moving On

Working in the System Folder used to be like playing with a house of cards, but as we've seen, System 7 brings new order and stability to this important part of your hard drive. The new subfolders are especially useful:

- The Apple Menu Items folder lets you customize your Apple Menu.

- The Extensions folder contains all the extensions and drivers that add features to your Mac and the system software.

- The Control Panels folder holds special "mini-applications" that set preferences for system software features, utilities and even hardware peripherals.

- The Startup Items folder lets you determine which files and applications are opened each time your Mac is turned on.

In the next chapter, we turn our attention to the effects this new system software has on software applications used on the Mac—from new ways of accessing your software to a new document type that makes it easier for you to create frequently used files. We'll also look at the enhanced dialog boxes you will encounter whenever you open or save files with System 7.

Chapter 5: System 7 & Your Software

Thus far, the System 7 features we have discussed are those that change the way you organize and manipulate data files on your Macintosh. But as important as file management is, it's not the reason you use a Macintosh. You use the Mac because its software applications—word processors, spreadsheets, databases, graphics programs and the rest—help you accomplish your work productively.

In this chapter, we'll look at some of the ways System 7 affects software applications, beginning with the important issue of compatibility. Then we'll see the expanded launching methods, new Stationery Pads and desktop-level enhancements System 7 provides. Other major enhancements that affect software applications, including data sharing, program-to-program communication and support for TrueType fonts, are discussed in Chapter 7, "The Edition Manager & IAC," and in Chapter 8, "Fonts in System 7."

System 7 Compatibility

It's always exciting to get a new software upgrade—it means more features, better performance and an easier-to-use interface. But as seasoned computer users know, along with improvements and solutions, software upgrades often introduce bugs and incompatibilities.

System software is particularly susceptible to upgrade compatibility problems because every Macintosh application is so heavily dependent on the system software. Each application must be fine-tuned and coordinated to work together smoothly with the system. The relationship between system software and an application is like that of two juggling partners, each throwing balls into the air that the other is expected to catch. Upgrading system software replaces a familiar partner with a new one, without changing the routine or allowing time to practice, while still expecting each toss and catch to occur precisely.

During its development, Apple worked hard to ensure that System 7 was compatible with as many existing applications as possible. In fact, they claimed that any application running under System 6.0.x would operate under System 7 without alteration, as long as it was programmed according to its widely published programming rules. For the most part, this was apparently true.

The majority of major applications were compatible with System 7 at the time of its initial release, and a great many utility programs were compatible too. Naturally, many utility programs whose function was to modify or extend the system software itself were not initially compatible.

Now—two years after the introduction of System 7—it's almost impossible to find an application or utility that isn't System 7-compatible. Every program written or updated in that time period has been created or modified with System 7 in mind.

The introduction of System 7.1 brings additional changes to the system software, yielding yet another set of potential problems, although very few programs—again, usually utilities that modify or extend the system—have proven incompatible.

What Is Compatibility?

Generally speaking, to be considered System 7-compatible, an application must run under System 7 and provide the same features, with the same degree of reliability, that it did under System 6.0x. But System 7 compatibility is not black and white—it can exist in varying degrees in different applications. Most compatible applications will launch and provide basic operations under System 7, and operate correctly in System 7's multitasking environment; but problems with 32-bit memory and File Sharing were more common in early releases of System 7-compatible software.

Applications written before System 7 was released, which are not System 7-compatible, will have to be upgraded by their developers in order to be System 7-compatible. If you have an application that doesn't operate properly in System 7, contact the software developer to obtain a System 7-compatible upgrade.

If a System 7-compatible application is (more or less) no better under System 7 than it was under System 6.0x, compatibility is obviously not the ultimate accomplishment. The ultimate goal is to take full advantage of all new System 7 features, a status which Apple calls "System 7-Savvy." To be System 7-Savvy, an application must be specifically written, or updated, for technical compatibility with System 7 and support for its new features.

In other words, applications that are System 7-compatible will survive, but applications that are System 7-Savvy will thrive. To be considered System 7-Savvy, applications must:

- **Support multitasking.** System 7 lets your Mac open multiple applications and process data simultaneously. Applications should be able to operate in both the foreground and the background, and should support background processing to the greatest degree possible. (More information on multitasking and background processing later in this chapter.)

- **Be 32-bit clean.** When the "32-Bit Addressing" option is turned on in the Memory control panel, certain Macintosh models can access large amounts of memory (see Chapter 11, "Memory Management"). Applications should operate correctly when this option is used.

- **Support the Edition Manager's Publish and Subscribe features.** The Edition Manager, described in Chapter 7, allows data to be transferred from one application to another while maintaining a link to the original file. Applications must include the basic Publish and Subscribe commands.

- **Support AppleEvents and Core events.** System 7's Inter-Application Communication (IAC), also described in Chapter 7, defines a basic set of Apple Events that allow one application to communicate with another.

- **Impose no limit on font sizes.** Applications should support all font sizes, from 1 to 32,000 in single-point increments. (See Chapter 8.)

- **Provide help balloons.** As described in Chapter 2, "The Finder," Balloon Help offers quick pop-up summaries of an application's menu commands, dialog box options and graphic elements.

- **Be AppleShare-compliant.** System 7 allows any user to access files shared on AppleShare servers or files from other System 7 Macintoshes using File Sharing. Applications should operate correctly when launched over an

AppleTalk network, or when reading or writing data stored on File Sharing or AppleShare volumes (see Chapter 9, "Introduction to File Sharing").

- **Support Stationery Pads.** Applications should be able to take full advantage of Stationery Pads, a new type of document template featured in System 7. (See the Stationery Pads discussion later in this chapter.)

Most of the Macintosh software that is being sold today includes a sticker on the box that designates the program as either System 7-Compatible or System 7-Savvy. Many mail-order catalogs also distinguish between incompatible, compatible and savvy software.

Of course, you have to be careful not to take the "savvy" label too seriously. Many great applications have been upgraded to take full advantage of System 7, but cannot be officially categorized as "savvy." The usual reason is that the program's developers intentionally decided to not implement one or more of the required items because such features were either unimportant or inapplicable for that application. For instance, many applications don't support Balloon Help or the Edition Manager.

Launching

Double-click, double-click, double-click. That's how most Macintosh users launch their software applications. Two clicks to open the drive or volume, two to open the application folder, and a double-click on the application icon to launch the software.

This method can quickly grow wearisome when it means clicking through many volumes and folder layers to reach an icon. As alternatives, a wide range of application launching utilities—including On-Cue, NowMenus, DiskTop and Master-Juggler—have appeared in recent years. With these utilities, you can launch by selecting application names from a list, instead of searching through folders for icons.

Applications can still be launched in System 7 by double-clicking on icons, but more icons are available, including aliases and stationery documents. It's now also possible to launch applications or documents from the Apple Menu or by dragging a document onto an application icon.

In fact, you can now launch applications in all of the following ways:

- **Double-click on an application icon.** You can double-click on an application icon, or the alias of an application icon, to launch that application.

- **Double-click on a document icon or its alias.** If the application that created a document is unavailable, the Application Not Found dialog box, shown in Figure 5-1, will appear. To open a document that presents this dialog box, you must either locate the original application or use another application that's capable of opening that type of document.

  For example, suppose a MacWrite II file displays the Application Not Found dialog box when double-clicked. You could open Microsoft Word, then access the file with the Open... command under Word's File menu. Similarly, SuperPaint can open MacPaint files and many applications can open TIFF or EPS files. Most applications can open documents of several different file types.

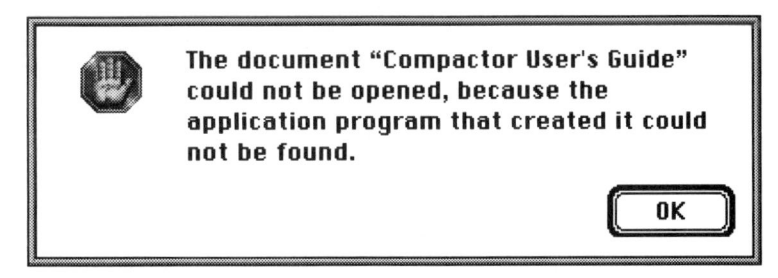

> The document "Compactor User's Guide" could not be opened, because the application program that created it could not be found.
>
> [OK]

Figure 5-1: The Application Not Found dialog box.

- **Double-click on a Stationery Pad document or its alias.** Stationery Pad documents are template documents that create untitled new documents automatically when opened. (More on Stationery Pads later in this chapter.)

- **Drag a document icon onto an application icon.** This method of launching will work only when the document is dragged onto the icon of the application that created it.

   If an application *will* launch, the application icon highlights when the document icon is above it. Application icons will highlight only when appropriate documents are positioned above them, as shown in Figure 5-2.

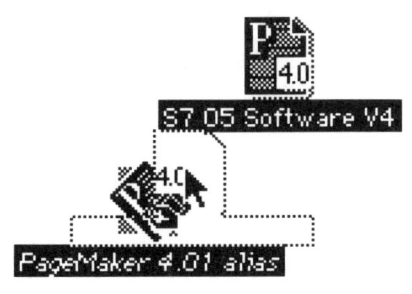

Figure 5-2: Application icons highlight when documents they can launch are dragged onto them.

- **Add applications or documents to the Startup Items Folder inside the System Folder.** To automatically launch an application or open a document and its application at startup, add the application or document icon or an alias of one of these icons, to the Startup Items folder inside the System Folder. This will cause the application or document to be launched automatically at startup. (See Chapter 4, "The System Folder," for more information on using the Startup Items folder.)

- **Choose an application or document name from the Apple Menu.** By placing an application or document in the Apple Menu Items Folder inside the System Folder, the application or document name will then appear in the Apple Menu and can be launched by choosing the application or document name. (Information on configuring the Apple Menu is found in Chapter 4.)

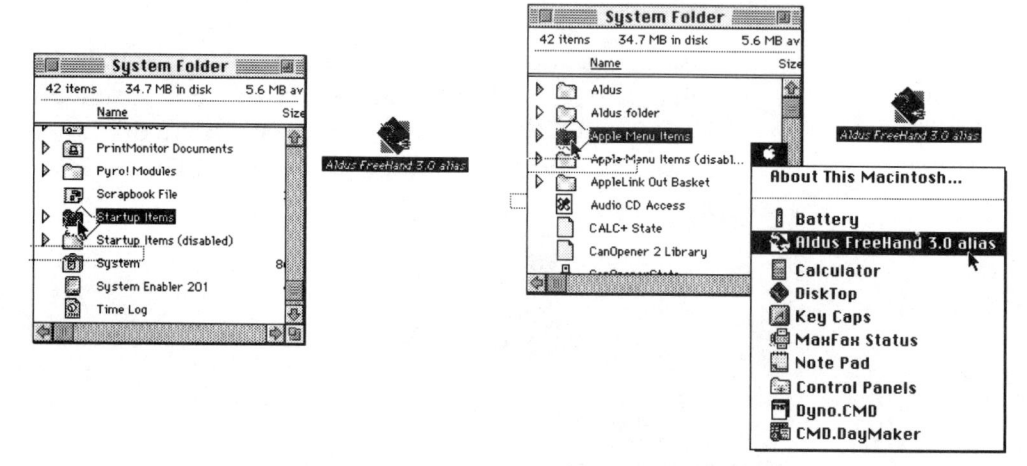

Figure 5-3: Items are launched at startup when added to the Startup Items folder (left), or when selected from the Apple Menu.

Launching Methods

There's no one best way to launch applications. You'll probably find that a combination of methods is the most efficient. Keep the following launching tips in mind:

- **The Apple Menu.** Add the applications and documents you use most frequently to the Apple Menu. (See Chapter 4. for more on the Apple Menu.)

- **Alias folders.** Assemble groups of application aliases into folders according to application type; add aliases of frequently used folders to the Apple Menu.

    You can select the folder name from the Apple Menu to open the folder and double-click on the application you want to launch. Hold down the option key while you double-click on the application icon to close the open folder window automatically during the launch.

Figure 5-4: Adding folders full of application icons to the Apple Menu makes them easy to access.

Figure 5-4 shows an Apple Menu configured using this method. An @ character has been added before the name of each folder alias, which forces these folders to group near the top of the Apple Menu.

- **Double-click on icons.** When browsing in Finder windows to locate specific files, use the tried-and-true double-click method to launch applications, aliases, documents or stationery icons.

- **Drag icons onto applications.** If you store documents and applications or their aliases in the same folder, or if you place application icons or aliases on the desktop, dragging icons onto applications (or drop-launching, as it's called) may prove useful, although double-clicking on the document is often easier.

Stationery Pads

Another innovation in System 7 is Stationery Pads, which is a fancy name for quickly making an existing document into a template. Templates, as you may know, give you a head start in creating new documents.

For example, the documents in your word processor probably fall into a handful of specific formats—letters, reports, memos, chapters, etc. Rather than starting each document with a new, unformatted file, the stationery document for a letter, for example, would provide date, salutation, body copy, closing character and paragraph formatting, correct margins and other basic formatting.

Template support has been available in several Macintosh applications for some time, but by adding the Stationery Pad feature to System 7, Apple makes templates available in every software package you use to create documents.

Figure 5-5: A letter that will become a Stationery Pad.

Creating a Stationery Pad

A Stationery Pad (a document that is going to be stationery) is usually created in three steps:

- First, you find an existing typical example of a document you commonly create.

- Then, you modify the typical document to make it a good generic representation and save it to disk.

- Finally, select the "Stationery pad" option in the file's Get Info dialog box.

As an example, to create a memo Stationery Pad, open an existing representative document, like the one shown in Figure 5-5. Although this memo is typical, it does have one unusual element, the embedded graphic. So we remove that element, since most of the memos we create do not call for such graphic elements. The remaining memo elements are left to serve as placeholders.

Before saving the memo Stationery Pad, it's a good idea to edit the text in all placeholders, so that they're appropriate to use in final documents. Replace placeholder text with nonsensical data ("greeking"), which helps ensure that no placeholder elements are accidentally used in finished documents. For the memo date, for example, use 0/0/00, and the memo address can read To: Recipient.

A date such as 7/15/91 might be overlooked and used instead of the current date each time the Stationery Pad is used. The 0/0/00 date, on the other hand, is almost certain to be noticed when the document is proofread. Figure 5-6 shows our sample memo with generic placeholders inserted.

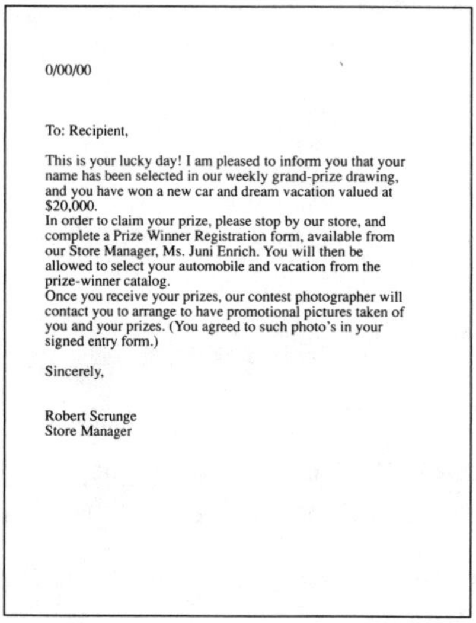

0/00/00

To: Recipient,

This is your lucky day! I am pleased to inform you that your name has been selected in our weekly grand-prize drawing, and you have won a new car and dream vacation valued at $20,000.
In order to claim your prize, please stop by our store, and complete a Prize Winner Registration form, available from our Store Manager, Ms. Juni Enrich. You will then be allowed to select your automobile and vacation from the prize-winner catalog.
Once you receive your prizes, our contest photographer will contact you to arrange to have promotional pictures taken of you and your prizes. (You agreed to such photo's in your signed entry form.)

Sincerely,

Robert Scrunge
Store Manager

Figure 5-6: After being edited, the document contains placeholders.

After editing the memo, the Save As... command saves the template document to disk. Use names that are easily identified in Finder windows and dialog box listings: for example, add the letters "STNY" to the end of each document name. You're not required to use naming conventions; you'll be able to distinguish Stationery Pads by their icons alone, but using distinct file names gives you an extra advantage.

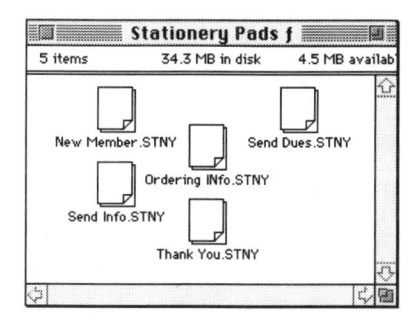

Figure 5-7: A folder full of Stationery Pads.

There's one final but critical step in creating a stationery document. After you've edited and saved your document, go to the Finder and select its icon and choose the Get Info command from the File menu. Click in the Stationery Pad check-box in the lower-right corner of the Get Info dialog box. Notice that the icon inside the Get Info dialog box changes to show that the document is now a Stationery Pad. When the Get Info dialog box is closed, the conversion is complete.

The document's icon at the Finder will also be updated to reflect its new status, but the icon that appears depends on the application used to create the document. These icons are discussed more completely later in this section.

Using Stationery

After you've created Stationery Pad documents, you can either launch them from the desktop by double-clicking on their icons, or you can open them with the Open command in an application's file menu.

When a Stationery Pad is launched from the desktop, the dialog box shown in **Figure 5-8** appears, prompting you to name and save the new document being created. After entering a new name, you can click the OK button and save the new document in the same location as the Stationery Pad, or, you can use the Save In... button to save the file in a new location before it's opened.

```
You have opened a stationery pad, so a
new document will be created.

Type a name for the new document:
[Thank You.STNY copy]

[ Save In... ]   [ Cancel ]   [   OK   ]
```

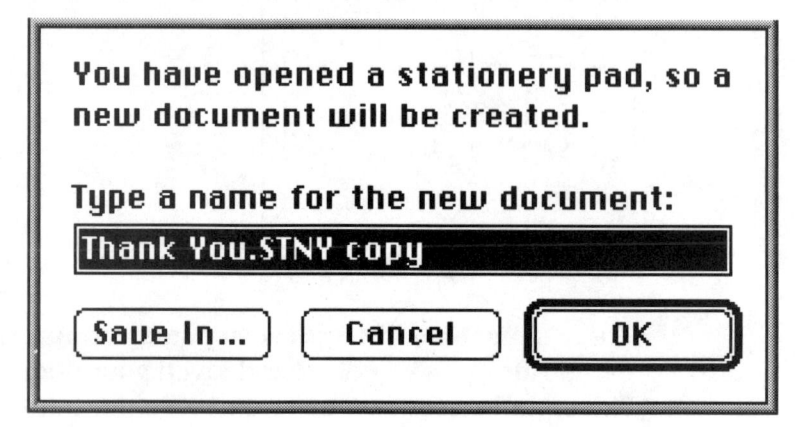

Figure 5-8: The Open Stationery Pad dialog box.

Since the Stationery Pad file is duplicated and renamed before it's opened, if you later decide you don't need this new document, you'll have to manually delete it from your disk.

Stationery Pads work differently when opened from within an application. In this case, a copy of the Stationery Pad is not created; instead, the original Stationery Pad file is opened. In Open dialog boxes, you can tell Stationery Pad documents by their icons, as shown in Figure 5-9. Since opening a Stationery Pad from the Open command modifies the original file, you can't use Stationery Pads as templates for new documents when opening them in this way. A warning dialog box appears when Stationery Pads are opened from the Open command, to remind you that you'll be modifying the Stationery Pad itself.

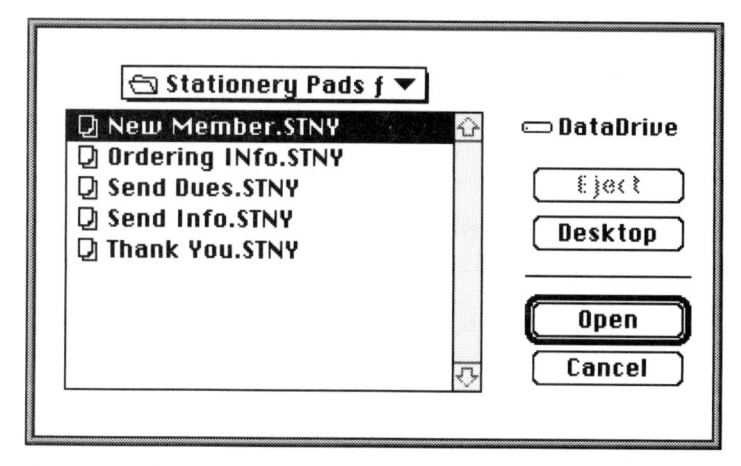

Figure 5-9: An Open dialog box with Stationery Pads visible.

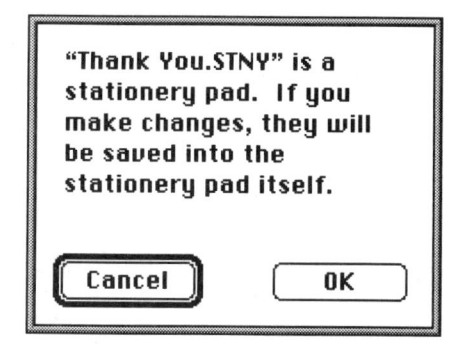

Figure 5-10: This dialog appears when a Stationery Pad is opened from inside an application.

If you want to use a Stationery Pad as a template, you must open it from the Finder. Of course, even when your application is already running, you can return to the Finder from the Applications menu, and launch your Stationery Pad without quitting the application.

Once you've opened a copy of a Stationery Pad document, you can customize it as required. Be sure to edit all placeholders that you set when creating the Stationery Pad document. You can delete unnecessary elements, add new ones, and edit the document in any other way you choose.

Stationery Pad Tips

- **Stationery Pad aliases.** Whether they were created before or after the "Stationery Pad" option was set, aliases of Stationery Pad documents access the Stationery Pad normally. The alias icon does not display the Stationery Pad icon.

- **Stationery comments.** Comments are transferred to any new document created with the Stationery Pad. To take advantage of this, you can write the name of each Stationery Pad document in the Stationery Pad's comment field. Later you can determine which Stationery Pad was used to create a document by simply checking the document's Get Info comment.

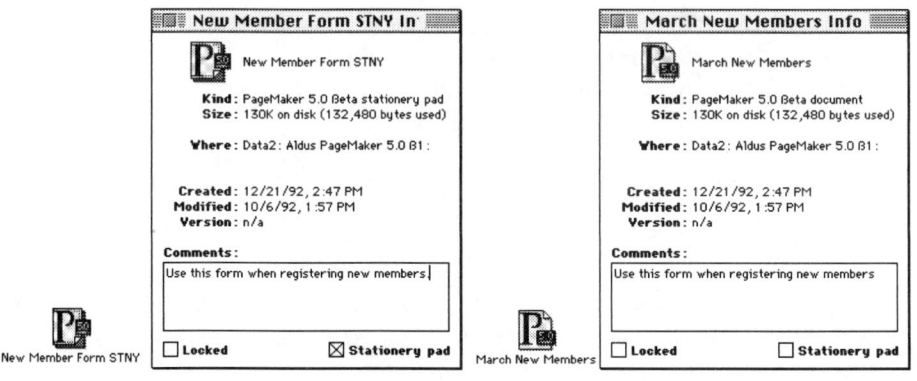

Figure 5-11: Comments are carried over to Stationery Pads.

- **Stationery Pad Folder.** Create a Stationery or Templates Folder and keep aliases of all your Stationery Pad documents in this folder. Keep the original documents organized as they were originally. This makes it easy to access Stationery Pads when you need them. If you use them frequently, you can also put an alias of this folder in your Apple Menu Items Folder.

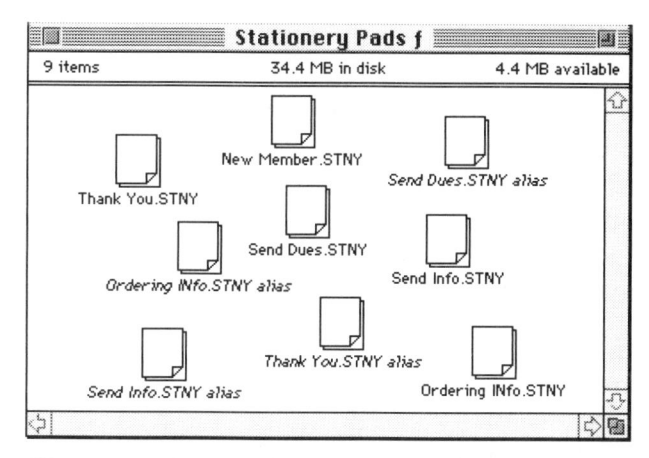

Figure 5-12: A folder containing Stationery Pads and Stationery Pad aliases.

- **Application support for multiple documents.** If an application does not support more than one open document at a time, opening a Stationery Pad from the Finder when the application and a document are already open may not work. In this case, close the current open document, then reopen the Stationery Pad using the Open command.

- **Opening Stationery from the Open command.** Opening a Stationery Pad document from inside an application that isn't "Stationery Pad aware" may cause problems. An application may open the Stationery Pad itself rather than creating a new Untitled copy. When you open Stationery Pads using the Open command, be sure to use a new file name and the Save As command, so you don't accidentally overwrite your Stationery Pad document.

- **Editing Stationery Pads.** Deselecting the "Stationery Pad" option in the Get Info dialog box will turn any Stationery Pad document back into a "normal" document—it will lose its Stationery Pad properties. You can then edit the Stationery Pad document, making changes to your master. After editing and saving this document, reselect the "Stationery pad" option in the Get Info dialog box to turn the file back into a Stationery Pad.

The Desktop Level

It is impossible to work on the Macintosh and not hear—and use—the word "desktop." In Macintosh terminology, the word "desktop" usually refers to the Finder desktop, which is the on-screen area where volume icons, windows and the Trash appear. Also, files and folders can be dragged from any mounted volume or folder and placed directly on the desktop.

In previous system software versions, the Finder desktop was ignored by the Open and Save dialog boxes. In these dialog boxes, each mounted volume was discrete, and all files were on disks or in folders.

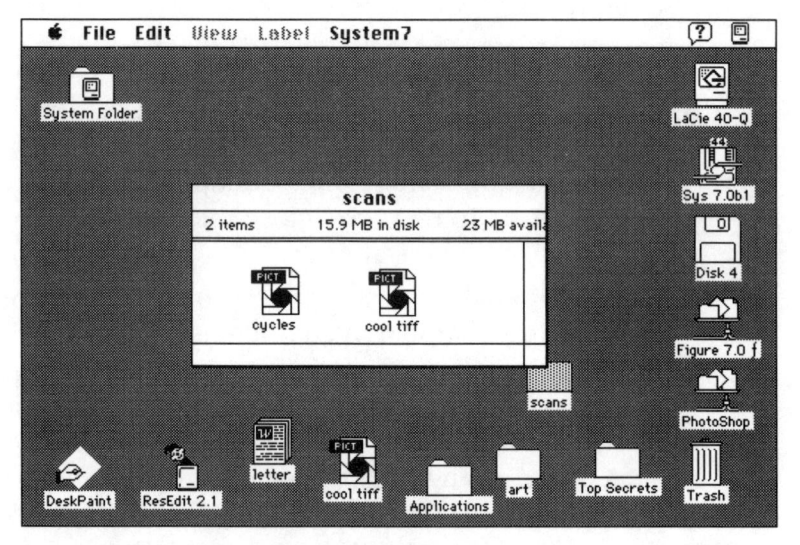

Figure 5-13: The Finder desktop.

In System 7, dialog boxes provide access to the Finder desktop and all volumes, files and folders that reside there. In fact, the Drive button has been replaced with a Desktop button that causes a new desktop view to appear in the scrolling file listing. This desktop view displays the name and icon of each volume, file and folder that exist on the Finder desktop.

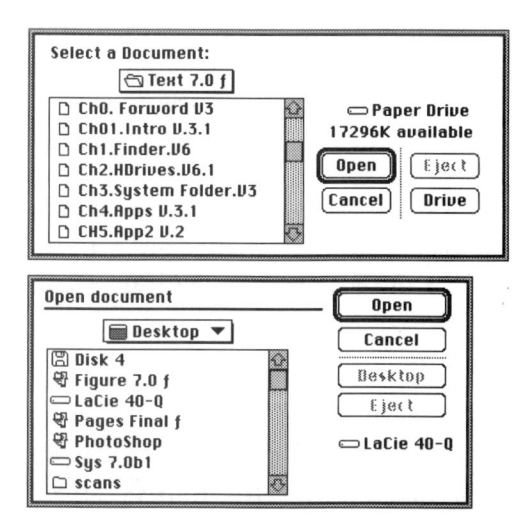

Figure 5-14: A sample dialog box from System 6.0x (top) and one from System 7 (bottom).

Figure 5-15: The desktop level offers a bird's-eye view of the available volumes, files and folders.

From the desktop view in these new dialog boxes, you can move into any volume, folder or file on the desktop by double-clicking a name in the scrolling list, or save files directly onto the desktop. Once any volume or folder is open, the list of files and folders at that location is displayed, and the dialog box operates normally. Saving a file onto the desktop causes its icon to appear on your Finder desktop, and leaves you free to later drag it onto any volume or folder.

Dialog Box Keyboard Equivalents

In addition to the new Desktop button, all Open and Save dialog boxes now support a number of keyboard equivalents that make it faster and easier to find and create files:

- **Desktop express.** Command-D is the equivalent of clicking the Desktop button.

- **Next or previous volume or drive.** To cycle through available volumes (formerly done by the Drive button), press Command-Right Arrow. You can now also cycle backward by pressing Command-Left Arrow.

- **File listing / File name options.** In Save As dialog boxes, pressing the Tab key toggles back and forth between the scrolling file listing and the file name option. You can tell which is activated by the presence of an extra black border, and you can also control the active window from the keyboard. (In earlier versions of the system software, pressing the Tab key was the equivalent of pressing the Drive button.)

  When the file name option is active, you can control the cursor position with the arrow keys, and of course enter any valid file name. When the scrolling file listing is active, use the keyboard equivalents listed below to locate, select and manipulate files and folders.

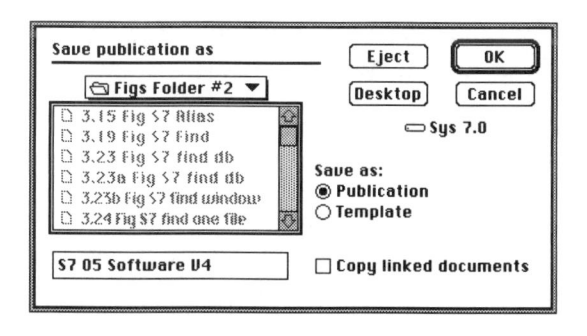

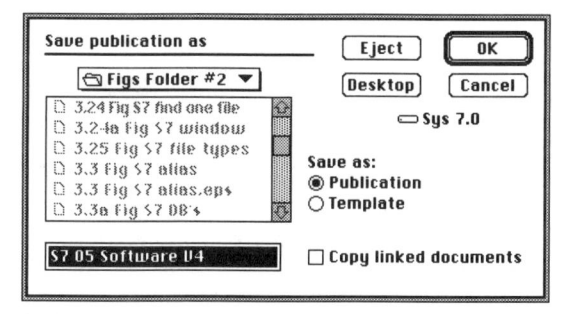

Figure 5-16: A dialog box with the scrolling list active (top) and with the Name option box active (bottom).

The following keyboard equivalents are available in the scrolling file listing of either Open or Save As dialog boxes:

- **Jump alphabetically.** Typing any single letter causes the first file name starting with that letter, or the letter closest to it, to be selected.

- **Jump alphabetically, then some.** If you quickly type more than one letter, the Mac will continue to narrow down the available file names accordingly. In other words, typing only the letter F will jump you to the first file name that starts with an F; typing FUL will pass by the file "Finder 7 Facts" and select the file "Fulfillment Info." When typing multiple characters to find files, you must not pause between characters, or the Mac will think you're starting a new search—instead of interpreting your second character as the second letter of a file name, it will treat it as the first letter of a new search.

- **Open folder.** While a folder is selected, press Command-Down Arrow to open that folder and view its contents.

- **Close folder.** While a folder is selected, press Command-Up Arrow to close that folder and view the contents of its enclosing folder or volume.

Desk Accessories

Desk accessories have always had a fond place in the hearts of Macintosh users. As they were originally designed, DAs came to symbolize the unique nature of the Mac—its customizability and much of its fun.

The main benefit of using desk accessories was being able to run an additional application (even if it was a small one) without quitting the main application—you could open a calculator, or delete files from your disk, without leaving your word processor, for example. With system software 5.0, MultiFinder became an inherent feature of the system software, giving users the ability to run multiple large and small applications.

The introduction of MultiFinder meant that desk accessories' days were numbered. System 7 pounds the last nail into the coffin, but not before assuring them an afterlife. The cause of death is System 7's inability to launch or install desk accessory files from the DA suitcase format. The resurrection is provided by System 7's ability to easily turn these old desk accessories into new double-clickable applications.

Existing desk accessories appear at the Finder with their familiar suitcase icons, as shown in Figure 5-17. In previous system software versions, these suitcases were opened and installed into the System file using the Font/DA Mover, or attached to the System file via utilities like Suitcase II and MasterJuggler. In System 7, however, these DA suitcases are relics whose only purpose is to store desk accessories until they're converted for use in System 7.

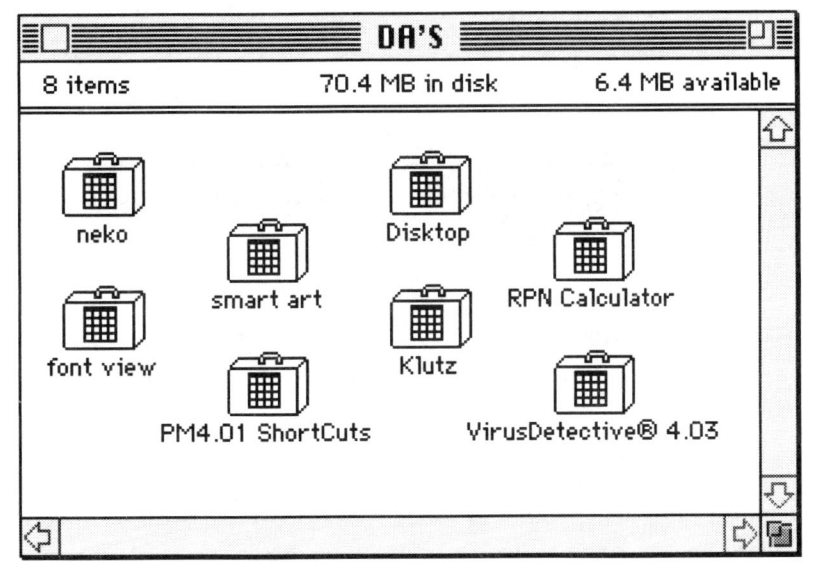

Figure 5-17: DA icons.

To convert desk accessories into System 7-compatible applications, double-click on the suitcase icon, and a window will open, as shown in Figure 5-18. This window displays each desk accessory in the suitcase, with its own Application icon. At this point, you may run the DA by simply double-clicking on it, or you can permanently convert the DA into an application by dragging it out of the suitcase and into any other folder or volume. As you copy the DA into a new folder or volume, it's transformed into a stand-alone application. From this point forward, it functions as an application, although it's still listed by the Finder's Kind item as a desk accessory.

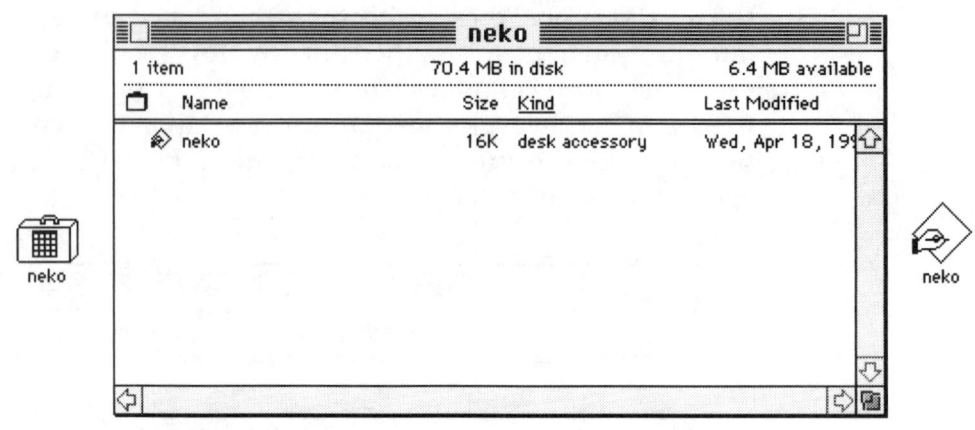

Figure 5-18: A DA icon, open DA window and DA application.

This process (removing DAs from their suitcases) is the only way to use DAs in System 7. Once "converted" into System 7-compatible applications, you can't use them as applications in System 6.0x or earlier. If you try to launch a converted desk accessory into earlier system software, the Name dialog box will appear. For this reason, you should keep copies of all your desk accessories, in their original desk accessory format, on disk in case you ever need to use them with an older version of the system software.

Once a DA has been converted into an application, it can be used just like any application. You can store it in any folder, and you'll usually launch it by double-clicking on its icon. Of course, you can launch the converted DA with any of the launching methods described earlier in this chapter. You'll also want to install the DA, or its alias, in the Apple Menu Items Folder so you can launch it from the Apple Menu.

After opening a converted DA, you can either close it when you're finished, hide it with the Applications menu's Hide command, or bring another application to the foreground and leave the DA open in the background. Most converted DAs are closed by clicking the close box in their window title bar, but you can also use the File menu's Quit command.

Moving On

Even the oldest Macintosh programs are improved by System 7, as we've seen throughout this chapter. Some improvements are dramatic and substantial, while others are more subtle or incidental:

- There are now even more ways than ever to launch your applications and their document files.

- A new document type, the Stationery Pad, is provided by the system software to every application.

- The Desktop level is given official presence in all Open and Save dialog boxes.

- Desk accessories leave the shelter of the Apple Menu and can now be used like normal applications.

Another important aspect of System 7 is the ability to open and use several applications simultaneously. Chapter 6 focuses on multitasking, describing the commands and features it supports, and looking at the ways it can be used to work more productively.

Chapter 6: Working With Multiple Applications

One "exciting new feature" of System 7 is actually an exciting old feature that some Macintosh users have been using for more than two years. Known as MultiFinder in previous system software versions, this feature lets you

- Run multiple applications at once.
- Switch between open applications as necessary.
- Leave one program working while you switch to another.

MultiFinder was a separate utility file, kept in the System Folder of previous system software versions. Because MultiFinder's features have been incorporated into System 7, the MultiFinder utility is no longer used. As you'll see, System 7 provides all the features of MultiFinder, plus some new ones.

Since the MultiFinder utility file is no longer used, the name "MultiFinder" is no longer appropriate. In this book, the set of features that allows you to open multiple applications simultaneously will be referred to as the *multitasking features of System 7*. Other people and publications will continue to refer to these as MultiFinder features, or you may also hear them described as the "Process Manager." Some may avoid using any specific name, simply referring to them as part of the system software or the Finder.

Technically speaking, it should be pointed out, there are two kinds of multitasking: *cooperative* and *preemptive*. System 7 provides cooperative multitasking, which means that all open applications have equal access to the Macintosh's computing power. Some purists consider preemptive multitasking, which ascribes priority to specific applications or tasks, to be the only "real" multitasking. The distinctions between these two are unimportant, and probably uninteresting, to most Macintosh users. For convenience, we'll use the term multitasking to describe the Mac's ability to open and operate multiple applications simultaneously.

What Is Multitasking?

Multitasking allows several programs to be opened and used simultaneously. You can have your word processor, page layout software and graphics package all running at the same time, and you can switch between them freely. It's even possible for an application to continue processing information while another application is being used. Figure 6-1 shows Adobe Illustrator, Microsoft Word, and Aldus PageMaker all open simultaneously on the Macintosh.

Chapter 6: Working With Multiple Applications

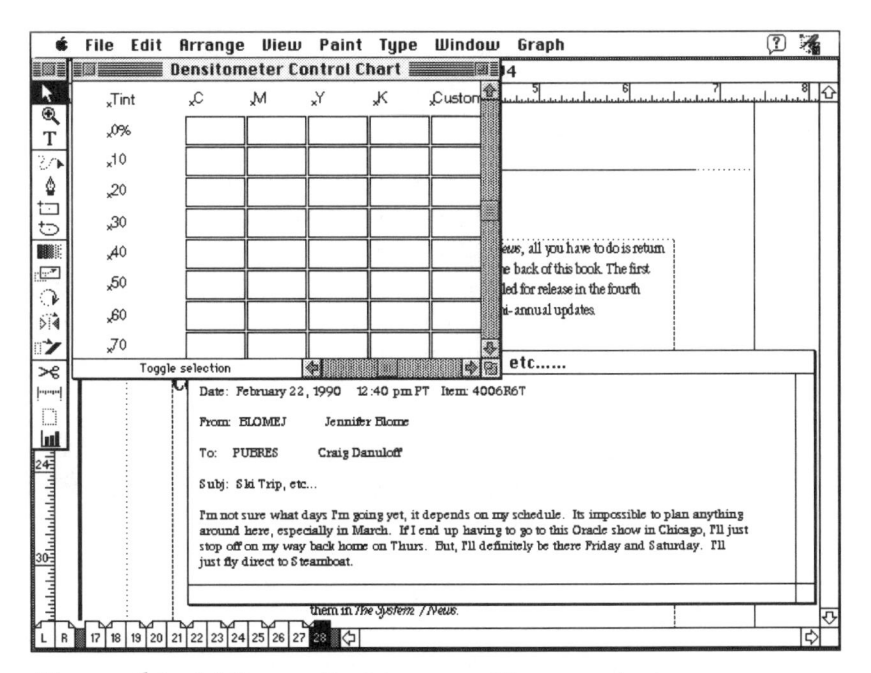

Figure 6-1: A Mac as it appears with several open applications.

Multitasking is a fantastic productivity booster, allowing you to use time and resources with maximum efficiency. For example, you're working in your word processor when you receive a telephone call from your mother. She wants to know whether she'd be better off investing the $10,000 she just won playing bingo in a 7-year CD paying 8.25 percent, or if she should sink it into T-bills paying 6.15 percent tax-free. To help dear old Mom out of her dilemma, you need access to a spreadsheet. So you quit your word processor, launch your spreadsheet, perform the necessary calculations, offer your advice, quit the spreadsheet, launch the word processor, reload your file and say goodbye to Mom.

All of this is fine—of course you want to help your mother— but all the time it took to quit your word processor, launch the spreadsheet, quit the spreadsheet, relaunch the word processor and reload your file could have been avoided.

Multitasking would have allowed you to run your spreadsheet without quitting your word processor.

This example points to one of the most obvious benefits of multitasking—the ability to handle interruptions with minimum loss of productivity. For most people, interruptions are an unavoidable part of working, and whether they're in the form of a ringing telephone, a knock on the door, an urgent e-mail message or your own memory lapses (you forgot to print that report and drop it in the mail), the least disruption possible is the key to productivity.

The second major benefit of multitasking is its ability to use two or more applications together to complete a single project. To prepare a mail merge, for example, you can export data from your database manager, prepare the merge lists, then execute the merge. In most cases, the raw data exported from your database will require some cleaning up before it's ready to be merged; and often you'll encounter a minor data formatting problem that requires you to repeat the whole export and data cleanup process. But by using multitasking, you avoid the delay and frustration of quitting the word processor to return to the database, then quitting the database to return to the word processor.

As other examples, you may need to read reports and view database or spreadsheet data while preparing presentation graphics; update graphic illustrations in a drawing package before importing them into a page layout; or use an optical character recognition package to read in articles for storage in a database. In these and many other cases, quickly switching from one application to another and using the Mac's Cut, Copy and Paste commands to transfer data between these open applications allow transfer of information between applications that can't otherwise share data.

The third benefit of multitasking is the most exciting—and certainly the one yielding the largest productivity gains: multitasking supports *background processing*. This means that an open application can continue to process data even when you switch away from that application to work in another. Any task that ties up your computer, forcing you to wait for it to finish, can probably benefit from background processing. Common examples are printing, transferring files to or from bulletin boards, large spreadsheet calculations and database report generation. Examples of background processing and ways you can take advantage of this tremendous capability are discussed later in this chapter.

MultiFinder in System 6.0x

If you're familiar with MultiFinder from earlier versions of the system software, you'll find only a few differences between MultiFinder and the multitasking features of System 7. The most notable difference is that multitasking is always available and, unlike MultiFinder, cannot be turned off.

If you didn't use MultiFinder in previous versions of the system software, it was probably for one of the following reasons:

- **Insufficient memory.** MultiFinder required two megabytes of RAM (at a minimum) and four or more megabytes of RAM to be useful. The same is true of the multitasking capabilities in System 7, although the recent dramatic lowering of RAM prices and the addition of virtual memory in System 7 make this less of an issue than in the past. (System 7 memory requirements are discussed later in this chapter, and in Chapter 11, "Memory Management.")

- **Reputation.** MultiFinder had a reputation for instability. Many people believed that using MultiFinder made the Macintosh prone to frequent crashes. As often happens with software and hardware, this reputation was undeserved—the rumors of crashes were not based on the real facts.

When MultiFinder was first released, many applications crashed when they were launched under MultiFinder. This was not the fault of MultiFinder; it was usually because the application had not been written according to Apple's programming rules. Once these incompatible applications were made MultiFinder-compatible, almost all problems vanished.

Another problem—again not MultiFinder's fault—was the increasing use of startup programs, which caused a memory conflict in the System Heap (an area of RAM used by the operating system), often resulting in crashes when using MultiFinder. This problem was easily cured with utilities such as HeapFix or HeapTool, which are freely available from user groups and bulletin boards. In any case, this type of problem is not apparent in System 7.

- **Complexity.** MultiFinder was considered too complex by many novice Macintosh users. This perception was understandable—after all, MultiFinder was offered as a virtually undocumented utility program. A Macintosh user had to be somewhat adventurous just to turn it on and learn how to use it. For the majority of users who don't spend their free time attending user groups, browsing on CompuServe or reading about Macintosh, MultiFinder seemed intimidating and too risky.

In System 7, multitasking is seamlessly integrated into the system software, making the simultaneous use of multiple applications a fundamental part of the working routine. Everyone who uses the Macintosh should take the time to learn, understand and benefit from this powerful tool.

Working With Multiple Applications

System 7 allows you to open multiple applications automatically, without any special configuration or initiation. In fact, when you launch your first application from the Finder, you'll immediately notice the effect: the Finder desktop (the volume icons, Trash, etc.) does not disappear as the new application is launched, as was the case in previous versions of the system software. The Finder remains visible in System 7 because both your new application and the Finder now run simultaneously.

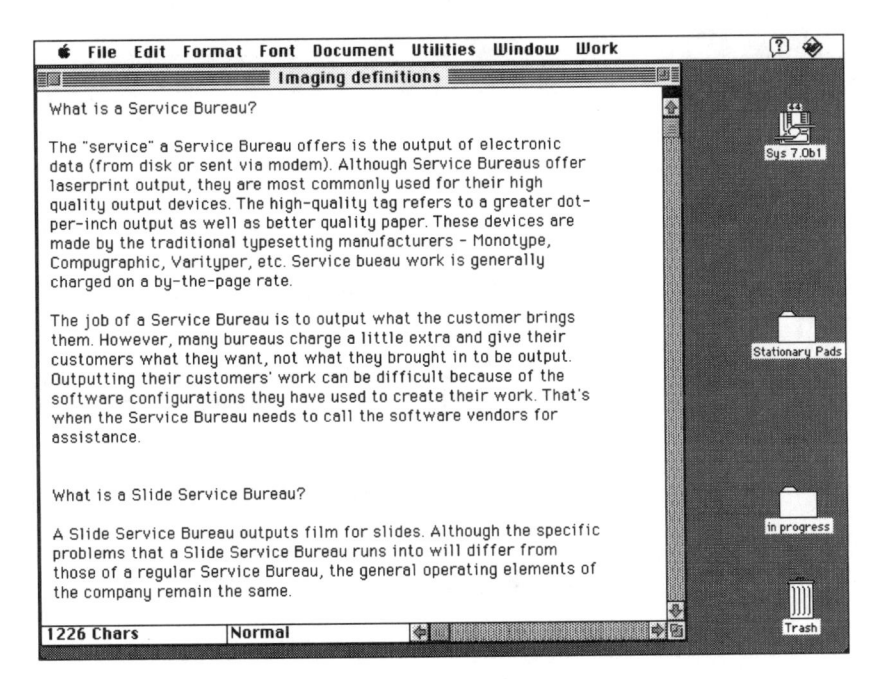

Figure 6-2: Word running with Finder elements visible.

Launching additional applications continues to demonstrate the abilities of multitasking. As each additional program opens, its menu bar and windows are displayed, and other open applications are unaffected.

When you first start using multiple applications simultaneously, the sight of several windows at the same time may be a little disconcerting. As you learn to arrange and manipulate these windows and enjoy the benefits of multiple open applications, you'll soon find yourself wondering how you ever got along using just one program at a time.

The number of applications you can launch simultaneously is limited only by the amount of memory you have available. If your launch will exceed available memory, a dialog box will alert you to the problem and the additional application will not be launched. (More on memory and running multiple applications later in this chapter.)

Foreground & Background Applications

Although more than one program can be open at once, only one program can be active at any one time. The active program is the *foreground application*, and other open but inactive applications are *background applications*, even if you can see portions of their windows or if they're simultaneously processing tasks.

You can tell which program is currently active in several ways:

- The menu bar displays the menu commands of the active program only.

- The active program's icon appears at the top of the Applications menu.

- The active program name is checked in the Applications menu.

- The Apple Menu About This Macintosh... command lists the active program name.

Chapter 6: Working With Multiple Applications 169

- Active program windows overlap other visible windows or elements.

- Active program windows display a highlighted title bar, which includes horizontal lines, the Close box and the Zoom box.

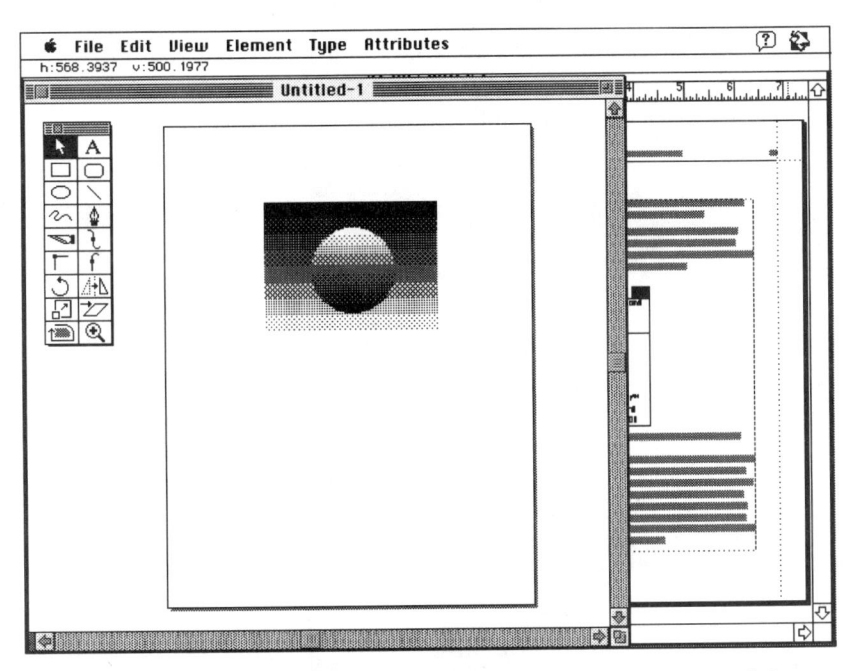

Figure 6-3: Aldus FreeHand is the active program in this window; PageMaker is in the background.

In contrast, a background application's menu bar does not appear, its icon is not checked in the Applications menu, none of its windows are highlighted, and some or all of its windows may be hidden or obscured.

Since only one program can be in the foreground, it's important to be able to quickly and easily switch from one foreground program to another. Switching between applications is commonly referred to as "sending to the back" and "bringing to the front."

There are two ways to switch between open applications:

- **Use the Applications menu.** Located in the upper-right corner of the menu bar, the Applications menu lists the names of all applications currently running. Choose the name of the application you want to switch to, and that program will bring its menu bar and windows to the front.

    For example, to switch from an application to the Finder, choose the word Finder from the Applications menu: the Finder's menu bar will appear, and any icons and windows on the desktop will become visible.

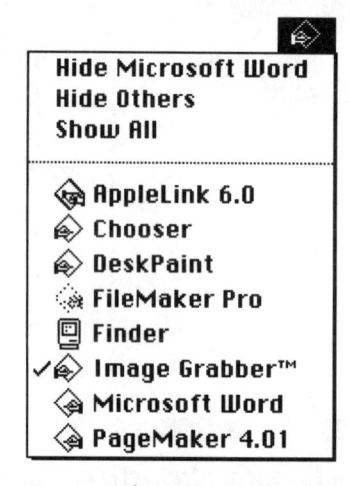

Figure 6-4: The Applications menu as it appears with numerous open applications.

- **Click the mouse on any visible window.** Clicking the mouse on any visible element on the screen brings the application owning that element to the front. For example, while working in your word processor, if you can still see the icons on the Finder desktop, clicking on one of these icons will bring the Finder to the front, making it the current application. After working in the Finder, return to the word processor by clicking on its window.

Background Processing

You can bring any application to the foreground, sending any other to the background, at any time except when dialog boxes are open. You can even send most applications to the background while they're processing data—they'll continue to calculate or process in the background. Background processing adds an entirely new dimension to simultaneously using open multiple applications.

If multiple open applications could be used only sequentially, one after the other, productivity increases would be limited to the time saved by avoiding repeated opening and quitting of applications. Background processing, however, lets you print a newsletter, calculate a spreadsheet and dial up a remote bulletin board at the same time. This is the ultimate in computer productivity.

Background processing is easy. Start by doing a lengthy process, like a spreadsheet calculation or a telecommunication session, then bring another open application to the foreground. The background task continues processing while the computer is used for another task in another application. Because foreground and background applications are sharing the hardware resources (there's only one central processing unit in the Macintosh), you may notice a slowdown or jerky motion in the foreground application. The severity of this effect will depend on your Macintosh's power and the number and requirements of the background tasks being performed; but there should be no detrimental effect on your foreground application.

You may need to periodically attend to a task left running in the background, or you may be given notice when it completes its task. If so, an Alert dialog box will be displayed, or a diamond will appear before the application's name in the Applications menu.

Using the PrintMonitor for Background Printing

The first background processing most people use is printing. Background printing is not quite the same as using two applications at once, but it's similar.

Without multitasking, you have to wait for the entire file to be printed—because of the time it takes for the printer to mechanically do the job. In background printing, files are printed to disk as fast as the application and printer driver can handle them, then a utility called a *print spooler* sends the print file from the disk to the printer. The advantage is that the print spooler takes over the task of feeding the pages to the printer and waits as the printer performs its slow mechanical tasks, while you continue working in your main application or even use another software application.

Background PostScript printing support is built into System 7 and controlled via the Chooser's Background Printing option. By default, Background Printing is turned on, but you can turn it off at any time by clicking the Off radio button, as shown in Figure 6-5.

With Background Printing turned on, files printed using the LaserWriter driver are spooled to your hard drive. At the same time, the PrintMonitor utility, automatically running in the background, begins printing the spooled file to the selected PostScript printer. While PrintMonitor is printing, you can bring it to the foreground by selecting its name from the Applications menu. (See Figure 6-6.)

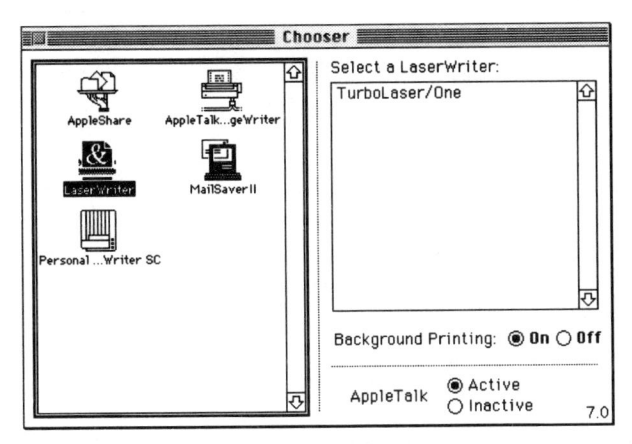

Figure 6-5: Chooser and Background Printing option.

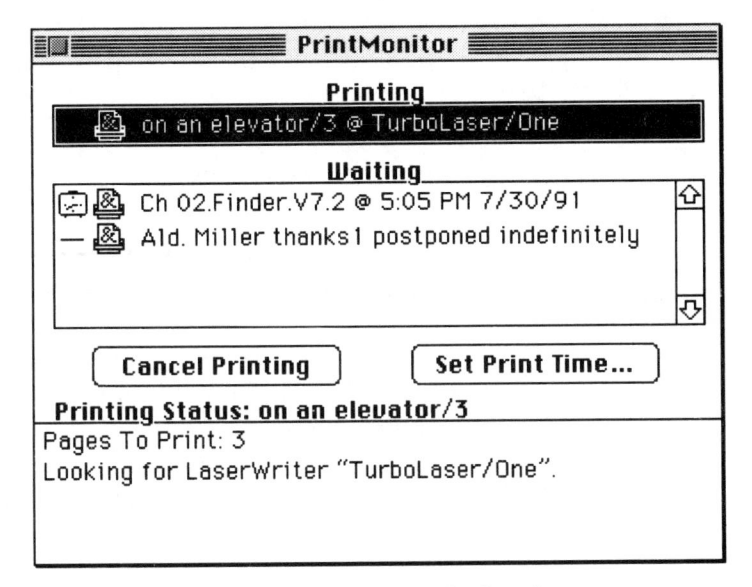

Figure 6-6: The PrintMonitor dialog box.

PrintMonitor provides several options: you can delay the printing of any spooled file for a specific or indefinite period of time; you can rearrange the printing order if several files have been spooled; and you can cancel the printing of a spooled file. PrintMonitor can also be used to simply monitor the status of background printing as it occurs.

To delay or postpone the printing of any spooled file, click its file name and then click the Set Print Time... button, as shown in Figure 6-7. When the Set Print Time dialog box appears, select the portion of the time or date you want to change, then click the up or down arrow next to that time or date to reset it. Click the Postpone Indefinitely radio button if you're not sure when you want to print the file but wish to save it so it can be printed later. After completing these settings, click the OK button to return to the PrintMonitor dialog box.

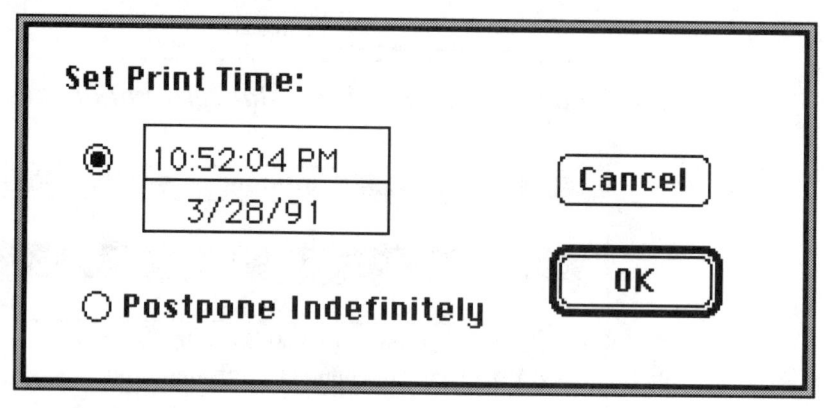

Figure 6-7: The Set Print Time dialog box.

To cancel after printing has begun, click the Cancel Printing button. It will take a few seconds for printing to stop, at which time the file name will be removed from the Printing message area at the top of the PrintMonitor dialog box. To cancel printing a file waiting in the print queue, select the file name from the Waiting area, then click the Remove From List button.

Normally, PrintMonitor completes its job invisibly in the background. If your Macintosh happens to crash, or be shut off, while PrintMonitor is handling a print job, PrintMonitor will run automatically when your Macintosh is restarted and advise you (by flashing its icon at the top of the Applications menu) that an error has occurred. Bring the PrintMonitor to the foreground, and it will tell you which file it was unable to finish printing, and ask if you want to re-attempt printing that file.

Copying Files in the Background

Copying files from one location to another is a basic tool the Finder has always provided, but through the successive Finder versions, the activity has continued to evolve.

Early versions of the Finder provided only a simple dialog box during file copying. Later, a counter of files being copied was added. Then names of copied files were added, and finally the progress bar became a part of this dialog box. Despite these improvements, which seemed to make time pass more quickly, you were still forced to wait while files were copied.

In System 7, the process of copying files takes a huge step forward: the wait has been eliminated altogether. You can now work in any open application while the Finder copies a file in the background. To use this feature,

- Open the application you want to use while the Finder is copying.

- Switch to the Finder using the Applications menu or by clicking on the Finder desktop.

- Start the copy process in the normal way by dragging the desired files from their source location to the icon of the destination folder or volume. The copying process will begin and the copying dialog box will appear.

- Then select the Applications menu with the stopwatch cursor and choose the name of the open application you want to use while the file copy is in progress. This application will come to the foreground and is ready for you to use, while the Finder continues its copy operation in the background.

- Switch back to the Finder any time you like, using the Applications menu or clicking on the Finder desktop.

Hiding Applications

Running several applications concurrently can result in an on-screen clutter of windows displayed by open applications. To alleviate this problem, System 7 lets you "hide" open application windows, thus removing them from the screen without changing their status or the background work they're doing. You can hide an application at the time you leave it to switch to another application, or while it's running in the background.

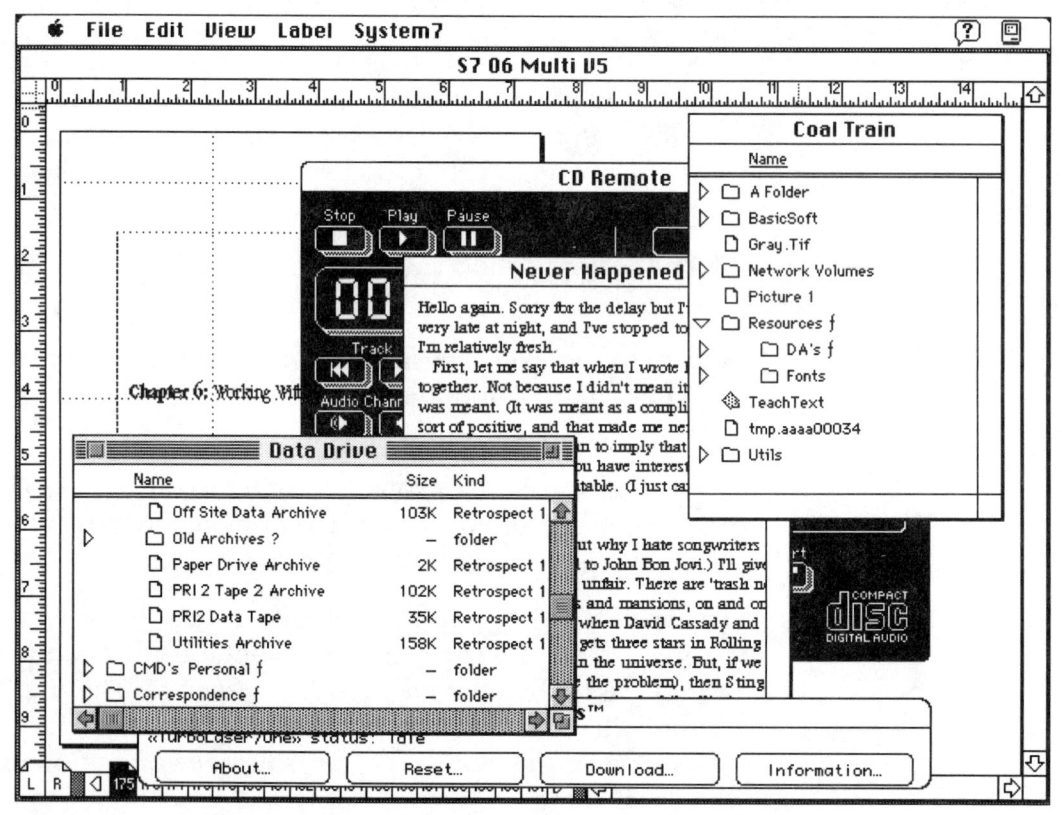

Figure 6-8: Without hiding, running multiple applications can result in a crowded display.

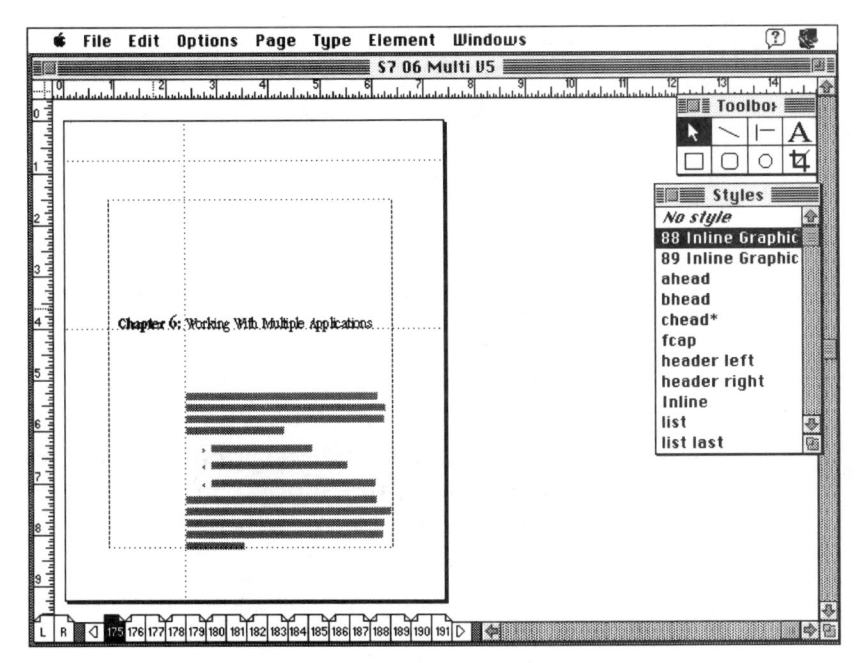

Figure 6-9: Using hiding, the same open applications result in a clear display.

The Applications menu provides three Hide commands: Hide Current Application (Current Application being the name of the current foreground application), Hide Others and Show All.

- **Hide Current Application.** Removes all windows of the current application from the screen, and brings another window of an open application to the foreground. Usually, the Finder is brought to the foreground; but if the Finder itself has been hidden, the next application in the Applications menu is brought forward instead.

  A hidden application's icon is dimmed in the Applications menu to signify that it's hidden. To unhide the application, either select its name from the Applications menu, which will bring it to the foreground, or choose the Show All command.

- **Hide Others.** Removes all windows from the screen except those of the current application. This is useful when on-screen clutter is bothersome, or if you're accidentally clicking on windows of background applications and bringing them forward. After the Hide Others command has been used, all open applications icons, except those of the foreground application, are dimmed in the Applications menu, as a visual reminder that these applications are hidden.

- **Show All.** Using this command makes all current applications visible (not hidden). You can tell which are currently hidden by their dimmed icons in the Applications menu. When the Show command is chosen, the current foreground application remains in the foreground and the windows of hidden background applications become visible but the applications remain in the background.

While an application is hidden, it continues to operate exactly the same as it would if it were running as a background application and not hidden. If an application can normally perform tasks in the background, it will still perform these tasks in the background while it's hidden. In fact, because of the effort saved by not having to upgrade the screen display, some tasks operate faster in the background when their application is hidden.

You can also hide the current foreground application when you send it to the background, by holding down the option key while bringing another application forward (either by choosing its name from the Applications menu or by clicking the mouse on its window). Applications hidden in this manner can be retrieved with the Show All command or by selecting their dimmed icons from the Applications menu.

Multitasking Tips

Once you start using the Hide commands to reduce screen clutter, you should be comfortable working with multiple open applications. The following tips can help:

- **Save before switching.** Before bringing another application to the foreground, save your work in the application you're leaving, so that if your Mac crashes or is turned off accidentally, you won't lose your work.

- **Resuming after crashing.** If an application crashes in System 7, you can usually force the Mac to close that application and regain access to your other applications by pressing Command-Option-Escape.

    Note that after resuming from this kind of a crash, your system may be unstable and prone to additional crashes. You should save any unsaved work in other open applications, and you may want to restart your Macintosh, just to be safe.

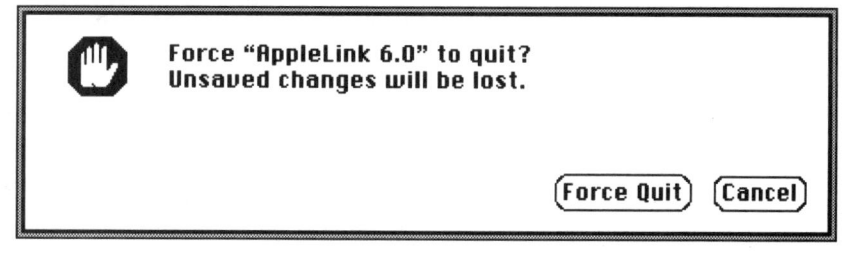

Figure 6-10: The Force Quit dialog box.

- **Shutting down or restarting.** Selecting the Shut Down or Restart commands from the Finder's Special menu while multiple applications are open will cause all open applications to be quit. If any open documents contain changes that haven't been saved, the application containing the document will be brought to the foreground, and you'll be asked if you want to save those changes. Click OK to save, No to discard the changes or Cancel to abort the Shut Down or Restart operation.

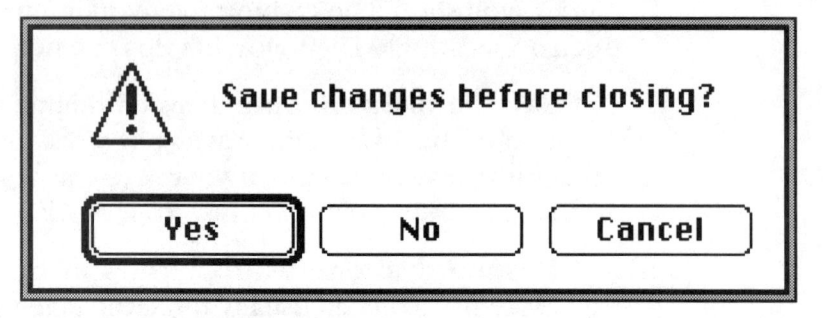

Figure 6-11: Save Changes dialog box.

- **Efficiency for background applications.** Applications in the background often run more efficiently if hidden with one of the Hide commands from the Applications menu. This is true because often the on-screen display can't keep up with the application's processing rate; as a result, the application has to wait for the screen to be drawn. The extent of this delay depends on your computer system and video display. Using the Hide command eliminates all video-related delay.

- **Switch and hide.** To hide an application while switching to another open application, hold down the Option key while clicking on the open application's window, or while selecting the name of another open application from the Applications menu.

The Memory Implications of Multitasking

Everything has its price. Macintosh users know this well (especially experienced Macintosh users). Multitasking is no exception—its price is *memory*.

Put simply, you can run only as many applications at once as your available Macintosh memory can handle. This is because a predefined amount of memory must be dedicated to the application while it's open. Running multiple applications simultaneously requires enough memory to satisfy the cumulative amounts of those applications. Your total amount of System 7 available memory includes what's supplied by the RAM chips installed on your computer's logic board or on NuBus cards, plus any virtual memory created with the Memory control panel. (See Chapter 11 for more information about virtual memory.)

When Macintosh System 7 is first turned on, some of your memory is taken up immediately by the system software and the Finder. This amount varies depending on how many fonts and sounds you've installed, your Disk Cache setting, the extensions you're using and whether you're using File Sharing. As many as three or four megabytes of memory can be consumed by the system software itself in some circumstances. Your Macintosh's memory usage is documented in the About This Macintosh dialog box, shown in Figure 6-12. If you would like to reduce the amount of memory your system software consumes, remove unused fonts or sounds, reduce the size of your RAM Disk and turn off File Sharing.

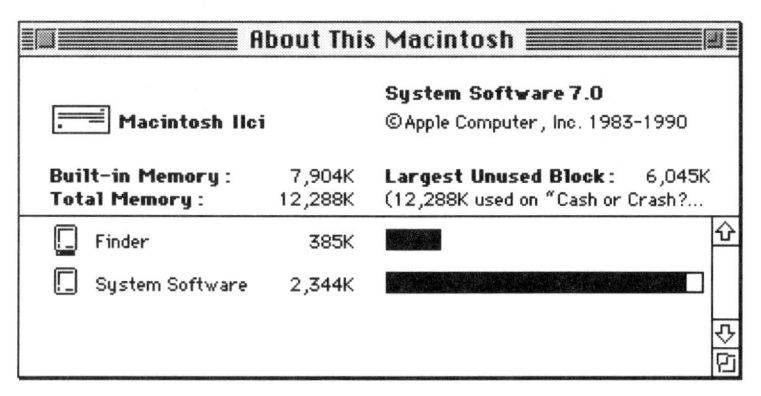

Figure 6-12: The About This Macintosh dialog box.

Each time you launch an application, it requests the amount of memory that it needs in order to run. If enough memory is available, the application is launched. If there isn't enough memory available, one of two dialog boxes will appear. The first, shown in Figure 6-13, informs you there's not enough memory available to launch the selected application. The second, shown in Figure 6-14, tells you the same thing but it also gives you the option of launching the application in the amount of RAM that is available. Normally, launching the application under these circumstances will allow you to use the application without incident.

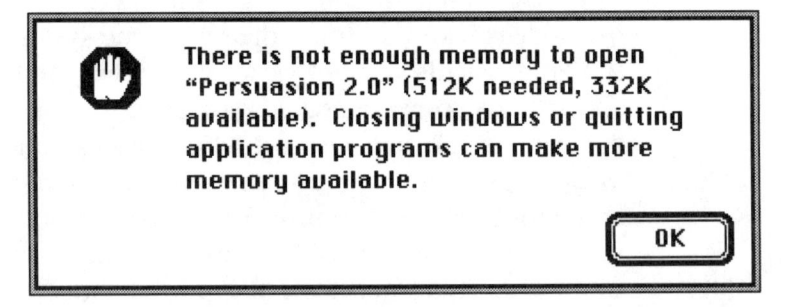

> There is not enough memory to open "Persuasion 2.0" (512K needed, 332K available). Closing windows or quitting application programs can make more memory available.
>
> [OK]

Figure 6-13: This dialog appears when launching an application with limited memory available.

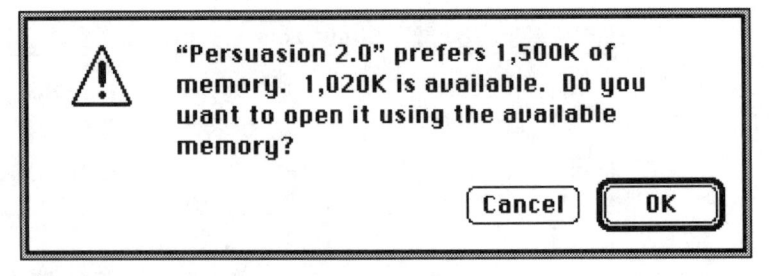

> "Persuasion 2.0" prefers 1,500K of memory. 1,020K is available. Do you want to open it using the available memory?
>
> [Cancel] [OK]

Figure 6-14: This dialog box appears when launching an application with almost *enough memory available.*

If available memory is insufficient to launch an application, quit one or more applications currently open to free up additional memory. Then try again to launch the application you want. If this isn't enough, quit additional open applications and retry the launch until you're successful.

(For more information on your Mac's memory, including ways you can expand available memory, tips on reducing the amount of memory each application consumes and more about using the About This Macintosh dialog box, see Chapter 11.)

Moving On

Working with several applications at once takes some getting used to, but it's the best way to make the most of your time and computing resources. As we've seen in this chapter, System 7's multitasking support is impressive:

- You can launch as many different applications as your available memory permits.

- Many applications can continue to process data while they're running in the background.

- "Hiding" open applications reduces on-screen clutter without affecting the operation of the applications themselves.

Like many other System 7 features, multitasking is available to every System 7-compatible program. Next, Chapter 7 introduces two advanced features available only to System 7-friendly applications, the Edition Manager and Inter-Application Communication.

Chapter 7: The Edition Manager & IAC

Launching several applications simultaneously can dramatically improve your productivity on the Macintosh, as you saw in Chapter 6. But System 7 makes it possible to integrate your applications more closely: text and graphic elements can be shared between documents; messages and commands can be passed from one application to another. These capabilities are made possible by the Edition Manager and Inter-Application Communication (IAC), respectively.

Although the power of the Edition Manager and IAC are provided by System 7, neither feature is automatically available to System 7-compatible applications. Each capability must be specifically added by software developers when their programs are updated for System 7. Support for the Edition Manager is widespread, since it is one of the requirements for System 7-Savvy status. Basic support for IAC is also a part of being System 7-Savvy, but as we'll see, full support for IAC is much more complex and is therefore appearing in applications more slowly.

The Edition Manager

Creating text and graphic elements within one application and using them in other applications has always been a hallmark of the Macintosh. Its legendary Cut and Paste commands are even being offered by other me-too graphical operating systems. But while others are matching the 1984 Macintosh's capabilities, System 7 raises the ante considerably for this type of feature with the introduction of the Edition Manager's Publish and Subscribe commands.

By using Publish and Subscribe in your System 7-Savvy applications, elements can be moved between applications, then manually or automatically updated as they're modified. In other words, when text, graphic, sound or video elements are moved from one document to another, original and duplicate elements remain linked. When the originals are changed, so are the duplicates.

The benefits are obvious:

- Charts created in spreadsheets or databases and used in word processors or page layout applications can be automatically updated any time the data changes.

- Legal disclaimers and other boilerplate text commonly used in documents can be automatically updated (like dates on a copyright notice, for example).

- Illustrated publications can be created using preliminary versions of graphic images that are automatically updated as these graphics are completed.

And Publish and Subscribe commands can be used for more than simple "live copy and paste" between two applications on your own Macintosh. They support Macintosh networks (using System 7's File Sharing feature or other networking systems), so your documents can include components created, manipulated and stored by many people on many network file servers.

(*Note*: While the term Edition Manager is the technical programming term for this set of capabilities, we'll use the term "Publish/Subscribe" for the remainder of this chapter to refer to the entire set of Edition Manager capabilities.)

How Publish/Subscribe Works

While Publish/Subscribe is a powerful feature, its basic premise is simple: any elements—text, graphics, sound or video—or combinations of them all can be transferred from one document to another using Publish/Subscribe. The transfer begins when elements to be shared are selected then published to a new edition file. (See Figure 7-1.) This process is similar to the Cut or Copy process, except that instead of being transferred into memory, the selected elements are saved to the edition file on disk. At the time you publish these elements, you name the edition file and specify where on your hard drive it will be stored.

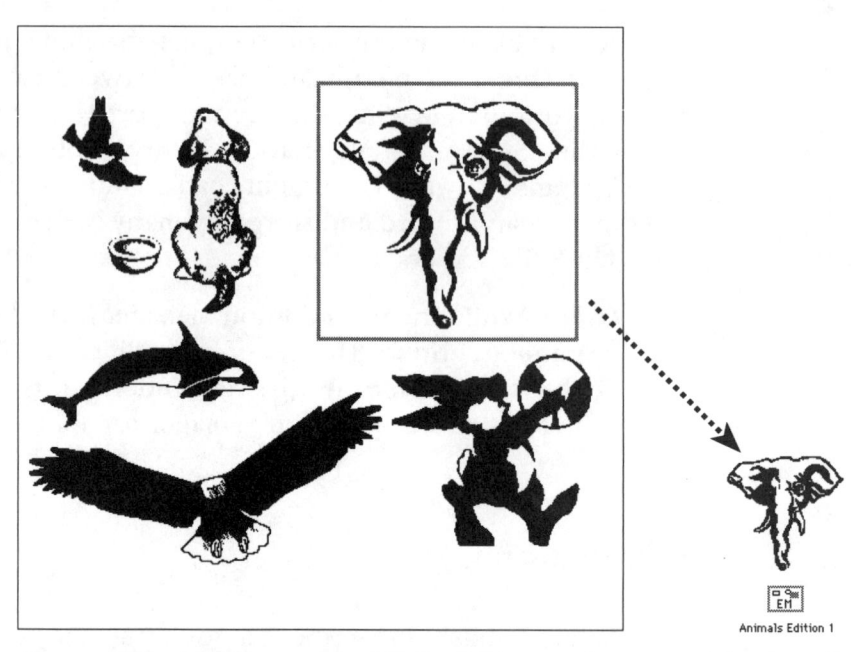

Figure 7-1: An element published from a document is stored in an edition file.

The section of your document used to create an edition is referred to as the Publisher. A link is automatically maintained between an edition file and the document that created it. When changes are made in the Publisher, the edition file is updated to reflect these changes. (See Figure 7-2.) Updates can be made any time the original document is changed, or at any other time you initiate them.

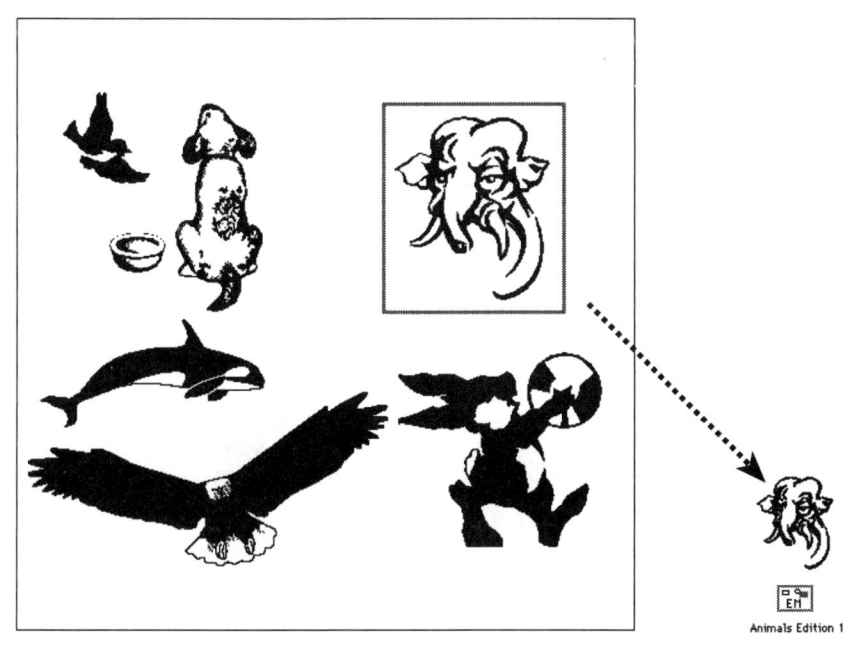

Figure 7-2: The edition file is automatically updated when the document changes.

To complete the transfer of elements between documents, the receiving document subscribes to the edition file by importing the edition file elements and establishing a link between the edition and the subscribing document. The document section imported from an edition becomes a Subscriber (to the edition). Figure 7-3 illustrates this.

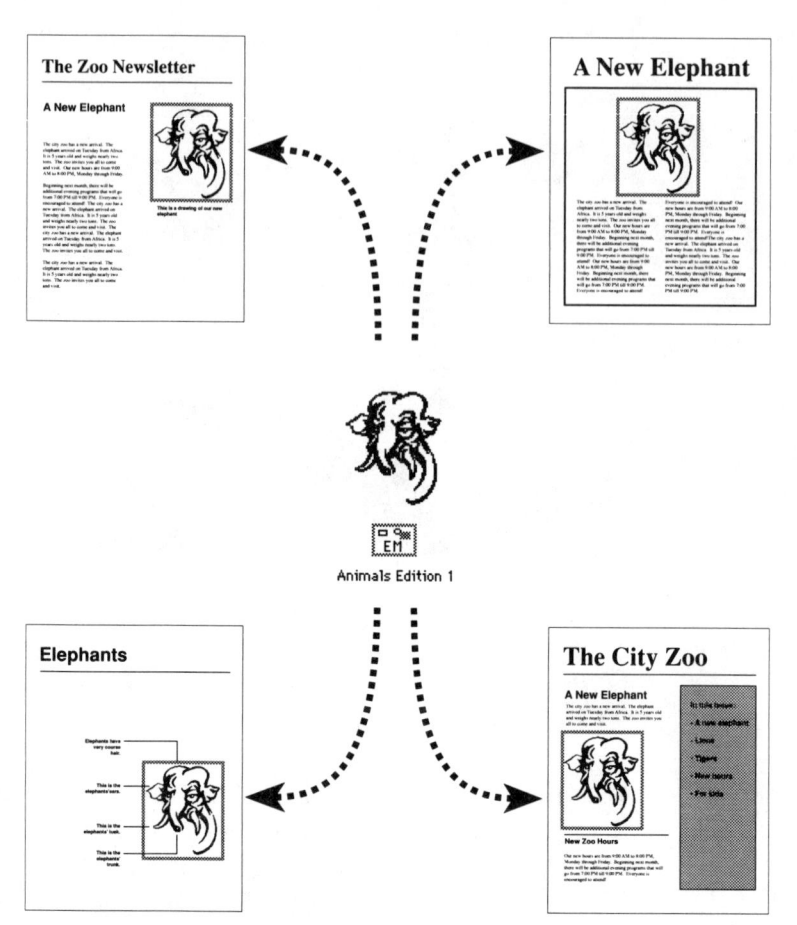

Figure 7-3: Edition files can be subscribed to by any number of other documents.

At this point, the edition file is an independent disk file, linked to the document that published it and any documents subscribing to it. (Any number of documents can subscribe to a single edition.) As elements in the publisher document change, the edition file is updated according to options set in that original document. As the edition file is updated, the edition data used by subscribers is also updated according to options set in the subscribing document. This entire process is shown in Figure 7-4.

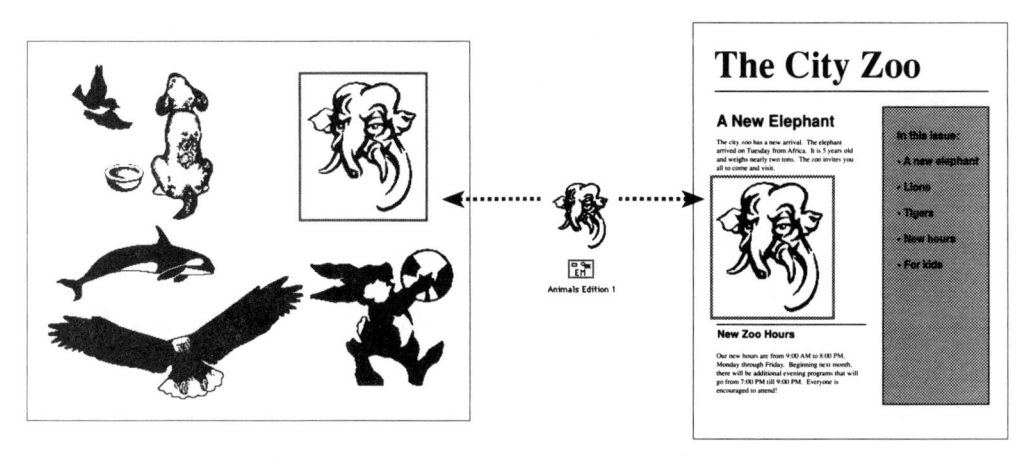

Figure 7-4: Both the publishing document and the subscribing document are linked to the edition file.

Publish / Subscribe Commands

In applications that support Publish/Subscribe, four new commands usually appear in the Edit menu: Create Publisher; Subscribe To; Publisher Options/Subscriber Options; and Show Borders. Some applications use other command names for these functions, but they should work essentially the same as that described below.

The Create Publisher Command

Create Publisher creates a new edition file, which you name and store in any desired location on any available volume. The edition file contains the text and graphic elements selected when the command is chosen. To publish any elements, select the areas of the current document that you wish to share, and choose the Create Publisher command. The Create Publisher dialog box, shown in Figure 7-5, then appears.

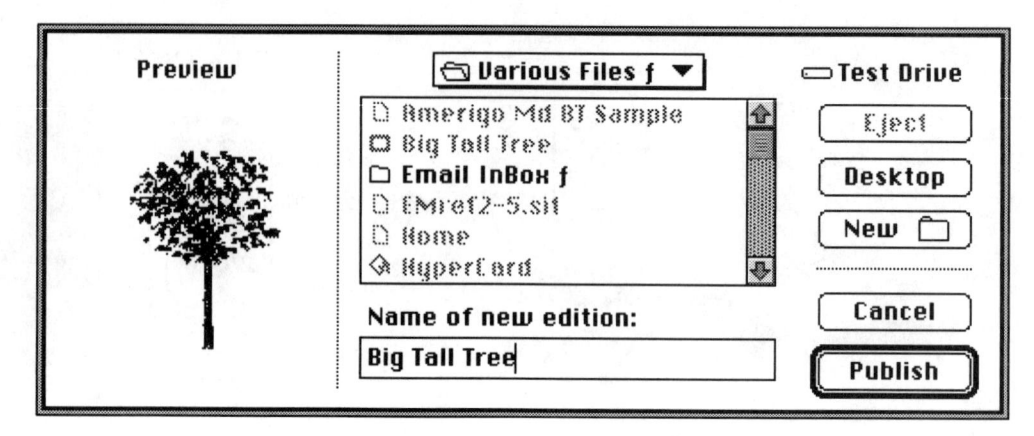

Figure 7-5: The Create Publisher dialog box.

The left side of this dialog box previews the elements that will be included in the edition. The edition contents depend not only on which elements were selected with the Create Publisher command, but also on the Select how publisher decides what to publish option setting. This option is described below along with the Publisher Options dialog box.

To complete the creation of the edition, enter a name in the Name of New Edition option box, and select a destination to which the file will be saved. Then click the Publish button, which saves your new edition to disk.

There's now a new file on disk (separate from the document you're currently working in) that contains a copy of the elements you selected to publish. It's this file—this edition—that will be placed into other documents and applications using the Subscribe To command. The edition will be updated to include any changes made to the elements it contains, according to the options set in the Publisher Options dialog box.

The Subscribe To Command

The *Subscribe To* command, the Publish/Subscribe equivalent of the Paste command, imports a copy of an edition file into the current document. When this command is chosen, the Subscribe To dialog box appears, as shown in Figure 7-6. The names of edition files appear in the scrolling list, and a preview of any edition appears when you select the file name. Select the edition you want, click the Subscribe button, and the chosen edition appears in your document.

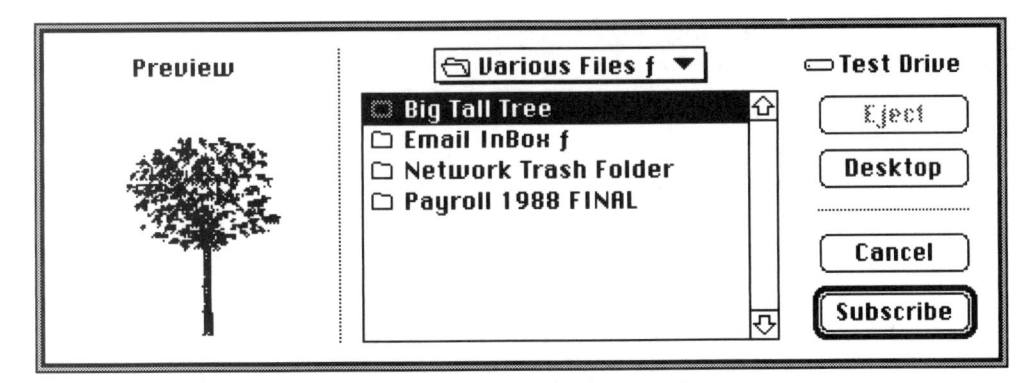

Figure 7-6: The Subscribe To dialog box.

When working in text-based applications, the edition appears at the place where the cursor was positioned when the Subscribe To command was chosen. In graphics applications, the edition file usually appears in the current screen display area. Details on how to use these included editions follow.

The Publisher Options Command

The third Edition Manager command is either *Publisher Options* or *Subscriber Options*, depending on the current selection. The Publisher Options command, available only when the rectangle surrounding published elements is selected, presents the dialog shown in Figure 7-7.

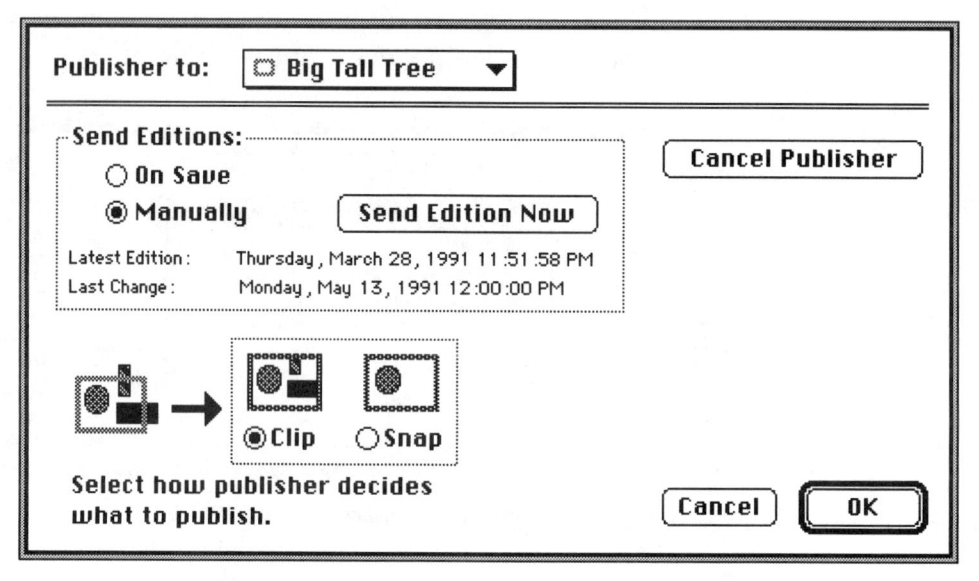

Figure 7-7: The Publisher Options dialog box.

The Publisher Options dialog box can also be accessed by double-clicking on the border of any published elements.

This dialog box presents five important options:

- **Publisher To.** This is not really an option, since it offers no alternatives; it simply shows you where the edition is stored and the path to that location. To see the storage location, click on the Publisher To pop-up menu.

- **Send Editions.** This lets you choose when the file associated with the selected edition will be updated. If you choose On Save, the edition file is updated each time the current document is saved; if you choose Manually, the Send Edition Now button must be clicked to update the edition file.

    This option also displays the date and time the edition file was last updated. If On Save is selected, this is probably the date and time the creating file was last saved. If Manually is selected, the time the elements included in the edition were last changed is also listed, letting you know how up-to-date the edition is in relation to the file's current status.

- **Send Edition Now.** Clicking this button updates the edition file to reflect the current status of the published elements. This button is normally used only when Send Editions Manually is selected.

- **Select how publisher decides what to publish.** As mentioned earlier, the light rectangle that appears after a publisher has been created defines the portions of the current document to be included in the edition. With this option, you decide if the edition will include only objects completely inside the box, or all elements (those partially enclosed as well as those fully enclosed).

    Select Clip if you want the edition to include all elements you select or partially select. Select Snap to include only fully enclosed elements.

Figure 7-8: Using the Snap option would exclude the whale from the edition created by the top example, and the eagle from the edition file created by the bottom example. The Clip option would include both animals in both examples.

Because the content of an edition is defined by a rectangle, you may notice some elements in the preview that were not selected when the Create Publisher command was selected. There's no way to exclude these elements, other than by altering the Select how publisher decides option.

- **Cancel Publisher.** The Cancel Publisher button removes the link between the published elements in the current application and the edition file. Canceling the publisher does not delete the edition file, so it doesn't directly affect any documents that subscribe to that edition.

You can't re-establish the link to an edition once it's been canceled (although you can use the Create Publisher command to create a new edition with the same name, saved in the same location), so the Cancel Publisher button should be used only in certain circumstances. It would be better to use the Send Editions Manually option, to temporarily prevent editions from being updated.

If you accidentally use the Cancel Publisher button, you may be able to undo it by exiting your document with the Close command, clicking the Don't Save button to avoid saving your changes, then re-opening the document with the Open command. (Of course, doing this means you lose any changes you've made.) The Revert command offered by some applications may also return your document to the state it was in before you canceled the publisher.

The Subscriber Options Command

The *Subscriber Options* command can be selected only when a subscribed edition is selected, as shown by the dark rectangle around the edition. When selected, the Subscriber Options dialog box, shown in Figure 7-9, appears.

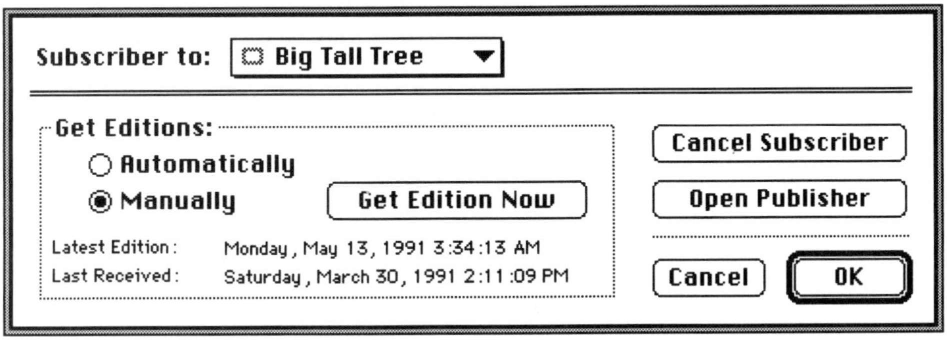

Figure 7-9: The Subscriber Options dialog box.

The Subscriber Options dialog box can also be accessed by double-clicking on the subscribed elements.

This dialog box presents five options:

- **Subscriber To.** This offers no alternatives; it simply lets you see where the edition is stored and the path to that location. To see the storage location, click on the Subscriber To pop-up menu.

- **Get Editions.** This lets you choose when the edition elements will be updated to reflect any changes made to the edition file. The Automatically option causes any changes to the edition file to be imported each time the document is opened or whenever the edition file changes; the Manually option requires the Get Edition Now button to be clicked in order for changes to the edition to be reflected in your document.

    If you choose Automatically, your document will always have the latest version of the text or graphic elements contained in the edition file. If you choose Manual, your document may not always reflect updates to the edition file, but you can choose when those updates are made.

    The date and time the current edition was last changed by the application that created it are displayed below the Get Editions option. If Manually was selected, the date and time the edition was imported into the current document are also listed. If these dates and times are not the same, the edition data contained in the current document is not up-to-date with the current edition file.

    If the dates and times are dimmed, the edition file can't be located: it's been deleted or moved to another volume. This means that the link between the current document and the edition file has been broken. More information on re-establishing this link is provided later in this chapter.

- **Get Edition Now.** Clicking this button imports the current edition file contents into your document. It's normally used only when the Manually option is selected.

- **Cancel Subscriber.** The Cancel Subscriber button removes the link between the imported elements and the edition file. The imported elements remain in the current application, but future changes to the edition will not be reflected in the current publication.

  You cannot re-establish the link to an edition once it's been canceled (although you can use the Subscribe To command to create a new link to that same edition), so using the Cancel Subscriber button should be limited to particular circumstances. A better strategy would be to use the Get Editions Manually option to temporarily prevent editions from being updated in the subscribing document.

  If you accidentally use the Cancel Subscriber button, you may be able to undo it by exiting your document with the Close command, clicking the Don't Save button to avoid saving your changes, then re-opening the document with the Open command. (Of course, following these steps means you lose any changes you've made.) The Revert command offered by some applications may also return your document to the state it was in before you canceled the subscriber.

- **Open Publisher.** The Open Publisher button performs an impressive task indeed, launching the application that created the selected edition and opening the document from which the edition was published. This allows you to edit the contents of the edition using all the tools and abilities of the application that originally created it.

  There is no difference between using the Open Publisher button to launch an application and open the document that created an edition, and performing these same tasks using the Finder. But the Open Publisher button makes the process convenient. Changes you make to the open document will be reflected in the disk file and related edition files, depending on the settings you use in the Publisher Options dialog box and whether you use the Save command.

It's possible to modify the edition file without changing the original document, using the following steps after launching the application with the Open Publisher button: 1) Set the Publisher options for the edition to Send Editions Manually; 2) Make the necessary changes to the text or graphic elements; 3) Click the Send Edition Now button in the Publisher Options dialog box; 4) Close the document or quit the application without saving your changes. The edition file will now be updated, but the original document and any other editions will remain unchanged.

The Show Borders Command

Rectangular borders distinguish elements in your document that have been published in an edition file from elements that are part of another edition file that's been subscribed to. The border around published elements is light (about a 50 percent screen); the border around subscribed elements is dark (about a 75 percent screen), as shown in Figure 7-10.

Figure 7-10: Borders surround published elements (right) and subscribed elements (left).

The Show Borders command toggles the display of these borders, allowing you to hide or display them as necessary. Regardless of the Show Borders command setting, borders always appear when a publisher or subscriber is selected. Borders never appear on printed versions of your documents—they're for on-screen use only.

Editing Subscribers

Because the contents of a subscriber are provided by an edition file, and are usually updated periodically (according to the setting in the Subscriber Options dialog box), there are limits to manipulating a subscriber within any document. In general, you can't make any changes that would be lost when a new version of the edition becomes available.

These are some of the limitations in editing subscribers:

- **Text subscribers.** With subscribers that include only text, you can't edit the text when subscribing to the edition. The only exception is that you can set the font, type size or type style of the text, as long as the change applies to the entire subscriber text. You can't make one word in the edition bold or set one sentence in a different font.

- **Graphic subscribers.** When using subscribers that include graphics, you can reposition the editions you've subscribed to, but in most cases you can't resize them. (If you *are* permitted to resize the subscriber, graphic handles appear on the corners of the subscriber border.)

- **Text in graphic subscribers.** The text in a graphic subscriber cannot be modified in any way. In the subscriber, the text is considered a part of the graphic element.

The correct way to edit a subscriber is to reopen the document that published the edition, make changes in that document, then save those changes or use the Send Edition Now button to update the edition. You can quickly access the original document for any edition by clicking the Open Publisher button in the Subscriber Options dialog box.

Edition Files at the Finder

The edition files created with the Create Publisher command look just like any other files on your disks. They use a small shaded rectangle icon like the one surrounding editions in publishing or subscribing applications; you can add comments to them using the Get Info command.

Double-clicking on an edition file in the Finder opens a window (shown in Figure 7-11) that contains the edition contents, the edition type (PICT, Text, etc.) and the Open Publisher button. The Open Publisher button launches the application that created the document the edition file was created from, and opens that document.

You work only on the document that created the edition, not on the edition file. Any changes made to the edition elements are then updated to the edition file (based on the options in the Publisher Options dialog box). This means that deleting a file that has published editions makes it impossible to ever modify or update those editions again—the data in the editions cannot be accessed from either the edition file or the subscriber document.

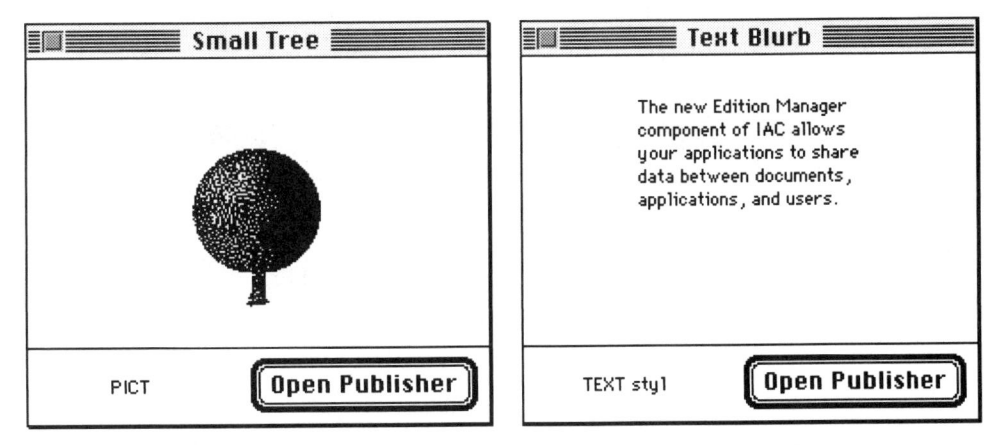

Figure 7-11: These windows are opened by clicking on edition files.

Edition File Links

The link between edition files and their publishers and subscribers is automatically maintained, even if these documents are renamed or moved to new locations on the current volume. If an edition file, publishing document or subscribing document is moved to a new volume and the copy on the original volume is deleted, the links to and from the file will be broken.

When links to or from an edition file are broken, it's impossible to automatically or manually update the edition file or the version of that edition file used in any subscribing documents. You can tell that a link is broken by the grayed-out appearance of certain type elements in the Publish To or Subscribe To dialog boxes, as shown in Figure 7-12.

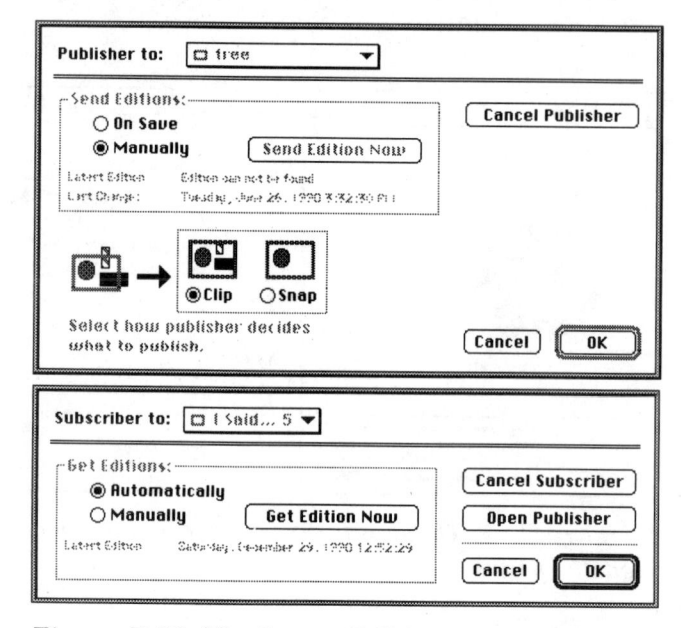

Figure 7-12: The Latest Edition and Last Change lines are dimmed when the edition has been deleted or moved to another volume.

Although there's no direct way to "reconnect" a broken Publisher or Subscriber link, you can re-create a link between an application and an edition published from it:

- Open the application and select the border surrounding the previously created edition. Even though the link has been broken, the border will still be visible.

- Select the Create Publisher command, and save the edition with the same name as the previous edition, to the same location as the previous edition, overwriting the unlinked copy that remains there.

- Any Subscribers using this edition will now update, according to their option settings, using the information in this new version of the edition.

To recreate a link between an edition and a subscribing application:

- Open the subscribing application and select the element that was imported as a subscribed edition.

- Select the Subscribe To command and locate the edition file you want to recreate a link to. Then click the Subscribe button.

- The data from the edition file as it now exists will appear in your document, replacing the older version that was selected. This edition is now linked to the edition file on disk, and will update according to the settings of the Publisher and Subscriber options.

Unavailable Edition Files

When a document containing subscribers is opened, the Macintosh attempts to locate edition files linked to each subscriber. If any of these edition files reside on unmounted floppy disks or removable volumes, you'll be prompted to insert the disks or volumes. Then the document will open normally and the links between the subscribers and their edition files will be maintained.

If you don't wish to insert the requested disks or volumes, click the Cancel button in the Please Insert the Disk... dialog box. The subscriber elements will still appear in the document, but the Subscriber Options dialog boxes will display an Edition Cannot Be Found dialog box. To establish a link to the edition, insert the correct disk, then click the Get Edition Now button.

Figure 7-13: The Edition is Missing dialog box.

Edition Files & Your Network

Edition files can be published to or subscribed from any available network or File Share volume. There's no real difference in the way they operate on network/File Share volumes, except that documents containing publishers and subscribers must access the editions over the network in order to keep all files updated properly.

To expedite sharing editions via a network, you can create aliases of editions stored on network volumes that you access frequently. You can then browse these aliases on your local hard drive (from the Subscribe To dialog box) and when the editions are used, the aliases will automatically connect to the appropriate network volumes and access the edition files.

To subscribe directly to editions on network volumes, these will also mount automatically when documents subscribing to the editions are opened.

Figure 7-14 shows one sample network: in this case, edition files could be stored on the AppleShare file server, or on either File Sharing Mac, and be used either directly or through aliases, by any network user.

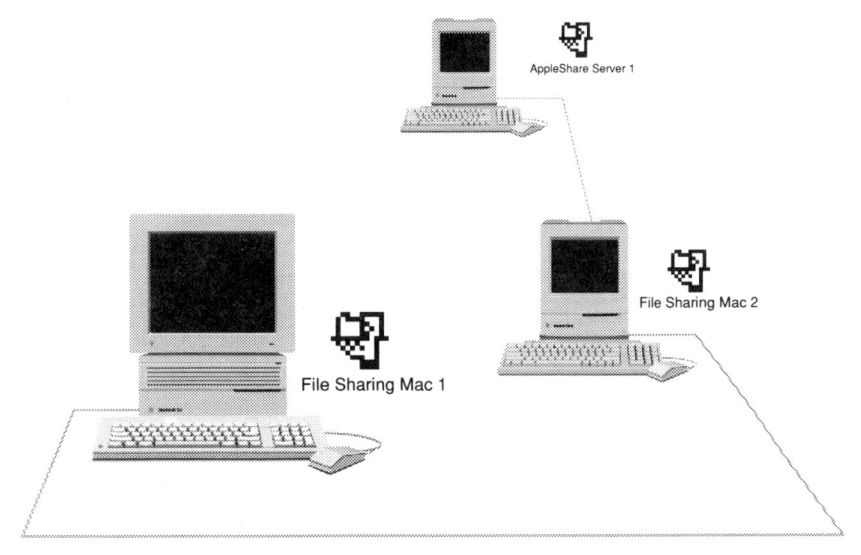

Figure 7-14: A sample network with an AppleShare server and File Sharing Macs.

Edition Manager Tips

- **Republishing an edition.** If you overwrite an edition (by creating a new edition with the same name in the same location as an existing edition), the new edition will be linked to all documents that subscribed to the old edition.

For example, if you wanted to replace an existing edition file named "Corporate Logo" with a new graphic, you could create a new edition named "Corporate Logo," using the Create Publisher command, and save it in the same volume and folder as the old "Corporate Logo" edition. (When you're asked to confirm that you want to overwrite the old file, click the Yes button.) At this point, all documents that subscribed to the old "Corporate Logo" edition file will begin using the new "Corporate Logo" edition file the next time they're updated.

- **Nested editions.** You can create editions that contain text or graphics subscribed to from other editions. After appropriate updating options are set in all associated Publish To and Subscribe To dialog boxes, changes made to elements in original documents will be correctly updated everywhere they occur.

  For example, if your page layout program subscribed to your "Corporate Logo" for the purpose of using it, along with some text and ornamental graphics, to create a corporate insignia, you could use the Create Publisher command to save an edition file named "Corporate Insignia." This edition could then be subscribed to for use on the first page of all corporate reports created in your word processing programs. If the Corporate Logo edition was updated, this update would appear in the page layout file (where the insignia was created), and extended to the Corporate Insignia edition when the page layout document was opened (assuming the Publisher options and Subscriber options are set correctly). The updated Corporate Insignia edition would then be updated in all documents it was used in (if the appropriate Subscriber option was set).

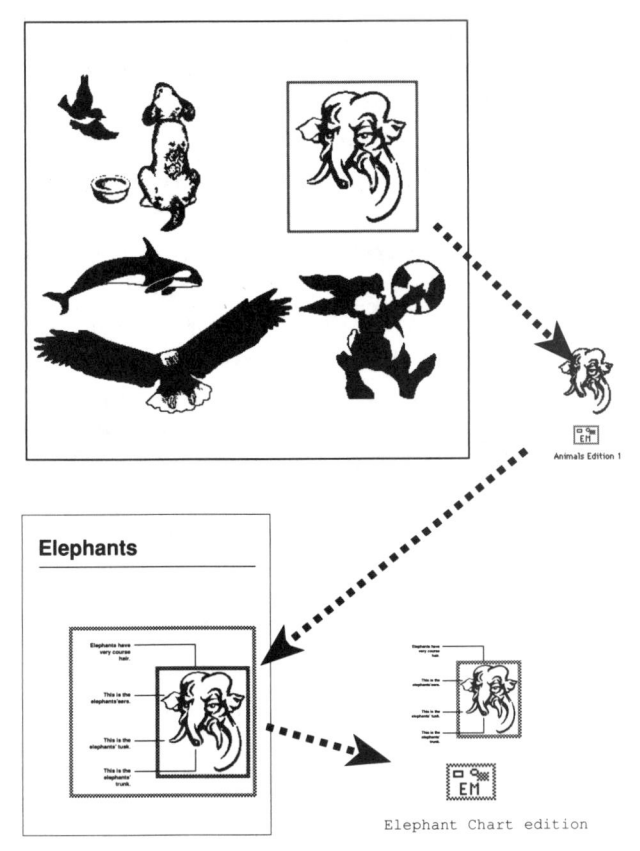

Figure 7-15: Edition files can contain other editions.

- **Double-click on edition borders to open option dialogs.** Double-clicking on a subscriber in a document will open the Subscriber To dialog box. Double-clicking on the border around any publisher will open the Publisher To dialog box.

- **Saving Publisher documents.** When an edition is created, the edition file appears on disk and can be subscribed to immediately. If the document that published the edition is closed without being saved, however, the edition file will be deleted, and all subscriber links will be broken.

An example: You open a drawing application and quickly create an illustration of a cow jumping over the moon. Using the Create Publisher command, you create an edition named "Cow Over Moon," then switch to your word processor where you subscribe to the Cow Over Moon edition and continue to work on your text document. Later, when you're ready to quit for the day, you choose the Shut Down command from the Finder's Special menu, and your drawing application asks if you want to save the Untitled file you used to create Cow Over Moon. At this point, if you don't name and save this file, the Cow Over Moon edition will be deleted from your disk. The image will remain in the word processing document that subscribed to it, but the link between the word processing document and the deleted edition file will be broken. It will be impossible to edit the graphic in the future without recreating it.

If you try to close a document with published editions without saving, the dialog box shown in Figure 7-16 will appear.

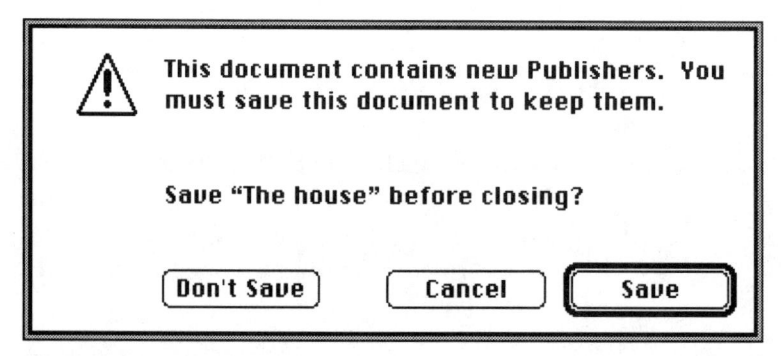

Figure 7-16: This dialog box warns you that quitting the unsaved document will result in the loss of edition files.

- **Edition aliases.** Edition file aliases can be subscribed to just like standard edition files. As always, the alias file will maintain a link to the original file, even if the alias or the original is moved or renamed. If the alias's original document is on a network server or File Sharing volume, the volume is mounted automatically.

Inter-Application Communication

Publish/Subscribe, like the Cut, Copy and Paste commands, are examples of how the Macintosh system software lets applications share data and communicate indirectly with each other. System 7 also provides even broader application-to-application communication, known as Inter-Application Communication (IAC).

IAC provides a structural framework within which software applications can send messages and data to other software applications. These capabilities make the Macintosh more powerful in many ways. They reduce the pressure on any one application to "do it all," allowing each application to specialize in what it does best.

Spell-checking is a good example. Almost every Macintosh application allows text to be created, and over the last few years many have added built-in spelling checkers, each with its own version and its own dictionary files. You have to learn and remember how each one works and make room for each data file on your hard drive. And the developers of each program have to spend time and money developing and testing utilities.

Suppose, instead, that one independent spelling checker was the best of them all, offering the biggest dictionaries, the most features and the best user interface. Using IAC, all your software applications could access this one spelling checker, saving you the hassle of learning multiple commands, customizing multiple dictionaries and wasting hard-drive space on duplicate files. And your software developers could spend their time and money on other things, such as improving their applications features.

Understanding Apple Events

The mechanics of IAC are quite technical, but fortunately you don't need to know anything about them unless you intend to write your own Macintosh programs. You'll be aware of IAC in the future when your updated software versions take advantage of its features; but even then, the entire IAC operation will be translated into friendly Macintosh commands and dialog boxes you're already familiar with. (So you can skip the rest of this section, if you'd like.)

Just in case you're interested, however, let's take a brief look at the way System 7 provides IAC capabilities to software applications.

IAC is a protocol that defines a new type of communication between applications, and provides a mechanism for the delivery and implementation of that communication. You can think of IAC as a set of grammatical rules that comprise an acceptable format for messages sent between applications. A message in this format is an Apple Event.

In addition to the Apple Events format, IAC provides a messenger service, to transmit the properly formatted message from one application to another.

While IAC defines the communication format, it doesn't specify the message content. The "language" of Apple Events is being defined by Apple and by the Macintosh software developer community, in cooperation with Apple. This is very important; a computer language designed to communicate between a variety of software applications developed by different companies must be carefully constructed in order to accomplish its goal of facilitating precise communication.

In order for an application to send an Apple Event, or to understand an Apple Event it receives, the program must be specifically programmed to handle that Apple Event properly. This is why it's impossible for non-System 7-Savvy applications to use IAC, and why even System 7-Savvy programs will provide only limited IAC support for some time to come. Only when the Apple Events language is clearly defined can software developers update their programs to properly engage in an Apple Events dialog.

To help software developers implement program support, Apple has classified Apple Events into four categories:

- **Required Apple Events.** Open Application, Open Document, Print Document and Quit Application are the four basic Apple Events and the only ones required for System 7-Savvy applications. (Think of them as the *Hello*, *Please*, *Thank You* and *Goodbye* of Apple Events.)

- **Core Apple Events.** These are not as universal or fundamental as the Required Apple Events, but they're general enough that almost every Macintosh application should support them. The list of Core Apple Events, quite large already, is growing as Apple and its software developers work to make sure every type of communication that may be needed is provided for.

- **Functional-area Apple Events.** Specifically addressed to a class of similar applications (like word processors or graphics programs), this type of Apple Event supports functions that are common within that class but not universal. Apple Events for word processing might include pagination, footnotes and hyphenation, for example, while Apple Events for graphics programs could support lines and curves, masking and custom fill patterns.

- **Custom Apple Events.** A Macintosh software developer might have a need for Apple Events designed for proprietary or cooperative use by their own applications. If a developer's word processor included a unique feature not controllable with any existing Core or Functional-area Apple Events, the company could define its own Custom Apple Event. This Apple Event could be kept secret and used only by the software developer's applications, or it could be shared with other software developers.

The entire current list of Apple Events, along with detailed descriptions of each, is regularly sent to all Macintosh software developers so they can incorporate these events into their software updates. Only time will tell whether defined Apple Events gain universal support.

Apple Events & Program Linking

When an application sends an Apple Event to another program, the receiving program is usually launched, then asked to perform a task. Of course, this assumes that the receiving program is available. In addition to programs that exist on the same hard drive, Apple Share events, through IAC, can communicate with programs that reside on other parts of the network as well.

Chapter 9, "Introduction to File Sharing," introduces the System 7 capability that lets any user on the network share data with any other user on the network.

In Chapter 10, "Working on a Network," you'll learn about the Program Linking option, which allows you to access software from other Macintoshes on the network via IAC commands.

Using this option, applications on one Macintosh can use Apple Events to communicate with applications on other Macs across the network. As with other aspects of IAC, it remains to be seen how this capability will be translated into new Macintosh software features.

Moving On

Some people are predicting that over time, the lines between individual applications will blur as the powers of the Edition Manager and IAC are fully utilized. As we've seen, the Edition Manager allows you to transfer text and graphics between applications, while maintaining a "live link" to the original data, using just a few simple commands:

- **Create Publisher.** This command saves the selected data to a new edition file on disk.

- **Subscribe to.** This command imports an edition file from disk into the current document.

- **Publisher/Subscriber options.** These commands control the way changes to original documents are updated to the edition file and documents subscribing to the edition file.

From the sophistication of Publish/Subscribe and IAC, we now return to an old familiar Macintosh topic—fonts. Chapter 8 looks at using fonts in System 7, including existing bit-mapped and PostScript fonts, and the relatively new font technology, TrueType.

Chapter 8: Fonts in System 7

Fonts are the blessing and curse of the Macintosh. No other computer offers such a variety of fonts or typographic capabilities; but because of technical problems and corporate politics, no other aspect of the Mac has caused so many headaches for so many people.

The release of System 7 has extended Macintosh font technology, simplifying font installation, improving the appearance of fonts on-screen, and introducing a new font format called TrueType. Unfortunately, many legitimate font issues remain unresolved. In this chapter, we'll look at each of the Macintosh font formats supported by System 7, font installation and management, and finally, the practical implications of font life in System 7.

Fonts on the Macintosh

The introduction of the Macintosh in 1984 brought with it many innovations, but one of the most important was the way Macintosh enhanced the appearance of text. While earlier personal computers reduced all communication to the drab, mechanical and impersonal look of pica-12 (the original dot-matrix font), the Macintosh produced text in a wide range of typefaces, both on-screen and on the printed page. Typography—long an important part of printed communication—became a part of personal computing.

The original Macintosh fonts (New York, Monaco, Geneva and Chicago) were bitmapped fonts, which means that each character in each font was predefined by the series of dots necessary to create that character at a specific point size. Most bitmapped fonts were produced at sizes of 9-, 10-, 12- and 14-point.

These original bitmapped fonts, and the many bitmapped fonts that soon joined them, were optimized for display on the Macintosh screen and for printing on the Apple ImageWriter (which was the only printer available at the time.) There were, however, limitations to working with these bitmapped fonts:

- **Dot-matrix bitmapped quality was unacceptable for most business uses.** While typeface variety was certainly a welcome improvement, most people still considered ImageWriter output quality unacceptable for business use regardless of the fonts.

- **Font variety was limited.** Although bitmapped fonts proliferated, almost all were "novelty" faces with little value beyond advertisements, invitations and entertainment.

- **400k system disks could hold only a limited selection of fonts.** Since hard drives were not generally available at that time, it was necessary to boot the Macintosh from a 400k floppy disk. After squeezing the System Folder plus an application or two onto a floppy, only a small amount of room was left for font styles and sizes.

- **Macintosh applications could support only a limited number of fonts at one time.** When too many fonts were installed in the System file, applications acted strangely, often providing only a random subset of the installed fonts.

These problems were solved, after some time, with new releases of system software, application software and third-party utility programs. The next big change in the Macintosh font world was not based on software, but on the introduction of the Apple LaserWriter printer with its built-in support for the PostScript page-description language.

PostScript Fonts

The introduction of the Apple LaserWriter printer brought a new type of font to the Macintosh; the PostScript font. These fonts were required in documents created for output to the LaserWriter (and all later PostScript printers) in order for type to be printed at high resolution. Bitmapped fonts were inadequate for these new printers. Eventually, PostScript fonts came to be known by a variety of names, including laser fonts, outline fonts and Type 1 fonts.

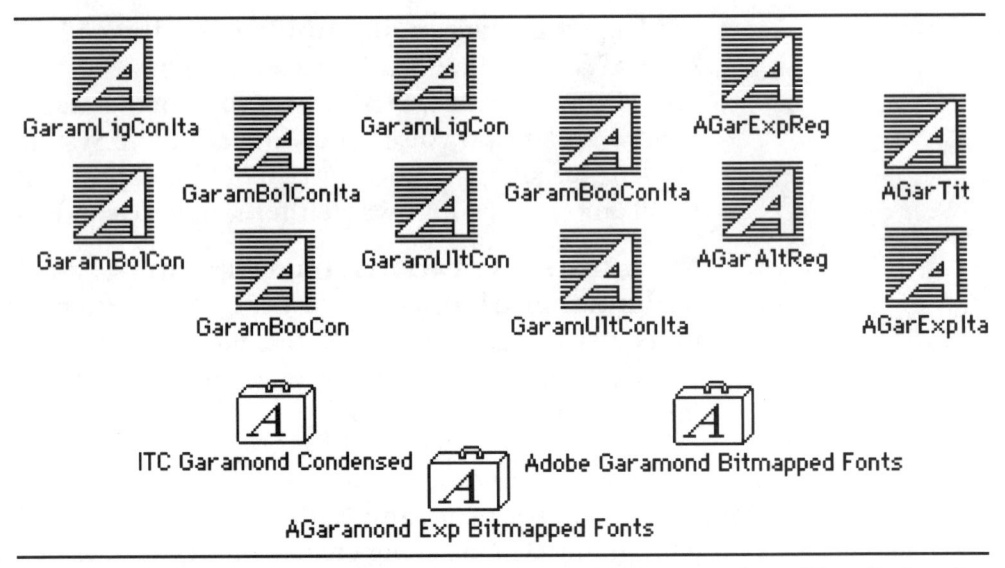

Figure 8-1: Icons for some popular screen font files (below) and printer font files (above).

Each PostScript font consists of two files: a screen font file and a printer font file. The screen font file for a PostScript font is nearly identical to the font file of bitmapped fonts, providing bitmapped versions of the font at specific sizes optimized for on-screen use. There are other similarities too:

- Both appear with a suitcase icon.
- Both are provided in different styles and sizes.
- Both were installed with the Font/DA Mover until the release of System 7.
- Both appear in the Font menu or dialog box in all applications.

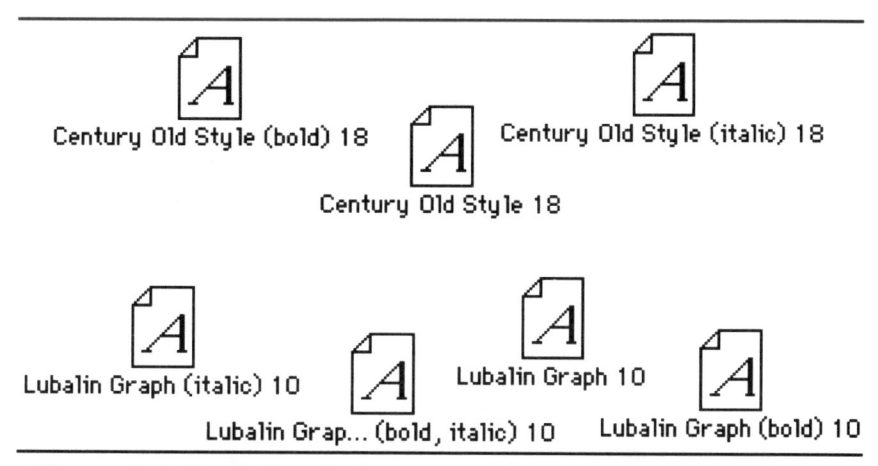

Figure 8-2: Each PostScript screen font represents a single font, size and style.

The difference between PostScript screen fonts and bitmapped screen fonts is that each PostScript screen font has a corresponding PostScript printer font. This printer font provides the PostScript printer with a mathematical description of each character in the font, as well as other information it needs to create and produce high-resolution output. When printing PostScript fonts, the screen font is used only as a pointer to the printer fonts.

Printer font files often display an icon that looks like the LaserWriter, but depending on the way the printer font was created, another icon may appear. Each printer font is usually around 50k in size, but can range from a minimum of 10k to a maximum of 75k. In most cases, there is a one-to-one correspondence between screen fonts and printer fonts (there's a unique printer font file for each unique screen font name). In some cases, however, printer fonts outnumber screen fonts, and vice versa.

Regardless of whether all screen fonts and printer fonts are matched, you don't always have to use all of the available screen fonts, but you must always use all printer fonts. In other words, you can create Helvetica Bold without installing the Helvetica Bold screen font (by using the Helvetica font and the Bold type style) but you cannot print Helvetica Bold without the Helvetica Bold printer font.

For a PostScript font to be printed correctly, the printer font file must be "available" to the PostScript printer when it appears in a file being printed. A font is available when it is built into the printer's ROM chips, stored on a printer's hard disk, or kept on the Macintosh hard disk and manually or automatically downloaded to the printer.

PostScript Font Challenges

For a variety of reasons, using PostScript fonts in the real-world Macintosh environment has never been easy. The main problem is that the software and hardware environment in which PostScript fonts are used and the PostScript fonts themselves have been in a constant state of evolution. Most of these problems have been overcome through system software upgrades, new font-management utilities or "work-around" methods that have become well known and commonly accepted as necessary for font survival.

The list below describes many of the challenges PostScript font users have faced, along with the corresponding solutions, resolutions or workarounds:

- **PostScript fonts vs. non-PostScript fonts.** Since PostScript screen fonts are not noticeably different from non-PostScript screen fonts, it is difficult for inexperienced users to distinguish between them when creating documents that will be output on high-resolution PostScript printers.

    This problem has been solved, at least partially, by PostScript's dominance in the Macintosh world; most Macintosh users now have access to PostScript printers. And

PostScript fonts are now the rule rather than the exception. Apple and Adobe should have provided a better solution, forcing PostScript screen fonts to indicate their PostScript status—perhaps a symbol character displayed before or after their font names. This would simplify determining which fonts can be used to prepare documents to be output on PostScript printers.

- **Screen font availability.** Once a document is created there's generally no easy way to determine which fonts it contains, in order to be sure all necessary screen and printer fonts are available at print time—especially if the person printing the file is not the one who created it.

    Over time, individual software vendors have developed schemes to help identify screen fonts used in a document. PageMaker displays the dimmed names of used but not-currently-available fonts in its font menu, and both PageMaker and QuarkXPress produce a list of fonts used, for example. Only Adobe has addressed the problem of screen font availability, allowing Illustrator to correctly print files even if the screen fonts used to create the file aren't available at the time the file is printed. Unfortunately this solution hasn't caught on with other vendors. (It's possible that Adobe's proprietary font knowledge allows them this advantage.)

- **Printer font availability.** The most fundamental requirement of PostScript fonts is that for each screen font used in a document, a corresponding printer font must be available at print time. This requirement has caused tremendous difficulty for Mac users, because there's no automated way to track the screen font/printer font correspondence.

    The advent of large font-storage printer hard drives, the Suitcase II and MasterJuggler font management utilities, the ability to download screen fonts and the NFNT font resource have made the "Font Not Found: Substituting

Courier" messages less common. But unfortunately, the only real solution to this problem lies with users and service bureau operators.

- **Too many font names in the font menus.** For non-PostScript screen fonts, a single font is provided in several different sizes, but bold and italic versions must be created using the Style command. PostScript fonts, on the other hand, provide a separate screen font for each size and style. This means that font menus are very long. For example, Helvetica includes four entries (B Helvetica Bold, I Helvetica Italic, Helvetica and BI Helvetica Bold Italic). Times has four as well, and so on.

Utilities like Suitcase's Font Harmony and Adobe's Type Reunion combine these font styles into a single font menu entry, reducing the four different Helvetica entries to one, and reinstating the Style command for additional font styles. But sometimes, during the process, the ID numbers that the System file uses to internally keep track of fonts are altered, resulting in fonts being "lost" when you move documents from one Mac to another.

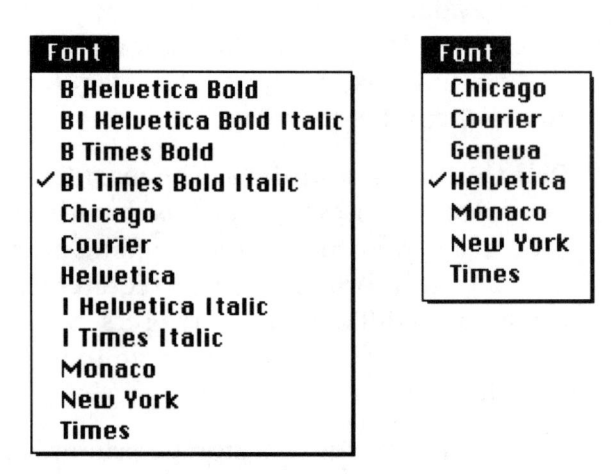

```
Font
  B Helvetica Bold
  BI Helvetica Bold Italic
  B Times Bold
✓ BI Times Bold Italic
  Chicago
  Courier
  Helvetica
  I Helvetica Italic
  I Times Italic
  Monaco
  New York
  Times
```

```
Font
  Chicago
  Courier
  Geneva
✓ Helvetica
  Monaco
  New York
  Times
```

Figure 8-3: Each style of a font is listed separately (left) when fonts are not harmonized, but not when they are harmonized (right).

- **Font ID Conflicts.** The original Macintosh system was designed to handle only a small number of fonts. With the font explosion that followed PostScript's introduction, there were soon more fonts than available Font ID numbers. The Apple Font/DA Mover resolved Font ID conflicts as new fonts were added to the System File, but unfortunately, the Font/DA Mover did this by randomly renumbering the fonts. This caused problems because some applications tracked fonts by Font ID number, and as a result, the same font would have different ID numbers on different Macintoshes.

  Because many applications used the Font-ID numbers to keep track of font assignments within documents, Font-ID instability caused documents to "forget" which fonts were used to create them when they were transferred from one Macintosh to another. Working with a wide range of fonts on the Macintosh bore a striking resemblance to a low-stakes game of Russian roulette.

  This problem was partially solved with the release of system software 6.0, which added more complete support for a Macintosh resource called NFNT (pronounced N-Font). NFNT offered a font-numbering scheme capable of handling over 32,000 different fonts. Of course, implementing the new system meant that millions of non-NFNT fonts already in use had to be replaced with new NFNT versions, and that a master set of new NFNT fonts had to be distributed for use in this replacement.

  To make matters worse, Apple and Adobe used the same uneven, unplanned and unprofessional distribution methods for the new font ID system that they used for Apple system software and shareware updates—user groups, bulletin boards and friendly file-sharing. Therefore, the problem was only partially solved.

  To further complicate the introduction of NFNT fonts, Apple and Adobe chose not to "harmonize" the NFNT fonts by allowing only a single Font Menu entry to appear for each font (as discussed previously). So it was left to users to perform this harmonization with their own utilities, which as mentioned above results in a non-universal set of fonts.

- **Different fonts with the same names.** As more vendors produced more PostScript fonts, another problem appeared: different versions of the same fonts released by different vendors.

  This not only caused Macintoshes to become "confused" about which screen fonts and printer fonts were used in documents; it also made it hard for service bureaus to know if the Garamond specified in a document was the Adobe, Bitstream or other font vendor version of the typeface. This point was crucial because font substitutions wouldn't work. And, even if they did, character width differences would play havoc with the output.

- **The Type 1 font secret.** Since Adobe Systems had developed PostScript, they kept the specifics of the optimized format known as "Type 1" for themselves. The Type 1 font format provided fonts with "hints" embedded in the font outline that made them look better when output in small type sizes on 300 dpi laser printers.

  The Type 1 format was also the only format compatible with Adobe's TypeAlign and Adobe Type Manager (ATM) utilities. This excluded all other vendors' PostScript fonts from using these utilities, since all non-Adobe PostScript fonts were in the "Type 3" format.

  After the political turmoil surrounding the announcement of TrueType, Adobe released the specification for the Type 1 font format, and most other font vendors have upgraded their fonts to the Type 1 format.

Printing PostScript Fonts

When a document containing PostScript fonts is printed to a PostScript printer, the LaserWriter printer driver queries the PostScript printer to determine if the printer fonts that the document requires are resident in the printer. These fonts may be built into a printer's ROM chips, or they may have been previously downloaded into the printer's RAM or onto the printer's hard disk. If the fonts are resident, the document is sent to the printer for output. If the fonts are not resident, the print driver checks to see if the printer font files are available on the Macintosh hard disk. If they are, they're downloaded into the printer's RAM temporarily. If they aren't, an error message in the Print Status dialog box alerts you that specific fonts are unavailable.

When the document is printed, the PostScript printer uses the printer font information to create each character. The information from the PostScript screen font is translated into new printer-font characters. Screen fonts are only placeholders on-screen. The process of creating the printed characters is called *rasterization*—the most complex part of the PostScript printing process. During rasterization, PostScript uses the PostScript printer font file's mathematical character descriptions to select the output device pixels necessary to produce the requested character at the highest possible resolution.

When a document containing PostScript fonts is printed to a non-PostScript printer, such as a QuickDraw or dot-matrix printer, screen font information is transferred directly to the printer and is the only source used to produce the printed characters. None of the advantages of PostScript are used. On a QuickDraw or dot-matrix printer, there is no difference between the use of a PostScript font and a non-PostScript font (except when ATM is being used, in which case PostScript fonts are superior).

Installing Fonts

Before the release of System 7, screen fonts were installed using a utility called the Font/DA Mover, which transferred them between their font suitcases and the System file. Over the years, however, the Font/DA Mover became a scapegoat for many of the larger problems of how the Mac managed fonts. Because of this, and due to the fact that the Font/DA Mover's interface was seen as inconsistent with the drag-and-drop method by which other files were moved from one location to another, a new method of installing screen fonts was introduced in System 7 version 7.0.

This new method requires no utility program—fonts are simply dragged onto the System Folder icon, or the icon of the System file. They are then placed into the System file automatically. This method works with all kinds of fonts (TrueType fonts, bitmapped fonts and PostScript screen fonts), and the only limitation is that fonts cannot be installed while any application other than the Finder is open. If you try to drag fonts into the System file or the System Folder while applications are open, the dialog box shown in Figure 8-4 appears.

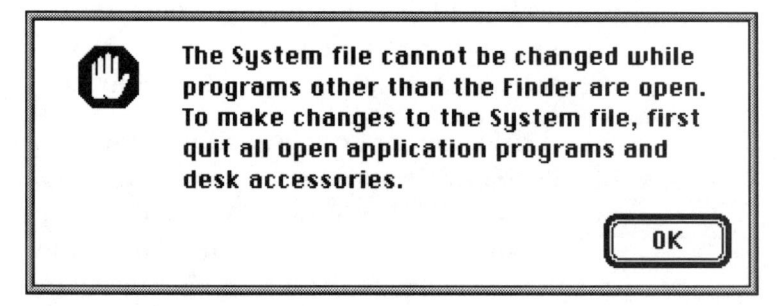

Figure 8-4: The System file Cannot Be Changed dialog box.

Another change in System 7 is that screen font suitcases can be opened directly from the Finder, by double-clicking on them as if they were folders. This opens a suitcase window, displaying individual icons for each screen font in the folder. You can distinguish PostScript screen fonts or bitmapped fonts from ones in the new TrueType format by the icon they display. TrueType fonts use an icon with three A's, and PostScript screen fonts or bitmapped fonts use an icon with a single A, as shown in Figure 8-5.

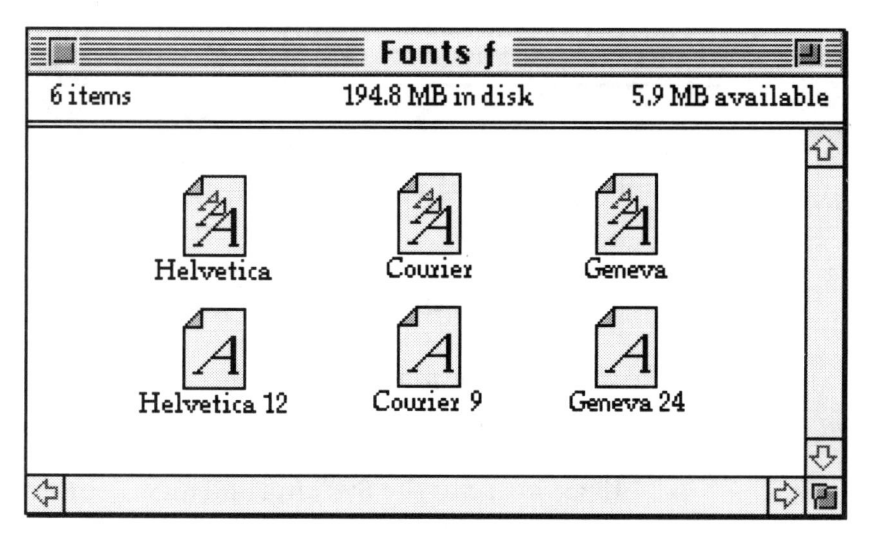

Figure 8-5: Font icons for TrueType and PostScript.

Double-clicking on an individual screen font icon opens a window showing a brief sample of the font. For TrueType fonts, this sample shows the font at 9-, 12- and 18-point sizes. Non-TrueType fonts display only a single sample.

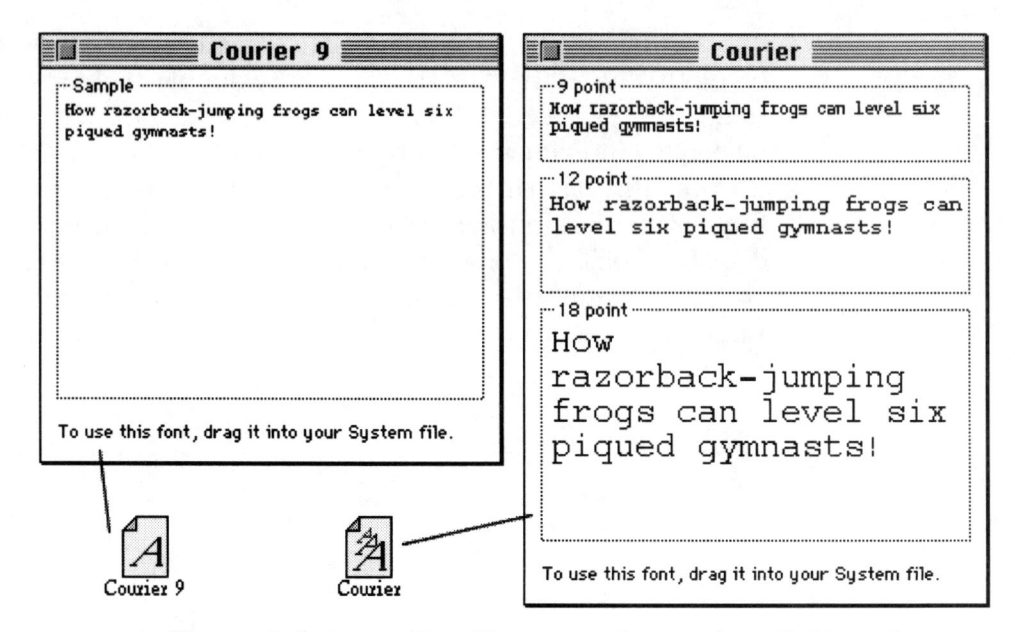

Figure 8-6: A non-TrueType sample window (left) and TrueType sample window (right).

When screen fonts are installed into the System file in System 7 version 7.0, the suitcase is discarded and only the individual font file icons are added. If you install fonts by dragging the suitcase to the System Folder icon or onto the System file, the suitcase itself will be discarded automatically. You can also drag individual font icons from an open suitcase window to the System Folder icon, the System file icon, to an open System file window, or to another suitcase icon or open suitcase window.

Individual font icons must always be stored in a font suitcase or in the System file; they cannot be stored as files in any other folder. System 7 provides no easy way to create new empty font suitcases, so if you need a new suitcase to store fonts in, you'll have to duplicate an existing suitcase file and then discard the fonts contained in that duplicate. You can then copy any fonts you want into that suitcase, and rename it as necessary. There are also shareware and commercial font-management utilities that can create empty suitcases.

Font Changes in System 7.1

Although System 7 version 7.0 eliminated the Font/DA Mover, it did little to correct the more fundamental problems of Macintosh font management. One of these fundamental problems was that installing fonts into the System file—when done by the system software or by some utility—resulted in large System files which tended to cause crashes. Sometimes, these crashes were so severe they required a complete system software reinstallation.

The release of System 7 version 7.1 corrected this problem by adding a "Fonts" subfolder to the System Folder; all screen fonts and printer fonts now reside in this folder—they are no longer stored in the System file. Up to 128 screen font files or font suitcases (each containing any number of fonts) stored in the Fonts folder will be loaded at startup and become available in the Font menu or dialog box of your applications.

Font suitcases or individual font files can be added to the Fonts folder by dragging them there just as with any other folder, or fonts may be dragged onto the System Folder icon and they will be placed into the Fonts folder automatically. If you open the Fonts folder window, you can merge the fonts from one font suitcase with another by dragging one suitcase onto another.

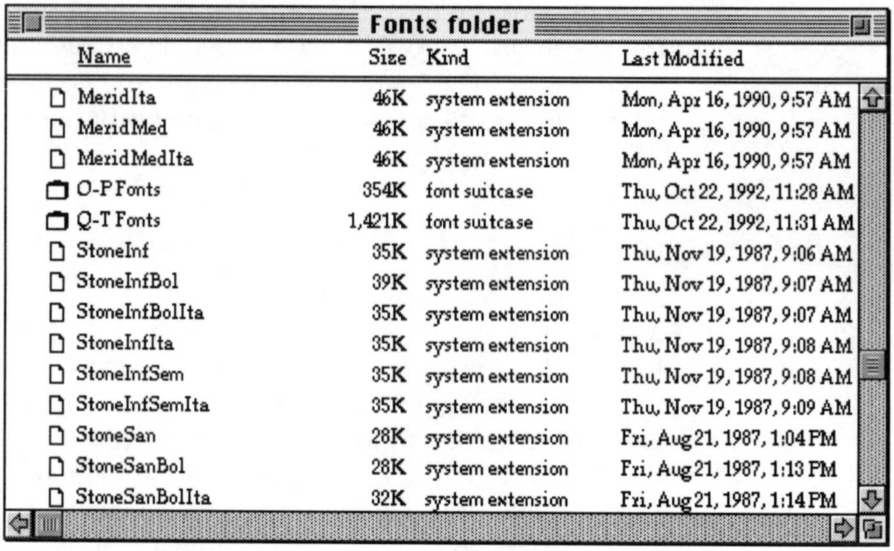

Name	Size	Kind	Last Modified
MeridIta	46K	system extension	Mon, Apr 16, 1990, 9:57 AM
MeridMed	46K	system extension	Mon, Apr 16, 1990, 9:57 AM
MeridMedIta	46K	system extension	Mon, Apr 16, 1990, 9:57 AM
O-P Fonts	354K	font suitcase	Thu, Oct 22, 1992, 11:28 AM
Q-T Fonts	1,421K	font suitcase	Thu, Oct 22, 1992, 11:31 AM
StoneInf	35K	system extension	Thu, Nov 19, 1987, 9:06 AM
StoneInfBol	39K	system extension	Thu, Nov 19, 1987, 9:07 AM
StoneInfBolIta	35K	system extension	Thu, Nov 19, 1987, 9:07 AM
StoneInfIta	35K	system extension	Thu, Nov 19, 1987, 9:08 AM
StoneInfSem	35K	system extension	Thu, Nov 19, 1987, 9:08 AM
StoneInfSemIta	35K	system extension	Thu, Nov 19, 1987, 9:09 AM
StoneSan	28K	system extension	Fri, Aug 21, 1987, 1:04 PM
StoneSanBol	28K	system extension	Fri, Aug 21, 1987, 1:13 PM
StoneSanBolIta	32K	system extension	Fri, Aug 21, 1987, 1:14 PM

Figure 8-7: An open fonts window viewed by name.

When fonts are added to the Fonts folder, they do not become available to any applications that are already open until you quit and relaunch those programs. Fonts or suitcases with the same name as existing fonts or suitcases cannot be added to the Fonts folder; you must first move the previously installed font to another folder or into the Trash.

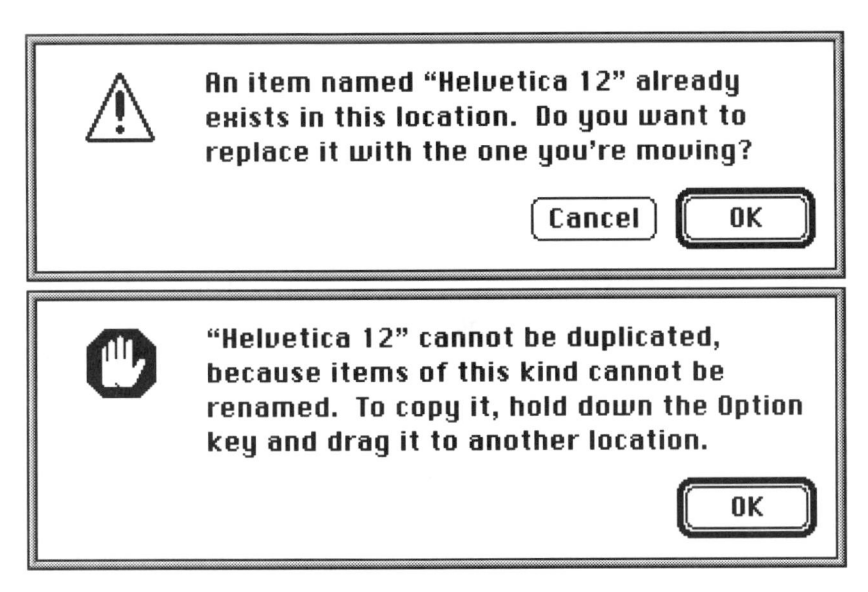

> ⚠ An item named "Helvetica 12" already exists in this location. Do you want to replace it with the one you're moving?
>
> [Cancel] [OK]

> ✋ "Helvetica 12" cannot be duplicated, because items of this kind cannot be renamed. To copy it, hold down the Option key and drag it to another location.
>
> [OK]

Figure 8-8: You'll see one of these error messages if you try to duplicate a font or replace it with a font of the same name.

Printer Fonts in System 7.0

Printer font files must be easily located by the system when they are needed for automatic downloading during a print job. In System 7 version 7.0, they must reside in the Extensions folder, or be loose in the System Folder itself. Under version 7.1, they must reside on the main level of the Fonts folder, or in the Extensions folder, or be loose in the System Folder itself.

Printer fonts dragged onto the System Folder icon in version 7.0 are placed into the Extensions folder, while in version 7.1, they are moved into the Fonts folder.

When using ATM versions prior to 2.0.3, printer fonts must reside in the System Folder itself, as ATM cannot locate them if they are installed in the Extensions folder or the Fonts folder. For maximum compatibility, ATM version 3.0 or later should be used with any version of System 7.

Removing Fonts

Fonts in System 7 version 7.0 and 7.1 are removed by a drag-and-drop method. In version 7.0, double-click on the System file to open a System file window and then drag the icons of any fonts you want to remove to another location or into the Trash. In version 7.1, simply open the Fonts folder and drag the icons of any fonts you want to remove to another location or into the Trash. In neither case can you remove fonts while applications other than the Finder are open.

TrueType

In addition to supporting the same bitmapped and PostScript fonts that Macintosh users have worked with for years, System 7 also introduces a new font format. TrueType fonts were designed to appear at high-resolution on the Macintosh screen at any point size, and to print at high-resolution on virtually any output device.

TrueType is a fundamental shift from bitmapped fonts and PostScript fonts. Each TrueType font exists as a single file which does the work of both the screen font and the printer font. And when used along with System 7, TrueType fonts appear on-screen without "jaggies" at any point size without the use of any extensions such as ATM. TrueType fonts can be printed at full resolution on any dot-matrix, QuickDraw, TrueType or PostScript printer.

TrueType is an open type format whose font specifications have been published for use by a wide variety of type vendors. It is supported by AGFA Compugraphic, Bitstream, International Typeface Corporation, Monotype and others. Future versions of Windows and OS/2 will continue to support the TrueType standard, providing for strong cross-platform compatibility.

TrueType & PostScript

TrueType is an alternative to PostScript, not a replacement for it; PostScript is fully supported in System 7, as described above. Neither is necessarily better than the other; let's just say they're different. Later in this chapter we'll examine the realities of working in a world of mixed PostScript and TrueType fonts, and offer some suggestions on the best ways to organize and utilize these font technologies on your system.

Although TrueType is in many ways a competitor for PostScript fonts, it's not a competitor for the complete PostScript language. TrueType printers use TrueType for fonts but QuickDraw descriptions for all other page elements. QuickDraw has proven itself on the Macintosh screen, but its use as a high-resolution printing model is new. It's unlikely that the PostScript standard will be replaced in the near future; it has firm support from developers of high-end software, hardware developers, service bureaus and end users. The PostScript language will likely continue to dominate personal computer printing.

LITHOS · 1234567890
ABCDEFGHIJKLMNOPQRSTUVWXYZ

FUTURA LIGHT · 1234567890
Aa Bb Cc Dd Ee Ff Gg Hh Ii Jj Kk Ll Mm Nn
Oo Pp Qq Rr Ss Tt Uu Vv Ww Xx Yy Zz

MISTRAL · 1234567890
Aa Bb Cc Dd Ee Ff Gg Hh Ii Jj Kk Ll Mm Nn Oo Pp Qq Rr
Ss Tt Uu Vv Ww Xx Yy Zz

WINDSOR · 1234567890
Aa Bb Cc Dd Ee Ff Gg Hh Ii Jj Kk Ll Mm
Nn Oo Pp Qq Rr Ss Tt Uu Vv Ww Xx Yy Zz

Geneva · New York · **Chicago** · Monaco

Figure 8-9: It's difficult to see a difference in output quality between PostScript and TrueType fonts, as shown by the assortment of Adobe Systems and Digital Typeface Corporation PostScript fonts (above and right), and Apple's TrueType versions of the standard Mac fonts (directly above).

BEESKNEES · 1234567890
ABCDEFGHIJKLMNOPQRSTUVWXYZ

FENICE · 1234567890
Aa Bb Cc Dd Ee Ff Gg Hh Ii Jj Kk Ll Mm Nn Oo
Pp Qq Rr Ss Tt Uu Vv Ww Xx Yy Zz

SALTO · 1234567890
Aa Bb Cc Dd Ee Ff Gg Hh Ii Jj Kk Ll Mm
Nn Oo Pp Qq Rr Ss Tt Uu Vv Ww Xx Yy Zz

BERNHARD FASHION · 1234567890
Aa Bb Cc Dd Ee Ff Gg Hh Ii Jj Kk Ll Mm Nn Oo Pp Qq
Rr Ss Tt Uu Vv Ww Xx Yy Zz

CLASSICAL SANS · 1234567890
Aa Bb Cc Dd Ee Ff Gg Hh Ii Jj Kk Ll Mm Nn Oo
Pp Qq Rr Ss Tt Uu Vv Ww Xx Yy Zz

TrueType Technology

TrueType fonts, like PostScript printer fonts, are outline fonts, which means that each character is described mathematically, as opposed to the bit-by-bit description used by existing screen fonts. TrueType mathematical descriptions are based on quadratic bézier curve equations rather than PostScript's standard bézier curve equations. The difference between these equations is in the number of points used to determine the position of the lines and curves that make up each character. Apple claims TrueType's method creates better-looking characters at a wider range of output and display resolutions.

Because TrueType uses mathematical descriptions for on-screen and printer font versions, a single file can serve both the display and any output devices. As mentioned above, PostScript requires two files, a screen font file and a printer font file, in order to print or display at full resolution. Although it is true that it's easier to manage one font file than two, Adobe claims that putting its screen fonts and printer fonts in separate files is an asset, since either can be updated or enhanced independently at any time without affecting existing documents or printer configurations.

When a document containing TrueType fonts is printed, the sequence of events depends on the type of printer used:

- **Dot-matrix printers.** When a document containing TrueType fonts is printed to a dot-matrix printer, the characters are reproduced in their natural contours, just as they appear on the screen. The output images are the results of the on-screen rasterization process, not the TrueType outlines. Therefore, dot-matrix output can only provide a more exact representation of the Mac's on-screen display.

- **QuickDraw printers.** When a document containing TrueType fonts is printed to a QuickDraw printer such as the LaserWriter II SC, the same process as described above for dot-matrix printers occurs—information from the on-screen rasterization process is sent to the printer.

- **68000-based PostScript printers with 2 Mb of RAM.** When a document containing TrueType fonts is sent to a PostScript printer or output device using a Motorola 68000 CPU and at least 2 Mb of RAM (such as the LaserWriter IINT, and most of today's imagesetters), the print driver queries the device to see if the TrueType font scaler is available. The TrueType font scaler may be built into the printer's ROM or it may have been previously downloaded onto the printer's hard disk or into printer RAM (using the LaserWriter Font Utility). If the TrueType font scaler is not available, it is automatically downloaded into the printer's RAM, where it will reside until the printer is reset. This font scaler will consume approximately 80k of printer memory.

  With the font scaler in place, the page is sent normally. Mathematical descriptions of any included TrueType fonts are sent to the printer and processed by the TrueType font scaler. The page is then output at full resolution, using any TrueType fonts rasterized by the font scaler software.

- **68000-based PostScript printers with less than 2 Mb of RAM, or RISC-based Adobe PostScript printers.** When a document containing TrueType fonts is printed to a PostScript printer or output device using a Motorola 68000 CPU and less than 2 Mb of RAM (such as the LaserWriter Plus), or to a RISC-based Adobe PostScript printer, TrueType fonts are encoded into PostScript Type 1 font format and sent to the printer where they're processed just like all other PostScript fonts. The encoded Type 1 fonts do not contain PostScript "hints."

- **Printers with built-in TrueType scaling.** When a document containing TrueType fonts is sent to a printer with a built-in TrueType font scaler, such as the LaserMaster 400XL, or MicroTek TrueLaser, the TrueType outline information is sent directly to the printer where the font is rasterized and imaged.

A Mixed World

In a laboratory environment, where some Macintoshes used only PostScript fonts and some used only TrueType fonts, where all documents using PostScript fonts were created only on the PostScript machines and those using TrueType fonts were created only on the TrueType machines, the daily use of these systems from a font-technology perspective would be very straightforward.

Unfortunately, none of us live or work in such a laboratory. Most Macintosh computers are more likely to be configured with PostScript fonts, TrueType fonts and non-PostScript non-TrueType bitmapped fonts. And most people will have some documents created with only PostScript fonts, some with only bitmapped fonts, some with only TrueType fonts and many documents with mixes of TrueType, PostScript and bitmapped fonts. So how is all of this going to work in the real world?

It depends—on the way you install fonts in your System file, the printer(s) you use and how software developers implement fonts in their updated System 7-compatible applications.

Picking Your Font Standard

When you install System 7, the Installer adds both the PostScript and TrueType versions of many default fonts, including

Helvetica, Times and Geneva. Over time, you will add additional fonts to your system, some PostScript, some TrueType, and sometimes you will add both PostScript and TrueType versions of the same fonts.

Once you've installed these fonts, their names will appear in the Font Menus or dialog boxes of all applications, but you will have no easy way to distinguish the TrueType fonts from the PostScript fonts, or those for which both versions have been installed: you cannot tell which formats are installed by looking at a name in a Font Menu. (Again, it's a shame Apple didn't make these distinctions visible.)

As you use fonts in your documents, when you choose a font that is installed in both PostScript and TrueType formats, the Macintosh will decide whether to use the PostScript screen font or a scaled TrueType font for each occurrence, depending on the point size at which the font is used. Assume, for example, that you have the PostScript screen fonts for Helvetica, Helvetica Bold, Helvetica Italic and Helvetica Bold Italic installed in your System file, each in 10-, 12- and 14-point sizes. Also assume that the TrueType Helvetica, Helvetica Bold, Helvetica Italic and Helvetica Bold Italic files are also installed. In this case, most applications would use the PostScript versions of Helvetica for any instances of 10-, 12- or 14-point type, and the TrueType version in all other cases. In other words, PostScript screen fonts are used when they're available at the size specified, and TrueType fonts are used for all other sizes.

Of course, when no TrueType font has been installed, PostScript versions are used at all sizes, just as they were before TrueType. If ATM is installed, ATM will scale the on-screen font display to provide smooth character representations. PostScript outlines will be used at print time to produce smooth type at the resolution of the output device (assuming the output device is equipped with a PostScript interpreter).

This process of alternating PostScript screen fonts and True-Type fonts is controlled by each application. Some software developers choose to use TrueType fonts even when PostScript screen fonts of the exact size requested are available. There's no way to tell whether TrueType or PostScript fonts are being used until the document is printed, so consult your application manuals for more information. It's doubtful that many developers will choose to use TrueType fonts when PostScript fonts are available.

This is clearly a confusing situation. It gets worse if you consider the possibility that some older documents on your hard drive were created using only PostScript fonts, and when you now open them you may be instead using TrueType versions of those same fonts. These old documents will then be forced to use TrueType fonts, and extensive text repositioning may occur as a result. The same thing will happen if you're using an application that ignores PostScript screen fonts and uses the TrueType fonts in all situations.

Text repositioning occurs because character widths for TrueType fonts will not always exactly match PostScript font character widths, even in the same font and family. The width of a 14-point Helvetica Bold "H" may be slightly different in TrueType than it was in PostScript. The cumulative result of the character width accommodations in your document will be text repositioning.

Because using both PostScript and TrueType versions of the same font at the same time makes it impossible to determine which version is being used at any one time, it is best *not* to install both PostScript and TrueType versions of the same fonts. This is especially true for fonts you'll use in documents being prepared for high-resolution output that will be printed at a remote site, such as a service bureau.

If you use the default System 7 fonts (Times, Helvetica, etc.) for high-resolution output, you may want to remove either the PostScript or the TrueType versions of these from your

System file (version 7.0) or Fonts folder (version 7.1) so both are not installed. If you just use these fonts on-screen, and from your local laser printer, however, it is probably not worth the trouble of removing one of them.

Moving On

Fonts continue to be an exciting part of the Macintosh, and as shown in this chapter, font technology remains a source of innovation and controversy. System 7 supports three different font formats:

- **Bitmapped fonts.** The end may be near for these fonts, which lack any type of outline and therefore have limited ability to produce smooth characters either on-screen or in print.

- **PostScript fonts.** This current standard is fully supported in System 7, but facing pressure from the abilities, or at least the publicity, of TrueType.

- **TrueType fonts.** The new font format developed by Apple, TrueType has already contributed by forcing innovations in PostScript, and by becoming an important font technology in its own right.

Another aspect of the Macintosh that has been in constant evolution is support for work on networks. In Chapter 9, you'll learn how to share the data on your Macintosh with others on the network.

Chapter 9: Introduction to File Sharing

Fonts were not the only area where the Macintosh was ahead of its time in 1984. The first Macintosh also had a built-in AppleTalk port, allowing any number of Macintosh computers to be strung together with inexpensive twisted-pair cable to form a network. Back then, however, there was no compelling reason to create a Macintosh network.

Today, an AppleTalk port remains standard equipment on every Macintosh, and there are many good reasons for putting a Mac on a network. But AppleTalk is no longer the only network available for the Mac; Ethernet and Token Ring networks are available as well.

The three main reasons why you might want to put your Macintosh on a network:

- **Computer-to-computer communications.** Networked Macintoshes can use electronic mail, messaging systems and transfer files directly from one computer to another.

- **Shared peripherals.** Laser printers, color printers, slide recorders, high-speed modems, fax/modems and scanners are all expensive peripheral devices that can be shared among networked Macintoshes.

- **Centralized or distributed file servers.** Storing large amounts of data on file servers provides an easy way to share information, allows a number of people to participate in work-group projects and reduces the data storage requirements of individual users. Apple's AppleShare is the dominant file-serving software, but other servers compliant with the AppleShare Filing Protocol (AFP) can also be used.

It's in this last category that System 7 provides greatly expanded abilities. In System 7, Macintosh users can share files from their hard drives with other computers on the network, and access files being shared by these other computers. This new feature is called File Sharing. In this chapter, you'll learn the basics of File Sharing, and how to use it to allow others to access your files. Chapter 10, "Working on a Network," discusses additional File Sharing features, including accessing the data shared by other Macs and ways you can connect to your own Macintosh from another computer on your network.

What Is File Sharing?

File Sharing is a System 7 feature that lets you designate up to 10 folders and volumes on your computer to be shared with other computers on your network. For each shared folder or volume, you can assign access privileges, which can limit the use of your shared data to only the computers you specify.

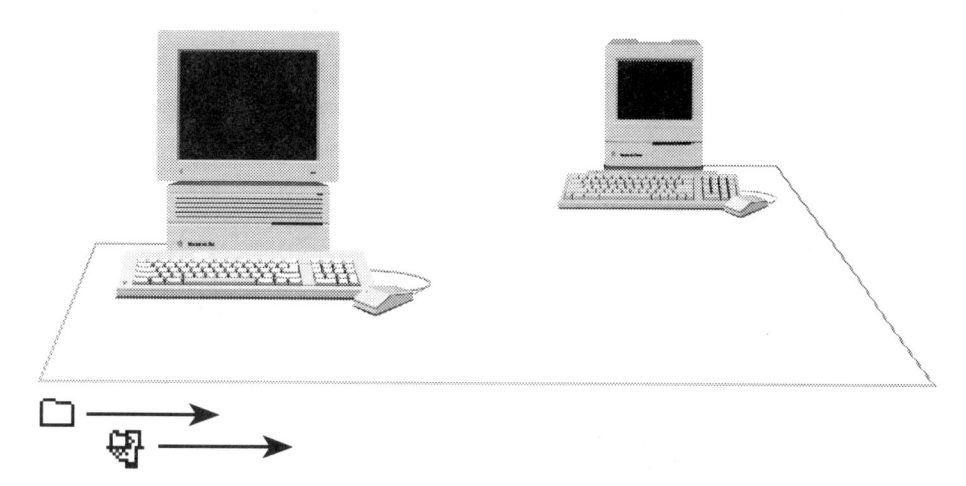

Figure 9-1: File Sharing lets you share your data with others.

File Sharing also lets you access folders and volumes other Macintoshes are sharing, provided you've been granted access privileges. Once accessed, folders and volumes from other Macs appear on your desktop and can be used as if they were your own.

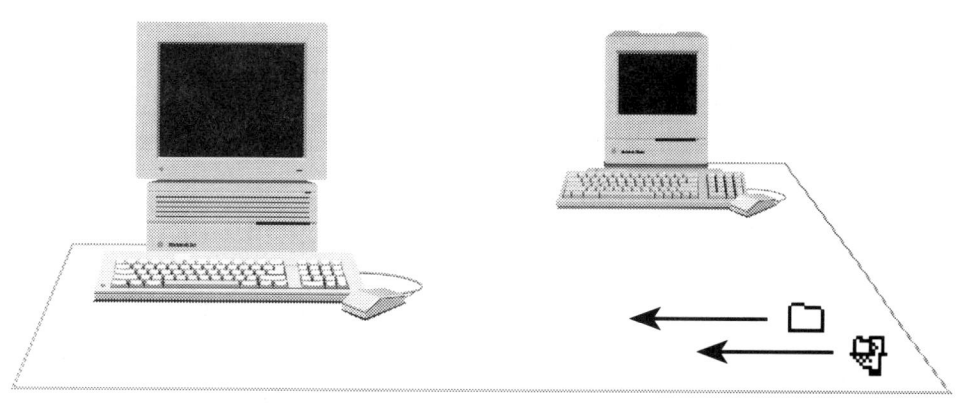

Figure 9-2: File Sharing lets you access data from other computers.

In networking parlance, when your computer is sharing files, it's acting as a server; when it's accessing files from another computer, it's acting as a client. File Sharing allows every user on a Macintosh network to become a server, a client or both server and client.

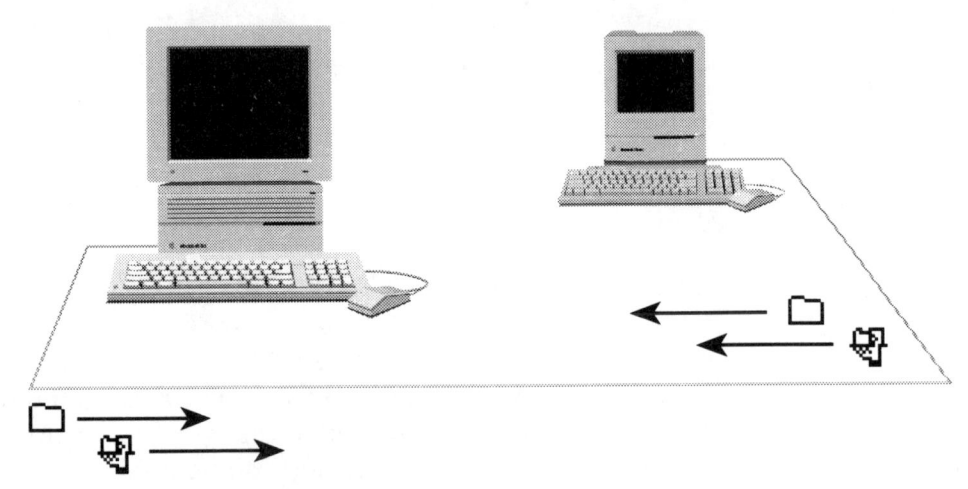

Figure 9-3: Using File Sharing, every Mac on the network can be both server and client.

Sharing data from your Macintosh, and accessing data shared by others on your network, can increase your capabilities and productivity in many ways. Here are some examples of resources that can be shared.

- **Central libraries.** Reference files such as clip art, templates (or Stationery Pads) and historical records can be kept in one location and shared with the entire network.

- **Drop-box folders that send and receive files.** Each network user can define an electronic "In box" and "Out box." By assigning access privileges, the In box lets everyone add files, but not look at the folder content, while the Out box does not allow files to be added, but does allow designated users to "pick-up" the files they need.

- **Shared edition files that create living "work-group" documents.** The Edition Manager features (described in Chapter 7, "The Edition Mananger & IAC") together with File Sharing give network users access to edition files created by many users and stored on several hard drives.

The Limits of File Sharing

Although the capabilities of File Sharing are impressive, it's important to understand that File Sharing is only a "personal" version of AppleShare, Apple's dedicated file-server software. For a small number of Macs, File Sharing is sufficient, while larger or heavily used networks should use a combination of AppleShare and File Sharing. In these situations, File Sharing will supplement AppleShare, not replace it.

There are several reasons why File Sharing in some cases should be limited in this way:

- **Administration requirements.** As you'll see later, the administrative requirements of sharing files are not incidental. When many users need frequent access to numerous files and folders, centralized file-sharing administration, provided by central file servers such as AppleShare, is usually more efficient than distributed administration.

- **Security risks.** To avoid the burden of administrative requirements, users often neglect security issues, leaving confidential or sensitive data unprotected and available to anyone on the network. This is less likely to occur on centralized, professionally managed file servers.

- **Performance degradation.** Even with a very fast Mac and a very fast hard drive, File Sharing takes a noticeable toll on computer performance. Macintoshes or peripherals that aren't particularly speedy to begin with make the problem even worse. The benefits outweigh the inconveniences for the casual or infrequent user; but continually having to deal with long delays can be annoying and counterproductive. A centralized server with resources dedicated to the burdens of serving network users is the practical alternative in these circumstances.

- **Access limitations.** File Sharing can serve only 10 folders or volumes from one Macintosh at a time, and support only 50 users at one time (and that would be pushing it). These constraints are too restrictive in many cases. Also, the sharing Macintoshes must be left on all the time to ensure files are always available on the network (files on a shut-down Mac are not accessible for sharing).

A File Sharing Quick Tour

File Sharing's capabilities are powerful, and therefore require more preparation and attention than most other System 7 features. Here are the steps necessary to use File Sharing:

- **Prepare your Macintosh.** This includes physically connecting to a network, installing the File Sharing files and activating AppleTalk.

- **Start File Sharing.** The Sharing Setup control panel provides configuration information and the master switch.

- **Configure Users & Groups.** Users must be defined, and user preferences and access privileges set in the Users & Groups control panel. In most situations, user groups will also need definition. You must also specify access privileges your Macintosh will enforce when network "guests" log on.

- **Specify folders/volumes to share.** To share any folder or volume, the Sharing command must be applied, and sharing options set.

- **Connect with others using File Sharing.** In order to access folders and volumes being shared by others, the Chooser is used to complete a log-on process.

- **Use the File Sharing Monitor to track access to your shared data.** A new control panel, called the File Sharing Monitor, constantly gives you updates on who's accessing what on your computer.

The remainder of this chapter looks in detail at the first four of these steps. The last two are covered in Chapter 10.

Preparing for File Sharing

File Sharing success depends on correctly connecting your Macintosh computers and installing network drivers. The simplest and most common Macintosh networking scheme uses LocalTalk or PhoneNet-style connectors and cabling that plug directly into the AppleTalk port on the back of the Mac.

More sophisticated networks require Ethernet or Token Ring adapters via NuBus or PDS slots (although some newer Macs have built-in Ethernet ports). When the network is physically connected, network availability and the presence of network software drivers must be verified by opening the Network control panel, which displays the available network drivers (shown in Figure 9-4).

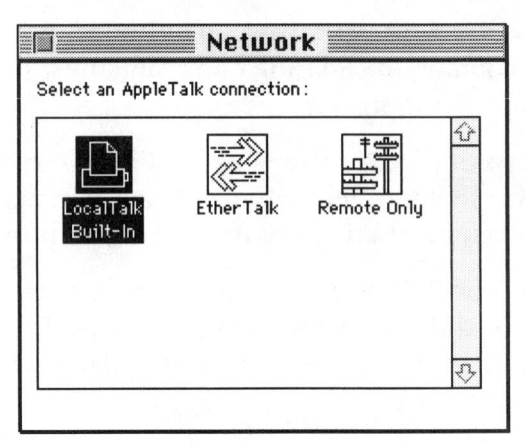

Figure 9-4: The Network control panel displays the icons for available networking systems.

After verifying installation, open the Chooser and call Apple-Talk by clicking the "Active" radio button. If your network is divided into zones, the Chooser also displays a list of available AppleTalk zones, as shown in Figure 9-5.

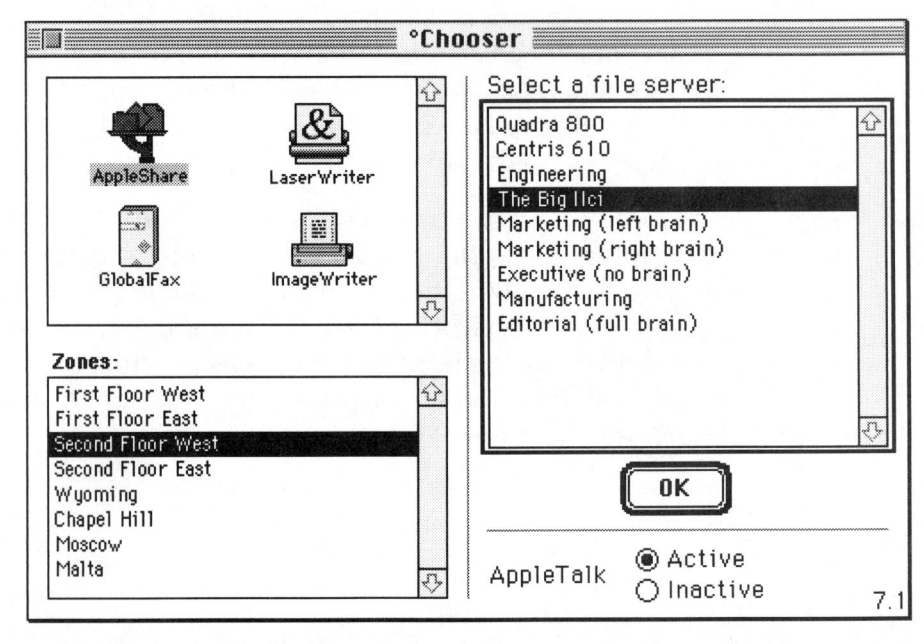

Figure 9-5: The Chooser turns on AppleTalk and selects network zones.

Chapter 9: Introduction to File Sharing   253

File Sharing also requires, not surprisingly, that the File Sharing software be installed by the Installer application. You can tell that File Sharing software has been installed when the Sharing command appears in the File menu. If it's not there, run the Installer again and choose the "File Sharing" option. (See Appendix A for more information on using the Installer to add File Sharing.)

Starting File Sharing

With your network physically ready and File Sharing installed, you can configure and turn on File Sharing with the Sharing Setup control panel located in your Control Panels folder. The Sharing Setup control panel (shown in Figure 9-6) lets you define your "network identity," turn File Sharing on and off, and start and stop Program Linking, using the Network Setup dialog box.

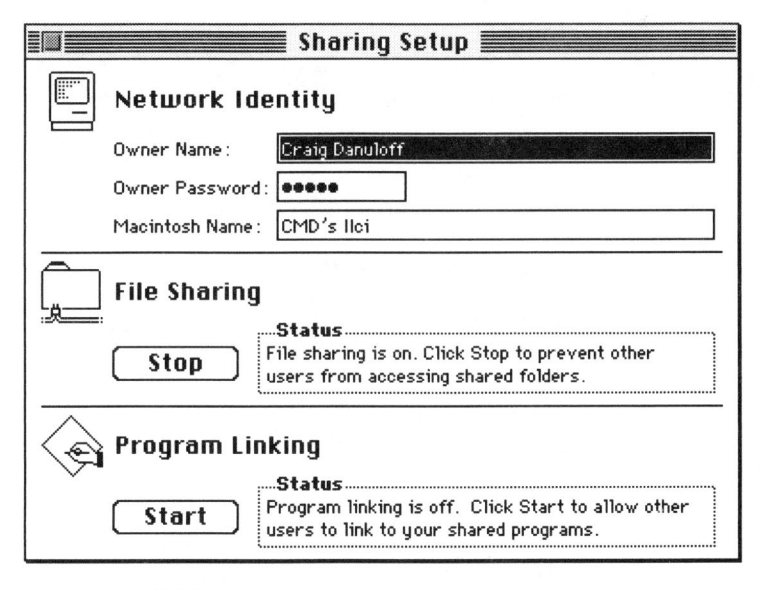

Figure 9-6: The Sharing Setup dialog box.

The options in this dialog box are

- **Owner Name.** The name your Macintosh displays to others when you seek access to their computers via File Sharing. It's also the name you use to access your computer from any other on the network. Any name of up to 32 characters is acceptable, and you can change the Owner Name at any time.

- **Owner Password.** A security gate, allowing you as owner to access this Macintosh's entire hard drive from anywhere on the network when File Sharing is turned on. It also allows you as an assigned owner to access any shared folders or volumes. (By default, you're assigned ownership of all folders and volumes shared by your Macintosh. You can then assign this ownership to others, if you wish, as described later in this chapter.)

    Note that this password can be changed at any time, and it's not necessary to know the old password to define a new one. This means you don't have to worry about forgetting your password—which may seem like a breach of security, and it is. But File Sharing controls only remote-user access to your Macintosh. It doesn't apply to anyone who sits down at your Mac's keyboard. Thus, the ability to change the password at any time is consistent with the Mac's total lack of local security.

- **The Macintosh Name.** The name other network users see when looking at your Macintosh from the network. It appears in the Chooser when they click on the AppleShare icon, and when they print to network printers. This "Macintosh Name" is the equivalent of the Chooser name used in earlier system software versions.

- **File Sharing (Start/Stop).** The master control switch. When the Start button is clicked, File Sharing is turned on and the folders and volumes on your Macintosh are available to the network, based on the access privileges assigned to them. As File Sharing starts, the message in the Status area documents the startup process.

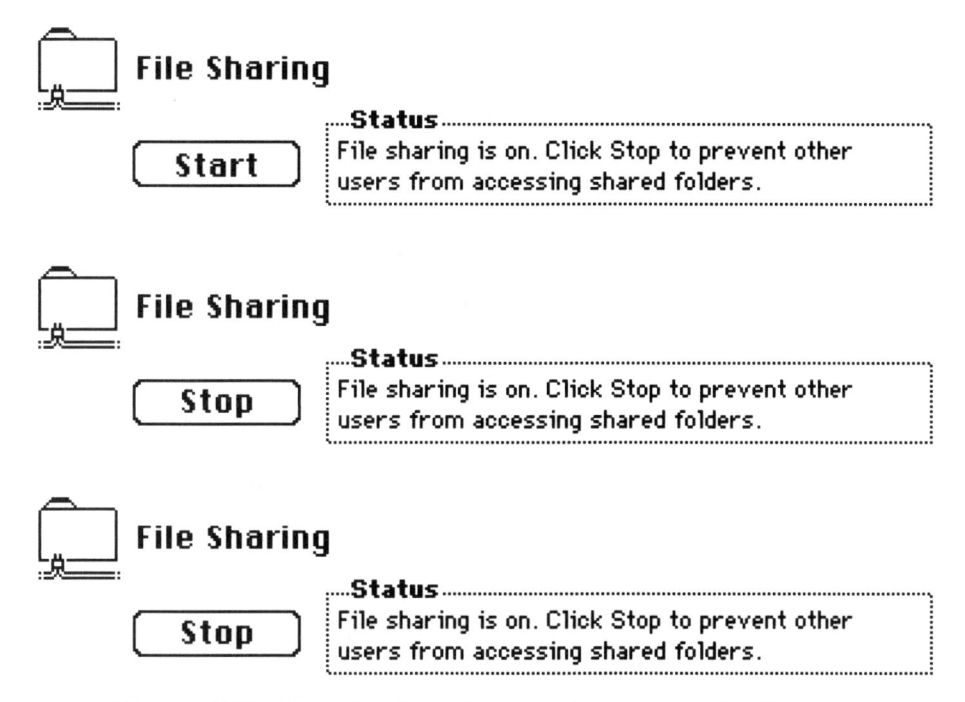

Figure 9-7: After the Start button is pressed, the Status message documents the progress of File Sharing.

Once File Sharing is running, the Start button becomes the Stop button. When the Stop button is clicked, you're asked how many minutes until shutdown. Enter a number between 0 (for immediate shutdown) and 999 (for delayed action).

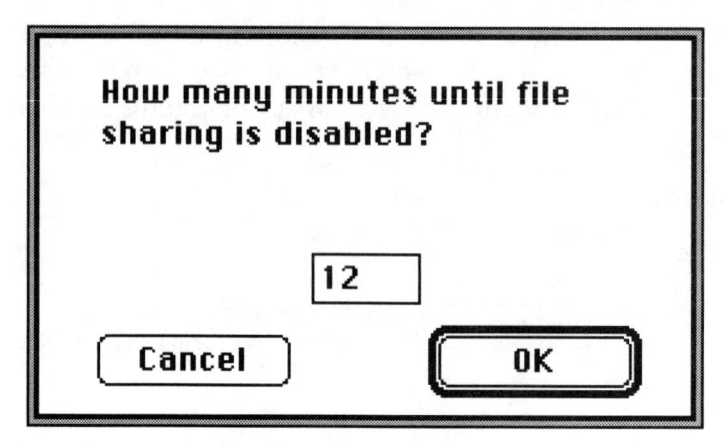

Figure 9-8: The Shutdown dialog box.

After you click OK in this dialog, the Status message tells you how many minutes remain before File Sharing is turned off. As turn-off time approaches, other users accessing your Macintosh files are warned of impending shutdown, so they can save their work and release any volumes or folders they're using. It's not necessary for users to release your files before the shutdown; contact with your Macintosh is terminated immediately in any case. However, the Mac simply extends the courtesy of warning other users, so they won't lose work or be abruptly interrupted. If you choose the 0 minutes option, cutoff will occur without warning. (To check the number of users connected to your Mac, use the File Sharing Monitor control panel, as described later in this chapter.)

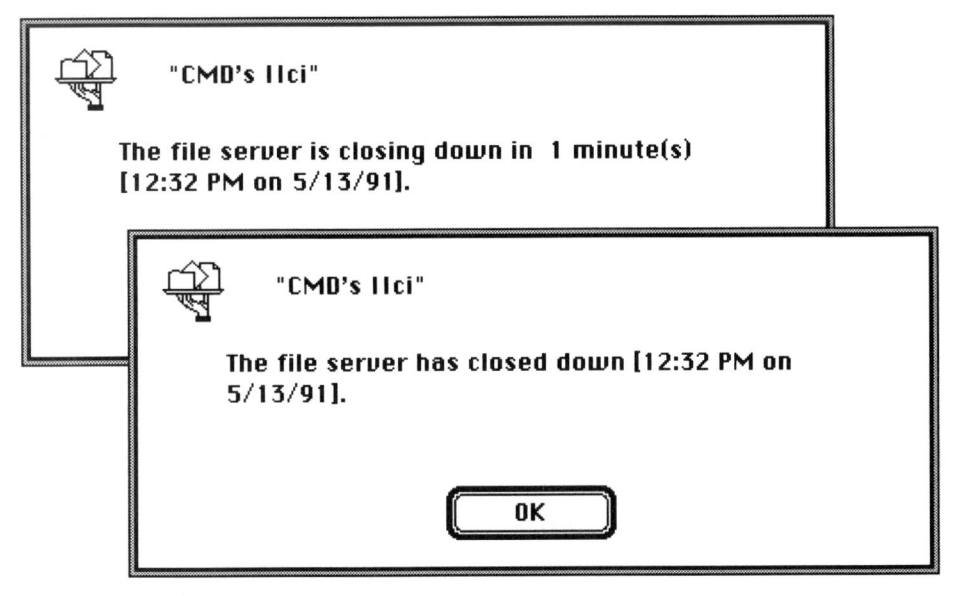

```
┌─────────────────────────────────────────────┐
│  📁   "CMD's IIci"                          │
│                                             │
│  The file server is closing down in 1 minute(s) │
│  [12:32 PM on 5/13/91].                     │
│         ┌─────────────────────────────────────────────┐
└─────────│  📁   "CMD's IIci"                          │
          │                                             │
          │  The file server has closed down [12:32 PM on │
          │  5/13/91].                                  │
          │                                             │
          │              ┌─────────┐                    │
          │              │   OK    │                    │
          │              └─────────┘                    │
          └─────────────────────────────────────────────┘
```

Figure 9-9: Clients are warned before a File Sharing server closes, and after it has closed down.

When File Sharing is on and users are connected to your Macintosh, the Shut Down or Restart command brings up the Alert dialog box shown in Figure 9-10. Again, be sure to give your network users enough time to save their work before shutting down. If possible, cancel the Shut Down or Restart and leave your Macintosh running so network use can continue.

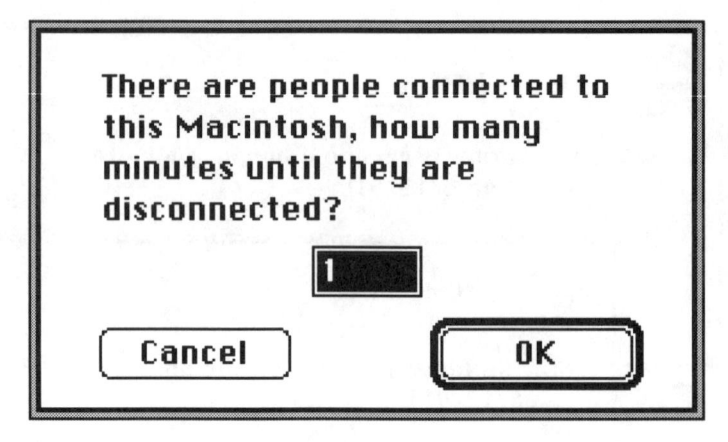

Figure 9-10: The alert that appears at Restart or Shut Down.

- **Program Linking (Start/Stop).** Discussed in depth in Chapter 10, this function allows inter-application communication (IAC) commands of remote users to control programs residing on your Macintosh.

Registering Users & Groups

If you plan to use File Sharing to make your Macintosh folders and/or volumes available to other network users, you must decide who may and may not share your files. You may want to share your files with every user on your network, but it is more likely that you will want to restrict access to some or all of your shared files.

To designate access you open the Users & Groups control panel (shown in Figure 9-11), which displays a window containing one icon for each user and one icon for each group registered to access your Macintosh, in addition to a Guest icon and an icon for you, the Macintosh Owner.

Of course, when you open the Users & Groups control panel for the first time, no users or groups are yet defined, so only the Guest and Macintosh Owner icons will appear.

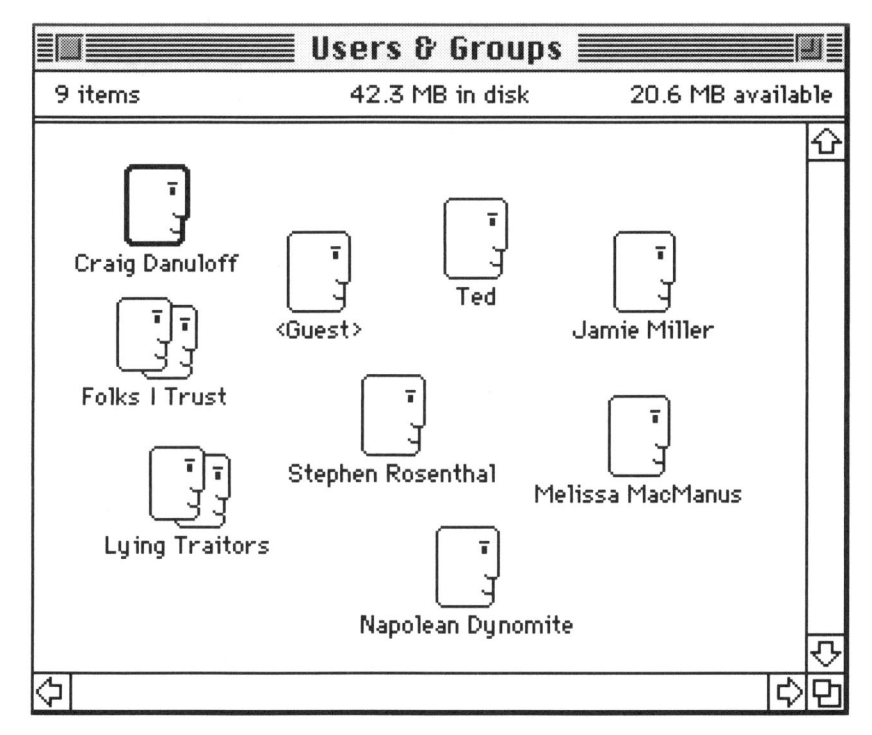

Figure 9-11: The Users & Groups control panel.

Although this control panel looks like a normal Finder window, it's not. You cannot drag-copy user icons or group icons out onto the desktop or to another folder or volume. Nor can you copy other files into this window. If you try to do so, an Alert dialog box will remind you that you can't.

Via the Users & Groups control panel, you can grant access to four user categories:

- **Registered Users.** These are specific people you want to have access to your shared folders or volumes. Registered Users are given access to your data as individuals or as members of a defined Group.

- **Groups.** A Group is a collection of defined Registered Users. Individual Registered Users can be included in any number of groups.

- **Guests.** Any user on your network who has not been defined as a Registered User can attempt to log onto your shared folders or volumes as a Guest. You define whether you want these non-Registered Users to have access to your data.

- **Macintosh Owner.** As the owner, you can give yourself special remote abilities and access privileges to your computer.

In addition to the definitions and privileges mentioned so far, the Sharing dialog box provides additional security safeguards. This dialog box specifies Registered Users and Groups who have access privileges to particular folders and volumes. (More on the Sharing dialog box later in this chapter.)

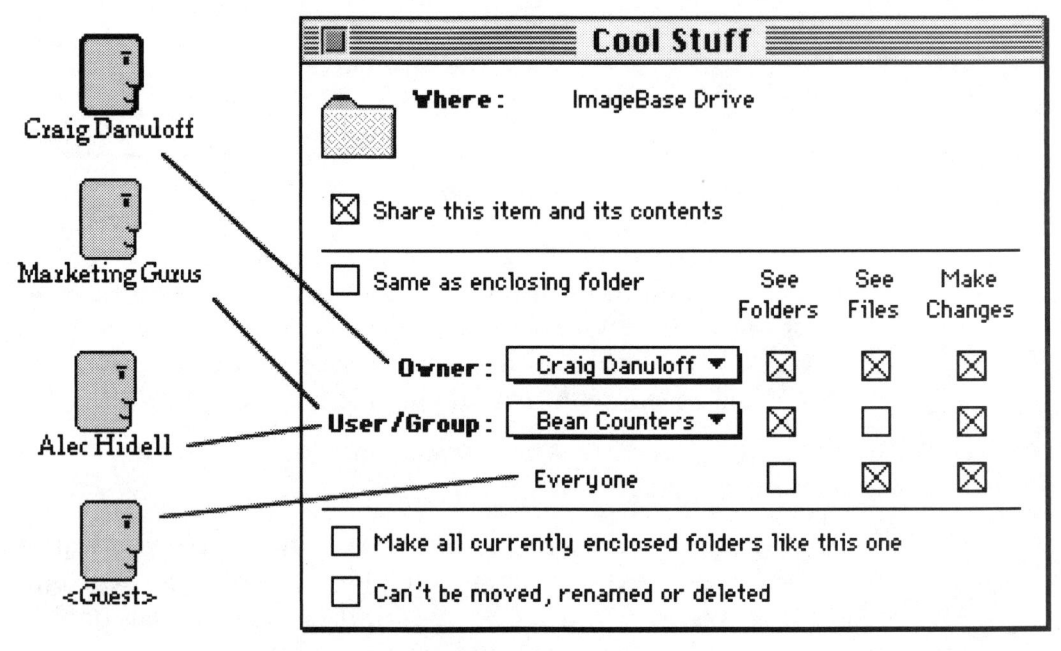

Figure 9-12: The defined users and groups are assigned access privileges via the Sharing dialog box.

Creating New Users

To create a new user, open the Users & Groups control panel, and choose the New User command from the File menu. This creates a new "untitled" Registered User icon in the Users & Groups window. Enter the name of the user you want this icon to represent.

It's best to enter the person's actual name, rather than a code name. A code name is more likely to be misspelled when the Registered User logs on.

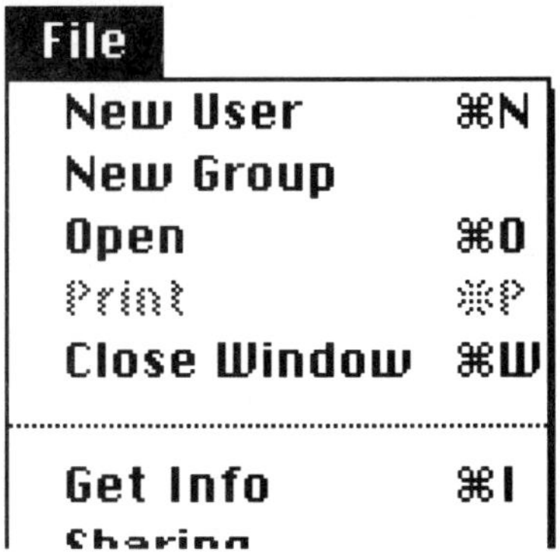

Figure 9-13: The File menu provides the New User and New Group commands.

Up to 100 Registered Users can be defined, but Apple recommends staying under 50. If more than 50 people need regular access to certain shared folders or volumes, consider moving that data to a dedicated AppleShare server, or allowing all Guests access to that data. (There is no limit to the number of Guests who can access your Macintosh, only to the number of Registered Users.)

You don't need to register users individually unless you want to limit access privileges. If you're going to allow everyone on the network to see and change your data, they can all log on as Guests. If not, you should define Users and Groups.

Configuring User Preferences

After registering a new user, or to alter a user's password or preferences, double-click on the user icon to open the File Sharing options window, as shown in Figure 9-14. This dialog box sets the user's password and allows or disallows the user to connect via File Sharing or Program Linking. This dialog box also displays a list of all groups the user is included in (you can't change or modify group memberships in this dialog box).

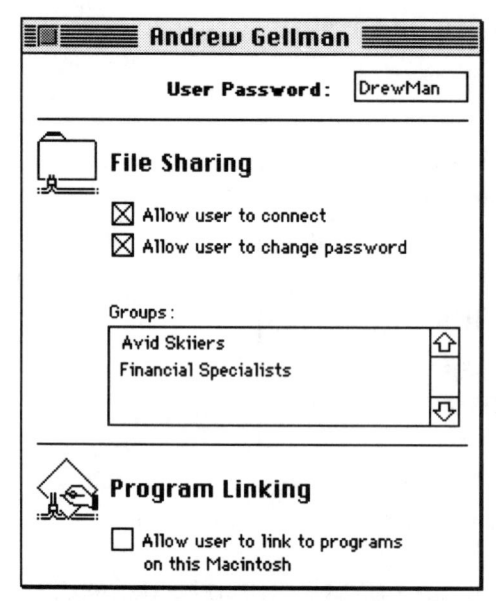

Figure 9-14: The User Preferences dialog box.

Lets look at the options in this dialog box:

- **User Password.** In order to access your data from another Macintosh on the network, a user name and, in most cases, a password must be entered. By default, the user has no password, and logs on by simply entering the user name and leaving the password option blank. (More information on the log-in process later.) This obviously doesn't provide much security assurance that the user logging on is supposed to have network access.

To add a password, type one into the User Password option box. For security, bullets will appear, instead of the password itself.

When you add or change a user password, you must notify the user, for obvious reasons. Another approach is to leave the user without a password, letting them define their own passwords the first time they log on. They can then change their password periodically after that. This is done with the Allow user to change password option, described below. A variation would be to start with an obvious password like the user's first name, then encourage the user to change it at the first opportunity.

You can change any user password at any time. For example, if a user forgets his or her password, there's no way for you to find it; you must "change" it to resolve this problem. Changing a password also lets you bar a particular user's access until you provide a new password.

Avoid using obvious passwords like names, zodiac signs and birthstones, and change passwords regularly.

- **Allow user to connect.** This check box is the "personal" master switch for File Sharing that makes it possible or impossible for a user to connect as a Registered User (they still may be able to connect as a Guest). This option is on by default, but occasionally you may want to turn it off. Using this option to revoke access privileges is less drastic than deleting the user, which makes later reinstatement more difficult.

- **Allow user to change password.** This option allows Registered Users to change their passwords using the Change Password button that appears in the Chooser as they log onto your Macintosh. In most cases, this option should be selected, because changing user passwords frequently increases the security of your data. Of course, since you as the Owner can always change passwords directly in this dialog box, you lose no privileges by allowing users this option.

- **Program Linking.** Users can take advantage of this option if the feature is turned on in the Sharing Setup control panel.

Creating & Working With Groups

Since a network comprises many individual users, assigning access privileges to each individual for each item would be a very tedious job. To avoid this, File Sharing lets you define Groups, add Registered Users to these groups, then assign access privileges that apply to all Group members.

New Groups are created by selecting the File menu's New Group command while the Users & Groups control panel is open, which places a new "untitled" Group icon in the Users & Groups window. Enter the name of the group you want this icon to represent (descriptive names are best). Registered Users never see the group names you assign, nor do they need to know which groups they're assigned to.

Groups cannot be combined and you can't make a Guest icon a member of any group; but you can add yourself as the Macintosh Owner to any group. This isn't as useless as it may seem: if you assign ownership of folders or volumes to another user or group, you won't have access to that folder (over the network) if you're not a member of a group that has access privileges (unless you add yourself to that group) or use the Allow user to see entire volume option in your Owner Preferences (described later).

To add Registered Users to the group, drag their icons onto the Group icon and release them. Or you can double-click on the Group icon to open the group's window and then drag user icons directly into this window. Adding a user to a group does not remove the user icon from the main Users & Groups window. You can drag a single user icon into any number of groups. To check which groups a user is part of, double-click the Registered User's icon and see the list in the User Preferences dialog box.

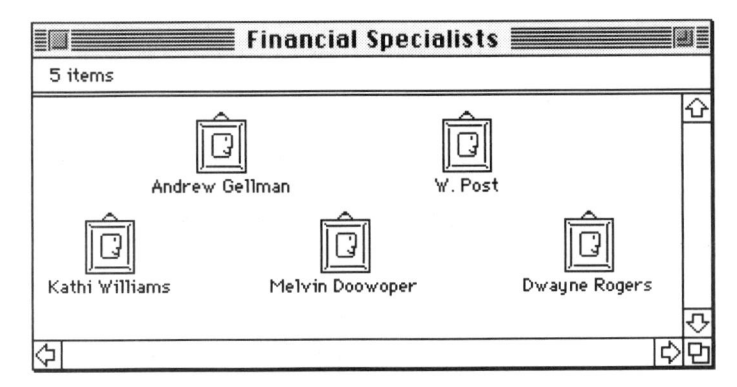

Figure 9-15: A defined Group containing five Registered Users.

To remove a user from a group, open the group window and drag the user's icon to the Trash. This deletes the user from the group; it does not remove the user entirely, and it doesn't remove the user from any other groups he or she belongs to. Similarly, you can delete an entire group by dragging the group icon to the Trash, which removes the group but does not affect any group member individually.

Configuring Guest Preferences

You may occasionally want to share files with someone on your network who isn't a Registered User. This is made possible by File Sharing's support of Guests. A single Guest icon is automatically included in the Users & Groups control panel, and this icon is used to control access to your shared data for all non-Registered Users. The Guest icon cannot be deleted. Double-clicking on the Guest icon brings up the Guest Preferences dialog box, as shown in Figure 9-16.

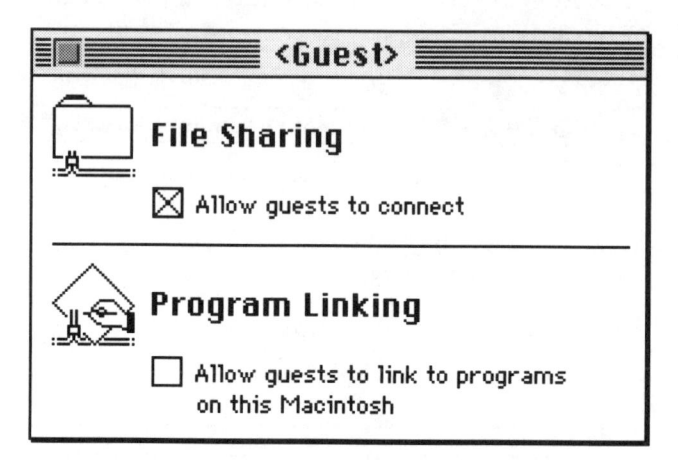

Figure 9-16: Guest Preferences.

There are only two options in this window:

- **Allow guests to connect.** This option (the default) is the master switch that lets guests log onto your Macintosh. When this option is deselected, network users can't log onto your Macintosh as guests.

    Allowing guests to log on does not automatically give them access to data. Guests can access folders and volumes based only on the "Everyone" access privileges in the Sharing dialog box, as described later in this chapter. If no folders or volumes are available to Everyone, guests who attempt to log on will find no data available.

- **Allow guests to link to your programs.** Program Linking, as described in Chapter 10, is used by System 7's IAC feature. If you select this option, guests can link to your programs; if you deselect it, they can't.

Configuring Owner Preferences

The preferences you set for yourself, the Macintosh Owner, affect the way you can access your Macintosh from elsewhere on the network. They have no affect on what you can do directly from your keyboard (and mouse). The Macintosh Owner icon is created automatically, and named with the Macintosh Owner Name, as set in the Sharing Setup control panel. The owner icon appears with a bold border in the Users & Groups window. Double-clicking on this icon opens the Macintosh Owner Preferences dialog, shown in Figure 9-17.

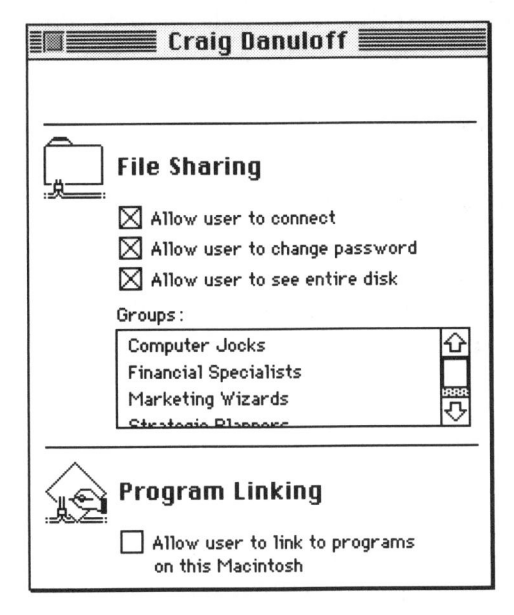

Figure 9-17: The Macintosh Owner Preferences dialog box.

The options in this dialog are the same as those described previously for any Registered User, with the exception of the Allow user to see entire volume option. This option lets you access entire volumes on your Macintosh from anywhere on the network at any time—even when the volumes have not been specifically shared with the Sharing command. When accessing volumes in this way, you have full access privileges to all files, folders and applications.

This feature is very powerful—and potentially dangerous. It allows you to work on your Macintosh, or access any data stored on your Macintosh, from any Mac on the network just as if you were at your own keyboard. The danger is that anyone else who knows your Owner Name and password could gain the same access.

If you don't need this feature, leave it deselected. If you do use this option, be very discreet with your password, and change it frequently. If you won't need to use this feature over an extended period of time, temporarily deselect it. Of course, there's always the possibility that someone might sit down at your Macintosh keyboard and access your data or change your password, then remotely access your Mac. File Sharing should not lull you into a false sense of security. If you have good reason to believe this could happen, other security measures should be taken.

Sharing Folders or Volumes

For any folder or volume to be shared with others on your network, the Sharing command must initiate sharing and specify access privileges. Any mounted volume, including hard disks, hard disk partitions, removable cartridges, CD-ROMs and any folder on any mounted volume can be shared. Floppy disks and folders on floppy disks cannot.

To initiate sharing, select the folder or volume and choose the Sharing command from the File menu, which brings up the Sharing dialog box (shown in Figure 9-18). This dialog box is used to turn on Sharing and assign access privileges to this item. Access privileges, as you learned earlier, determine who can see the folders and volumes, who can see the files inside those folders and volumes, and who can make changes to existing files or store new files. (More on access privileges later in this chapter.)

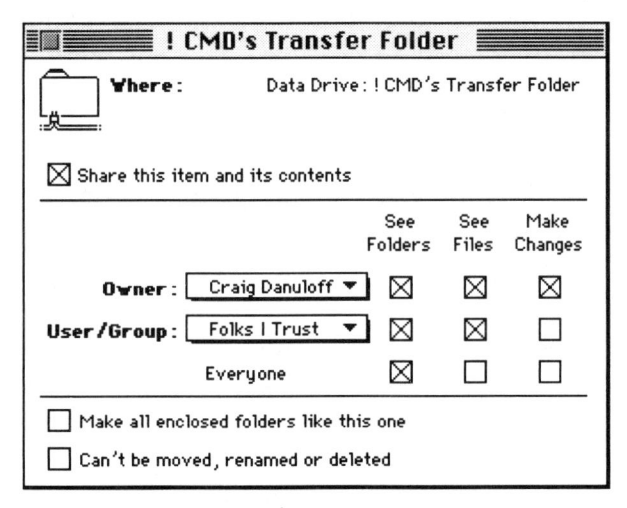

Figure 9-18: A Sharing dialog box.

The Sharing dialog box presents a number of important options:

- **Share this folder and its contents.** This check box is the master switch that turns sharing on or off for the selected folder or volume and the contents of that folder or volume. Until this option is selected, all other options in this dialog box are dimmed.

- **Owner.** This option specifies the owner of the selected folder or volume and the owner's access privileges. In most cases, you (as the Macintosh Owner) will remain the owner of shared folders and volumes.

However, using the pop-up menu, you can designate any other Registered User as the owner of the selected folder or volume. The assignee can then reset access privileges for the item. Your access to the folder or volume from another Macintosh on the network is then dependent on your inclusion in the User/Group option (discussed in the following subsection). Of course, your access to the folder or volume from your own Macintosh will not be affected; these options affect only network access.

Once an owner has been specified, use the check boxes to assign access privileges. (More on available access privileges and their use in the next section of this chapter.)

- **User/Group.** This option grants one user or one group access to the selected folder or volume (via the pop-up menu), and defines the access privileges available to this user or group. In many ways, this is the most important Sharing option, because it usually designates the person or group of users that will most frequently access the shared data. (See the "Access Privileges" section of this chapter for the ways this feature can be used, including bulletin boards, drop boxes, read-only filing systems and true work-group file sharing and storage systems.)

- **Everyone.** This option specifies access privileges granted to Guest users on your Macintosh. As mentioned before, anyone on your network can log onto your Mac as a Guest, providing you've specified that Guest log-ins are permitted. In that case, the "Everyone" option determines which volumes and folders they can access.

- **Make all enclosed folders like this one.** When you share a folder or volume, all enclosed folders are also automatically accessible to users with access privileges. You cannot "unshare" a folder enclosed in a shared folder or on a shared volume, but you can change the access privileges of an enclosed folder so that they don't match those of the enclosing folder. This option also can reset the access privileges of the enclosed folders so they match those of the currently selected folder or volume.

    For example, a folder called Out box is shared, with full access privileges, by everyone on the network. Inside this folder is a folder called Project A. We want to limit access to Project A so that only members of the Project A group can share it. To do this, after using the Sharing command for the Out box folder, you'd select the Project A folder and choose the Sharing command again. Now, access privileges are reset, limiting access to group members only. Figure 9-19 displays the Sharing dialog box for the "CMD's Outbox" folder and "Project A" folders.

    Notice that the Share this folder and its contents option has been replaced in the "Project A" folder dialog box with a Same as enclosing folder option. This occurs because the "Project A" folder is inside a folder that is already shared. By default, this new option is selected, and the access privileges match those specified for the enclosing "CMD's Outbox" folder. Deselecting this option makes it possible to change the access privileges.

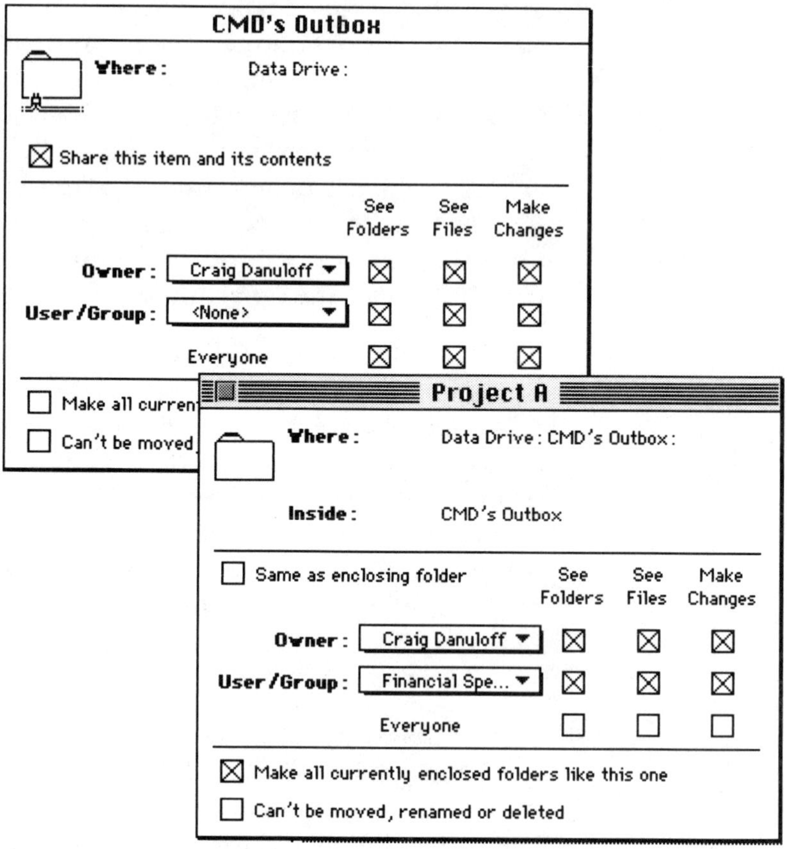

Figure 9-19: The Sharing dialog box for a parent and child folder.

- **Can't be moved, renamed or deleted.** This option gives you a safety net to ensure that the folder or volume you share is not moved, renamed or deleted by any network user—including the owner. It's a good idea to select this option in all cases, unless you know that repositioning, renaming or deleting the item will be necessary. This will prevent accidental changes with unpleasant results.

After completing these options, click the close box in the title bar to close the dialog box, and apply these options to the selected item. If you've made changes to the ownership or access privileges of the item, dialog boxes appear asking you to confirm or cancel the changes requested. A dialog box will also appear if you chose the Make all enclosed folders like this one option. Figure 9-20 displays these warning dialogs.

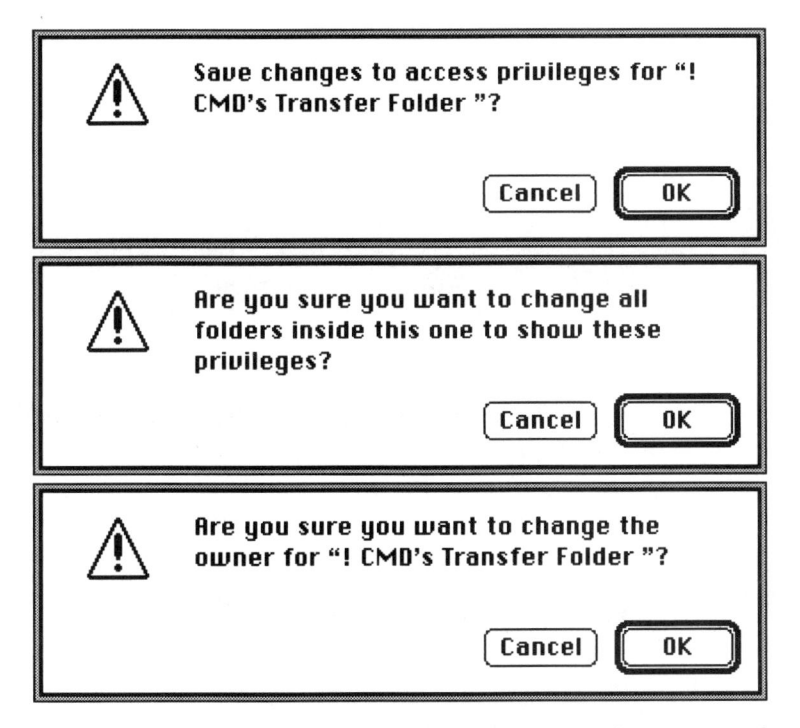

⚠ Save changes to access privileges for "! CMD's Transfer Folder "?

[Cancel] [OK]

⚠ Are you sure you want to change all folders inside this one to show these privileges?

[Cancel] [OK]

⚠ Are you sure you want to change the owner for "! CMD's Transfer Folder "?

[Cancel] [OK]

Figure 9-20: Three confirming dialog boxes appear after changing Sharing options.

Icons of Shared Items

After you have specified and implemented sharing options, icons of the shared folders will modify, confirming their shared status. Figure 9-21 shows a folder icon and its changes.

Figure 9-21: A folder as it appears before Sharing (left), after Sharing (center) and when users are connected (right).

Unsharing

There are two ways to make shared items unavailable to network users: you can turn File Sharing off completely, or you can turn File Sharing off for individual folders and volumes.

To turn File Sharing off completely, open the Sharing Setup control panel and click the File Sharing Stop button, as described earlier. When File Sharing is turned off, the settings and access privileges set with the Sharing command are retained for all shared folders and volumes, and will go back into effect when File Sharing is again turned on.

To turn off the sharing of a particular folder or volume only, select the appropriate folder or volume icon, choose the Sharing command and deselect the Share this item and its contents option. When you close the Sharing dialog box, the selected folder or volume will become unavailable for network access. (An Alert dialog box will appear if users are currently accessing the shared item, as shown in Figure 9-22.) Note that all access privilege settings are lost when sharing is turned off for a particular folder or volume; you'll have to reset them the next time the item is shared.

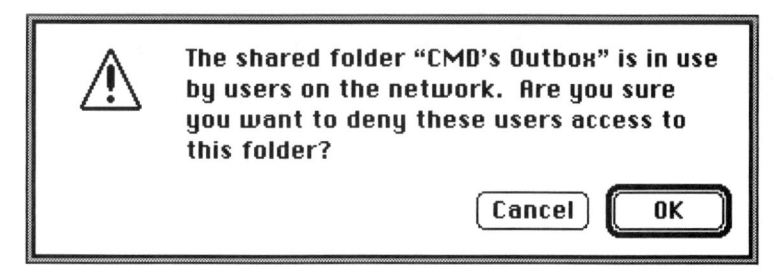

> ⚠ The shared folder "CMD's Outbox" is in use by users on the network. Are you sure you want to deny these users access to this folder?
>
> [Cancel] [OK]

Figure 9-22: Unsharing with users.

As an alternative to turning off File Sharing either completely or for particular folders or volumes, you could also change the Allow user to connect and Allow guest to connect options in the user icons found in the Users & Groups control panel. This method is not generally recommended, but it does allow access privilege settings to remain in force while temporarily making it impossible for some or all users to connect.

Access Privileges

Shared folders, volumes and folders enclosed within those shared folders and volumes are provided to other network users according to access privilege settings you apply in the Sharing dialog box. These privileges, along with users and groups designated in the Users & Groups control panel, are the key to controlling File Sharing.

As shown in Figure 9-23, the three access privilege options are assigned to three different users or groups. Option settings and combinations you apply determine how network users can access and modify your shared data and storage space. Let's look at these access privileges, the users and groups they can be assigned to, and the results of applying them in different combinations.

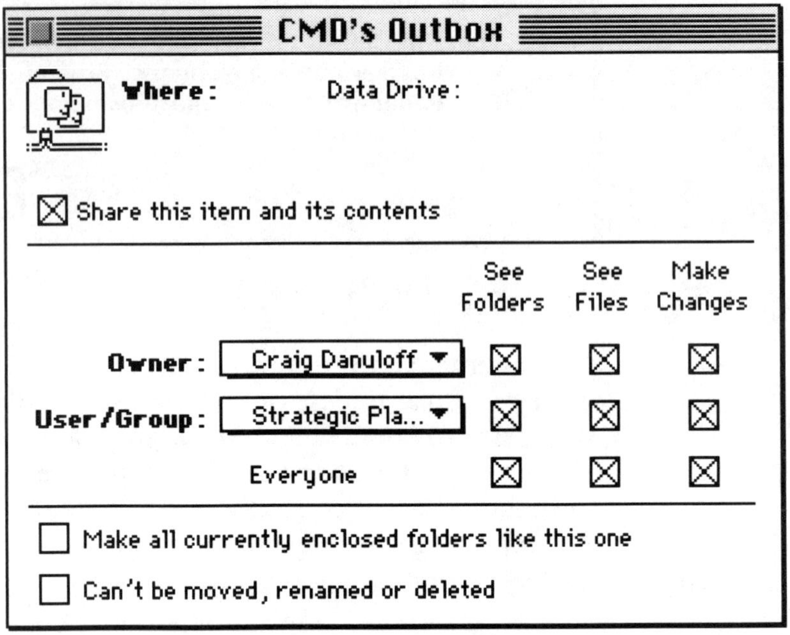

Figure 9-23: The access privilege options.

- **See Folders.** When this option is set, all folders within the selected folder or volume are shown to the specified user or group. Deselecting the See Folders option hides all folders from the specified user or group—users don't even know which folders exist in the selected folder or volume. When the See Folders option is deselected, an icon appears in the upper-left corner of the title bars of all windows accessed via File Sharing, letting the user know that folders are not being displayed.

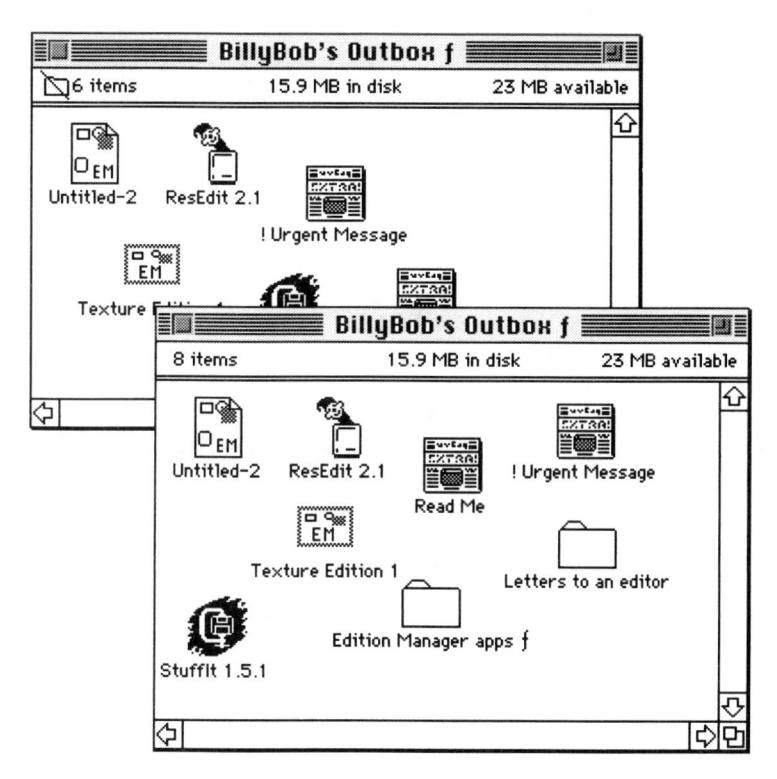

Figure 9-24: A shared folder with and without See Folders privilege.

- **See Files.** All files contained in the selected folder or volume appear normally to the specified user or group. Deselecting this option hides all files from the specified user or group—users don't know which files exist in the selected folder or volume. When the See Files option is deselected, an icon appears in the upper-left corner of the title bars of all windows accessed via File Sharing, letting the user know that files are not being displayed.

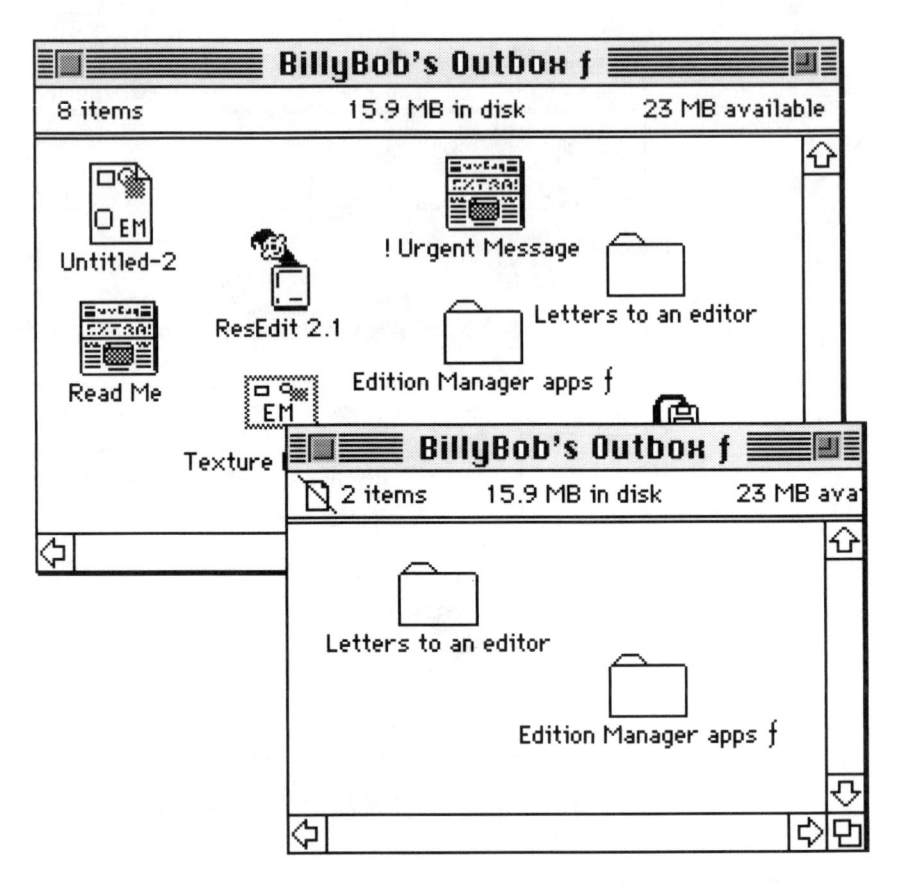

Figure 9-25: A shared folder with and without See Files privilege.

- **Make Changes.** When the Make Changes option is set, the user can save new files, change existing files and create new folders. When the Make Changes option is deselected, the folder or volume is *write protected:* no new files, folders and changed files can be written. When the Make Changes option is deselected, an icon appears in the upper-left corner of the title bars of all windows accessed via File Sharing, letting the user know that the folder or volume is write protected.

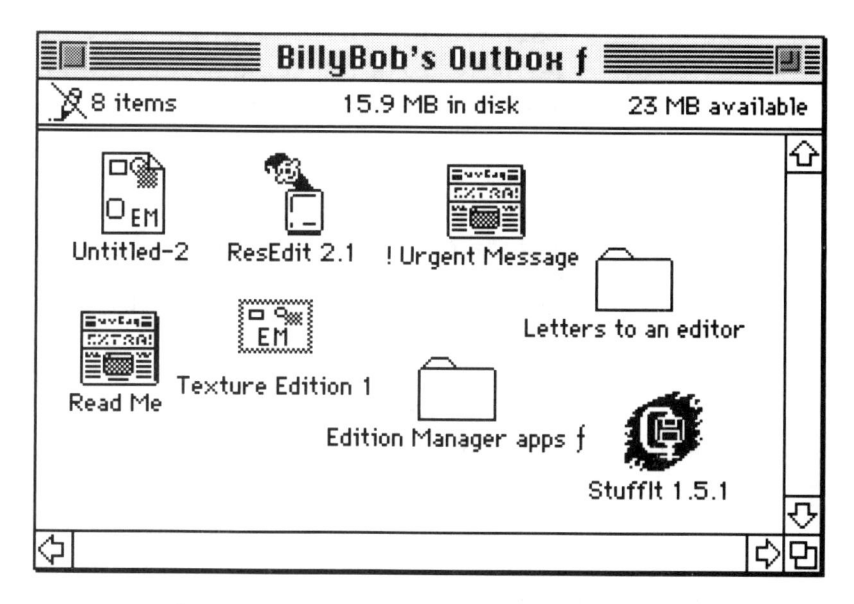

Figure 9-26: Shared folder without Make Changes privilege.

These three options are assigned individually to three user categories:

- **Owner.** The owner of a folder or volume is the person or group who can change the access privileges of that folder or volume while accessing it over the network. The person who creates a folder is automatically the owner of it; therefore, you are default owner of the folders and volumes on your Macintosh. When a user creates new folders in shared folders or volumes, however, that user becomes the owner of the new folders.

    Using the pop-up menu, the owner can be designated as any defined user or group. Or, selecting the <any user> option gives any guest who accesses the folder or volume full owner privileges (including the right to reassign access privileges). When setting access privileges on remote volumes, the "Owner" pop-up menu does not appear and the Owner Name must be entered manually.

- **User/Group.** The User/Group category assigns access privileges to one specific user or group. When sharing folders or volumes, select the desired User/Group from the pop-up menu listing of all registered users and groups. When setting access privileges on remote volumes, the "User/Group" pop-up menu does not appear and the Owner Name must be entered manually.

- **Everyone.** The Everyone category grants access privileges to all Guests who connect to the Macintosh that contains the selected folder or volume. Of course, in order for Guests to log on, the Allow guests to connect option must be set in the Users & Groups control panel.

Access Privilege Strategies

This elaborate matrix of categories and access privilege levels allows precise control over the way shared files can be used. Several common ways of using access privileges are described below:

- **Create an Out box folder.** The key aspect of an Out box is that those who pick up the files can see them but not make changes to them. This is accomplished by providing "See Files" and "See Folders" privileges but withholding "Make Changes," as shown in Figure 9-27. Of course, those who should not have access to the files in the Out box should not even see files or folders.

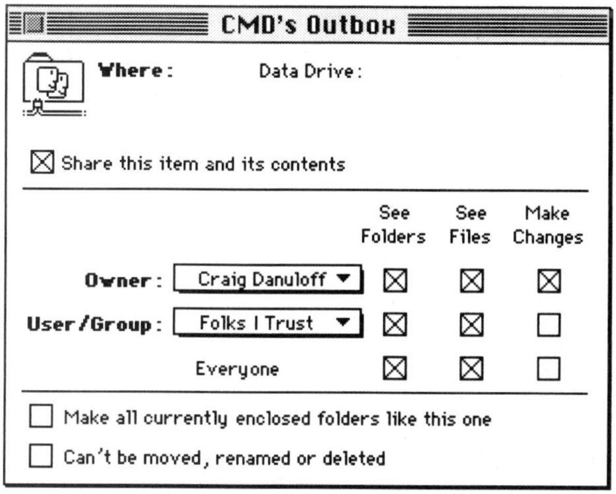

Figure 9-27: A set of access privileges that define an Out box.

- **Create an In box Folder.** The opposite of an Out box, an In box allows users to add files, but not to see anything that's already there—it's like a mail slot. This is defined using the opposite set of access privileges that an Out box has, as shown in Figure 9-28.

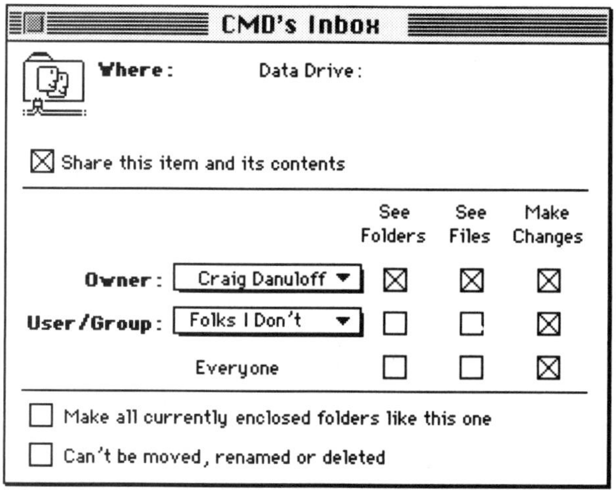

Figure 9-28: A set of access privileges that define an In box.

- **Create a bulletin board.** Combining the attributes of Out boxes and In boxes in various folders and enclosed folders, you can create a place where people can read and retrieve some files and add and modify others, depending on who they are and which folder they're accessing. Figure 9-29 shows a set of enclosed folders and the privileges that provide such an arrangement.

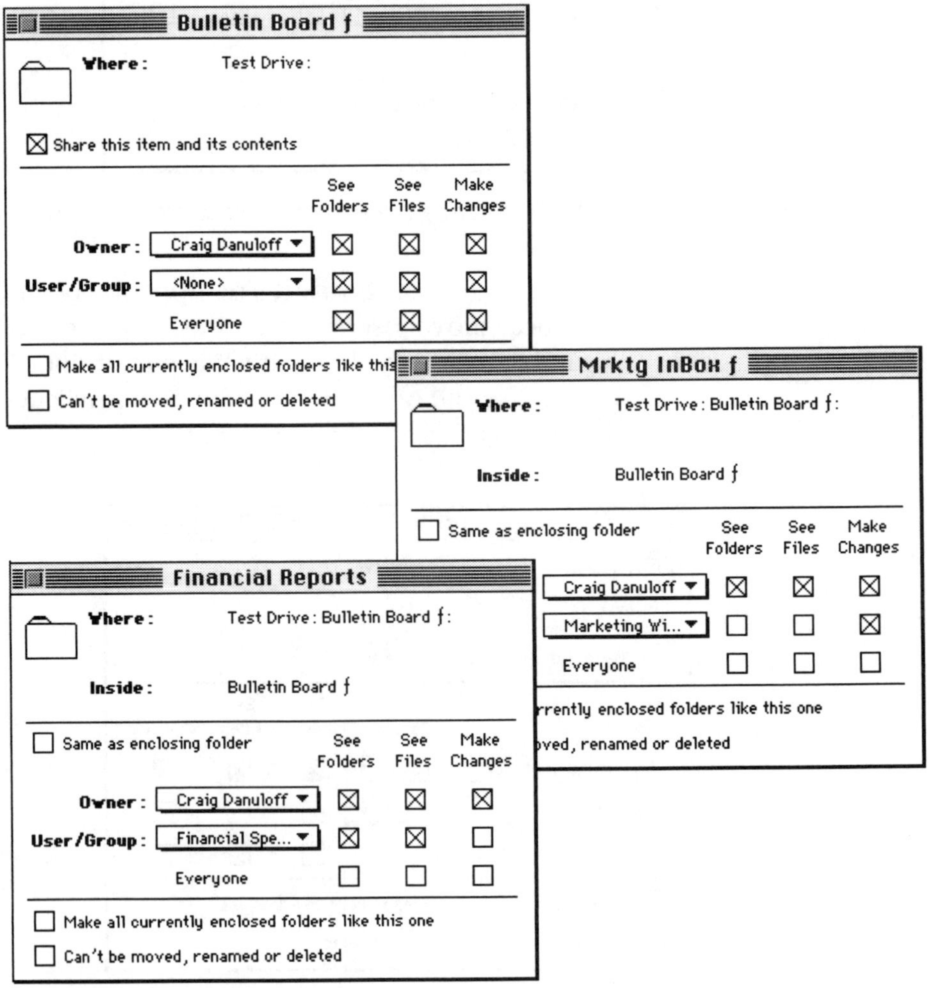

Figure 9-29: Privileges for several folders in a bulletin board.

- **Provide a group work area.** A simpler but more common way to use access privileges is to make a set of files available to specific users and groups. For example, you may have a folder to which the members of the "Engineers" Group have full privileges, while members of the "Sales Reps" team can see the files but not modify them.

Monitoring File Sharing

The File Sharing Monitor control panel gives you information about the items shared, the users connected to your computer, and the activities of these users. Open the File Sharing Monitor, and the control panel shown in Figure 9-30 appears.

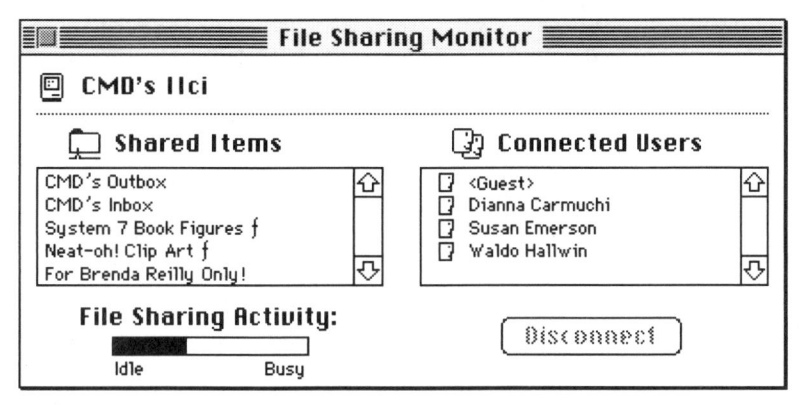

Figure 9-30: The File Sharing Monitor dialog box.

The scrolling window on the left side of this dialog box presents a list of the folders and volumes you've shared. The one on the right side lists network users currently connected to your Macintosh. You can disconnect any user by selecting the user's name from this list and clicking the Disconnect button. A dialog box lets you give the selected user warning by delaying disconnection for the number of minutes you select, or you can use the default 0 minutes and disconnect immediately.

The last item in this control panel is the File Sharing Activity Monitor. This gauge fluctuates with the demands on your computer system as connected users access your Macintosh. When the demand is high, the local operation of your Macintosh slows. If slowdowns caused by remote users are a persistent problem, you may need to limit the access of Registered Users and Guests by reducing the amount of shared data you make available. Or you can shift some shared data to dedicated AppleShare file servers.

Moving On

The power and possibility File Sharing offers will undoubtedly change the way you work on a Macintosh network. File Sharing removes almost all the barriers—physical and psychological—that previously inhibited the flow of data between computers. With File Sharing, you can

- Make any folder or volume on your computer available to anyone connected to your Macintosh network.
- Designate who can access the files and folders you share.
- Specify privileges extended to each regular user, and network guest.

In Chapter 10, you'll see the other side of the File Sharing coin—accessing data shared by other Macs, and by centralized file servers. You'll also look at other aspects of network life, such as coexistence with Macs running system software 6.0x.

Chapter 10: Working on a Network

Macintosh users have long known the benefits of computer networking. Shared printers, and other peripheral Mac-to-Mac communications, and remote access to network file servers are commonplace on almost every Mac network. System 7 offers additional networking capabilities, such as File Sharing, support for aliasing, the Edition Manager and IAC.

This chapter focuses on using your Macintosh network to access AppleShare and File Sharing volumes; the effects of access privileges; and how you control files stored on remote volumes. We'll also look at IAC's Program Linking and networks that include Macs still running system software 6.0x.

Accessing Network Volumes

As described in Chapter 9, "Introduction to File Sharing," every System 7 Macintosh on your network can share up to 10 folders or volumes with other network users, based on user and group access privilege designations for each Mac that shares network data. In addition, dedicated AppleShare file servers can make any number of complete volumes available to all network users, according to specified access privileges.

Connecting to other System 7 Macs for File Sharing and AppleShare file server access is easy. This section describes how to do it and how to manage shared data.

Connecting With the Chooser

The first step in accessing network data is to open the Chooser (in the Apple Menu) and click on the AppleShare icon as shown in the upper-left corner of Figure 10-1. (If this icon does not appear in your Chooser, run the Installer and choose the AppleShare (workstation) option in the Customize dialog box.)

The available network file servers appear on the right side of the window, and if your network is divided into zones, those zones are listed in the lower left corner of the Chooser. If a zone list appears in your Chooser, select the zone in which that Macintosh is registered; available server volumes in that zone will appear.

The list of file server names that appears includes both dedicated AppleShare file servers and Macs on your network using

System 7's File Sharing. There's no easy way to tell from the listing which are AppleShare servers and which are File Sharing Macintoshes. In any case, as a client accessing data over the network, it makes no difference to you whether you're accessing data from a dedicated AppleShare file server or from a File Sharing Macintosh.

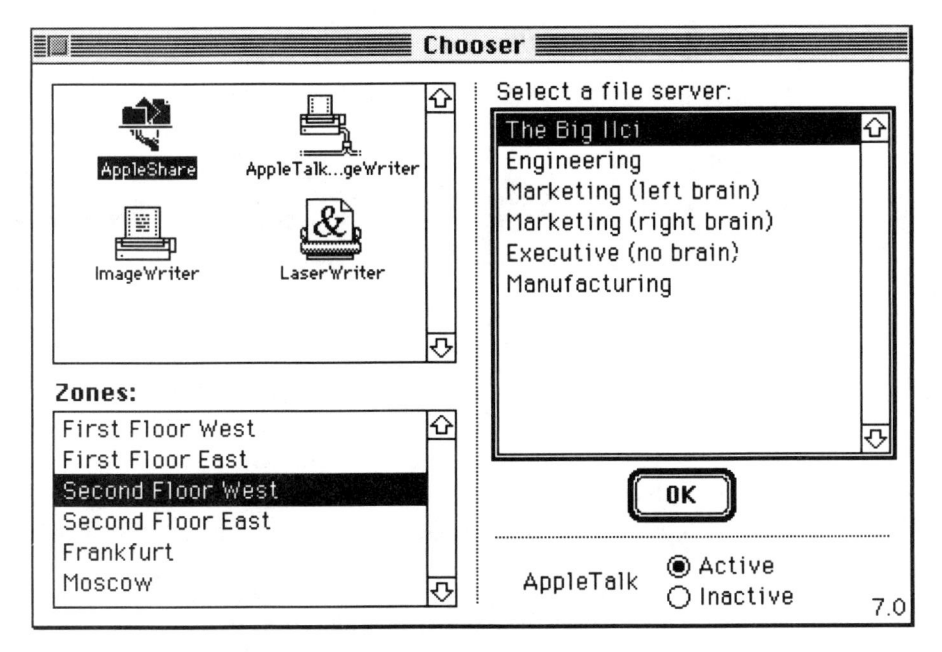

Figure 10-1: The Chooser with zone and file server listings.

When you've located the name of the file server you wish to access, double-click on the file name, or click the OK button below the file server list. The Connect dialog box appears (shown in Figure 10-2). This dialog box gives you the option of connecting to the selected file server as a Guest or as a Registered User.

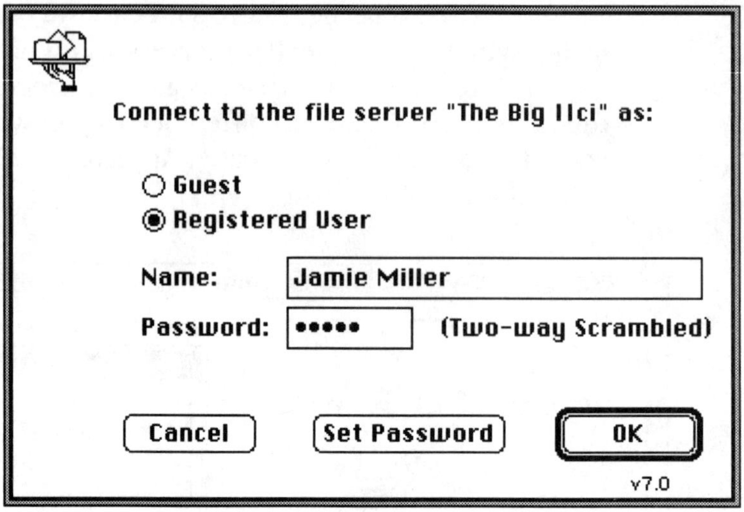

Figure 10-2: The Connect dialog box.

In order to connect as a Registered User, a user icon with your name and password must exist on the AppleShare server or File Sharing Macintosh. This shows that the system administrator or Macintosh owner has created and defined your Macintosh as a Registered User, as described in Chapter 9.

You can now click the Registered User option. The Owner Name specified in your Sharing Setup control panel will appear as the default in the Name option box. If this is not the name under which you're registered, make required changes to the Name option. If a password has been assigned, enter it in the Password option. If none is needed, leave the option blank. Then click the OK button.

Connecting as a Guest is simpler but may restrict your access privileges. Of course, this is your only option if you're not a Registered User. To connect as a Guest, click the Guest option, then click the OK button. If the selected file server does not allow Guests to connect, the Guest option will be dimmed. In this case, the only way to connect is to contact the Macintosh owner or server administrator and ask to become a Registered User.

The final option in the Connect dialog box is the Set Password button which allows Registered Users with appropriate access privileges to reset their passwords for a particular file server. Changing your password affects only the currently selected file server, not all servers on which you're a Registered User.

Selecting Specific Volumes

After identifying yourself as either Registered User or Guest (and clicking the OK button) a list of available volumes on the selected server appears, as shown in Figure 10-3. (If an incorrect name or password was entered, an Alert dialog box appears and you'll be returned to the Connect dialog box.)

This dialog box lists all volumes that the selected server is sharing with the network. (When accessing File Sharing volumes, it's not possible to differentiate between shared folders and shared volumes, so we'll use the term volumes generically.) The names of any volumes you're not allowed to access will be dimmed. You can mount any one non-dimmed volume by double-clicking on the volume name or selecting the volume name and clicking the OK button. To mount more than one volume, hold down the Shift key while selecting volume names, then click the OK button.

```
┌─────────────────────────────────────────────┐
│  📬   The Big IIci                          │
│       Select the items you want to use:     │
│       ┌─────────────────────────────┬───┬─┐ │
│       │ Monthly Reports             │ ☒ │⇧│ │
│       │ Stationary & Editions       │ ☐ │ │ │
│       │ Raunchy Clip Art            │ ☐ │ │ │
│       │ In Box (DPA Mac.)           │ ☐ │⇩│ │
│       └─────────────────────────────┴───┴─┘ │
│       Checked items (   ) will be opened at │
│       system startup time.                  │
│            ⦿ Save My Name Only              │
│            ○ Save My Name and Password      │
│       ┌──────────┐         ┌──────────────┐ │
│       │  Cancel  │         │      OK      │ │
│       └──────────┘         └──────────────┘ │
│                                       v7.0  │
└─────────────────────────────────────────────┘
```

Figure 10-3: Available Server Listing.

You can also configure the volume to mount automatically each time you start up your Macintosh, by clicking on the check box next to a volume name. But you'll have to enter your password manually each time you start your Macintosh and the volume is mounted, since by default your password is not stored as part of this automatic-mount process. To simplify the automatic mount (but at the same time reducing security), click the "Save My Name and Password" option, then double-click the volume name or click the OK button.

After mounting a volume, you're returned to the Connect dialog box. To mount additional volumes from the selected file server, click the OK button again to return to the volume list, and repeat the mounting process for another volume.

Remote Volumes & Access Privileges

Any remote volumes you've mounted appear on your desktop as AppleShare Volume icons, as shown in Figure 10-4. This icon also accompanies these volumes in Open or Save As dialog boxes. These volumes are used just like local volumes (those physically connected to your Mac) except for any restrictions imposed by your access privileges. When your Macintosh is communicating with remote volumes, arrows flash just to the left of your Apple Menu, as shown in Figure 10-4.

Figure 10-4: A volume icon on the desktop (left), and the activity arrows that flash while remote volumes are accessed (right).

As described in Chapter 9, access privileges determine whether you can See Folders, See Files and Make Changes to available volumes. The Finder windows for remotely accessed volumes indicate your access privileges by displaying small icons in the upper left corner, just below the title bar (shown in Figure 10-5). To see your assigned access privileges, choose the Sharing command from the File menu while the folder is selected or open.

Figure 10-5: The Cannot Write, Cannot See Folders and Cannot See Files icons.

When you don't have Make Changes privileges, you can't save or copy a file to a volume. In Save dialog boxes, the Save button is dimmed when the selected volume is write protected in this way; and, at the Finder, any attempt to copy or create files will bring up the dialog box shown in Figure 10-6.

This same dialog box will appear if you attempt to create a new folder on a volume for which you don't have See Folders privileges.

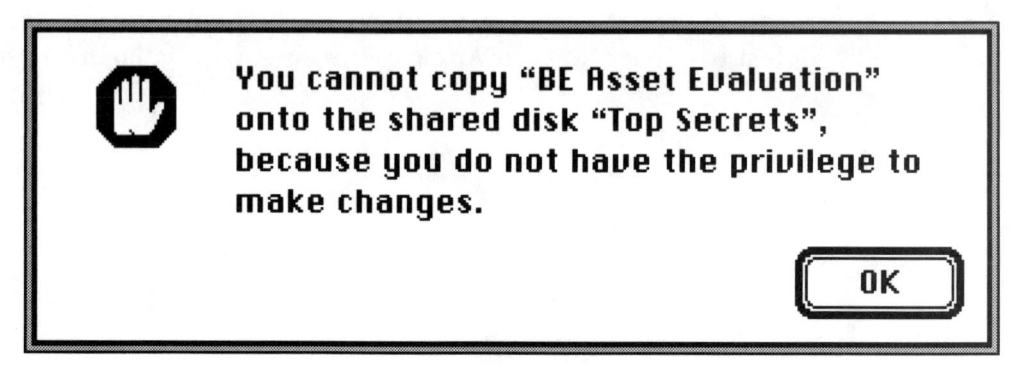

> **You cannot copy "BE Asset Evaluation" onto the shared disk "Top Secrets", because you do not have the privilege to make changes.**
>
> [OK]

Figure 10-6: Not Enough Access Privileges dialog box.

Use the Sharing command to see the complete access privileges for any volume you can mount. Select the volume icon and choose the Sharing command from the File menu. If you own the volume, you can change these access privileges. If you create a folder on a shared volume, you're automatically assigned as the folder's owner and allowed to use the File menu's Sharing command to reset the access privileges.

A Volume Access Shortcut

To avoid this lengthy process every time you mount a networked volume, you can create an alias of the volume icon that appears on your desktop, and store that icon in a convenient spot on your hard drive. In fact, you can create a folder full of network volume icons (see Figure 10-7).

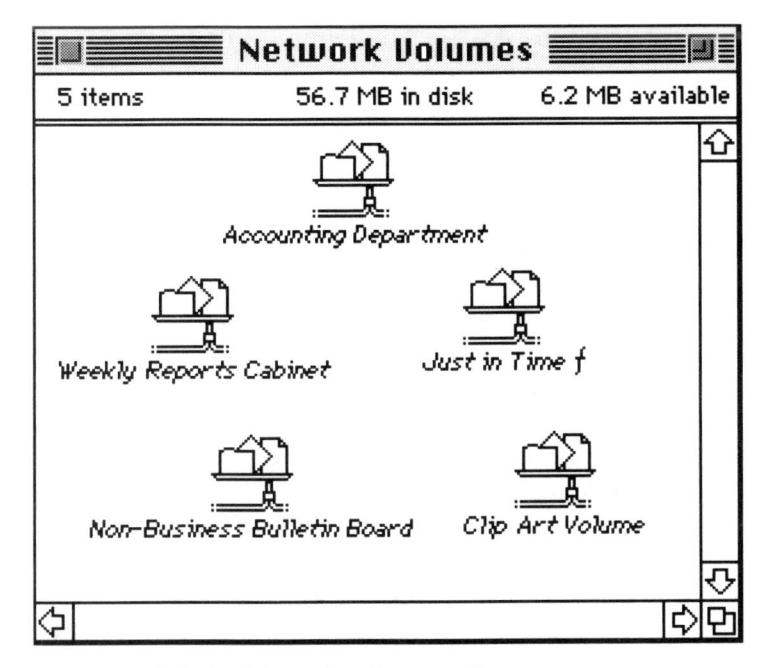

Figure 10-7: Folder of volume aliases.

Double-clicking on the network volume alias icon mounts the volume, after you supply any necessary passwords. This shortcut can save lots of time and effort.

Disconnecting From Remote Volumes

There are three ways to disconnect a mounted network volume:

- **Trash the volume.** Simply drag the volume icon into the Trash. Just as this action ejects removable disks, it releases mounted file server volumes.

- **Shut Down or Restart.** All mounted volumes are also released when you use the Shut Down or Restart command.

- **Put Away.** The File menu's Put Away command, or its keyboard equivalent, Command-Y, dismounts any selected volumes.

Accessing Your Hard Drive Remotely

When File Sharing is on, you can access your entire hard drive and all volumes currently mounted from anywhere on your network—unless you've deselected the Allow user to see entire volume option in the Owner Preferences window of the Users & Groups control panel. This option is accessed by double-clicking on the user icon that displays your Owner name.

To reach your hard drive from another Mac on your network, select the Chooser just as you would to log onto any network volume. Locate the name of your Macintosh in the scrolling file server list, and double-click on it. A new dialog box appears, listing the name of each hard drive connected to your Macintosh. These are not volumes you've shared with the Sharing command; they're complete hard drives as they appear on the Macintosh desktop. To mount your drive, double-click on the drive name, or select the drive name and click the OK button.

Your hard drive then appears on the desktop of the Macintosh you're using, with AppleShare volume icons. You now have complete access to your drive, including all files and folders, with no limitations based on access privileges. You can create files and folders, delete files, redefine Users & Groups, set File Sharing access privileges or do anything else you could do if you were sitting at your own Mac keyboard.

When you're finished using a remotely mounted hard drive, you can release it, just like you would any other volume, by dragging it to the trash, using the Put Away command, or shutting down and restarting.

Program Linking

As mentioned in Chapter 7, "The Edition Manager and IAC," applications specifically programmed to support Apple Events can communicate with application programs residing on any AppleShare server or File Sharing volume on the network. If you use any programs that can take advantage of Program Linking, and want these programs to communicate with the applications on your hard drive, you must specifically enable Program Linking.

The master control for Program Linking is found in the Sharing Setup control panel, as shown in Figure 10-8. The message in the Status area will document the Program Linking start-up process. Once Program Linking is running, the Start button becomes the Stop button.

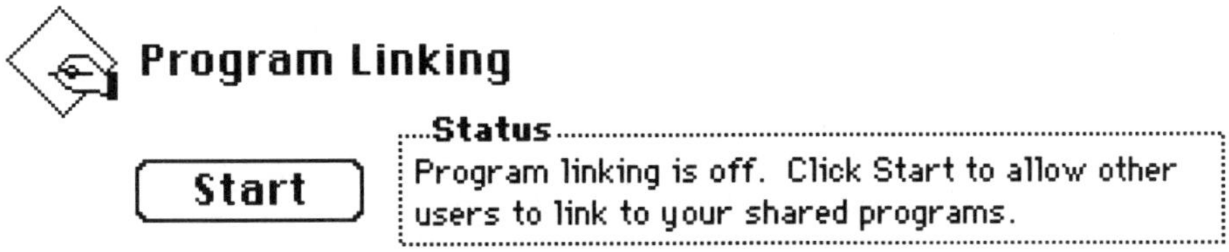

Program Linking

[Start] Status: Program linking is off. Click Start to allow other users to link to your shared programs.

Figure 10-8: The Sharing Setup dialog box provides the master control for Program Linking.

Program Linking must also be enabled in the Macintosh owner icon found in the Users & Groups control panel. (The Macintosh owner icon has a dark border around it and displays the name entered in the Sharing Setup dialog box.) Double-clicking on this icon displays the dialog box shown in Figure 10-9. The Program Linking option, in the lower portion of this dialog box, enables Program Linking.

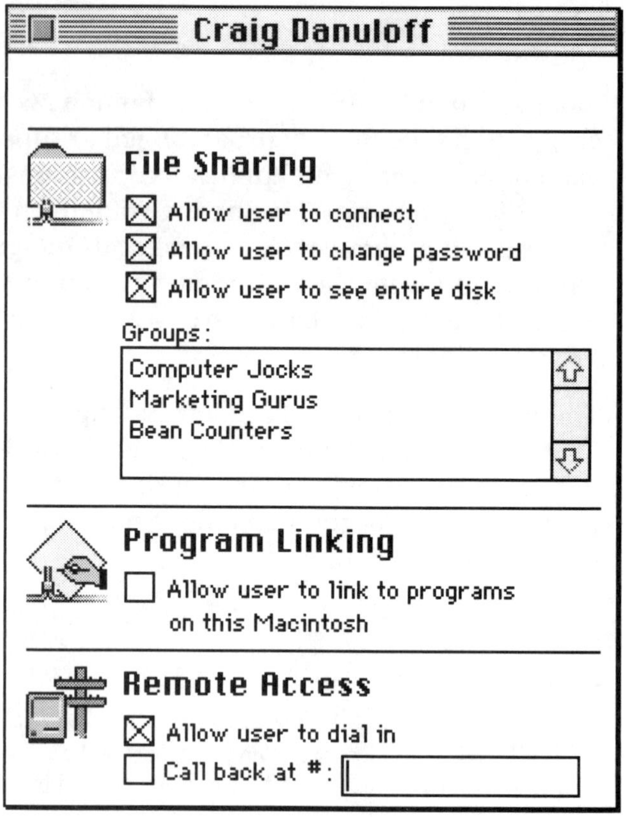

```
┌──────────────────────────────────────────┐
│ ▣ ═══════ Craig Danuloff ═══════         │
│                                          │
│  ┌─────  File Sharing                    │
│  │▨▨▨│  ☒ Allow user to connect          │
│  └─────  ☒ Allow user to change password │
│          ☒ Allow user to see entire disk │
│          Groups:                         │
│          ┌────────────────────────┬─┐    │
│          │ Computer Jocks         │▲│    │
│          │ Marketing Gurus        │ │    │
│          │ Bean Counters          │ │    │
│          │                        │▼│    │
│          └────────────────────────┴─┘    │
│                                          │
│  ┌─────  Program Linking                 │
│  │ ✍  │  ☐ Allow user to link to programs│
│  └─────     on this Macintosh            │
│                                          │
│  ┌─────  Remote Access                   │
│  │ 🖥  │  ☒ Allow user to dial in         │
│  └─────  ☐ Call back at #: [_____]   │
└──────────────────────────────────────────┘
```

Figure 10-9: The User Options dialog box for the Macintosh owner.

Even when Program Linking has been turned on and enabled in the File Sharing dialog box, it is only available to applications that support it. This remains a very small number of System 7-Savvy applications.

To initiate Program Linking for an application that supports it, highlight the application you wish to use, then choose the Sharing command from the File menu. A Sharing dialog box appears (see Figure 10-10).

Figure 10-10: An application's Sharing dialog box.

If the application you selected supports Program Linking, the Allow remote program linking check box is displayed. Otherwise, this option will be dimmed. To make the application available for Program Linking, click the check box, then close the Sharing dialog.

Networks With Macs Running System 6.0x

If some of the Macintoshes on your network aren't upgraded to System 7, you can still run them on the network. It's no problem to run system software 6.0x and System 7 on the same network, with one small exception. The exception is the LaserWriter driver file that's installed with System 7.

Updating LaserWriter Drivers

In order to allow everyone on your network to share the same laser printers without having to constantly restart them, you'll have to copy the new LaserWriter driver (version 7.0 or later) into the System Folder of all Macintoshes still using system software 6.0x. There are three files you will need to copy; the LaserWriter driver, LaserPrep and Backgrounder. You can either manually copy these files from the System 7 Printing disk or from the System 7 CD-ROM, or run the Printer Update script which will use the Installer to add these files to any existing System Folder.

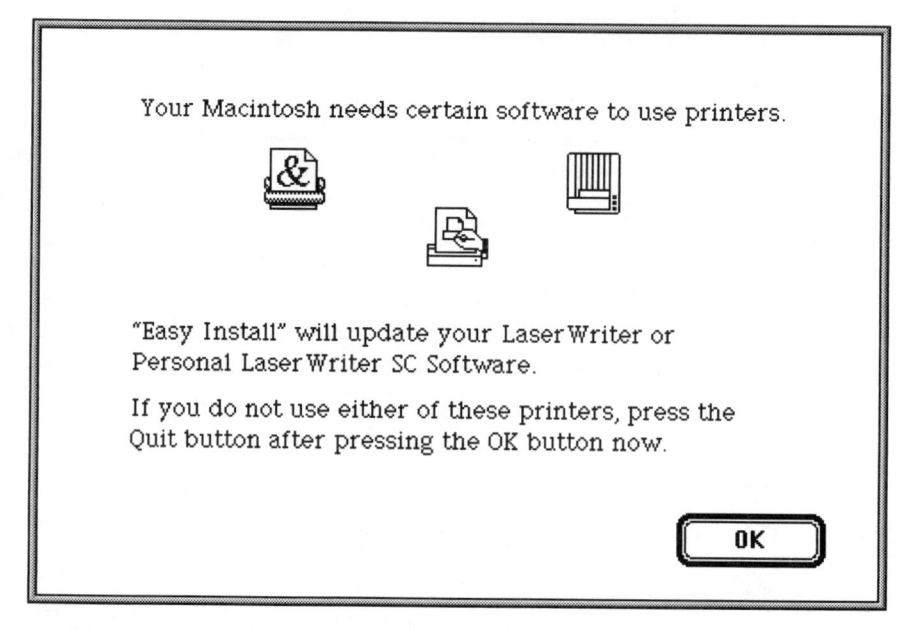

Figure 10-11: The Printer Update Installer screen.

Replacing existing LaserWriter drivers with the LaserWriter driver version 7.0 will work fine—they won't even notice the difference. It's easy to tell when the LaserWriter driver Version 7.0 is being used because its icon is different from the one used by earlier versions. The icons for LaserWriter driver Version 7.0 and Version 5.2 (which is commonly used with system software 6.0x) are shown in Figure 10-12.

Figure 10-12: The LaserWriter 7.0 (left) and 5.2 (right) icons.

It's not impossible to use the older LaserWriter drivers with System 7, which you might be tempted to do if only a few people on your network have upgraded, but this can cause problems with background printing, and is not advised.

If you don't use the same versions of the LaserWriter drivers throughout your network, those who have the different version will be greeted by the Restart Printer dialog box (shown in Figure 10-13) whenever they attempt to print. There's no technical problem with constantly reinitializing your laser printer, but it wastes lots of time. It also causes any downloaded fonts to be removed from the printer's memory at each restart. So, upgrading all LaserWriter drivers to 7.0 is the practical solution.

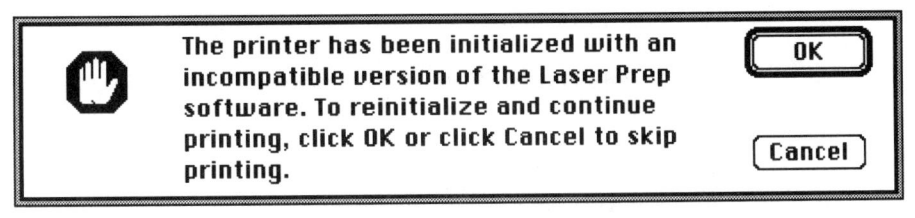

> The printer has been initialized with an incompatible version of the Laser Prep software. To reinitialize and continue printing, click OK or click Cancel to skip printing.

Figure 10-13: The Restart Printer dialog box.

Accessing File Sharing Volumes From System 6.0x

As explained in Chapter 9, any System 7 Macintosh can share up to 10 folders or volumes with the Macintosh Network. These shared volumes are available to Macs running earlier system software versions (such as System 6) as well as those using System 7.

The only requirement is that the AppleShare INIT be installed in the System Folder. The Access Privileges desk accessory should also be installed. Running any version of the system software Installer and choosing the AppleShare (workstation software) option will install all the necessary files.

Once these files are installed, volumes shared by a System 7 Mac using File Sharing, as well as volumes from any network AppleShare servers, can be accessed and used by the System 6 Mac exactly as described in this chapter.

Moving On

Most Macintosh users are first interested in connecting to a network in order to share peripheral devices, such as laser printers, or perhaps network modems. But networks also make it possible for computers to communicate with each other, and for data to be shared either between computers or by accessing centralized file servers.

In this chapter you've seen how to make the most of these abilities:

- Using the Chooser to select an available File Sharing Macintosh or AppleShare server.

- Mounting volumes and setting up automatic mounting connections.

- Working with assigned access privileges.

Next, in Chapter 11, "Memory Management," we focus on the important issue of effectively using the memory available in your Macintosh. We'll examine several System 7 tools that enhance your available memory, and ways you can control the memory used by your applications.

Chapter 11: Memory Management

When someone asks you about your Macintosh, you probably say something like, "I've got a IIci with 5 megs of memory and an 80-meg hard drive." It's no accident that the three variables you use to describe your computer are its model name, the amount of installed RAM and its hard disk size. These are the factors that determine what you can do—the speed and range of activities you can perform—with your computer.

With System 7, the amount of RAM installed in your Mac is still important, but it's no longer the total measure of memory or the only important memory issue. In this chapter, we look at the overall picture of Macintosh memory, including the new Memory control panel options, the About This Macintosh... dialog box and ways you can configure applications to use memory most efficiently.

Memory vs. Storage

Before we jump into the new memory options and implications of System 7, let's clarify the difference between memory (RAM) and storage (disk space). This distinction may be clear to experienced Macintosh users, but if you are not certain that you understand the difference, please read this section carefully.

In the simplest terms, memory is the chips in your computer where data is temporarily stored while it is being used by the Macintosh. This is in contrast to your hard disk, floppy disks and other storage devices where data is permanently stored when it is not being used by your Macintosh.

The differences between memory (or RAM) and hard drives, floppies and other media (which are known as storage) are very important. Both memory and storage hold data—application programs, system software and data files—but the similarities end there. RAM stores data electronically on a set of chips, and as a result, these chips "forget" their contents as soon as the power is turned off, or the Mac is restarted. Storage devices like hard drives and floppy disks operate magnetically, or using new optical technology, and only lose information if it is intentionally erased.

More importantly, the Macintosh can only work with data stored in RAM, it cannot directly manipulate data on any storage device. In order to open an application or file, it must be read from storage and written into memory. Once in memory, the application can be executed or the file can be changed, but to make these changes permanent, the information in RAM must be written back out to the storage device—this is what happens when you choose the Save command.

RAM & You

If we compare the way your Mac uses memory and storage with the way you work and think, perhaps the difference will become more apparent and easier to remember. In this analogy, the computer (and it's processor) plays the part of the human brain, memory (RAM) is equated with our own memory, and floppy and hard disk storage is equated with written or typed notes.

As you know, no information can gain access to your brain without also entering your memory; regardless of whether information originates from your eyes, ears or other senses, it is immediately put into memory (RAM) so that your brain (the Macintosh processor) can access it. But what do we do with information that we want to use in the future? We transfer it to some storage medium, like paper (disk). This way we know that when this information is needed in the future we can transfer it back into memory by reading it. Of course, the fact that humans have both short-term and long-term memory weakens this analogy, but it is generally a useful way to make the distinction between memory and storage.

The Memory Control Panel

One of the realities Macintosh users have to confront is the finite amount of memory available in their computers. Today's software seems to have an insatiable appetite for RAM, and new technologies—like multitasking, 24-bit color and sound—intensify the problem. The crusade for additional memory has traditionally encountered certain roadblocks: the operating system's limited ability to address the need for large amounts of memory, the computer's physical limitations and the high price of memory chips.

System 7 begins the process of breaking down these barriers, or at least temporarily pushing them back. The Memory control panel is one of System 7's new memory-related features. This control panel offers the new virtual memory, 32-bit addressing and RAM disk options, as well as the disk cache option, which is System 7's version of the RAM cache found in the General control panel of earlier Systems. The Memory control panel does not provide all of these options on all Macintosh models, however. When a certain Mac model doesn't support an option, it doesn't appear in the control panel. Each of these options and their compatibility details is described in detail below.

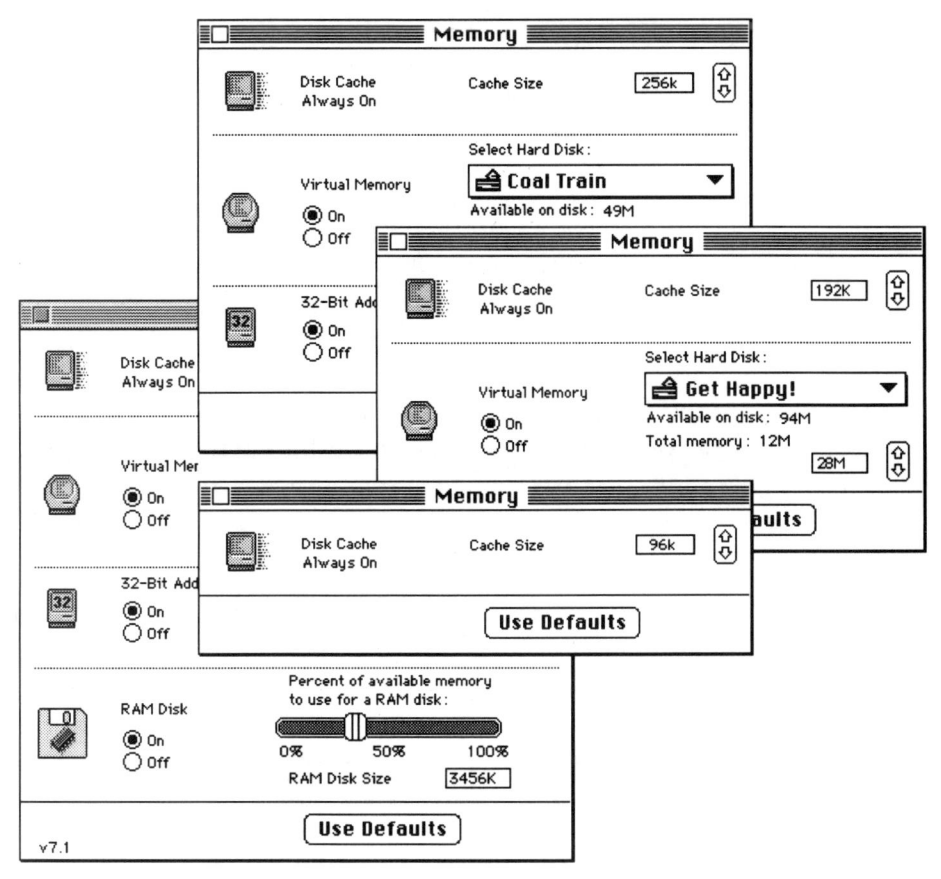

Figure 11-1: The four versions of the Memory control panel that appear on Macintoshes.

Disk Cache

A disk cache is a small section of Macintosh RAM set aside to store a copy of the most recent data read from disk (or volume) into memory. Storing this copy makes the data readily available when it's needed again. Reaccessing data via the RAM-based cache, rather than having to reread it from disk, saves considerable time.

By default, your Macintosh uses 32k of cache for every one megabyte of RAM installed in your Mac. If you have 4 megabytes of RAM, for example, 128k would be the default cache setting. Using the arrows, you can increase or decrease your disk cache size as required.

For most users, settings between 96k and 256k are sufficient. Unless you have specific memory limitations, you shouldn't reduce the cache below its default setting, since the small amount of memory the cache consumes significantly improves your Macintosh's performance. In most cases, you should not increase the size of your cache too much either, as there is a distinct point of diminishing returns after which more disk cache will actually slow down your Macintosh. Settings over 384k or perhaps 512k should be used only in very specific situations.

The perfect disk cache size is a matter of great debate even among the most technically knowledgeable Macintosh users. Your Macintosh hardware and software configuration, and the way you use your Mac has a big effect on your optimal setting, so trial and error is really the only way to find what works best for you.

Virtual Memory

Virtual memory is a software trick. It uses space on your hard drive to "fool" the Macintosh into thinking there's more available memory than there really is. Using virtual memory, a Macintosh with only 2 or 4 Mb of actual RAM can act like it has 12 Mb or more. In fact, in conjunction with 32-bit addressing (discussed later in this chapter), virtual memory can provide your Macintosh up to 1 gigabyte (1000 Mb) of memory.

Virtual memory substitutes hard disk space for RAM. One benefit of using this device is that hard drive space is generally much less expensive than actual RAM. In addition, with

32-bit addressing, virtual memory can provide access to more memory than is possible with RAM chips alone. (The 32-bit addressing option is described later in this chapter.)

However, using virtual memory has two main drawbacks. First, performance is slower than with real RAM, since the mechanical actions required of your hard drive are no match for the electronic speed of RAM chips. Second, virtual memory appropriates hard disk space normally available for other activities.

In order to use virtual memory, your Macintosh must be equipped with a 68030 or better processor, such as the Macintosh SE/30, Macintosh IIci, IIsi or IIfx. Virtual memory can also be used with a 68020 Macintosh II, with a PMMU chip installed. Virtual memory cannot be used with the Macintosh Plus, Classic, SE, LC or Portable.

Without 32-bit addressing, virtual memory provides the following amounts of memory to your Macintosh:

▪ Macintosh Plus, Classic, SE, Portable, LC, II, PowerBook 100	None
▪ Mac IIx, IIcx, SE/30 or II w/PMMU	14 Mb less 1 Mb per installed NuBus card
▪ Other Macintoshes	14 Mb less 1 Mb per installed NuBus card

With 32-bit addressing, the virtual memory option provides these amounts of memory:

▪ Macintosh Plus, Classic, SE, Portable, LC or II, PowerBook 100	None
▪ Mac IIx, IIcx, SE/30 or II w/PMMU	14 Mb less 1 Mb per installed NuBus card
▪ Other Macintoshes	1 gigabyte

Enabling Virtual Memory

If your Macintosh supports virtual memory, go to the Memory control panel to activate this feature. After clicking the On button, the Select Hard Disk option becomes available. From the pop-up menu, select the hard disk volume on which the virtual memory storage file will be created and stored.

The amount of available space on the selected hard disk is displayed below the hard disk pop-up menu. The amount of free space available determines the amount of virtual memory that can be configured. A virtual memory storage file, equal to the total amount of memory available while using virtual memory, will be placed on the selected disk. In other words, if your Macintosh has 4 Mb of actual RAM, and you wish to reach 12 Mb by using 8 Mb of virtual memory, a 12 Mb virtual memory storage file must be created on the selected volume.

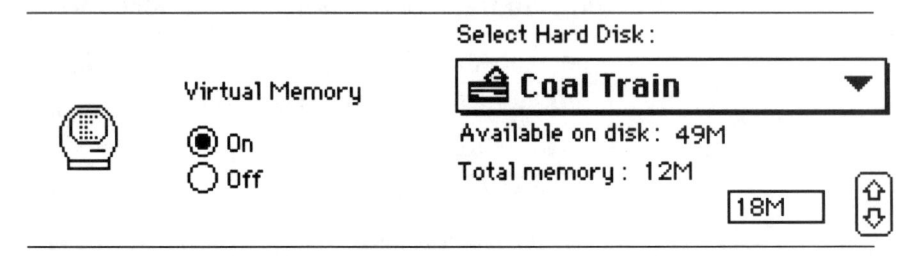

Figure 11-2: The virtual memory option in the Memory control panel determines the size and location of the virtual memory file.

Appearing below the Available on disk option is the total amount of memory currently available. The After restart option indicates the amount of memory specified, including actual RAM and virtual memory. Click on the arrows to modify this specification. If the After restart option is not visible, click one of the arrows until it appears.

The amount of memory you can specify depends on your hardware configuration and the 32-bit addressing option setting. Without 32-bit addressing, you can specify up to 14 Mb of memory *minus* one megabyte for each NuBus card installed in your Macintosh. If 32-bit addressing is turned on, up to 1 gigabyte of memory can be specified, depending on which Mac you have and the free space available on the selected hard disk.

Any changes made to the virtual memory option will not take effect until your Macintosh is restarted. When you finish setting the Memory control panel options, close the control panel and restart. To verify that virtual memory is on, choose the About This Macintosh command to display the current memory status. (More information on the About This Macintosh dialog box later in this chapter.)

Virtual Memory Performance

Virtual memory works by moving information between a disk-based swap file and the RAM inside the computer; even when virtual memory is being used, the Macintosh communicates only with the real RAM. This movement of data between hard disk and RAM, technically known as *paging*, causes the Macintosh to perform slower than it does when using actual RAM alone.

The amount of paging slowdown depends on how much actual RAM is available and how virtual memory is being used. The more available RAM, the less paging interference. The type of activity called for also affects paging; working on multi-megabyte data files and frequent switching between open applications are examples of activities that usually require more paging and therefore decrease performance.

A good rule of thumb in determining your own RAM/virtual memory mix is that you should have enough actual RAM to cover your normal memory needs and enough supplemental virtual memory to handle occasional abnormally large requirements. If you find that approximately 4 Mb of RAM let you work comfortably in the three or four open applications you use regularly, but you occasionally need 8 Mb to open additional applications or work with large data files, then 4 Mb of real RAM and a total of 10 Mb of RAM and virtual memory would probably appropriate. Trying to get by with just 2 Mb of real RAM and 10 Mb of virtual memory would result in prohibitively slow performance and the potential for crashes caused by the heavy paging.

Disabling Virtual Memory

Virtual memory can be turned off by clicking on the Off button in the virtual memory area of the Memory control panel and restarting your Macintosh. After disabling virtual memory, the virtual memory storage file is usually deleted from your hard drive automatically. If it isn't, you can remove it by dragging it to the Trash.

32-Bit Addressing

In the past, 8 Mb was the maximum amount of RAM that could be installed (or used) on the Macintosh. This limitation was posed by the way the available memory chips were addressed by the Macintosh system software, including those parts that reside on the ROM chips on the computer's logic board. When used on Macintosh computers containing newer versions of the ROM chips, System 7 breaks the 8-megabyte barrier, allowing up to 1 gigabyte of RAM (a gigabyte equals 1000 Mb!).

This extended ability to use memory is called *32-bit addressing*, referring to the number of digits used in the new memory-addressing scheme. The Mac's older memory scheme is *24-bit addressing*, since only 24 digits are used. Twenty four-bit addressing is still used on most Macintosh models, and is also supported by System 7.

The ROM chips required for 32-bit addressing are *32-bit clean ROMs*, and are currently included in all shipping Macintoshes except the Macintosh Classic and the PowerBook 100. Several certain "older" models, specifically, the Plus, Classic, SE, SE/30, Portable, II, IIx, IIcx and LC, do not have 32-bit clean ROMs, and therefore can't normally use 32-bit addressing. The SE/30 and Macintosh II, IIx and IIcx can be upgraded to 32-bit clean capacity using an extension called MODE32, or the 32-bit Addressing system enabler, both of which are available without charge from Apple via user groups and online services.

When used on a 32-bit compatible Mac, the Memory control panel includes the 32-bit addressing option, as shown in Figure 11-3. When the option is set to Off, the Macintosh uses 24-bit addressing and only 8 Mb of RAM can be used (or up to 14 Mb of virtual memory). When set to On, the Mac uses 32-bit addressing and all installed RAM (within the limits discussed below) becomes available to the system software. Changes to this option take effect only after restarting the Macintosh. The 32-bit addressing option does not appear on Macs which are not 32-bit compatible.

Figure 11-3: The 32-bit addressing option.

Most Macs using 32-bit addressing can access up to 128 Mb of real RAM and up to 1 gigabyte of virtual memory (as described earlier in this chapter). Some older software applications written and released before the introduction of System 7 are not compatible with 32-bit addressing, and so you will have to turn 32-bit addressing off to use them. These incompatible applications are fairly rare, but if you notice unpredictable behavior on your Mac, or frequent crashes, and you're using one or more older applications, utilities or extensions, try turning 32-bit addressing off to see if the problems are related to 32-bit addressing incompatibility.

In some cases, launching an application that's not compatible with 32-bit addressing will cause a dialog box to appear, warning you that you must restart your Macintosh with 32-bit addressing turned off. Most of the time, however, this dialog box will not appear and you'll have to find this out the hard way, by experiencing a system crash or unpredictable behavior.

If your Mac has more than 8 Mb of RAM installed, or you want to use more than 16 Mb of virtual memory, you should activate 32-bit addressing. If more than 8 Mb of RAM is installed and you don't turn 32-bit addressing on, the About This Macintosh dialog box will report that your system software is consuming all of your RAM over 8 Mb. (This dialog box is discussed more fully later in this chapter.) If you have 8 Mb of RAM or less, and don't need to use 16 Mb of virtual memory or more, you should leave the 32-bit addressing disabled.

Memory Control Panel Tips

- **Use at least the minimum recommended disk cache.** The disk cache speeds up operation, so you should leave it set to at least 32k for every megabyte of RAM installed in your Mac. (That means 64 for 2 Mb, 128k for 4 Mb and 256k for 8 Mb.)

- **Install enough real RAM in your Macintosh.** Real RAM chips should provide enough memory to cover your normal daily memory needs—at least 4 Mb and in some cases up to 8 Mb. Although virtual memory can provide inexpensive additional memory, 80 percent of your memory needs should be covered by real RAM. The performance drawbacks of relying too heavily on virtual memory don't justify the relatively small amount of money saved.

- **Extend your available memory with virtual memory.** Once you've installed enough RAM to satisfy your everyday needs, use the virtual memory to give yourself extra memory to cover special occasional situations, such as working with large color images, animation or more than the usual number of simultaneously open programs.

  If you have 4 or 8 Mb of real RAM in your Mac, 10 to 12 Mb of supplemental virtual memory is recommended. Users with 32-bit compatible Macs can go beyond the 14-megabyte limit up to 1 gigabyte, although amounts of 20 to 30 megabytes will usually suffice.

- **Use 32-bit addressing carefully.** Although most old applications and nearly every new application is compatible with 32-bit addressing, there are a few programs out there that still don't run well (or at all) with 32-bit addressing activated. When using a program for the first time after turning on 32-bit addressing, save your data frequently until you're sure the program is working properly. Leave 32-bit addressing turned off if you don't need to use it.

Controlling Memory

Once you've determined how much memory you need and made it available to System 7 (by installing RAM, using virtual memory and 32-bit addressing), you'll want to manage that memory wisely and use it economically. Managing your Mac's memory allows you to make sure that each application has enough RAM to operate properly, and that enough total memory is available to open as many different applications as necessary.

System 7 provides two excellent tools for memory management—the About This Macintosh dialog box and the Get Info dialog box. We'll look at both of these tools in this section.

About This Macintosh

In System 7, the familiar About The Finder command has been changed to About This Macintosh, and the dialog box associated with it has been improved. As shown in Figure 11-4, the About This Macintosh dialog box provides information about the Macintosh being used, your system software version, installed and available memory, and the amount of memory used by each open application.

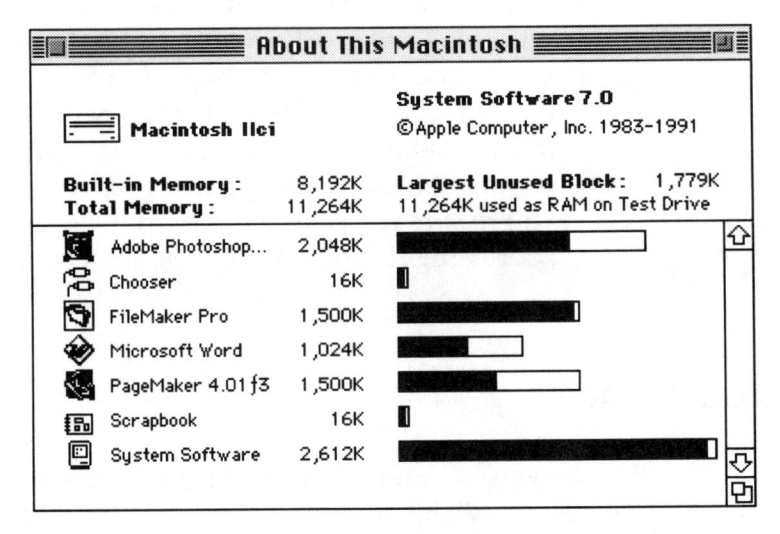

Figure 11-4: The About This Macintosh dialog box.

The upper section of the dialog box gives the icon and name for your Macintosh, the version of system software currently in use, and the following data related to the memory available in your Mac:

- **Built-in Memory.** The amount of actual RAM installed in your Macintosh, not including virtual memory. This listing does not appear on Macintoshes that don't support virtual memory, such as the Plus, Classic, Portable and LC.

- **Total Memory.** Documents the total memory available in your Macintosh, including installed RAM plus available virtual memory. If virtual memory is being used, the name of the hard disk storing that file and the amount of hard drive space being used are listed to the right of the Total Memory listing.

  Virtual memory and hard drive designations are set via the Memory control panel, as described earlier in this chapter.

- **Largest Unused Block.** The largest contiguous section of memory currently not being used by open software applications. This number is important because it determines both the number and size of additional software applications you can open.

  In some cases, the Largest Unused Block will not equal the amount of total memory available, less the size of all open applications. That's because as applications are launched and quit, memory becomes fragmented—gaps are created between sections of memory that are used and those that are available. To defragment your memory and create larger unused blocks, quit all open applications and then relaunch them. As they're relaunched, applications will use available memory sequentially, leaving the largest possible unused block.

Each software application requires a particular amount of memory in order to be opened successfully. The amount of memory is documented, and can be controlled, in the Get Info dialog box, as described later in this chapter. When a program is launched, if its memory requirement is larger than the Largest Unused Block, it can't be opened. So you need to know approximately how much memory an application needs.

The lower portion of the About This Macintosh dialog box displays information about each open application, including its name, icon and amount of memory allocated and used.

- **Application name and icon.** Each open application is listed in alphabetical order along with a small version of its icon.

- **Amount of memory allocated.** Just to the right of the application name, the total amount of memory that was allocated to that program when it was opened, along with a bar graph showing this amount in relation to amounts used by other open applications. The total bar represents total allocated memory; the filled portion of the bar represents the portion of that allocated memory currently in use.

- **Amount of memory used.** In most cases when an application is opened, only a portion of its total allocated memory is used immediately. Usually, some of the memory is used by the application itself, some is used to hold open document files, and some is left over for use by the software's commands and features. Only the memory currently being used appears as the filled-in percentage of the memory allocation bar.

An About This Macintosh Tip

- **A secret dialog box.** Holding down the option key changes the About This Macintosh command into the About The Finder command, which brings up a copyright screen (shown in Figure 11-5), that first appeared in Finder 1.0 in 1984.

Figure 11-5: The About The Finder dialog box.

The Get Info Dialog Box

The Get Info dialog box allows you to use the information provided in the About This Macintosh dialog box to take charge of your Macintosh's memory use. You do this by adjusting the amount of memory each program uses, to minimize problems related to memory shortages or better allocate your available RAM to the different applications you want to open simultaneously.

The memory related options of the Get Info dialog box are different in System 7 version 7.0 and version 7.1, so we will examine each of these separately.

Get Info in Version 7.0

The Get Info dialog box's Memory option is shown as it appears in version 7.0 in Figure 11-6. The Memory option has two parts: Suggested Memory Size and Current Size.

- **Suggested Size.** The amount of RAM memory the developer recommends to properly run the application. You can't change this option, but it's very valuable as a reminder of the original Current Size setting.

- **Current Size.** Specifies the actual amount of RAM memory that the application will request when it's launched. (By default, the Current Size is equal to the Suggested Size.) You can change the amount of memory that will be allocated by entering a new value in this option, then closing the Get Info dialog box.

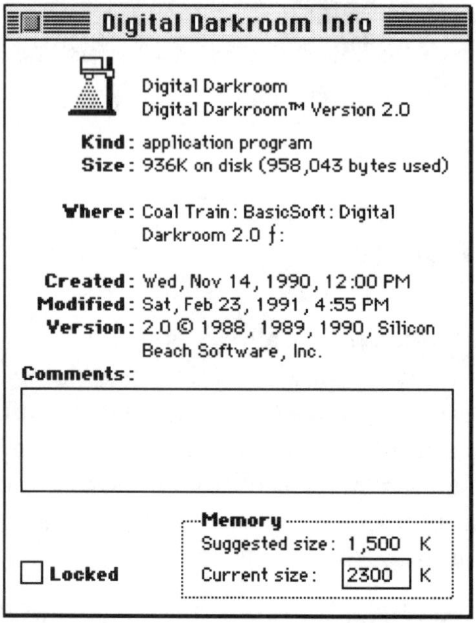

Figure 11-6: An application's Get Info dialog box in System 7.0.

When an application is launched, the program requests the amount of memory specified in the "Current Size" option. If this amount is available in an unused block, the memory is allocated and the program is opened. You can check the size of the largest available block in the About This Macintosh dialog box, as described earlier.

If the amount of memory requested is larger than the largest available unused block, a dialog box will appear, stating that not enough memory is available (shown in Figure 11-7), asking if you want to try to run the application using less memory (shown in Figure 11-8), or suggesting that you quit an open application to create enough free memory (see Figure 11-9).

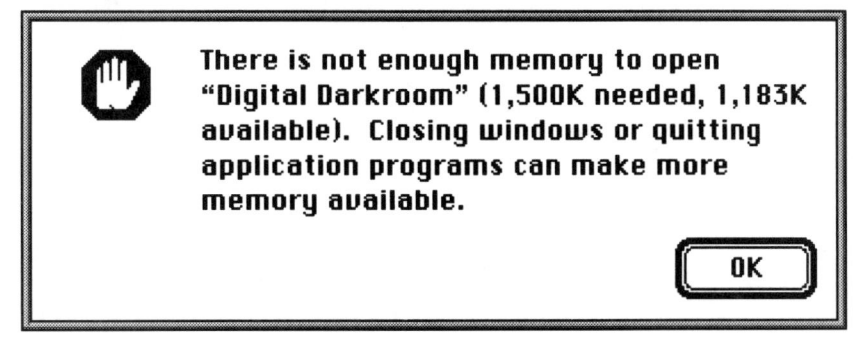

> There is not enough memory to open "Digital Darkroom" (1,500K needed, 1,183K available). Closing windows or quitting application programs can make more memory available.
>
> [OK]

Figure 11-7: The not enough memory dialog box.

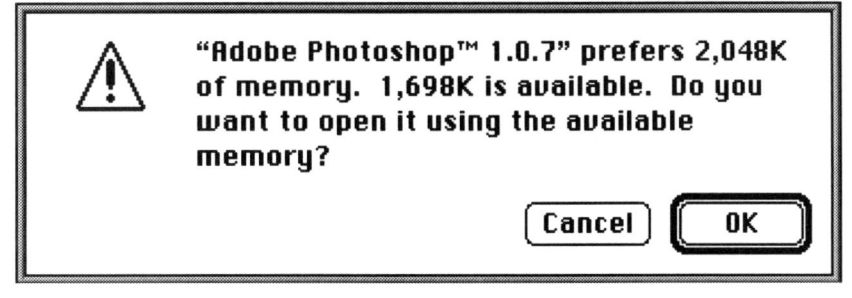

> "Adobe Photoshop™ 1.0.7" prefers 2,048K of memory. 1,698K is available. Do you want to open it using the available memory?
>
> [Cancel] [OK]

Figure 11-8: The almost enough memory dialog box.

> There is not enough memory to open "FileMaker Pro" (3,530K needed, 3,523K available).
>
> To make more memory available, try quitting "Adobe Photoshop® 2.0.1".
>
> [OK]

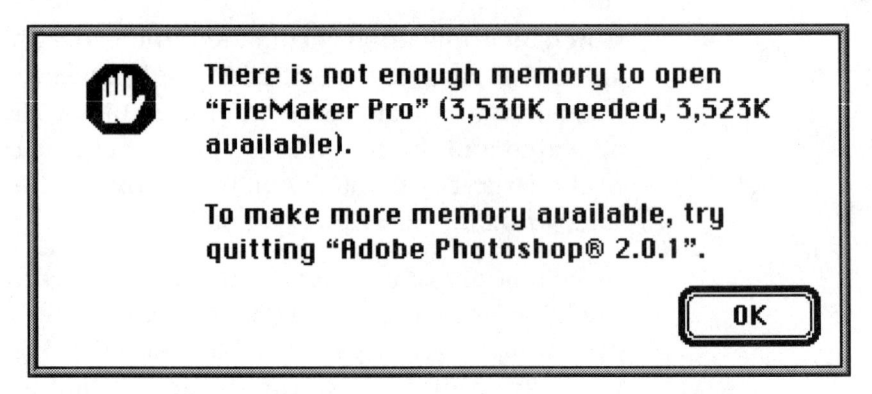

Figure 11-9: The enough memory if you quit dialog box.

Get Info in Version 7.1

In System 7 version 7.1, the Get Info dialog box's options eliminate the need to change settings for different memory situations by allowing you to set options that determine the amount of memory that will be used depending on the amount of memory available at launch time. The version 7.1 Memory option is shown in Figure 11-10.

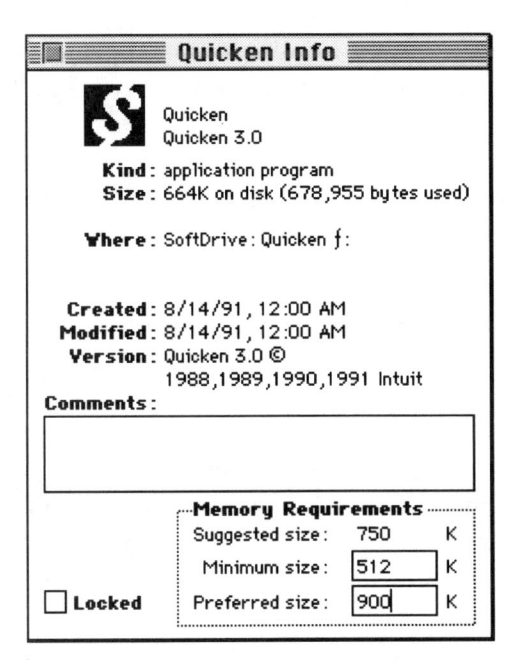

Figure 11-10: An application's Get Info dialog box in System 7.1.

The Memory option here has three parts: Suggested Size, Minimum Size and Preferred Size.

- **Suggested Size.** The amount of RAM memory the developer recommends to properly run the application. You can't change this option—it's a reminder of the memory requirements as set by the application developer.

- **Minimum Size.** The smallest amount of RAM in which the application will run properly. You can change this option by entering a new value.

- **Preferred Size.** Specifies the actual amount of RAM memory that the application will request when it's launched. You can change the amount of memory that will be allocated by entering a new value in this option, then closing the Get Info dialog box.

When an application is launched, the program requests the amount of memory specified in the Preferred Size option. If this amount is available in an unused block, the memory is allocated and the program is opened. You can check the size of the largest available block in the About This Macintosh dialog box, as described earlier.

If the amount of memory requested by the Preferred Size option is not available, but more memory is available than the Minimum Size option, the application will launch using all available memory. If the amount of RAM specified in the Minimum size option is unavailable, one of two dialog boxes will appear; one which offers to quit an open application which has no open files in order to free enough memory to complete the launch (see Figure 11-11), or one which states that not enough memory is available to complete the launch (see Figure 11-12).

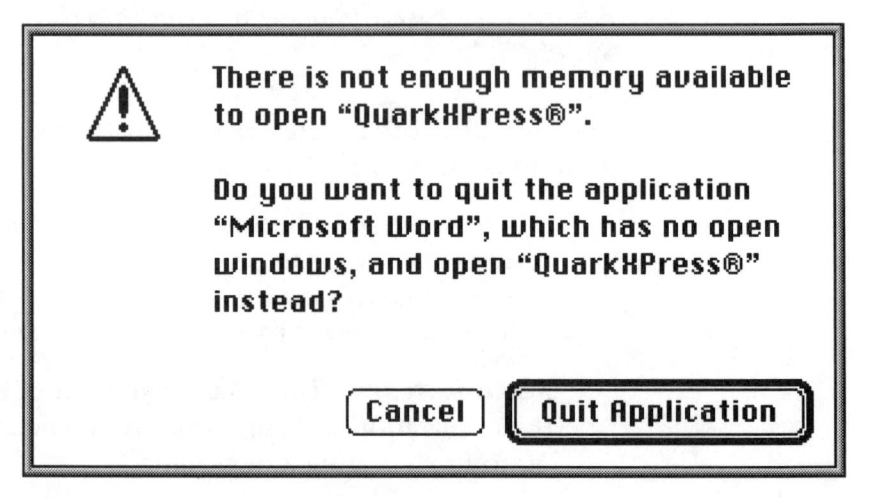

Figure 11-11: The not enough memory unless you quit something else dialog box.

Chapter 11: Memory Management   323

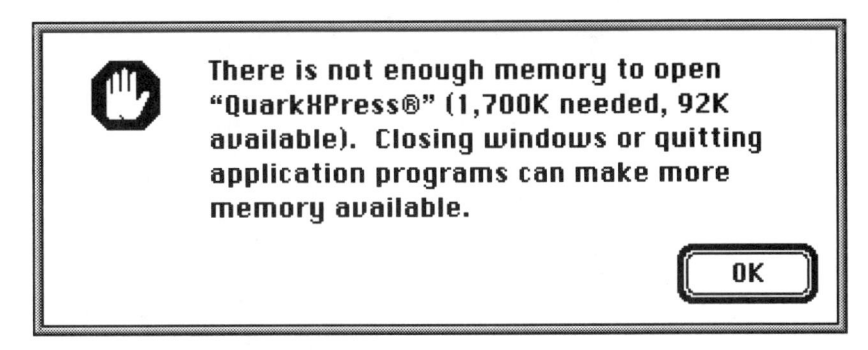

> 🛑 There is not enough memory to open
> "QuarkXPress®" (1,700K needed, 92K
> available). Closing windows or quitting
> application programs can make more
> memory available.
>
> [OK]

Figure 11-12: The not enough memory dialog box.

Setting Memory Options

Optimally, 15 to 25 percent of the space in the memory allocation bar displayed next to an application name in the About This Macintosh dialog box should remain open, or unused, while the application is running. (As explained earlier, the bar graph displays total allocated RAM in white and the portion of memory actually being used in black.)

Most applications will not use all their allocated memory at all times—usage will vary as commands and features are used. So to determine the actual, average and maximum amount of memory used, keep the About This Macintosh window open while you work, and monitor the changes in memory use by your applications.

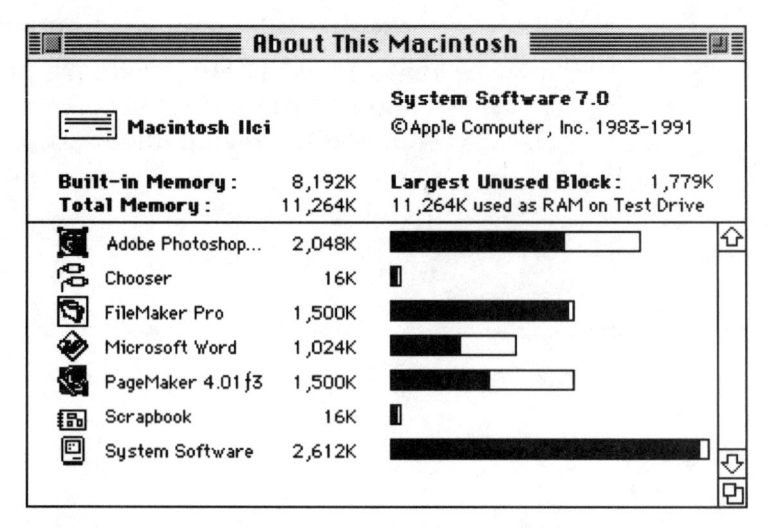

```
┌─────────────────────────────────────────────────┐
│ ▓▓▓▓▓▓▓▓▓▓▓▓▓ About This Macintosh ▓▓▓▓▓▓▓▓▓ ▣ │
├─────────────────────────────────────────────────┤
│                        System Software 7.0      │
│   [▭] Macintosh IIci   ©Apple Computer, Inc. 1983-1991 │
│                                                 │
│   Built-in Memory:  8,192K   Largest Unused Block:  1,779K │
│   Total Memory:    11,264K   11,264K used as RAM on Test Drive │
│                                                 │
│   [icon] Adobe Photoshop…  2,048K  [███████      ] │
│   [icon] Chooser              16K  [▌            ] │
│   [icon] FileMaker Pro     1,500K  [█████████    ] │
│   [icon] Microsoft Word    1,024K  [████         ] │
│   [icon] PageMaker 4.01 f3 1,500K  [█████        ] │
│   [icon] Scrapbook            16K  [▌            ] │
│   [icon] System Software   2,612K  [████████████ ] │
└─────────────────────────────────────────────────┘
```

Figure 11-13: Application memory use is documented in the About This Macintosh dialog box.

Given that 15 to 25 percent unused space is the goal, watching the amount of actual memory used will show if the current memory allocation is too low, too high or about right. As a result, you may need to increase a program's memory allocation, or you may be able to decrease it. Either of these modifications is done with the Current Size (version 7.0) or Preferred Size (version 7.1) options.

Increasing memory allocation provides additional memory that can in many cases improve application performance, allow larger and more complete document files to be opened and reduce or eliminate the possibility of memory-related crashes. These effects are hardly surprising, when you consider how an application uses its allocated memory: it must control and manage its own code, data from any open document files and all data manipulations performed by its commands and features. And it must do all this with an allocated memory that's less than the total size of the application program and its data files, let alone what it needs to manipulate its data. As a result, software must constantly shift parts of its own code and data from open documents back and forth between disk-storage memory and real memory. Providing additional memory minimizes this activity and allows the program to concentrate on operating efficiently.

For most programs, increasing the Current Size or Preferred Size option by 20 to 25 percent is optimal, but if you experience frequent "out of memory" errors in any software application, continue increasing until these errors are eliminated.

Decreasing memory allocation allows you to successfully launch applications with less memory, thereby running more programs simultaneously. This is not generally a recommended practice, but in many cases software will operate successfully using less RAM than the developer suggested.

There is no easy way to determine what the true Minimum size should be, although it will rarely be more than 20 percent smaller than the Suggested size. Don't be afraid to try it—just be sure to test the application in this configuration before working on important data, and save frequently once you begin working. Start by reducing the Current or Minimum size by just 5 to 10 percent; if you find the About This Macintosh dialog box shows large amounts of unused space, you may be able to reduce the allocation even more.

With the advent of virtual memory support, the need for most Macintosh users to reduce these sizes should become less common. Even if you have only 2 Mb of RAM installed, using virtual memory is preferable to reducing the Current or Minimum size options. You're less likely to experience crashes or loss of data using virtual memory than with Current sizes reduced. (See the discussion of virtual memory earlier in this chapter.)

Of course, the best long-range solution is to add enough RAM to your Macintosh so you won't have to depend on either virtual memory or Memory Requirements reductions.

Moving On

The amount of memory available on your Macintosh determines, in large measure, what you can do with your computer. As we've seen in this chapter, System 7 gives you much more control over memory availability and how that memory is utilized.

- Virtual memory lets you "create" memory by using space on your hard drive as if it were RAM.

- 32-bit addressing makes it possible to access a vast amount of memory.

- The Get Info dialog box helps you control the amount of memory an application uses.

- The About This Macintosh dialog box provides constant feedback about what's happening with your Mac's memory.

As System 7 has grown, so has Apple's practice of releasing extensions to update and improve important aspects of how the Macintosh functions. In the next chapter, we'll take a look at the many extensions Apple has created to enhance the Mac's system software.

Chapter 12: Apple's System 7 Extensions

INITs, control panels and extensions have been an important part of the Macintosh system software for years, but only since the release of System 7 has Apple itself chosen to deliver significant new features in the form of extensions. QuickTime, PC Exchange, At Ease, ColorSync and ATM are all extensions that Apple has made available as of this writing. Others, including AppleScript, AOCE and QuickDraw GX are expected shortly.

This modular approach to system software features has several benefits for both Apple and Mac users; it makes new capabilities optional, so those who don't need a particular new feature don't have to waste the hard drive space and RAM it requires, it also allows new capabilities to be offered very quickly, without waiting for the next major system software update, and finally it makes it possible for Apple to charge for separate features individually. Obviously this last point may not be considered a benefit by everyone!

Apple's extensions range from bug fixes (MODE 32) to hardware enablers (PC Exchange) to radical new technologies (QuickTime). Below we'll look at each Apple offering, with an especially detailed look at the revolutionary QuickTime extension.

MODE 32

As described in Chapter 11, "Memory Management," a number of Macintosh models contain ROM chips that render them incompatible with the 32-bit addressing capabilities in System 7. MODE 32 is an extension, developed by the Connectix Corporation, that corrects this incompatibility for the Macintosh IIx, IIcx, SE/30 and Mac II (with optional PMMU chip installed) when using System 7 version 7.0 or version 7.01. MODE 32 is available without charge from Apple dealers, online services and user groups.

Since version 1.2 of MODE 32 is incompatible with virtual memory under Version 7.1, Apple has released a new *system enabler*—a special kind of extension—that will allow certain older Macs without 32-bit clean ROMs to become 32-bit compatible with System 7 Version 7.1.

PC Exchange

Mac hardware has had the ability to read PC disks for more than five years, but in that time, Apple's only software support for this capability was Apple File Exchange, a Font/DA Mover-like utility that made it possible to copy files from PC disks onto Mac disks or hard drives.

But while everyone else was wondering why PC disks wouldn't just mount at the desktop so files can be dragged to and from them disks directly, Apple ignored the issue in release after release of the system software. With PC Exchange, a $79 extension, Apple finally provides this capability.

When installed, PC disks appear on the Mac desktop just like other Mac disks. Via the control panel, you can specify which Macintosh application you want to use to open files from PC disks. Files dragged to PC disks will automatically have their names changed to comply with PC file naming conventions (eight characters and a three character extension).

Adobe Type Manager

Not long after Apple's announcement of System 7 and TrueType, Adobe Systems released Adobe Type Manager (ATM), a utility that allows PostScript fonts to be drawn more smoothly at any resolution on-screen, or on any non-PostScript output device. This development eliminated the biggest advantages that TrueType fonts initially had over PostScript fonts. It also proved that competition is often good for the consumer.

Adobe Type Manager (ATM), is an extension that allows PostScript printer font data to be viewed on-screen. When ATM is installed, PostScript fonts display at the best possible resolution on-screen at any point size, for any font whose screen and printer fonts are installed. ATM also improves the output quality of PostScript fonts on non-PostScript printers. With ATM, almost any PostScript font can be printed successfully at any size on any dot matrix, ink jet or QuickDraw laser printer.

The primary drawback of ATM is that a printer font corresponding to each installed screen font must be kept on your hard drive. This requires more space and increases the cost of working with lots of fonts. Screen fonts can be obtained without charge from service bureaus or online sources, but most printer fonts must be purchased at costs ranging from a few dollars to a few hundred dollars per type family.

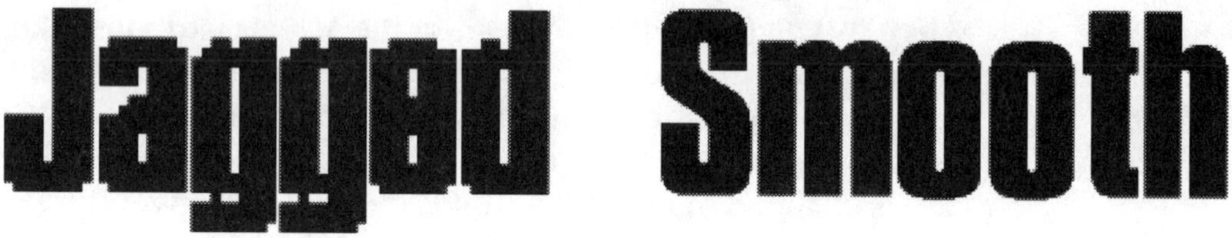

Jagged Smooth

Figure 12-1: Without ATM (left), fonts appear jagged on-screen at most point sizes. With ATM (right), the same fonts are smooth at any size

ATM quickly became a huge success, and most people who worked with more than a few PostScript fonts either purchased the utility, or received it in a bundle with some other software application or application upgrade. Some time after the initial shipment of System 7, Apple began offering ATM to anyone who purchased System 7 or a System 7 upgrade package. But Apple did not add ATM to the System 7 install disks, making it necessary to order the "free" copy of ATM from a toll free number (800/521-1976 ext. 4400) for a shipping and handling charge of $7.50.

Using ATM

ATM consists of two files, an ATM control panel and a file called "~ATM 68020/030," which must be in your System folder. In order to use ATM, you must also have the printer font files for any PostScript files you want ATM to work with.

Several of the fonts provided with System 7 are PostScript screen fonts, but the printer font portions are missing—Times, Helvetica, Courier, and Symbol are examples. These printer fonts must be obtained or purchased separately.

There are several versions of ATM in circulation, and each has different System 7 considerations:

- **ATM version 2.0.** This version is System 7 compatible, but not 32-bit clean. (It will cause crashes if 32-bit addressing is turned on.) Printer fonts must reside in the System Folder itself, even though printer fonts dragged to the System Folder icon will be automatically placed in the Extensions folder (if this happens, you need to manually drag them back into the System Folder itself.) It is not recommended that you use this version with System 7.

- **ATM version 2.02.** This version is System 7 compatible, and 32-bit clean, but does not recognize printer fonts in the Extensions folder or Fonts folder—they must reside in the System Folder itself.

- **ATM version 2.03.** This version is System 7 compatible, 32-bit clean, and recognizes the printer fonts in the Extensions folder but not the Fonts folder. It is a safe version to use with System 7 version 7.0 or version 7.01, but not recommended for version 7.1.

- **ATM version 3.0.** This version is fully compatible with—and recommended for—System 7 versions 7.0, 7.01 or 7.1. In addition to adding support for System 7.1's Fonts folder, ATM 3.0 supports Adobe's Multiple Master font technology.

- **Super ATM version 3.5.** This version of ATM not only supports Multiple Master fonts, it also takes advantage of them to construct fonts when you open or print documents containing missing fonts. It is fully compatible with System 7 versions 7.0, 7.01 and 7.1.

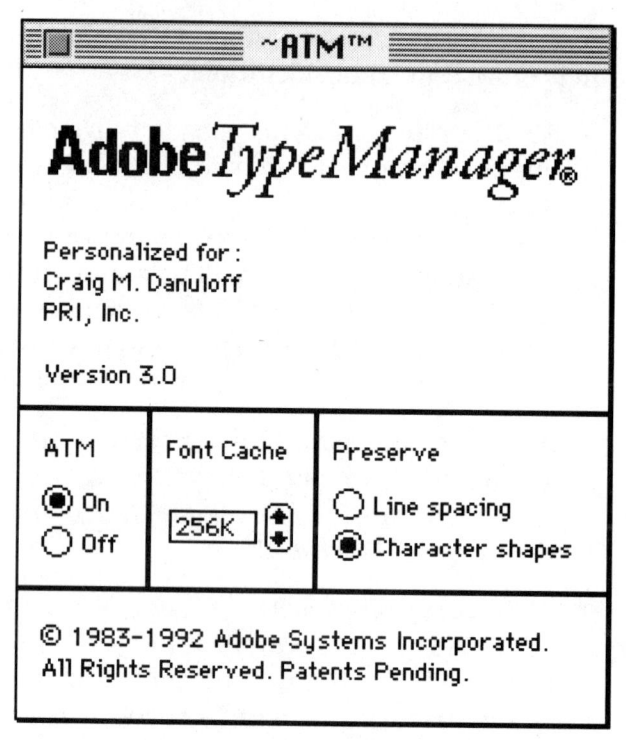

Figure 12-2: The ATM control panel.

At Ease

This extension is a very simple application launcher, which also provides basic security by limiting access to the Finder and control panels. At Ease is bundled with system software version 7.01P and version 7.1P, which ship with Macintosh Performa models. It is also available separately for $59 and can be used along with any version of System 7.

At Ease is controlled via a control panel called At Ease Setup. When it is turned on, the control panel can be used to add applications or documents to the At Ease launcher windows. When At Ease is running, two tabbed index cards appear on-screen, looking a lot like an old HyperCard stack. Clicking (not double-clicking, as is usually the case) on any application or document icon from one of these cards launches the application or document.

When At Ease is running, launching any application immediately hides all other applications. The control panels folder is also removed from the Apple menu. In order to access the Finder, or the Control Panels folder, the Go To Finder command must be chosen from At Ease's File menu. If a password was specified, it must be entered in order to gain Finder access.

At Ease is a very nice utility to simplify Macintosh operations so that children can use two or three Mac programs unattended without causing their parents any computer-related grief. But as a utility for older, more experienced users, At Ease is far too limiting and much less powerful than many other launcher-style Finder replacement utilities.

QuickTime

The Macintosh has led the way for personal computers in typography, graphics, sound and high-resolution color. With the introduction of QuickTime, the Macintosh continues this tradition by leading the way in video and multimedia.

QuickTime is an extension that gives your Macintosh the ability to play and record moving video images, animation and sound in ways never before possible. It makes moving images and sounds a basic type of Macintosh data. All types of applications—word processors, databases, presentation graphics packages, page-layout programs—can now (or will soon be able to) incorporate these moving images as easily as they now use standard graphics.

Any Macintosh model containing a 68020 or later processor that uses System 6.07 or later (including Systems 7.0 and 7.1) can use QuickTime—all you need is the QuickTime extension. QuickTime version 1.0 has been available since January 1992, and an improved version, QuickTime 1.5, was released in November 1992. There is no charge for the QuickTime extension, although in typical Apple fashion that doesn't mean you will be able to get it easily or without cost. QuickTime is being distributed in a number of different formats and channels

- QuickTime is included as part of the System 7 Personal Upgrade Kit and the System 7 Network Upgrade Kit.

- The QuickTime Starter Kit features the QuickTime extension, a player utility, a few sample movies and more and can be purchased from any Apple reseller, or most mail-order software dealers, for around $160.

- QuickTime can be downloaded from online services, or obtained from most Macintosh user groups.

- You can legally copy QuickTime from another Macintosh user who has it.

- Many QuickTime-dependent applications include the QuickTime extension on their distribution disks.

- QuickTime is included with all Macintosh Performa systems (but not with any other Macintosh models).

QuickTime Movies

The QuickTime extension adds support to your Macintosh for a new file format, called Movie (file type MooV.) Like other file formats, such as PICT, EPS or TIFF, the Movie file format saves a certain kind of data—in this case moving video, animation or sound (or all of these)—in a way that can be viewed at a specified rate and quality. By defining this new file format at the system software level, Apple makes it easy for application developers to support this kind of data, which encourages them to develop sophisticated ways to create and use data that changes or reacts over time (such as moving images or sounds) on the Macintosh.

A QuickTime movie acts much like any other text or graphic element—you can select it, cut, copy or paste it either within or between QuickTime-savvy applications, and store it in the latest version of the Scrapbook. In some cases, you can't even tell that an object is a movie until you select it; before that, it looks just like any other graphic element. When a movie is selected, however, it displays an identifying set of controls that allow you to adjust the volume and play the movie, as well as fast-forward, reverse or randomly adjust the movie.

Figure 12-3: A QuickTime movie with its controls.

The image you see in a movie element when the movie isn't playing is called its *poster*. The poster is a selected image from the movie. Because it's often not the first frame of the movie, you'll see the image of the poster jump to another image when the movie begins.

If the poster is a still-frame from the movie, a *preview* is a moving representative of the movie. Not all movies have previews, but most longer ones do. A preview gives you a quick look at the movie highlights. Many standard file dialog boxes let you see the poster or a preview, before opening a movie.

QuickTime & Data Compression

One of QuickTime's most important technological breakthroughs is the real-time compression and decompression it provides video, animation, photographs and other graphics. QuickTime supports several built-in compression schemes, and can easily support others as necessary. The built-in com-pression is a software-only solution, capable of achieving ratios as great as 25:1 without any visible loss in image quality. With specialized hardware, compression ratios as high as 160:1 are possible.

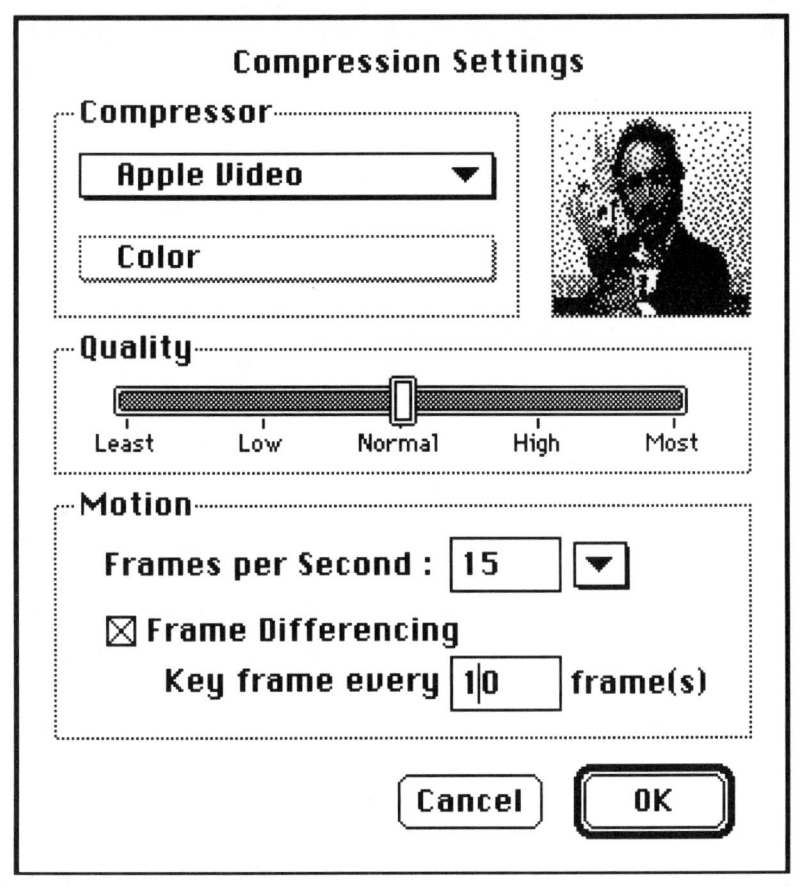

Figure 12-4: A QuickTime Compression Options dialog box.

Compression is particularly important because of all the data needed to generate moving images and accompanying sounds. A good rule of thumb for estimating movie size is that every minute of motion consumes 10 Mb of disk space. As another example, a seven-minute, full-size, full-resolution video movie could consume 200 Mb in its uncompressed form. Compressed, that same movie might need only 45 Mb. Of course, most movies are significantly shorter (lasting between 5 and 30 seconds), so files in the 200k to 1 Mb range are common.

The actual size of a QuickTime movie depends on the following:

- **Image size.** Measured in horizontal and vertical pixels, determines how large the movie will appear on-screen. The larger the image, the larger the movie file. Movies defaulted to 160 x 120 pixels in QuickTime 1.0, but version 1.5 expands this default to 240 x 180 pixels.

- **Resolution.** QuickTime supports all the Mac's resolutions—or depths of color—including 1, 2, 4, 8, 16, 24 and 32-bit. The higher the resolution, the larger the movie file.

- **Frames per second.** Most QuickTime movies are recorded using 10, 12, 15 or 30 frames per second (fps). Without additional hardware, 15 fps is the QuickTime standard, although 30 fps, which is the standard for commercial-quality video, is supported by QuickTime 1.5. The higher the frame rate, the larger the resulting movie file.

- **Audio sampling rate.** This can be thought of as the "resolution" of the sound. The Macintosh supports 8, 11, 22 or 44 Khz audio sampling, although anything higher than 22 Khz requires additional hardware. The higher the sampling rate, the larger the sound portion of a movie file.

- **Compression.** As mentioned earlier, QuickTime supports a number of compression schemes; and for each you can select the degree of compression used. Increasing compression reduces movie size but sometimes affects playback quality. New compression schemes introduced with QuickTime 1.5 should reduce or eliminate these kinds of problems.

- **Content.** Beyond the above-mentioned technical factors, the actual set of sounds and images contained in a movie is what will finally determine its size. This makes it difficult to estimate the size of a QuickTime move solely based on its length or technical characteristics.

Using QuickTime

You can use QuickTime to watch movies (which may be included on CD-ROM disks, obtained from user groups or on-line services, or come embedded in documents you get from other Mac users), or you can create your own QuickTime movies. It's easy for almost anyone with a Mac to view a QuickTime movie, but creating one requires a fairly substantial investment in hardware, software and the development of what may be brand new skills.

Most QuickTime movies now being delivered are part of CD-ROM-based information discs, providing education or information on music, history, sports, news, entertainment or computer-related topics. CD-ROM is the perfect media for QuickTime, since it huge storage capabilities (650 MB), can be inexpensively reproduced, and has access times sufficient to deliver good quality playback of QuickTime movies. CD-ROM support for QuickTime has recently been enhanced by faster CD drives (such as the Apple CD 300) and performance improvements included in QuickTime 1.5.

Most movies delivered as part of these CD-ROM discs are viewed using some controlling application, such as HyperCard or MacroMedia Director, that is included on the CD. Movies included as part of other documents can be viewed from within their applications, such as Microsoft Word, Aldus Persuasion and others. To watch movies which exist only as stand-alone Movie files, you'll need a player application.

Several movie player applications are available as shareware or freeware. One from Apple is called Simple Player, and another is called Movie Player. Aladdin Systems, makers of the StuffIt line of compression utilities, offers a player called Popcorn (the perfect movie companion), which is available online and from most user groups. If you ever need to view a movie but you don't have one of these movie player utilities handy, just create a document using any QuickTime-compatible application, import the movie and play it from within the document.

ColorSync

The Mac's proficiency and popularity as a publishing computer is well known. And in the past few years, advances in processing power, storage capacities, scanning and output technology have earned the Mac a significant place in even the most demanding high-quality color publishing situations. Publications from *The New Yorker*, to *People*, to *Playboy* are now produced fully or partially on the Macintosh.

Despite this acceptance, and the overall improvements in color publishing technology, one aspect of using Macs for color publishing has remained a challenge: matching colors that appear on-screen to those that are printed on color proofing devices and, finally, to the colors of the finished product, which is usually based on film output. Keeping colors consistent as they move from an on-screen display to different output devices has been difficult for two basic reasons.

First, computer monitors produce colors by adding together differing percentages of red, green and blue light. This method of mixing light from original sources is called *additive color*.

Output devices, on the other hand, work by applying color to a page that will selectively absorb light waves when the document is illuminated via an external white light (such as light bulbs, or the sun). This method of creating colors is called *subtractive color*. There are fundamental differences in the ranges of colors that additive and subtractive color can produce. This is why, for example, on-screen color (additive) offers bright, highly saturated colors which invariably appear darker when printed (subtractive) on paper or other materials.

Second, variations between different printers, monitors and presses make it impossible for them all to produce the exact same range and quality of colors. An inexpensive ink-jet printer is going to have one set of printable colors, a color laser printer another, a dye sublimation printer yet another, a web press another and a high-quality sheet-fed press another still.

Differences in the color models and technical characteristics of color devices result in each having its own specific *gamut*, or range of colors. The trick to achieving consistent color across different devices is to map colors from one device to another so that when a file is displayed or produced on each device, the differences between the devices' gamuts are accounted and compensated for, and the color remains as consistent as possible.

This is exactly what Apple's ColorSync extension does. When ColorSync is installed, colors are converted from their original definitions into a device-independent definition based on the international CIE XYZ color standard. This conversion is done using a device profile, which is a small file that tells ColorSync about the color characteristics and capabilities of the input device or monitor. Once a color is defined in CIE XYZ, it can then be translated for output using the device profile of the output device.

Apple will provide device profiles for its own monitors, scanners and color printers, but the success of ColorSync will be dependent upon third party developers producing and distributing their own device profiles for their scanners, monitors and printers. In order for you to use ColorSync effectively, you must have device profiles for the exact scanners, monitors and printers you are using (or intend to use) for any given project.

When ColorSync translates colors into or out of the CIE XYZ color model, it does so with the goal of providing the best possible match between the original color and the final color. Differences in devices do not always make an exact match possible, as explained earlier. The algorithm ColorSync uses to perform this translation was designed for optimum results, but it was also designed to use a small amount of memory and provide good performance. Other companies such as EFI and Kodak have developed other conversion methods—based on lookup tables rather than algorithms—which will produce superior results but require much more memory, information and expertise about each input and output device. These methods are compatible with ColorSync, however, and can be taken advantage of by anyone working in high-quality color who desires improved results.

Moving On

With the advent of System 7 and the use of extensions, Apple has embarked on an innovative new method of delivering improvements and corrections to its system software. Extensions allow Apple and other developers to deliver specialized capabilities and enhancements only to those users who want and need them, without forcing uninterested users to waste drive space and memory working with an unwanted extension. Extensions also allow Apple to deliver new features without waiting until the next major system upgrade. Apple has released a diverse array of extensions since System 7 was introduced.

- **ATM** improves the display and print quality of PostScript typefaces on any Mac, helping to answer some of the challenges that TrueType brought to PostScript.

- **MODE32** (or the 32-bit system enabler) allows ceratain older Macs to use 32-bit addressing (and therefore, more memory) by making their ROMs 32-bit clean.

- **PC Exchange** lets Mac users easily mount on the desktop floppies formatted for the DOS environment. It also helps map documents created by DOS applications to certain Mac applications.

- **At Ease** presents a less complicated interface to children and first-time Mac users. It also guards against the possibility of important files being deleted or changed inadvertently.

- **QuickTime** brings video, animation and sound to the Mac in a format that is standard across the entire Macintosh line.

- **ColorSync** helps compensate for the differences between various input, viewing and output devices when working with color files.

But despite Apple's continuing efforts to enhance the Mac's operating system through the release of new extensions, many users are still wishing for everything except what they already have. As has often been the case in the development of the Macintosh, a host of third parties have filled the gaps left by Apple by releasing special utilities that pick up where System 7 leaves off. In the next chapter, we'll take a look at some of the best shareware and commercial utilities available for System 7.

Chapter 13: Third Party Utilities

Apple isn't the only company that has released utilities to augment System 7. Dozens of programmers—from small firms to large corporations—have found ways to improve Apple's system software. These modifications affect nearly every aspect of the system, including the Apple Menu, Balloon Help, dialog boxes, fonts, the Finder, icons, file sharing and more.

In this chapter, we'll look at dozens of the best utilities available for System 7. Some of these utilities are available without charge from online services or user groups, some are shareware (which means you can try them out for free but must send in a specified payment to their author if you decide to keep them), and others are commercial packages available from your favorite software reseller.

The System 7 Companion Disk is available from Ventana Press by calling (919) 942-0220. It includes many of the freeware and shareware programs described in this chapter. Programs included on the disk are highlighted by a floppy disk icon. See the order form in the back of this book for details.

Apple Menu Utilities

Some of the first utilities for System 7 overcame a shortcoming most people found immediately obvious: folders in the Apple Menu should hierarchically display their contents. Most of these early programs were public domain or shareware programs that allowed displays of up to five levels of subfolders. Since their origination, these utilities have matured, offering a range of options at a range of prices.

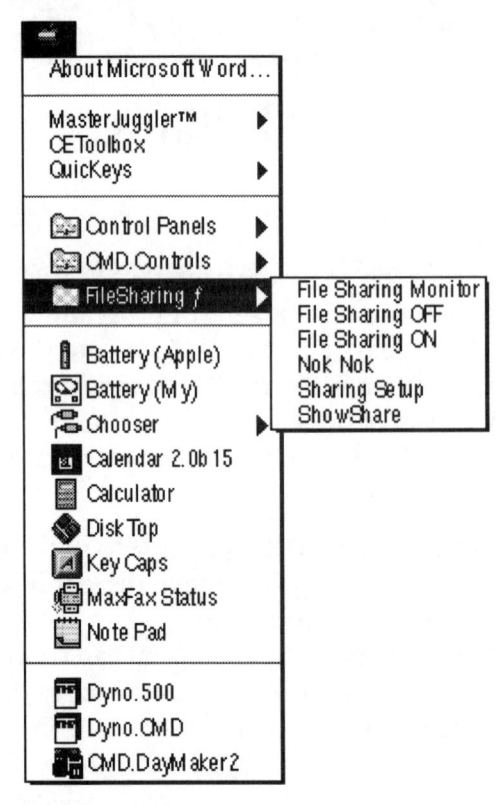

Figure 13-1: NowMenus provides a wide range of options for creating hierarchical menus.

HAM 1.0
Inline Design; $99

HAM is the only stand-alone commercial hierarchical menu utility reviewed here; the others I discuss are part of some larger utility package. As such, it's no surprise that HAM offers the widest range of menu control options, or that it is the largest utility of its kind—more than 100k for the control panel plus up to 100k for its preferences file—and the most expensive.

In addition to enabling hierarchical display, HAM lets you sort Apple Menu items by name, size, kind or label, or reorder the items in a custom order. This ability to customize the order of items is unique, and really improves the functionality of the Apple Menu. HAM also adds its own item to your Apple Menu, the Recent Items folder. This folder lets you quickly access the applications, files, folders and servers you have opened most recently. Finally, HAM offers the ability to launch a group of applications and documents with a single selection by grouping them into a single Apple Menu item.

NowMenus 4.01 (part of Now Utilities)
Now Software; $149

NowMenus is a descendant of HierDA, the first utility that ever presented hierarchical Apple Menus. HierDA, which was later renamed DA Menuz, provided hierarchical access to control panels, the Chooser and other desk accessories under System 6. This extensively redesigned version is a part of the great Now Utilities package.

NowMenus lets you do almost anything you could ever dream of doing with the Apple Menu. You can freely reorder items, add separator bars, and even include special hierarchical menus listing the most recent applications or documents you have used. Or you can include an Other... command that lets you launch any program you have not added to your Apple Menu.

Beyond these Apple Menu customizations, NowMenus also supports two other drop-down menus from your menu bar—one at the far right and one at the far left—both of which can be customized as application launchers. Finally, it provides a great memory map that can help you track how your RAM is being used, and a utility for changing the RAM requirements of your applications.

MenuExtend (part of Alsoft Power Utilities)
Alsoft; $129

This straightforward utility adds hierarchical support to the Apple Menu, and provides an option that sorts each submenu so files and folders are listed separately. Not much flash, but a solid utility that doesn't hog much memory. Perfect for Power-Books, or whenever memory and disk space are limited.

PowerMenus (sold separately or bundled with PowerWindows)
Kiwi Software; $39.95

Another small and fast program, PowerMenus offers several very nice options including control over the font used in your Apple Menu, and the ability to show more than 5 levels of hierarchical menus. It also allows you to specify if menu changes should be updated manually or automatically, which makes it possible to access Apple Menus on the PowerBook without causing the hard drive to spin up.

MenuChoice
Kerry Clendinning; shareware $15

Its shareware status makes this hierarchical menu utility a good low-cost offering. Hierarchical menus are provided for all Apple Menu folders, and a Recent Items folder is added automatically, but no control over the order of Apple Menu items is provided.

Trash Utilities

There's room for improvement everywhere, even in the Trash. Although Apple made some Trash-related improvements in System 7, the utilities below take waste management to entirely new levels.

TrashMaster 1.1
Utilitron; $69.95

This utility adds just about every function we can imagine to the Trash. Most noticeably, it adds a hierarchical menu to your Empty Trash command, that lists the name of each mounted volume separately and then the names of files from each of those volumes which are currently in the Trash. By selecting volumes or file names, you can selectively delete items from the Trash, leaving unselected items alone. A progress dialog lists the name of each file or folder as the Trash is emptied.

The TrashMaster control panel lets you take further control of the way trash is treated, allowing you to define filters that can specify when your trash will be emptied based on the length of time files have been in the Trash, the size of trashed files, the type of trashed files, or the applications that created these files. You could, for example, specify that files over 100k be emptied from the Trash every day, that files created by Microsoft Excel be emptied every hour, and that all files be emptied once they've been in the Trash for a week. The Incinerator option allows you to actually overwrite the space a file occupies on a hard disk when it is emptied from the Trash. You can use this option for any or all files emptied from the Trash as specified by your filters.

TrashPicker 1.0

Bill Johnson & Ron Duritsch; shareware $10

TrashPicker is slightly less extensive than TrashMaster, but does a great job of adding the kind of intelligence to the Trash that Apple probably should have added. You can specify if and when the trash should be emptied (for instance, it can be emptied as soon as items are thrown away), and you can also instruct TrashPicker to empty the Trash on startup or shutdown, at any timed intervals or only when available disk space falls below a certain level.

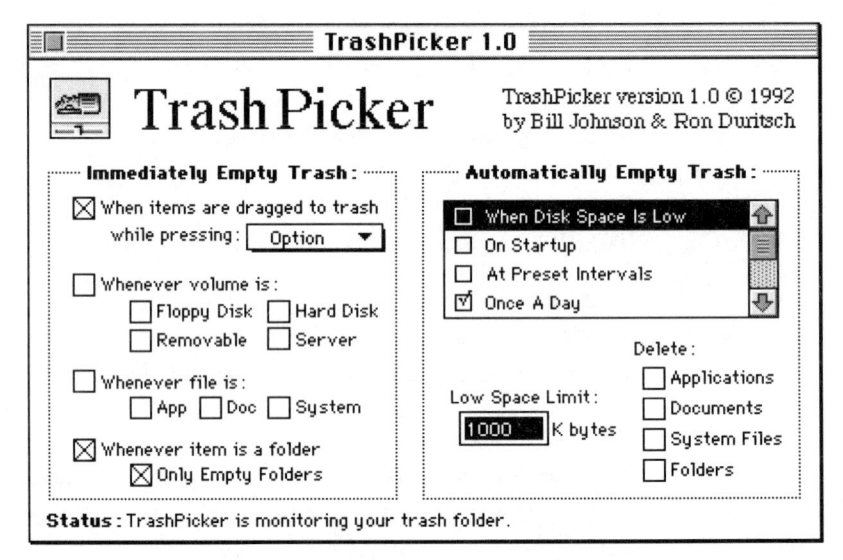

Figure 13-2: The TrashPicker control panel.

TrashMan

Dan Walkowski; shareware $5

An even less extensive trash dumper, TrashMan lets you specify the number of days and hours a file should be in the trash before it is automatically deleted. Small, efficient, and to-the-point.

Trash Chute 2.0
Melissa Rogers; freeware

This little System 7 utility is basically an icon for the Empty Trash command. If you place it into your Startup Items folder, the Trash is emptied each time you start up. If you put an icon of it on the desktop, you can drop files onto it just like you drag them into the Trash, but they will be trashed and emptied immediately. Watch out when using this capability for aliases, however, as the alias icon *and* the original file the alias refers to will both be deleted.

The Grouch 2.5B3
Rock Ridge Enterprises; freeware

Animation comes to the Trash with this fun little extension—every time you choose the Empty Trash command, it brings Oscar the Grouch out of your trash can singing, "I love trash."

Alias Utilities

Aliases are one of the important new features introduced by System 7, but exploiting their full power requires a number of capabilities beyond those provided by Apple. The utilities in this section offer lots of powerful features, helping you keep track of aliases, make sure they are connected to their original files, create new aliases more easily and even make sure aliases get deleted when they are no longer useful.

Alias Stylist
Bill Monk/Ziff Davis Publishing; freeware

This simple program lets you change the default type style for new aliases, from italic to any combination of bold, italic, outline, shadow, condensed or whatever you'd like.

AliasBOSS
Scott Johnson; shareware $20

This program makes it easy to both create new aliases for groups of files and to manage the aliases that you have already created. It allows you to search for files by name, type or creator and then create new aliases of just a few or all of the found files. You can even have the aliases created onto any location you specify, not just within the same folder, as is normally the case. You can search for existing aliases and verify that they are still linked to their original files. If they are not, you can re-link them to old, new or different files. This is a capability that Apple definitely forgot!

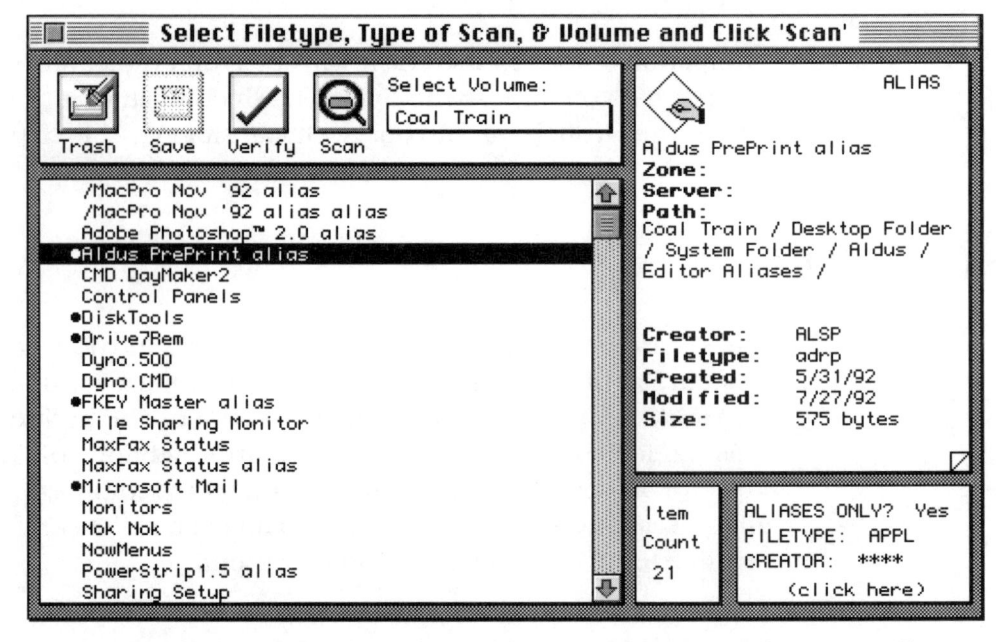

Figure 13-3: AliasBOSS offers many options for controlling your aliases.

AliasZoo

Optimize Information Control; shareware $15

This program could be called "Alias Killer," because it searches a drive for aliases, lists all that are found, and allows you to delete any aliases that you no longer want. Orphaned aliases—those that are no longer linked to their original files—are listed in bold, as shown in Figure 13-4.

Figure 13-4: AliasZoo lists orphaned aliases in bold.

Mount Alias

Jeff Miller; freeware

This little control panel automates one of the tips from Chapter 3, "Managing Your Hard Drive." It automatically aliases any AppleShare or File Sharing volumes that you mount, so that you can remount those volumes easily in the future by just clicking on the aliases. Via the control panel, you can specify which folder these aliases are stored in, and how the aliases are named.

ZMakeAlias
Mike Throckmorton/Ziff Davis Publishing; freeware

Installing this extension adds a button to your Save dialog boxes, allowing you to create and position aliases of the current file without returning to the Finder and doing it manually. Another utility that shows Apple how it should have been done!

TrashAlias 1.1.1
Maurice Volaski; freeware

One of the little annoyances of the way aliases are implemented in System 7 is that when you delete a file which has been aliased, the alias(es) remains on your hard drive even though it is no longer functional. This extension eliminates that problem, automatically deleting aliases when the files they point to are deleted.

Is this really worth a stand-alone utility? Probably not, unless you work with aliases extensively. It is a nice idea though, and we hope Apple builds this functionality into future versions of the system software.

Font Managers

With the introduction of System 7's ability to add fonts without the Font/DA Mover, and version 7.1's Fonts folder, some people thought that the need for third party font management utilities was going to subside. Nothing could be further from the truth. Unless you seldom add or delete fonts, you need one of the font utilities described below.

These programs allow you to access and use fonts that are not actually loaded in your System file or located in the Fonts folder. The fonts stay in their font suitcases, located anywhere on any mounted volume, but act as if they were in the System file or Fonts folder. They also let you add or remove fonts very quickly and easily, and since they don't really copy fonts in and out of the System file, there is no chance of harming the System file itself. They also let you add and remove desk accessories, and provide a number of other enhancements to your Macintosh.

Suitcase
Fifth Generation Software; $79

This is the utility that introduced the idea of font management to the Macintosh, and remains the most popular font utility. Beyond the basic capability of adding and removing fonts, Suitcase lets you:

- **Work with Font Sets.** You can name and save groups of font suitcases—which you might need to use for different projects—and then load or unload all of the fonts in a set with a single mouse click.

- **Resolve Name/ID conflicts.** Suitcase alerts you to any conflicts between fonts you try to open, and provides a dialog box that allows you to rename one of the fonts, or cancel the font opening.

- **Create empty suitcases.** System 7 users soon discover that there is no way to create new empty suitcases without Font/DA Mover version 4.2, and since Apple does not provide this with System 7, Suitcase provides a handy command to solve the problem.

- **Share fonts for networks.** Many large font users store their fonts on network file servers which are shared by many users. Suitcase specifically supports network font use, allowing you to open shared fonts so other Macs can use them simultaneously.

MasterJuggler
Alsoft; $49

MasterJuggler has always been the upstart competitor to Suitcase, and offers a user interface I prefer over Suitcase. All of the basic functions are the same—it can remember where font suitcases are located, show you samples of any selected fonts, compress fonts to save hard drive space, work with FKEYs and DAs, automatically resolve font ID conflicts, and it lets downloadable fonts work from any folder on your hard drive.

In addition, MasterJuggler lets you attach sound files, and assign different sounds to 9 different System activities (disk eject, shutdown, launch, etc.). It also features the FontShow utility (that can provide extensive font samples), methods of launching applications from either a dialog box or pop-up program list, and a utility to locate and correct any name or ID number conflicts in your font, DA, FKEY or sound files.

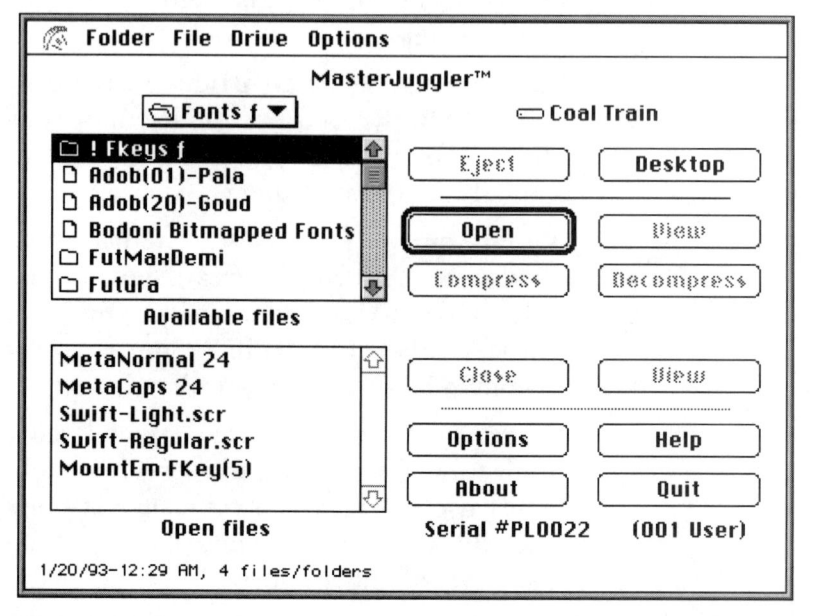

Figure 13-5: MasterJuggler has some features Suitcase can't match.

Carpetbag

James Walker; shareware $5

Another shareware alternative offering basic functionality at a very low price, Carpetbag lets you specify folders that contain your fonts, and it will either automatically open fonts in those folders at startup, or you can use the control panel to open or close fonts at any time. If you use fonts extensively, one of the commercial programs is probably more appropriate, but for the marginal font fanatic, CarpetBag is a nice (and cheap) alternative.

System Software Selectors

Although the recommended procedure for moving to System 7 is to have it replace System 6 entirely, some people prefer to keep both system software versions installed, or must do so in order to keep using applications that are incompatible with System 7. It is possible to have both system software versions installed on one hard drive, and alternate between them without problems, using one of the utilities described below.

Installing System 7 without removing System 6 is relatively easy: simply move the Finder out of the System 6 System Folder to some other location (but don't trash it) and then install System 7. This will create a new System 7 System Folder. Then copy the System 6 Finder back into the System 6 System Folder. Use one of the utilities described below to "bless" one of these folders as the one you want used at startup.

System Switcher
Canon Sales; freeware

A list of available volumes is presented by System Switcher, and clicking the Open button for any selected volumes lists available System Folders. To select the folder you want to designate as the System Folder when you next restart, highlight the folder and click the Switch button.

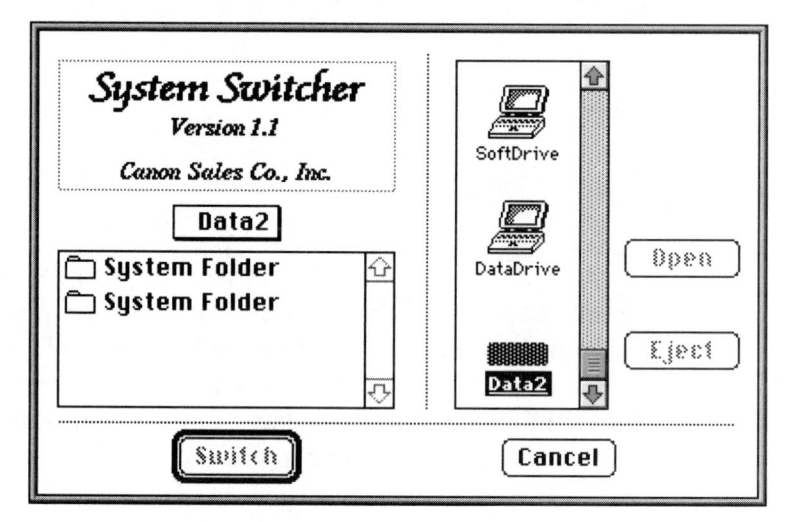

Figure 13-6: System Switcher lets you "bless" one of many System Folders.

System Picker
Kevin Aitkin; freeware

System picker performs the same function as System Switcher, but it works a little differently. When System Picker is launched, it automatically searches for all System Folders on all mounted volumes, and presents a pull-down menu that you can use to select the one you want to use.

Figure 13-7: System Picker scans for System Folders and lets you pick one as the active folder.

File Sharing Utilities

One of the first items to appear on the wish list of any File Sharing user is a better way to know who is connected to your Mac (and when they are connected). Another frequent wish is for a quicker way to turn File Sharing on and off. These and other capabilities are added by the utilities described below.

Nok Nok
Trik; $49.95 (AppleShare 3.0 version, $295)

When this control panel is installed, you can choose to be informed of users logging onto your Mac with a dialog box, a flashing icon in the menu bar, a sound, the opening of the File Sharing Monitor or some combination of these. A special version is available for use on AppleShare 3.0 networks.

ShowShare
Robert Hess; freeware

This rather comprehensive utility adds a File Sharing icon to your menu bar which shows you the status of file sharing (starting up, on, off, shutting down or error) and provides a drop-down menu with commands that let you set user preferences, check user information, and even send messages to logged on users via the network.

File Sharing Toggle
Adam Stein; shareware $10

These two small applications (10k each) let you quickly and easily turn File Sharing on and off without going to the Sharing Setup control panel. This lets you use File Sharing just when you need it, which saves RAM, improves performance, and enhances security. You can leave these apps on your desktop, alias them to the Apple Menu, or use them with your favorite launching or macro utility to make them easily accessible.

Extension Managers

You know you've arrived as a Mac user when your extensions get out of control. There are so many great extensions and control panels available (and not-great-but-interesting ones) that it's easy to find that you have installed too many, which leads to conflicts, slowdowns and general confusion.

Each of the utilities described below let you take control over the chaos of your startup documents, selectively turning them on or off without having to move them in or out of their respective folders. Most also let you build sets of extensions, so you can load the group of extensions relevant to the work you intend to do. You can also use an extension manager to avoid memory-intensive extensions (and thus, possible conflicts) when you know you won't need them. For example, you could use one group when you're going to use all your telecommunications programs, another when you want to use File Sharing, another when you want just the minimum number loaded, and so on.

Init Picker
MicroSeeds; $59.95

The best of the first-generation extension managers, Init Picker remains a powerful tool, although it is no longer the most powerful program available. In addition to the basic extension manager features described above, it allows you to select one of your extension groups by holding down a key at startup, and to configure a key that temporarily disables all extensions. Another nice feature of Init Picker is that—unlike other extension managers—it does not change the file type of the extension it disables.

Startup Manager (part of Now Utilities)
Now Software; $149

My current favorite extension manager, Startup Manager boasts all the basic capabilities an extension manager needs plus several powerful enhancements: icon wrapping is included (taking care of the problem of having more extensions than can fit along the bottom of your screen at startup); you can force the display of icons for extensions that don't normally display icons; extension conflicts can be controlled using a very handy linking feature, which prevents conflicting extensions from running simultaneously or loading in the wrong order; and any extension that crashes at startup is automatically temporarily disabled.

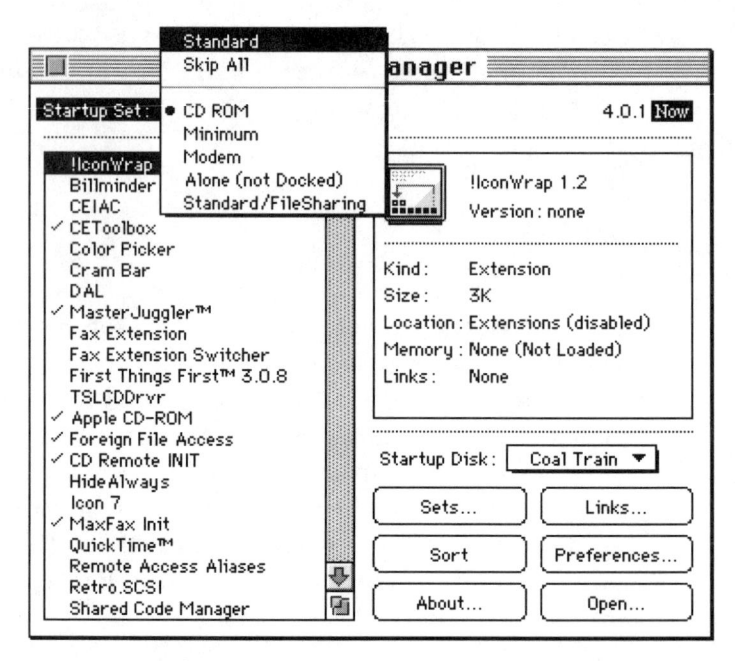

Figure 13-8: Startup Manager packs lots of features into an extension manager.

On Startup
Icom Simulations (On Cue II); $99.95

This extension manager provides all the basic capabilities you'll need, including startup access, and extension groups. It can automatically turn off extensions that cause crashes at startup, and provides a handy way to select from extension groups at startup (just hold down the mouse button after the Welcome to Macintosh dialog box appears).

Extension Manager
Apple Computer; freeware

Even if Apple has officially ignored the Mac's need for an extension manager, at least one of their employees hasn't.

Richard Batista's Extension Manager is a nice freeware program, offering all the basic capabilities, including reordering items, creating and choosing extension groups, and the ability to configure extension loading at startup.

Init Loader
Ian Hendry; freeware

This System 7 utility isn't really an extension manager, but it adds the capability of loading extensions that are stored in folders other than the Extensions folder, Control Panels folder, or the System Folder itself. It allows you to designate any other folders that hold extensions and have those extensions load, even if those folders are on other volumes—even remote network volumes.

Finder Performance Boosters

The utilities in this grouping provide a whole range of minor Finder modifications, each of which is helpful and, when taken together, are not to be missed.

System 7 Pack
Adam Stein; shareware $29.95

This great utility, written by a young man who was in high-school when it was first introduced, has continued to evolve and improve. (Version 3.01 is current as of this writing.) Here are just some of the Finder enhancements provided:

- **File copying speed improvement.** By allowing the Finder to use more RAM when copying files, the time it takes to copy files from one volume to another is reduced dramatically.

- **Remove zooming rectangles.** A simple check box turns off the Finder's zooming animation which appears when folders are open, saving a few fractions of a second during folder display.

- **Quit Finder menu.** You can add this Quit menu to your Finder, making it possible to Quit the Finder just like any other application, thereby freeing the memory the Finder normally uses for other purposes.

- **Set Rename Delay.** Modify the delay after a file or folder has been selected before you can rename it.

- **Change alias suffix.** I'm not sure what else besides "alias" you would like to call your aliases, but here's your chance.

- **Application linking.** Specify which application will open different document types when you don't have the creating application on your hard drive. Set Microsoft Word to open MacWrite files, for example.

- **Finder command keys.** You can modify or assign command keys to any command in any Finder menu.

- **Rename Finder commands.** For certain commands in the Finder, you can completely rename them to amuse yourself or confuse your friends.

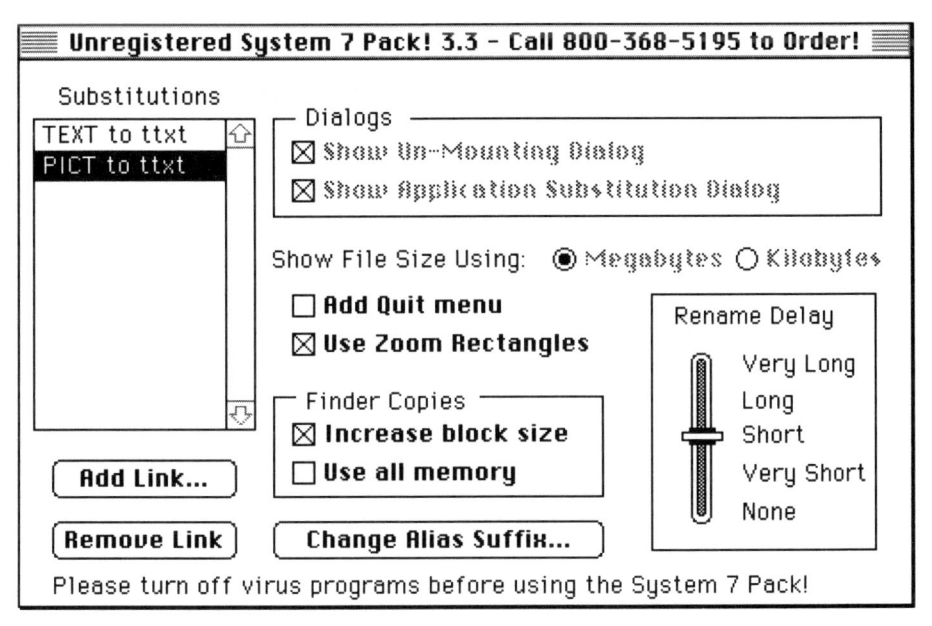

Figure 13-9: The System 7 Pack grants users the ability to change several aspects of their Finder.

SpeedyFinder7
Victor Tan; shareware $20

Another great Finder utility written by a college student, this one lets you make a number of modifications: speed up Finder copying and Trash emptying (which can be painfully slow in System 7), remove zoom rectangles, remove the rename delay and set links between stranded documents and your application programs. It can also add menu commands to certain Finder commands, add nice icons for your floppy disks, resolve "lost" aliases, change alias names and hide the Balloon Help menu while still allowing instant access to help balloons. This is a great utility with a nice user interface.

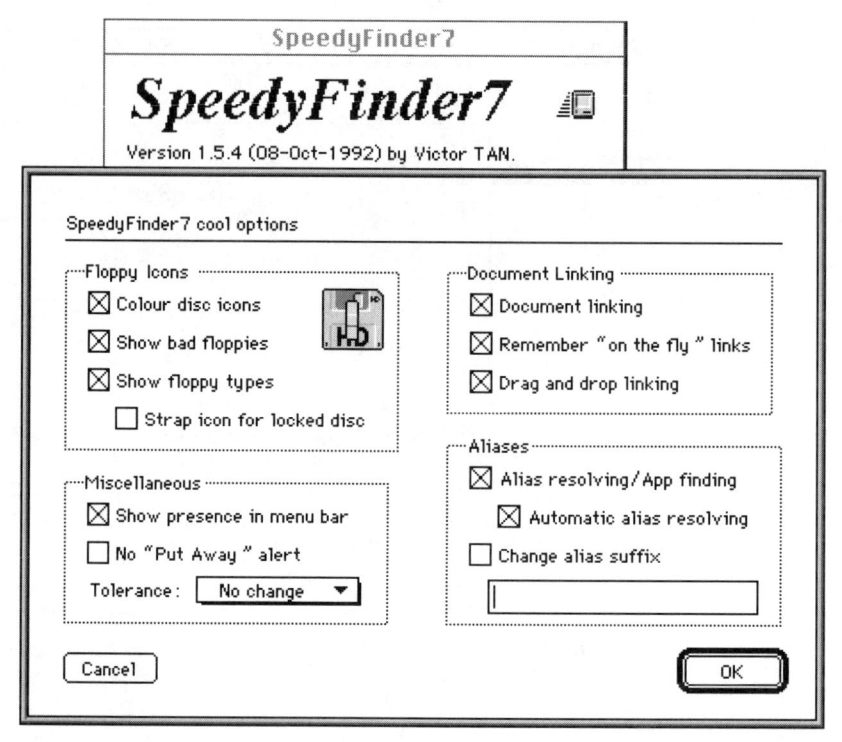

Figure 13-10: SpeedyFinder7 dialogs feature an attractive interface.

Utility Collections

Many System 7 utilities only offer a single function or feature, and when viewed individually, may seem rather minor. Lately, it has become popular to put together a collection of programs that all enhance System 7 in some way. Below are some of the best of these collections.

7 for Seven

Peter Kaplan; freeware

This package includes seven handy modifications for the System 7 Finder:

- **Set Rename Delay.** This option allows you to change the number of seconds you must wait after selecting a file name before the I-beam cursor appears. It is intended to undo a change in System 7 that annoys many people.

- **Change Alias Style.** By default, aliases have their file names set in italics. This option lets you pick any other type style (or type style combination) for your aliases.

- **Balloon Help Size.** If you find the 9 point size of text in balloon help too small, this option lets you pick a larger point size instead.

- **Application Linker.** This option lets you build links between certain document types and the application programs you would like to use to open those documents. If you use Microsoft Word as your word processor, for example, you can use this option to have MacWrite documents open in Word when double-clicked.

- **Add Quit to Finder.** The fact that the Finder is always open in System 7 means that it is also always using some RAM (about 200k). Adding a Quit command to the Finder lets you reclaim this RAM for use by other applications in memory-tight situations.

- **Show/Hide Command Key.** This option adds a command key equivalent to the Hide Others and Show All commands in the Application menu.

- **Remove ZoomRects.** When you open a window in the Finder, a slight animation effect called zooming rectangles occurs. This option lets you disable that animation, which improves Finder speed slightly.

7.0 PLUS Utilities
Robert Gibson; shareware $29.95

This series of utilities—they aren't usually packaged together but are instead available individually from online services and user groups—provides a wide variety of new and enhanced functions for System 7. Most take advantage of System 7's drag-and-drop (or drop-launching) capabilities. With drop-launching, you can, for instance, drag a document file icon onto the icon of an application and the application will launch and open the document. In the case of these utilities, the drop-launching performs a specific function other than simply opening a file. The 7.0 PLUS Utilities include

- **Blindfold.** This program makes files or folders visible or invisible at the Finder. This allows you to hide files from others who may use your Mac.

- **Catapult.** Drag a document icon onto Catapult and you can then choose which application you want to use to open it. This is a form of on-the-fly application linking useful for occasions when you get a file created by an application you don't have.

- **Custom Killer.** System 7 allows custom icons to be applied to files, folders, or disks. This utility removes them, restoring original icons.

- **DeIcon.** If you like to leave a lot of files on your Finder desktop, you may sometimes wish there were a way to limit the amount of desktop space these files consume. With DeIcon, your files appear on the desktop with names only—no icons appear. This allows you to fit more files on the desktop in less space.

- **Deflate.** For the extremely space conscious, this utility will remove the help resources from application files, thereby making them slightly smaller without compromising functionality (except help capabilities).

- **Desktop Deleter.** The invisible desktop file that System 6 created on your hard drive (assuming you previously used System 6 and have not reformatted your hard drive since) is sitting uselessly around wasting disk space, until you use this utility to remove it.

- **GetInfo.** Not to be confused with the Finder's Get Info command, this utility lets you view and change technical information about a file, such as its creator, Finder flags and locked bit.

- **Locksmith.** Locksmith allows you to lock or unlock files, folders and disks quickly and easily without the trouble of the Finder's Get Info windows. Locked files and disks cannot be modified until they are unlocked. No locked item can be renamed or deleted until it is unlocked. When used with System 7's drop-launching capabilities, you can modify entire groups of items.

- **Obliterate.** This is a great utility that provides an alternate Trash can that automatically empties as soon as any files or folders are put in it. This saves you the trouble of using the Empty Trash command when you throw things away that you want deleted immediately. Obliterate does not, however, actually remove files from your disk, as its name might suggest. Obliterated files can still be retrieved with undelete utilities, so it should not be used for security purposes.

- **Pesticide.** Empty folders, files without data, and aliases whose original items have been deleted can clutter your hard disk. Pesticide deletes these types of files, so you don't have to worry about them.

- **Recoverup.** This utility is designed to help fix the "missing files" bug that affected some people using System 7 version 7.0 and version 7.0.1. Tune-Up version 1.1.1 fixed the problem, however.

- **Scale.** This utility could be called "Group Get Info," because its main use is to find the combined size of a group of files and/or folders. Normally, you must accomplish this task by either dumping all the items into a single folder and checking its size or selecting the items and Getting Info on each of them and manually adding up their sizes.

- **SCSI Startup.** Rather than using the Startup Disk control panel to specify a startup drive, this program lets you drag-and-drop a drive icon to designate your intended startup disk. Unless you change startup drives constantly, this may be the least useful utility in this set.

- **Sound Roundup.** A scavenger for beep sounds, this program makes a copy of sounds contained in any files or applications you drag onto it, and puts them in a new folder or suitcase. You can then use these sounds in your System file, or with any sound utility.

- **Stationer.** When you drag a file's icon onto this utilities icon, it toggles the Stationery Pad check box normally found in the Get Info window. This makes it easier to turn groups of files into Stationary Pads.

- **Pink Slip.** A control panel that adds a Quit command to the Finder, allowing you to recover the memory that the Finder uses while open.

- **Wait!** A control panel for changing the delay when renaming files and folders.

- **Zap!** A control panel for resetting the parameter RAM of your Mac, which holds information set by other control panels, such as the startup disk, time, date, keyboard preferences, mouse preferences, screen bit-depth, volume and port configurations. Without this utility, the only way to reset the parameter RAM is to hold down Command-Shift-Option-P-R during startup.

7th Heaven
Logical Solutions; $99.95

A commercial package of utilities, 7th Heaven focuses on adding functionality to the Finder and making System 7 a little more fun. The utilities in 7th Heaven are

- **FinderExpress.** A utility to improve the allocation of memory to the Finder during file copies, thereby speeding up file copying dramatically.

- **FileMapper.** Another utility to define which application should be used to open documents whose creating applications are not available. FileMapper has a better user interface than either Catapult or the Application Linker option of Seven for 7, and allows linking lists to be imported and exported, so once a list has been created it can be shared among different Macs.

- **Red Alert.** The Alert, Info and Warning icons in System 7 get updated to your choice of new, more dramatic color icons with this utility.

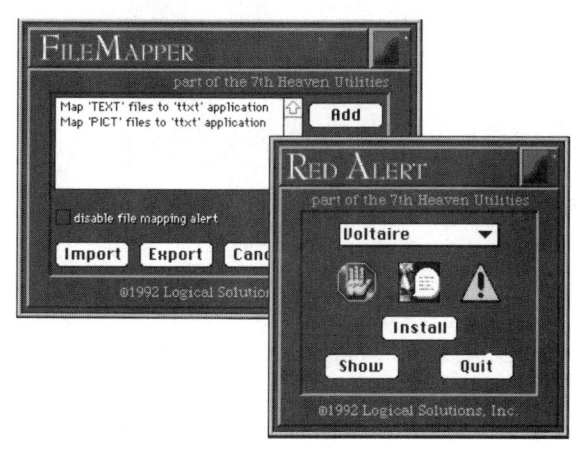

Figure 13-11: FileMapper and Red Alert.

- **Informant.** Providing all the info Apple left out of the About This Macintosh... dialog box, this program tells you just about everything about your Mac, extensions, SCSI drives and NuBus cards.

- **Calendar.** The desk accessory Apple forgot—a 10,000 year calendar that can show one or three months, as well as the current time. It can even function as a decorative calendar, with a new image or graphic every month.

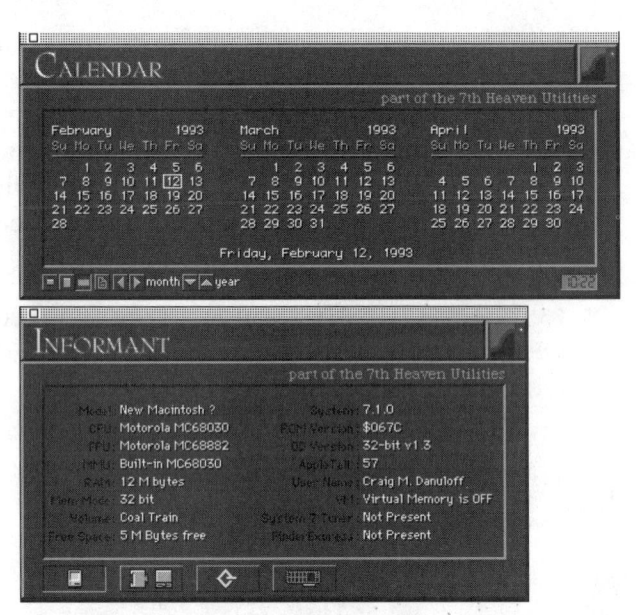

Figure 13-12: Calendar and Informant.

- **Chameleon.** Desktop patterns go high-resolution and beautiful with this utility, which lets you install one of dozens of predesigned patterns to replace your normal desktop. You can also import other patterns from professional designers or create your own.

Figure 13-13: Chameleon is a nice change of pace from the normal desktop.

- **Vector Plasma.** A rather low-tech screen saver, offering just one display (a constantly moving and changing object), no automatic launching options, no security options, and no waking options. It does, however, use very little memory or processing power, and supports color and multiple monitors.

Super Seven Utilities
Atticus Software; $99.95

Another commercial package (but one focusing more on core system software enhancements and adding the little niceties that Apple forgot), the Super Seven Utilities offer a number of unique control panels:

- **Helium Pro.** This upgraded version of the shareware utility Helium 2.1.1 adds functionality to Balloon Help, by allowing you to access help balloons anytime, without using the Balloon Help menu (just hold down a Command key combination and all balloons appear until you release the keys). You can also use Helium Pro to customize the font and size of help balloons and remove the balloon icon from your menu bar altogether.

- **Mighty Menus.** One of several features Apple talked about for System 7 that didn't make the final release was tear-off menus (like in HyperCard) for the Finder and all other applications. This utility provides tear-off menus, turning any menu into a floating palette you can access easily at any time.

- **Desktop Extras.** The new Finder menu provided by this utility includes commands to copy, move, alias and trash selected files. Using this menu, you can perform these operations without having to open the destination windows on the desktop.

- **Printer Picker.** Anyone working on a network with more than one printer will appreciate this utility, which adds a printer chooser menu just to the left of the Balloon Help menu. It allows you to change your target printer from this menu, without having to use the standard Chooser.

- **Speed Beep Pro.** Sound is one of those capabilities that Apple touts as a Macintosh strength, but barely supports with its system software. This control panel lets you control the volume of individual sounds, set random sound selection for system events, group different sounds for different applications, and play sounds without tying up your Mac, so you don't have to wait for long sounds to finish before continuing to work.

- **Super Comments.** Another early System 7 promise that Apple failed to keep is the survivability of Get Info comments when the Desktop file is rebuilt. This control panel makes comments more useful in System 7, letting you add them when you save a file, see them when you open files, and preserve them when the Desktop file is rebuilt.

- **Trash Alias.** Normally, when you delete a file, any aliases to that file are stranded on your hard drive, taking up space needlessly. When this control panel is installed, aliases are automatically deleted along with original applications, files or folder.

And so we conclude our look at System 7. Through the course of this book, we've examined nearly every aspect of the system software and, I hope, provided the explanations, information, tips, tricks and suggestions you were looking for when you first grabbed this book off the bookstore shelf.

As with so many aspects of the Mac, exploiting the operating system is a talent that has as many different approaches as there are Macintosh users. I welcome your comments, suggestions and discoveries; see the Introduction for information on how to reach me.

Appendix A: Installing or Updating System 7

When you decide to install System 7 for the first time, or to update from one version of System 7 to another, it is important that you carefully perform a number of steps in order to ensure that all of your hardware and software will be compatible with your new system software.

This appendix looks at everything you should know, before and during system software upgrades or updates. (Generally speaking, an upgrade involves moving up a whole number—like from System 6 to System 7—while an update means moving up a decimal place—like from Version 7.0 to 7.1.) We'll cover preparing your hard drive, using the Apple Compatibility Checker program, tips for using the Installer application, and strategies for arranging files on your hard drive after the installation.

Hardware Requirements

Before even starting the installation process, you should be sure your hardware is System 7-compatible. Fortunately satisfying this requirement is easy: any Macintosh with at least 2 Mb of memory (although 4 Mb or more is highly advised) and a hard drive is fine. You'll need between 3 and 5 Mb of free hard drive space (depending on the installation options you choose) to hold System 7 and all its related files.

Although all Macs can use System 7, some models cannot use the virtual memory or 32-bit addressing features. These limitations are fully explained in Chapter 11, "Memory Management."

System 7 is compatible with all existing Macintosh SCSI peripherals, although some of the INITs or control panels these peripherals use may be incompatible. In most cases, you'll be able to get new System 7-compatible software from hardware vendors. Most third-party video monitors and display adapters should also be compatible, although software driver updates may be required for these, too. Any printers you currently use with your Macintosh will continue to be compatible.

Replacing System 6.x With System 7

If you've upgraded or updated your system software before, you may be tempted to add System 7 by simply running the Installer application. This is not a good idea. Some of the fundamental changes made in System 7 make it necessary to first prepare your hard drive, and the Installer application doesn't always remove and replace the correct files when System 7 is installed over System 6, so manually removing certain files is recommended.

Below is a list of the installation steps I recommend. Each of these is described in detail in the following sections of this appendix. Please read through all of the steps before starting your installation.

- Back up your entire hard drive
- Update your hard disk driver
- Run the Apple Disk First Aid utility
- Run the Apple Compatibility Checker
- Delete certain existing system software files
- Run the System 7 Installer
- Configure your new System Folder

Back Up Your Hard Drive

As you prepare for the installation of System 7, your first step should be a complete back up of all data on your hard drive. There's always the remote possibility that the installation process could leave your hard drive inaccessible. It would be foolish to install System 7 without first backing up your data!

In fact, you should always back up your data before performing any major modification to your hard drive or system software. If you have a regular backup scheme in place, the effort required to do a backup should be minimal. If you don't have a regular backup scheme in place, then the effort required will be worth it, and if you're smart you'll use this opportunity to start a new habit of complete and regular backups.

If your hard drive is partitioned, be sure to back up each partition. Although the System 7 installation will be targeted as a single partition only, it will affect the hard drive in ways that could put all your data at risk. Again, this is highly unlikely but worth the effort of taking precautions.

So, have you backed up your data yet? **Do not continue** until you've done a complete back up!

Prepare Your Hard Drive

After you've backed up your data, it is important to verify the integrity of your hard disk and to make sure its hard disk driver is current. To do this, you'll need the Apple Disk First Aid utility that is included on the Disk Tools disk, and the software program that was used to format your hard disk.

To use Disk First Aid, restart your computer using the Disk Tools disk as a startup disk. Launch Disk First Aid, and select the name of the disk onto which you intend to install System 7 from the dialog box. Select the Repair Automatically command from the Options menu, and then click the Start button.

Disk First Aid will then verify your disk, and should report: No Repair Necessary. If it indeed finds some problem with your disk, it will attempt to repair it, and will notify you if it cannot repair the problem. In this case, you will need to either reformat your hard drive, or attempt repairs using Norton Utilities, MacTools or some other commercial repair utility. In any case, you should not install System 7 until Disk First Aid gives your drive a clean bill of health.

Next, you need to make sure that a System 7-compatible hard disk driver is installed on your hard drive. If your hard drive has not been reformatted with a current formatting utility in the last two years, you will probably have to update your driver. An incompatible hard disk driver will probably not make it impossible for you to use System 7, although it may make virtual memory unusable. In any case, installing a current driver is a good idea—it will probably improve the perfomance of your hard drive.

You can update your hard disk driver without reformatting your drive by using your formatting utility. If you purchased a hard drive that was preformatted by Apple, the Apple HD Setup utility was probably used to format your drive. A copy is included on the System 7 Disk Tools disk. If you purchased your hard drive from your Apple dealer, or from a mail-order reseller, you should have been given a copy of the hard disk formatting software. Whichever software was used, launch the utility and choose the Update Drivers or Install New Drivers option.

Note: If you are not certain which utility was used to format your drive, you should be very careful when updating drivers and under no circumstances should you perform the update without first backing up your hard drive. The drivers from one formatting utility may work properly on a drive formatted with another utility, but they may not. In this situation, the best advice is to actually reformat your drive, install new drivers, and then restore all of your data from your backup.

If you are using the Apple HD Setup utility, you may want to take advantage of this opportunity to instead use one of the commercially available formatting utilities, such as Drive7, SilverLining or Hard Disk Toolkit. While it may seem unusual to purchase a utility program to replace one that Apple provides without charge, each of these programs provides better drive performance, compatibility with a wider range of devices (including removable cartridges such as Syquest or Bernoulli), and better drive repair, salvage and troubleshooting support. Reformatting your drive with one of these utilities is a good investment in your Mac system.

Run Apple's Compatibility Checker

To help you discover which pieces of software you're currently using are compatible with System 7, Apple developed the Compatibility Checker 2.0, that provides a very good, although not comprehensive, survey of the files on your hard drive and a summary of the way these files will react once System 7 is installed.

The program has a handy tool for moving all your System Folder files known to be incompatible, or untested by Apple for compatibility, to a special folder where they will not conflict with System 7. You can then test each of these files individually, or replace them with newer System 7-Savvy versions.

Earlier versions of the Compatibility Checker required HyperCard, but version 2.0 is a stand alone application. After you launch the Compatibility Checker, you select the drives you want to check. In most cases, you should select all of the volumes you'll use on your new system.

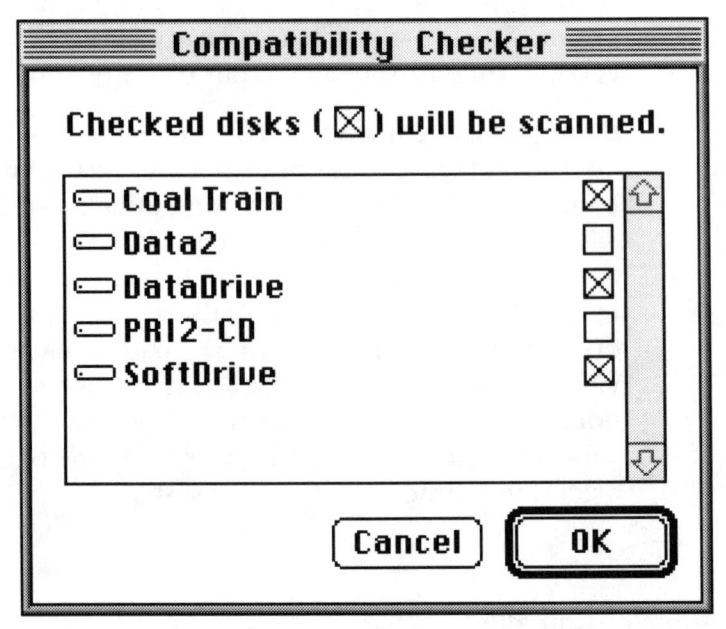

Figure A-1: The Compatibility Checker's Select Drives dialog.

As the Compatibility Checker examines your volumes, a progress bar documents percentage of completion. When all volumes and the current System Folder have been checked, an incompatibility list, like the one shown in Figure A-2, will appear on-screen if a problem or a suspected incompatible file has been found in the System Folder.

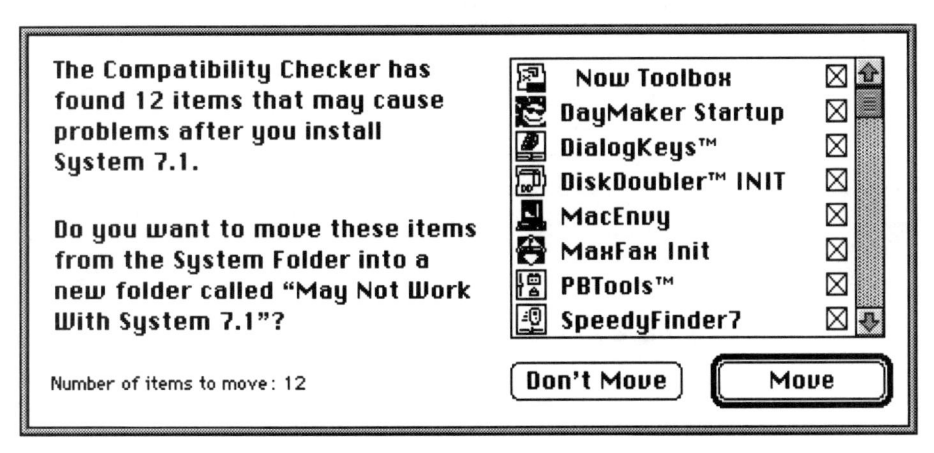

Figure A-2: Incompatibility Warning list.

The Compatibility Checker can move these files to a safe location—the May Not Work With System 7.1 folder—where they can't cause problems. This is done by clicking the Move button. You can later replace those that are incompatible with newer System 7-compatible versions, and test those that Apple has not tested.

Next, the complete Compatibility Report (shown in Figure A-3) appears, which lists each executable file found on the selected volumes, plus each INIT or Control Panel device, and documents its status as identified by Apple.

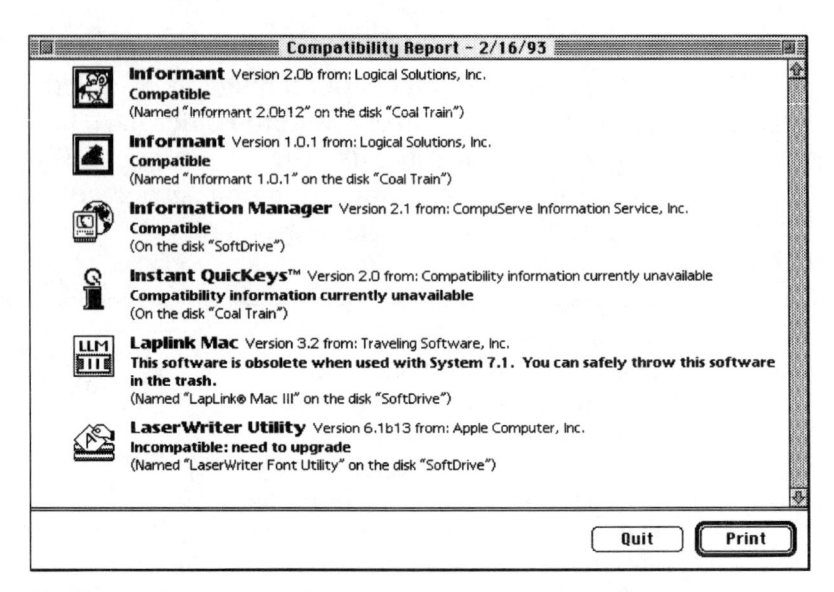

```
┌─────────────────────── Compatibility Report - 2/16/93 ───────────────────────┐
│ Informant  Version 2.0b from: Logical Solutions, Inc.                        │
│ Compatible                                                                   │
│ (Named "Informant 2.0b12" on the disk "Coal Train")                          │
│                                                                              │
│ Informant  Version 1.0.1 from: Logical Solutions, Inc.                       │
│ Compatible                                                                   │
│ (Named "Informant 1.0.1" on the disk "Coal Train")                           │
│                                                                              │
│ Information Manager  Version 2.1 from: CompuServe Information Service, Inc.  │
│ Compatible                                                                   │
│ (On the disk "SoftDrive")                                                    │
│                                                                              │
│ Instant QuicKeys™  Version 2.0 from: Compatibility information currently unavailable │
│ Compatibility information currently unavailable                              │
│ (On the disk "Coal Train")                                                   │
│                                                                              │
│ Laplink Mac  Version 3.2 from: Traveling Software, Inc.                      │
│ This software is obsolete when used with System 7.1. You can safely throw this software │
│ in the trash.                                                                │
│ (Named "LapLink® Mac III" on the disk "SoftDrive")                           │
│                                                                              │
│ LaserWriter Utility  Version 6.1b13 from: Apple Computer, Inc.               │
│ Incompatible: need to upgrade                                                │
│ (Named "LaserWriter Font Utility" on the disk "SoftDrive")                   │
│                                                                              │
│                                                    [ Quit ]  [ Print ]       │
└──────────────────────────────────────────────────────────────────────────────┘
```

Figure A-3: Compatibility Report as it appears on-screen.

There are four main status categories in this report:

- **Compatible.** An application is either System 7-compatible or System 7-Savvy, and you'll have no problems using it with System 7.

- **Upgrade available.** Although your version is System 7-compatible, the software developer recommends using a more recent version with System 7.

- **Must upgrade.** The software is incompatible with System 7. You must use a newer version with your new system software.

- **Unknown.** The software has not been tested for compatibility. Most of these items will prove compatible with System 7, but you'll have to make that determination yourself, as described later in this chapter.

Other codes also appear next to some status names. They're explained in the lower portion of the Compatibility Report.

It's a good idea to print the entire Compatibility Report, by clicking the Print button, since you'll probably need this information later. You can also write the report to disk, which lets you view the report in your favorite word processor. When you've finished, choose the Quit command to exit.

Delete Existing System Software

The last important step to take before actually running the installer is to delete some or all of the files from your existing system software. This step is taken to eliminate the possibility that the Installer application will not completely replace these files with new ones. (Although you can technically just run the Installer without deleting old files, experience has shown that these installations are not very stable.)

Before you begin trashing files, you may want to run your Font/DA Mover for one last time, and transfer any non-standard fonts (anything except Chicago, Geneva, New York, Monaco, Times, Helvetica, Courier and Symbol) that are in your System file into a suitcase file elsewhere on your hard disk, so that you can reinstall them after your System 7 installation. You should also save copies of any non-standard desk accessories from your System file, as well as any FKEYs that have been installed.

To delete your existing system software, just drag the Finder, System file and other Apple system software files to the Trash. You won't be able to empty the trash since many of these files are in use, but that isn't a problem. Be careful not to trash any non-Apple files, such as third-party INITs, Control Panel devices, or other files that you may need once System 7 is installed. If you're not sure what a file is, just leave it. As long as you delete the Finder and/or System file, the installation will occur properly.

After you have dragged the system software files to the trash, rename your existing System Folder as something like "OLD System Folder," so its name will not conflict with the new System Folder added by the Installer.

You're now ready to use the System 7 Installer to install System 7. A new System Folder will be created on your hard disk. (Complete details on using the System 7 Installer, how to re-install the fonts, DA's and other files you removed from your old System Folder are included in the "Configuring the System 7 System Folder" section later in this appendix.)

Run the Installer

The System 7 Installer application can be run from the System 7 CD-ROM, from floppy disk or from a mounted AppleShare file server. Unlike earlier versions of the Installer, you can actually install System 7 onto the hard drive that's your current Startup Disk (the one containing the system software the Mac is currently using).

If you are going to install over existing system software (which I don't recommend), you should disable any virus-checking utilities you regularly use, since these would likely be triggered repeatedly by the actions of the Installer, making it difficult or impossible for the Installer to complete its tasks successfully.

If you are going to install from an AppleShare volume containing the System 7 Installer, mount that volume normally, using the Chooser. If you're installing from a System 7 CD-ROM, insert the CD so it appears on your Finder desktop. To install from the System 7 floppy disk set, restart your Mac using Install Disk 1 as a startup disk.

Launch the Installer application by double-clicking on its icon. You're now ready to install System 7. The first screen of the Installer is the Easy Install dialog box, which includes a recommended set of installation options. It also displays the name of the drive the system software will be installed on. If the selected disk is not the one you want, click the Switch Disk button until the name of the desired hard drive appears.

There are three options from the Easy Install dialog box:

- **Install.** Click the Install button to install the listed software onto the named hard disk or volume. Use this option if you're sure you want the recommended options, or you're not sure which options you want installed. (The discussion later in this chapter should help you avoid that situation.)

- **Customize.** Clicking the Customize option lets you select the specific drivers and other files you want installed along with your system software.

- **Quit.** Forget this whole thing, let's go back to System Software 6.0x! This option will leave your original system software untouched and exit the Installer.

The scrolling window in the Customize dialog box provides options covering the system software, printing software, File Sharing software and network driver software. Click on the options you want, holding down the shift key to select multiple items.

The Customize dialog box options include

- **System Software.** These options include System Software For Any Macintosh, System Software For (Specific Macintosh), Minimal System Software For Any Macintosh and Minimal System Software For (Specific Macintosh). You can choose only one of these options.

Choose System Software For Any Macintosh if the destination drive will be connected to different Macintosh computers at different times. If you were to choose one of the system software options specific to one Macintosh model, that hard disk would not be able to support some Macintosh models. This option might add a few more files than you really need for your Macintosh, but these files consume only a small amount of disk space and will cause no problems for you.

Choose System Software For (Specific Macintosh) if you're sure the hard drive you're installing on will be used with one specific Macintosh model only.

Choose Minimal System Software For Any Macintosh if you're installing on a hard drive that will be used on more than one Macintosh model, but you have limited free space on that hard drive.

This option can also be used to create a 1.44 Mb floppy disk of System 7.

Choose Minimal System Software For (Specific Macintosh) if you're sure that the hard drive you're installing on will be used with one specific Macintosh model only, and there's limited free space on that hard drive.

- **Printer drivers.** The options for printer drivers include Software For All Apple Printers, Software For LaserWriter, Software For Personal LaserWriter SC, Software For ImageWriter and Software For AppleTalk ImageWriter. Choose according to the printers you'll use with your Macintosh. There's no limit to how many of these options you can select for installation at one time.

- **File Sharing software.** If you will be operating System 7 on a network and want to share folders or volumes with other Macintoshes or access your hard drive from another network Macintosh, select this option.

- **Network drivers.** If an Ethertalk or Tokentalk network card is installed in your Macintosh, select the appropriate network driver option. You can install both of these drivers, but you'll likely need only one of them at most. If you're using an AppleTalk network, you don't have to select either option.

After selecting the appropriate options, click the button to begin the installation. You can also use the Easy Install button to return to the previous dialog box, or the Quit button to cancel the entire installation.

Once the installation begins, its progress is displayed. If you're installing from floppy disks, you'll be prompted for disks as required. When the installation is complete, the Installation Successful dialog box appears. Click the Continue button if you need to return to the Easy Install dialog box, or the Quit button, to return to the Finder.

After quitting the Installer, you should restart your Macintosh to confirm that installation was successful and that System 7 will launch properly. Welcome to System 7!

Configure the System 7 System Folder

Now you can customize your system software by adding fonts, additional extensions, control panels and other files to the System Folder. If you created the "OLD System Folder" as described above, carefully move all files from this folder into your new System Folder. Make sure you don't move any files that are part of your old system software. You should drag files in small groups, and cancel the copying if a dialog box appears telling you that files with the same names as the files you are moving already exist. This probably means you are trying to move a file from System 6 that already exists in a System 7 version. (See "Configuring Your System" in Chapter 8, "Fonts in System 7," for details on the font installation process.)

Extensions (formerly called INITs) and control panels are installed into the System Folder by dragging their icons onto the System Folder icon. The Macintosh will then automatically place them in the Extensions or Control Panels folder. Alternatively, you can manually drag them into the Extensions or Control Panels folder yourself. (See "Adding Files to the System Folder" in Chapter 4, "The System Folder," for more information on installing extensions and control panels.)

Since extensions and control panels can contain special code that is executed at startup and that modifies the System file as it's loaded into memory, it's important to avoid those that are incompatible with System 7. The report you created with the Compatibility Checker will identify extensions and control panels that are compatible and those that require an upgrade before they can be used with System 7.

Copy all files the Compatibility Checker listed as compatible to the System Folder. Don't install those requiring an upgrade; contact the software developer at the address listed in the Compatibility Report to obtain a compatible version.

Many of your files will be listed by the Compatibility Checker as "Unknown," which leaves it up to you to test their compatibility. The only way to do this is to add these files one at a time to your System Folder, then restart your Macintosh and test for compatibility.

It's easy to tell that a file is incompatible—your Mac crashes on startup. If this happens, press the reset switch on your Macintosh or turn its power off and on, then hold down the Shift key during startup. This will disable all extensions, allowing you to open the System Folder and remove the problem file.

If the Macintosh starts up without incident, test the extension by using it in one or two different situations. In most cases, if incompatibilities didn't show up during startup, they'll become apparent as soon as the extension or control panel is used. If you find an incompatible file, remove it from your System Folder. Continue this testing process for each new control panel and extension until all the ones you want to use have been added.

Next, move all the miscellaneous files from your previous System Folder (things like dictionaries, help files, preferences files or even entire folders) into the newly installed System Folder. Most of these files should go into the System Folder itself, although preferences files should be moved into the Preferences folder.

To install your desk accessories, you can either drag them to the System Folder, which will place them into the Apple menu folder automatically, or convert them into stand-alone applications that you can launch by double-clicking. To do this, double-click on any DA Suitcase, and all enclosed DAs will appear with individual application icons. Dragging them out of the DA window and into any other folder or volume converts them into double-clickable applications. (See Chapter 5, "System 7 & Your Software," for a more complete discussion of converting DAs.)

Once a DA has been converted into an application, it can be used just like any application. You can store the converted DA in any folder; you can usually launch it by double-clicking on its icon; and you can install the DA or its alias in the Apple Menu folder so it can be launched from the Apple Menu.

Updating System 7

Moving from one version of System 7 to another is far easier than moving from System 6 to System 7, although there are a few special recommended steps:

- Run Apple Disk First Aid before updating. This utility can find problems with your hard drive before they cause real problems with new system software.

- Drag the Finder to the trash and rename your old System Folder, before booting from the Install 1 disk to run the Installer. This will cause the new system software to be installed in a new System Folder. If you don't do this, the new system software will be installed over the old system software, and while this is the way Apple intends for updates to be handled, it has not proven very reliable.

- After the installation, carefully drag all non-Apple system software files from your old System Folder to the new System Folder. Be especially careful not to overwrite any new system software files with old ones, or to move old system software files that are no longer needed.

Appendix B: A Brief History of System 7

Since its initial release, System 7 has been enhanced, extended and updated several times. At the time of this writing, there are three main System 7 versions (7.0, 7.0.1 and 7.1), three bug-fix/performance improvement extensions (Tune-Up 1.0, 1.11 and Macintosh Hardware System Update 1.0), two special versions (7.0.1P and 7.1P, for the Macintosh Performa line) and a slew of system enablers.

The Many Faces of System 7

This book covers all these versions of System 7. Any time the reference "System 7" is used, the features being described are common to all versions listed above. Whenever a feature unique to one version is described, the software is referred to by its specific version name, such as "Version 7.0.1" or "Version 7.1P."

Details about each version of System 7, the Tune-Ups and enablers are provided in this appendix.

System 7.0

System 7.0 was the original "golden master" release of Apple's new system software. It is the foundation on which all subsequent versions are based, and the overwhelming majority of its features are common throughout all versions of System 7.

System 7.0.1

System 7.0.1 was released to support the Mac Classic II, Quadra 700, Quadra 900 and the PowerBooks (models 100, 140, 145 and 170). While it is compatible with any Macintosh, only users of the models listed above, or the IIci, IIfx or IIsi, would benefit from upgrading from Version 7.0 to Version 7.0.1.

Beyond the changes made to support the Classic II, Quadra 700, Quadra 900 and PowerBooks, Version 7.0.1 updates the ROM-based Standard Apple Numeric Environment (SANE), which improves computational speed on Mac's equipped with math coprocessors.

Version 7.0.1 was shipped with the Classic II, Quadra 700, Quadra 900 and PowerBooks. It was not offered for sale because Apple did not recommend users of all Mac models upgrade from Version 7.0 to Version 7.0.1. Version 7.0.1 is available, however, without charge from many user groups and online services. In addition, you may legally install someone else's copy of Version 7.0.1 on your Macintosh.

System 7 Tune-Up

Tune-Up is a System 7 bug-fix and performance improvement, which installs an extension called System 7 Tuner, as well as new versions of the Chooser, File Sharing extension, LaserWriter and StyleWriter files into your System 7 System Folder. Installing the Tune-Up files improves the performance of System 7.0 or 7.0.1, and fixes a number of bugs in the first two releases of System 7.

There are two versions of Tune-Up, Version 1.0 and Version 1.1.1. Both are compatible with System 7 Version 7.0 and Version 7.0.1. Fixes and improvements in Tune-Up 1.0 include: faster Finder copying, better printing speeds (50 to 200 percent), enhanced memory management (especially in low-memory situations), savings of 100k when AppleTalk is turned off in the Chooser and correction of several file sharing problems. Tune-Up 1.1.1 corrects a bug which causes folders to disappear from the Finder, and provides a new LaserWriter driver (Version 7.1.1) which improves performance on the LaserWriter Plus, LaserWriter NTR and LaserWriter IIf and IIg.

When Tune-Up is installed, a dot appears next to the System Software version number in the About This Macintosh dialog box. You cannot tell by looking at this dot whether Version 1.0 or Version 1.1.1 of the Tune-Up file is installed. Neither version of Tune-Up is required when using Version 7.1 or later (all Tune-Up features have been built into these versions).

Anyone using System 7 Version 7.0 or Version 7.0.1 should obtain and install Tune-Up. The System 7 Tune-Up disk is also free and is available from Apple, Apple dealers, user groups, online services and bulletin boards.

System 7.1

System 7.1 has been positioned as the first major update to System 7.0, but for most users it isn't very significant. It does, however, have some underlying technological changes that will become more important in the future.

The biggest new feature of Version 7.1, from Apple's point-of-view, is called *WorldScript*, a technology that allows System 7 to be customized more easily for foreign languages, including Japanese, Chinese and other languages with large character sets. This may be important to Apple, but it is hardly significant to most Macintosh users in the United States.

The change every Mac user will notice is the new Fonts folder inside the System Folder. The new Fonts folder becomes the official home of all fonts—screen, printer, bitmapped, PostScript and TrueType—in Version 7.1. This new folder means fonts are no longer stored in the System file or loose in the System Folder. Use of the new Fonts folder is fully described in Chapter 8, "Fonts in System 7."

One of the changes in Version 7.1 that users will eventually notice is that new Macintosh models will no longer require new versions of the system software, as they frequently have in the past. Instead, special files called system *enablers* will be shipped with future Macintoshes, allowing these new machines to be used with Version 7.1. Most existing Macintoshes use Version 7.1 without system enablers (which function much like extensions), although the Macintosh Performa line is already using enablers.

The features found in the Tune-Up releases described above have been built-into Version 7.1, so neither release of Tune-Up is needed. QuickTime 1.5, an extension that allows a number of multimedia capabilities to become part of the Macintosh system software is bundled with Version 7.1 (see Chapter 12, "Apple's System 7 Extensions" for a complete discussion of QuickTime), and the DAL extension that was provided with Version 7.0 and Version 7.0.1 is no longer included with Version 7.1. DAL is used for database server access, and will be available with other software products requiring it.

System 7 Version 7.1 differs from previous system software releases in one important way—it is not available as a free-of-charge update. Apple's upgrade policy and pricing is as follows:

- If you do not receive Version 7.1 along with your Macintosh when you purchase it, you must purchase a System 7.1 Upgrade Kit in order to legally obtain Version 7.1.

- Upgrade kits containing only the Version 7.1 disks are available directly from Apple for $34.95 at 800-769-2775.

- A complete System 7.1 Personal Upgrade Kit, including manuals, is available at most Apple dealers for $99. A System 7.1 10-user MultiPack Upgrade Kit is available through dealers for $499.

- Customers who purchased Version 7.0 of the System 7 Personal Upgrade Kit or the System 7 Group Upgrade Kit after September 1, 1992, will receive the Version 7.1 product free of charge by providing proof of purchase. For more information, call 800-769-2775.

This change of policy is significant to many Mac users, and has caused much debate. Generally speaking, pricing is the only reason not to upgrade to Version 7.1 for most users. Purely as an act of protest against Apple's poor execution of the decision to charge for their system software, sticking with Version 7.0.1 and Tune-Up 1.1.1 is commendable. And in the short run—until the release of new 7.1-dependent applications or extensions—there is little harm in doing so. In the long run, however, everyone will have to upgrade and hopefully Apple will create a fair and realistic system of handling system software updates.

System 7.1 Hardware System Update 1.0

To prove that it is working tirelessly to continually improve System 7, Apple released Macintosh Hardware System Update 1.0, which is like a tune-up extension for Version 7.1. It is shipped along with Version 7.1.1 of the Memory control panel. Using these two files improves high speed serial communications, system clock accuracy, floppy ejection during shutdown and system performance in low memory situations. The extension is recommended for all Mac II, LC, PowerBook and Quadra models, as well as the Classic II. Performa users should not use this extension, as these features are built into the current system enablers for Performas. (See the last section of this appendix of details on enablers.)

System 7.0.1P, System 7.1P

The introduction of the Macintosh Performa series brought with it two new variants of System 7, Version 7.0.1P and Version 7.1P. These versions are identical to Versions 7.0.1 and 7.1 as described above, and throughout this book, with a few exceptions:

- **Application Launcher.** An application launcher control panel is included, which provides a window at the Finder displaying large icons for frequently used software. This makes it easier for users to launch these programs. Application icons can be added to the launcher window by placing aliases of the applications in the Launcher folder inside the System Folder.

- **Default Folders.** When using the standard Open or Save dialog boxes, default folders named "document folder" and "application folder" are located automatically. This is intended to make it easier for new users to find files they want to open and to save files in the correct location. Of course, users are still free to navigate to any other folder or volume if the default locations are not correct.

- **Application Hiding.** When any application is launched, all other applications, including the Finder, are hidden. This has the same effect as automatically using the Hide Others command in the Application Menu. This change makes the screen less cluttered and confusing for new Macintosh users.

- **Desktop Patterns.** The General control panel has been modified to make selection of a desktop pattern easier.

- **Backup and Restore.** A very simple backup program is included, allowing the entire hard disk, or just the System Folder, to be backed up or restored.

- **8-Bit Default.** When using a Performa 400 or 600, the Monitors control panel is automatically set to 8-bit color (instead of 2-bit black and white) by default.

- **At Ease.** This Apple extension is bundled with all "P" versions (and is also sold separately for anyone else who may want it). It provides a simpler interface for the Finder, making it easier to launch applications, find and save files, and limit access to the standard Finder and the Trash. Restricting access to the Finder is designed to prevent unsophisticated users (such as children) from accidentally deleting or moving files. Chapter 12, "Apple's System 7 Extensions," provides more details on At Ease.

Which Version Should I Use?

It's not hard to understand why many people are confused about which version of System 7 they should be using:

- The many well-known problems with past releases of new system software made some users wary of the first release of System 7—simply because it was the first release. "I never use any software whose version number ends in a zero," was the familiar refrain from some skeptics, who sat and waited for some sort of update, regardless of the reason for it.

- Those who did make the move to System 7 were just settling in to Version 7.0 when Version 7.0.1 came along, accompanied by conflicting reports about who should use it. Distribution limitations and uncertainty about Apple's policy regarding this release further inhibited its use.

- The Tune-Up extensions were fairly well publicized, (if you read *Macworld* or *MacUser*), but details on who needed them and why were scarce. Word quickly spread that Tune-Up 1.0 didn't fix all the initial problems, and Tune-Up 1.1 was quickly released and then discontinued. Understandably, people were a bit queasy about Tune-Up 1.1.1. Distribution of Tune-Up disks was better than that for 7.0.1, but for folks without easy access to online services or user groups, it was still a little hard to come by.

- The release of Version 7.1, with all the significance of that first decimal place and the valiant but ineffectual attempt by Apple to suggest that this release was technically significant, actually did convince many holdouts that it was time to move to System 7, and provided Version 7.0 users with hope that the comedy of 7.0.1 and the Tune-Ups was over. This ground swell of support was quickly dashed, however, when Apple announced that their long-rumored plan to charge for system software updates would be implemented beginning with those updating to Version 7.0.1. In other words, users who supported Apple's System 7 from the start were asked to pay $30 (or more) for WorldScript and the Fonts folder. Many have understandably opted to stick with 7.0.1 and Tune-Up 1.1.1 instead.

- The release of the Macintosh Performa series—based on the supposition that anyone who shops at Sears won't actually visit a computer store—brought the "P" variants of System 7: Version 7.0.1P and Version 7.1P. Most Mac users haven't heard of these versions, and when they do, they will probably be confused. Most Performa users do not realize they have a special version of the system software, and will therefore be very confused when the next update comes out and they install it and find their training wheels missing.

- The somewhat mysterious "system enablers" introduced along with System 7.1 are needed for Macs released after System 7.1. The Performas, Duos and Centrises have them, as does the Quadra 800 and PowerBook 160, 165c and 180. Enablers are discussed in greater detail later in this appendix.

Given all this, what system software version should you use? Ideally, you should always use the latest version of the system software that is appropriate for your machine. At the time of this writing, that means Version 7.1 (or 7.1P, if you have a Performa and need or want the modifications). Even as time passes, and the version numbers and incidents described here become distant memories, new version numbers and new incidents will almost certainly replace them.

But a few general rules can help keep you out of trouble when upgrading or updating your system software:

- New versions of system software are released to provide more features, and generally make things better. There are exceptions to this rule, but it is the rule. This is why you should always use the latest version.

- Don't use a new version of system software for at least one month after it is released. Let the daredevils and the press figure out if it has any bugs first. If there are bugs, read the articles in the trade magazines carefully to determine how serious and widespread they are. While the press does a good job in making these kinds of problems known, it generally overstates and exaggerates them. (No one said this was going to be easy.)

- The primary factor behind needing to change your system software (beyond basic hardware compatibility and overall performance) is the applications and utilities you use. In other words, if you don't regularly update your software or use new programs or utilities, there is less reason to continually update your system software. In this case, your Mac is a closed environment, so if it ain't broke, don't fix it. Of course, to get the most from your Mac, you will inevitably have to update your applications, try new ones, and add utilites. When you do (or better yet, before you do) move to the latest version of the system software as well.

Enablers

Historically, each time Apple releases a new Macintosh model, it has had to release a new version of their system software. These new hardware-specific releases changed the second decimal place of the current version number when they occurred with System 6 (Versions 6.0.5, 6.0.6, 6.0.7, etc.), and usually included a few bug fixes and performance improvements in addition to the additional hardware support.

For System 7, Apple has decided to avoid releasing new versions of the system software for each new Macintosh model, turning instead to a new form of system file, called a *system enabler*. These files work much like extensions—they reside in the System Folder and are loaded at startup.

Enablers are not required for Macintosh models released before the introduction of Version 7.1, but are required by all subsequent models. The chart below lists the current system enabler version for each Mac model.

Macintosh	System Enabler	Version
Centris 610	system enabler 040	1.0
Centris 650	system enabler 040	1.0
Color Classic	system enabler 401	1.0.4
IIvx	system enabler 001	1.0.1
LC III	system enabler 003	1.0
PowerBook 160	system enabler 111	1.0.2
PowerBook 165c	system enabler 121	1.0
PowerBook 180	system enabler 111	1.0.2
PowerBook Duo 210	system enabler 201	1.0.1
PowerBook Duo 230	system enabler 201	1.0.1
Quadra 800	system enabler 040	1.0
Plus	none required	
SE	none required	
SE/30	none required	
Classic	none required	
II/IIx/IIcx/IIfx/IIci/IIsi	none required	
Quadra 700/900/950	none required	
LC/LCII	none required	
PowerBook 140/145/170	none required	

System enablers are a major sore spot in the Apple system software distribution scheme. Their logistical implications are incredible. Requiring different enablers for different Macs might make theoretical sense, but a much simpler solution would be to have a single enabler that can be used on all Macs released since a specific system software version release.

Building emergency startup floppies that can be quickly used to boot any Mac has become almost impossible. Already overwhelmed Mac users and system administrators now have another set of files (with crystal clear names like "system enabler Version 1.2.1") to keep track of, each with their own functions and version numbers. So now you must know the version number of your system software, the tune-up number and version (when applicable), and the system enabler number and version (when applicable). What could be easier?

Enablers are included along with all models that require them, but at the time of this writing, Apple does not allow them to be freely distributed via online services, user groups, or dealers. Since several specific enablers have already been updated themselves, there appears no clear way for a Mac user without either an AppleLink account or Apple Internet FTP to keep their enablers current.

I hope Apple will soon change its policy and consolidate enablers into a single file supporting all Mac models, number their versions clearly, and make them widely and freely available.

Glossary

Alias   An alias is a duplicate icon for any file, folder or volume. The alias icon is linked to the original icon used to create it, and opening the alias opens the original file. Even if an alias is moved or renamed, the link to the original file remains.

Apple Menu folder   A folder inside the System Folder used to hold all applications, documents, folders, volumes and desk accessories that you want to appear in the Apple Menu. Up to 50 files or aliases can be stored in this folder.

Comments   Short descriptive notes attached to any file, folder or volume. Comments are entered into the Get Info dialog box by choosing the Get Info command. To display comments in Finder windows, use the Views control panel to select the "Show Comments" option. You can search for a file by text contained in its comment using the Find command.

Control Panels folder   A folder inside the System Folder which contains all control panel files used on a Macintosh. Control panels must reside in this folder so that they are properly loaded at startup, although you can create aliases of them and store those aliases in other locations.

Desktop (level)   The top of the Mac's disk and file hierarchy, equivalent to the display seen at the Finder desktop. The desktop level includes all mounted hard disks and volumes, mounted floppy disks and any files or folders that have been placed on the Finder desktop.

Edition files   Edition files are normal Macintosh files that contain text or graphic elements saved by the Create Publisher command. Edition files are imported into other documents using the Subscribe To command.

Edition Manager   A feature that allows software applications to exchange data using the Publish and Subscribe commands. This umbrella term covers both the specific commands associated with data exchange and the underlying technology that manages edition files after they have been created.

Extension   A small program that modifies or extends the capabilities of the system software. This includes startup programs (INITS), printer drivers, network drivers and other types of files. All extensions must be kept in the Extensions folder inside the System Folder in order to load properly at startup.

Font scaler   A small program that is automatically sent to PostScript printers when documents containing TrueType fonts are printed.

File Sharing   A feature that allows any Macintosh running System 7 to make folders and volumes available to other network users, and to access shared data from other File Sharing Macs, or from AppleShare file servers.

Help balloons   Small information windows that pop-up to provide simple explanations of commands, dialog box options and on-screen icons. Help balloons only appear when the Show Balloons command is selected, and can be removed by choosing the Hide Balloons command.

Hiding Removing the windows of an open application from the screen without quitting the application. This is done with the Hide commands found in the Applications Menu. To see windows after they are hidden, the Show commands are used.

Hierarchical view The ability of a Finder window to display a folder and the files inside that folder in a single window.

IAC An abbreviation for Inter-Application Communication. This is a set of protocols that make it possible for Macintosh applications to communicate and control each other. IAC is used by Apple Events, which are commands issued and understood by some software applications that have been specifically upgraded for System 7.

INITS See Extensions.

Labels A set of user-defined categories that can be applied to any file, folder or volume as a means of classification. Labels are defined with a title and color using the Labels control panel, and applied by selecting an icon, or group of icons, and choosing the appropriate label from the Labels menu.

Publish/Subscribe See the Edition Manager.

Startup Items folder A folder inside the System Folder used to store applications, folders or documents that you want opened automatically at startup.

Stationery Pads Any document in System 7 can be designated a Stationery Pad, or template. Stationery Pads are automatically duplicated when opened, providing their content as the starting elements that make it easier to create other documents.

System 7-Savvy Software applications that pass Apple's checklist for compatibility and compliance with System 7. This checklist includes support for MultiFinder, the Edition Manager, IAC, Balloon Help, File Sharing, 32-bit addressing, Stationery Pads and more.

32-bit addressing A method of addressing memory which makes it possible for users of certain Macs to use up to 128 Mb of actual memory, and up to 1 gigabyte of virtual memory. Some software is incompatible with 32-bit addressing. The current standard is 24-bit addressing, which is still used on all other Macs, and with software that is not compatible with 32-bit addressing.

TrueType An outline font format created by Apple for System 7. TrueType fonts are scaled on-screen to provide smooth high-resolution display, and print at the resolution of the output device on either PostScript or QuickDraw printers.

Virtual memory A scheme which allows hard drive space to act like RAM, providing applications with additional memory. Because it uses hard drive space in place of SIMMs, virtual memory comes as close to providing something for nothing as anything you're likely to find on the Macintosh.

Index

A

About The Finder dialog box   317
About This Macintosh dialog
  box   181, 314-17, 324
Access privileges   290-92
    examples of use   280-83
    Groups   280
    Guests   280
    options   275-83
    owner of folders & volumes   279
    Registered Users   280
    seeing assigned   291
Adobe Type Manager   329-32
    acquiring   330
    control panel   332
    disadvantages   329-30
    requirements for use   330-31
    versions   331-32
Alert dialogs
    defined   12-13
Alias Stylist   351
AliasBOSS   352
Aliases   76-96
    aliasing aliases   84-85
    control panels   120
    creating   31, 81, 354
    defined   76-77
    deleting   85, 353-54, 369, 375
    edition files   206, 211
    features   77-78
    file organizing   79-80
    Find command   105

finding information   67-73
folders   88-89
Get Info dialog box   72-73, 86-87
hard drive remote access   95
launching applications   78, 90-92, 143-44
managing   352
moving   82
multiple   84, 92-93
names   81-82
network file access   81, 94-95, 292-93, 353
original files
    deleting   86
    finding   86-87
    moving   82-83, 85-86
    renaming   82-83
removable file access   80, 93-94
renaming   81, 83
replacing icons   87
Stationery Pads   150
summary   95-96
Trash   94
type style   351
uses of   78-81, 90-95
utilities   351-54
volumes   89-90
AliasZoo   353
Always snap to grid option   39
Apple color wheel   110
Apple Events   212-15
    Core   213
    Custom   214

defined   212
Functional-area   213
language   212-13
required   213
System 7 Savvy   138
Apple Installer   129
Apple Menu
alphabetizing files   118-19
launching applications   91-92, 142-43
modifying contents   117
utilities   346-48
Apple Menu Items folder   116-19
adding items   117
file types   117
AppleShare
System 7 Savvy   138-39
AppleTalk   252
See also File Sharing; Networks
Application Not Found dialog box   140-41
Applications
active   168-69
background   168-69
closing   179-80
finding information   67-73
foreground   168-69
hiding   176-78, 180
launching   139-44, 332-33, 399
from Apple Menu   91-92, 142-43
automatically at startup   142
memory required   182-83
methods   140-44
using aliases   78, 90-92, 143-44
linking information between
See Edition Manager; IAC
memory size   70, 318-23, 325
memory usage   324-25
monitoring memory   316, 323-24
multiple, automatic updating in
See Edition Manager
multiple, working with
See Multitasking
opening various doc types   368, 371
switching between   170, 179
Applications menu   33-34, 170
At Ease   332-33, 399

B

Background printing   172-74
cancelling   174
delaying   174
turning off   172
Background processing   171-78
copying files   175
defined   164-65
hiding applications   176-78
printing
See Background printing
Backups
before installing System 7   379-80
quick and dirty   106
using labels   108
Balloon Help   61-64
displaying   62
Helium Pro   374
limitations   63
removing   62
System 7 Savvy   138
See also Help menu
Balloon Help menu   33
Bitmapped fonts
compared with PostScript   220-21
defined   218
limitations   218-19

Blindfold   368
Borders   200–201
Bulletin board folder   282

C

Calculate folder sizes option   40–41
Calendar   372
Cancel Publisher option   196–97
Cancel Subscriber option   199
Carpetbag   357
Catapult   368
CD-ROMs
    movies   339–40
Cdevs
    See Control panels
Chameleon   372–73
Check boxes, defined   12
Chooser   286–87
    defined   19
CIE XYZ color standard   341
Clean Up All command   59–60
Clean Up By Name (By Size, etc.)
    command   60–61
Clean Up command   33
Clean Up Desktop command   59
Clean Up options   59–61
Clean Up Selection command   61
Clean Up Window command   60
Clicking, defined   16
Client, defined   248
Clip option   195–96
Clipboard   23–24
Color
    additive   341
    Apple color wheel   110
    icons   371

    labels   32, 109–10
    matching print & screen   340–42
    monitor display   20–21
    subtractive   341
ColorSync   340–42
    how it works   341–42
Commands, menu   14–15
Comments   110–12, 375
    searching by   111
    Stationery Pads   150
Compatibility
    Compatibility Checker   382–85
Compressing data
    See Movies, compressing
Connect dialog box   288–89
Control panels   20–23
    aliases   120
    defined   6, 20, 36, 119
    System Folder   390
    See also specific names of control
        panels
Control Panels folder   119–21
Copy command   24
Copying   23–26
Copyright screen   317
Crashes
    installing System 7   390–91
    multitasking   179
    startup   122–23, 390–91
    32-bit addressing   312
Create Publisher command   191–92
Create Publisher dialog box   192
Cursor   15–16
    actions with   16
    speed of   21–22
Custom Killer   368
Customize dialog box   387–89
Cut command   23–24

D

Deflate 368
DeIcon 368
Desk accessories 156-58
    closing 158
    converting to System 7
      applications 157-58, 391
    defined 6-7
    icons 157
    launching 158
Desktop 152-54
    cleaning 59-60
    defined 152
    managing 374
    patterns 372-73
    System 7 29
    System 6 28, 369
Desktop Deleter 369
Desktop Extras 374
Dialog boxes 11-13
    defined 11
    keyboard equivalents 154-56
    opening Edition Manager 209
    options 12
    System 6 153
    System 7 153
    See also specific names of
      dialog boxes
Disk cache 312
    defined 305
    size 306
Disk First Aid 380-81
Disks
    displaying information about 41-42
    formatting 18-19
    See also Hard drive
Dot-matrix printers
    TrueType fonts 238

Double-clicking, defined 16
Dragging, defined 16

E

Easy Install dialog box 387
Edition files
    accessing 202
      removable media 205-6
    aliases 206, 211
    borders 200-201
    creating 191-92
    defining included items 195-96
    editing 199-200
      without changing original
        document 200
    Finder 202-7
    how they work 187-91
    importing to current
      document 193, 199
    links 203-5
      cancelling 196-97, 199, 204
      recreating 204-5
    locating 194-95, 198
    nesting 208-9
    networks 206-7
    overwriting 207-8
    saving 209-10
    updating 195, 198, 203
Edition is Missing dialog box 206
Edition Manager 185-211
    advantages 186-87
    features 186
    how it works 187-91
    opening dialog boxes 209
    support in applications 185
    System 7 Savvy 138
    tips 207-11

Empty Trash command 33, 64-65
Enablers
    See System enablers
Extension Manager 362-63
Extensions 121-23, 327-43
    advantages 327
    defined 6
    disabling at startup 123
    folder 121-23
    incompatibility 122-23
    managing 360-63
    positioning 123
    System Folder 130, 390

F

File Sharing 31, 245-84
    access privileges 268-73
        See also Access privileges
    allowing changes 278-80
    allowing user to connect 263
    computer name 254
    configuring 253-68
    defined 246-47
    displaying files 277
    displaying folders 276-77
    Groups
        See Groups
    Guests
        See Guests
    icons 273-74
    installing 253, 388
    items to share 248-49
    limitations 249-50
    Macs running System 6 299-300
    manipulating folders &
        volumes 272-73
    menus 359-60
    monitoring 283-84
    monitoring users 359
    owner
        See Macintosh Owner
    passwords 254, 262-63
        changing 263-64
    preparing to use 250-83
        summary 250-51
    Program Linking
        See Program Linking
    Registered Users
        See Registered Users
    security 254, 268
    slowdowns 284
    starting 254-55
    System 7 Savvy 138-39
    toggling on & off 360
    turning off 255-58, 274-75
    utilities 359-60
    See also Networks
File Sharing Monitor dialog box 283
File Sharing Toggle 360
FileMapper 371
Files
    categorizing with labels 108-9
    comments 110-12
    copying 175, 371
    deleting 33, 369
        See also Trash
    displaying in File Sharing 277
    dragging 54-56
    editing technical info 369
    finding 31-32, 58, 96-107
        by comments 111
        group size 370
        information 67-73
        multiple criteria 107
        by name 98-100
        search options 101-4
        by specific application 106

hiding 368
jumping to 52
kinds 45-46
labels 107-10
locking 69-70, 369
managing 75-112
manipulating 17-18
multiple, working with 55-57
names, editing 53
organizing with aliases 79-80
recovering missing 369
renaming 370
retrieving deleted 66
security requirements 109
selecting by keyboard 52
sharing
   See File Sharing
sorting by
   comment 48
   date 47
   kind 45-46
   label 46
   size 44-45
   version 47
Find Again command 31, 100, 103, 105
Find button 103
Find command 31, 96-107
   accessing from applications 97-98
   aliases 105
   system files 105
   tips 105-7
Find dialog box 98-100
   accessing from Find Item dialog box 104
Find File desk accessory 96-97
Find Item dialog box 100-105
   search options 101-4
Find Original button 86-87

Finder 27-73
   defined 5
   desktop
      See Desktop
   edition files 202-7
   improving performance 363-67
   menus 29-34
   purpose 27
   quitting 370
   restricting access 332-33, 399
Finder Shortcuts dialog box 63
Finder windows 34-61
   attributes 34-35
   Clean Up commands 59-61
   comments displayed 112
   controlling appearance 36-43
   customizing 42-43
   fonts 37-38
   scrolling 56-57
FinderExpress 371
Floppy disks
   See Disks
Folders
   access privileges 258-60, 268-73
      See also Access privileges
   aliasing 88-89
   deleting empty 369
   designating owner 269-70
   displaying contents 48-51
      hierarchy 57-59
      See also Hierarchical views
   displaying in File Sharing 276-77
   finding 106
   finding group size 370
   finding information 67-73
   fonts 357
   manipulating 17-18, 272-73
   owners 279

renaming 370
size displayed 40-41
Stationery Pads 150-51
unsharing nested 271-72
See also specific types of folders
Fonts 217-43
adding to System file 128, 228
bitmapped 218-19
See also Bitmapped fonts
deleting 234
Finder windows 37-38
formats 243
history 218-26
icons 230
ID numbers 225-26
installing 228-34
duplicate names 232-33
managing 231-33, 242-43
utilities 354-57
multiple formats, working with 240-43
PostScript 219-27
See also PostScript fonts
removing from System file 128
sizes, System 7 Savvy 138
specifying folders 357
transferring 225-26
TrueType 234-40
See also TrueType fonts
Fonts folder 123-24, 231-33
Force Quit dialog box 179

G

General control panel 20
Get Edition Now option 199
Get Editions option 198

Get Info dialog box 67-73, 317-25
aliases 72-73, 86-87
information provided 68-69
options 69-71
Stationery Pads 147
System 7 318-20
System 7.1 320-23
Trash 71-72
versions 68
GetInfo 369
Graphical User Interface 9-16
Grouch 351
Groups
access privileges 270, 280
See also Access privileges
adding Macintosh owner 264
adding users 264-65
checking user membership 265
creating 264-65
defined 259
deleting users 265
Guests
access privileges 270, 280
See also Access privileges
connecting to networks 288-89
defined 260
preferences 265-66

H

HAM 347
Hard disk driver
System 7 compatible 380-81
Hard drive
accessing remotely 95, 294
backups before installing
System 7 379-80

checking 380-81
freeing space 102-3
managing 75-112
Helium Pro 374
Help
    removing 368
    See also Balloon Help; Help menu
Help balloons
    See Balloon Help
Help menu 61-64
    See also Balloon Help
Helping Hand 131-32
Hide Balloons command 62
Hide Current Application command 177
Hide Others command 178
Hierarchical views 48-51
    advantages 49-50
    capabilities 50
    collapsing 51
    keyboard commands 53

I

IAC (Inter-Application Communication) 211-15
    defined 212
    support in applications 185, 213
Icon Views 38-39
Icons
    color 371
    customizing 68-69
    defined 9
    desk accessories 157
    fonts 230
    positioning 33, 38-39, 59
    removing from desktop 368
    replacing aliases 87
    restoring original 368

samples 10
shared items 273-74
size 40
suitcase 156-57
In Box folder 281
Informant 372
Init Loader 363
Init Picker 361
INIT See Extensions
Installation 377-91
    customizing options 387-89
    deleting old system software 385-86
    hard drive backup 379-80
    hard drive checking 380-81
    hardware requirements 378
    incompatible files 383, 390-91
    running installer 386-89
    software compatibility 381-85, 390-91
    summary of steps 379
    transferring System Folder 389-91
Inter-Application Communication
    See IAC

K

Keyboard
    commands 51-53, 154-56
    System file 127-28

L

Label control panel 32
Label menu 32
    configuring 107-8

Labels 32, 107-10
    color 109-10
    uses 108-9
Labels control panel 107-8
LaserWriter drivers
    updating 297-99
Linking information between applications
    See Edition Manager; IAC
List Views option 39
Locksmith 369

M

Macintosh
    basic operations 9-26
    copyright screen 317
    font history 218-26
    learning about 30
    monitoring system
        resources 314-17, 372
    Performa series 398-99
Macintosh Owner 254, 260
    Preferences dialog box 267-68
Make Alias command 31
Make Changes option 278-80
Marquee 55
MasterJuggler 356
Memory 301-26
    applications 70, 316, 318-23, 325
    computer vs. human 303
    defined 302
    how applications use 324-25
    launching applications 182-83
    managing 313-26
    monitoring 181, 314-17
        applications' usage 323-24
    multitasking 168, 180-83
    setting options 323-25

total available 315
unused blocks 315-16
usage 181
See also RAM; Virtual memory
Memory control panel 303-13
    tips 312-13
MenuChoice 348
MenuExtend 348
Menus 14-16
    creating hierarchical 346-48
    defined 14
    File Sharing 359-60
    Finder 29-34
    tear-off 374
    See also specific names of menus
Mighty Menus 374
MODE 32 328
Monitors control panel 20-21
Mount Alias 353
Mouse
    operating 15-16, 21-22
Mouse control panel 21-22
Movies 333-40
    CD-ROMs 339-40
    compressing 337-39
    controls 336
    estimating size 338-39
    manipulating 335-36
    poster 336
    previews 336
    watching stand-alone 340
MultiFinder 156, 161-62
    disadvantages 165-66
    See also Multitasking
Multimedia
    See Movies
Multitasking 33-34, 161-83
    advantages 163-65
    defined 162
    memory 168, 180-83

resuming after crashing 179
System 7 Savvy 138
tips 179-80
See also Background processing

N

Names
    aliases 81-83
    File Sharing computers 254
    files, editing 53
    Macintosh Owner 254
    PostScript fonts 226
    Stationery Pads 146-47
Network control panel 252
Network drivers
    defined 5
    installing 389
Networks 285-300
    accessing your computer remotely 268
    advantages 245-46, 285
    connecting to 286-89
    edition files 206-7
    file access with aliases 81, 94-95, 292-93, 353
    installing 251-52
    Macs running System 6 299-300
    mounting volumes automatically 290
    selecting volumes 289-90
    See also File Sharing
NFNT 225-26
Nok Nok 359
NowMenus 4.01 347-48

O

Obliterate 369
On Startup 362
Open Publisher option 199-200
Open Stationery Pad dialog box 148
Operating system *See* System software
Option boxes, defined 12
    See also specific names of options
Out box folder 280-81

P

Paging 309
Palette 13
Passwords
    File Sharing 254, 262-63
    changing 263-64
Paste command 24
PC disks
    mounting on desktop 328-29
PC Exchange 328-29
Performa
    See Macintosh, Performa series
Pesticide 369
Pink Slip 370
Placeholders 146
Pointing the cursor 16
Pop-up menus 12
PostScript fonts 219-27
    compared with bitmapped 220-21
    drawing smoothly on screen 329-32
    examples 236-37
    identifying on screen 222-23

menus   224
names   226
printing   221-24, 227
problems   222-26
Type 1 format   226
vs. TrueType   235-37
PostScript printers
   PostScript fonts   227
   TrueType fonts   239
PowerMenus   348
Preferences folder   124-25
Printer drivers
   defined   5
   installing   388
Printer fonts   221-22
   availability   223-24
   locating   233-34
Printer Picker   374
Printers
   dot-matrix   238
   PostScript   227, 239
   QuickDraw   238-39
   selecting   374
   sharing laser   297-99
   TrueType   240
Printing
   PostScript fonts   221-24, 227
   TrueType fonts   238-40
   See also Background printing
PrintMonitor   172-74
PrintMonitor dialog box   173
Program Linking   214-15, 258, 264
   enabling   295-96
   initiating   296-97
Publish/Subscribe
   See Edition Manager
Publisher   188
Publisher Options command   194-97

Publisher Options dialog box   194-97
Publisher To option   194-95

Q

QuickDraw printers
   TrueType fonts   238-39
QuickTime movies   333-40
   acquiring   334-35
   using   339-40
   see also Movies
QuickTime Compression Options
  dialog box   337

R

Radio buttons   12
RAM
   amount installed   315
   amount needed   313
   amount possible   310, 312
   defined   302
   setting parameters   370
   See also Memory
Rasterization   227
Recoverup   369
Red Alert   371
Registered Users   259-64
   access privileges   270, 280
     See also Access privileges
   connecting to networks   288
   creating   261
   defined   259
   preferences   262-64

ROM
      defined   5
      32-bit addressing   310-11

S

Save Changes dialog box   180
Scale   370
Scrapbook   25-26
Screen fonts
      displaying samples   229-30
      identifying   223
      identifying format   229
      installing   228-31
      menus   224
      PostScript vs. bitmapped   220-21
      PostScript vs. non-PostScript   222-23
      suitcases   229-31
Screen savers   373
SCSI Startup   370
Security
      File Sharing   254, 268
      using labels   109
See Files option   277
See Folders option   276-77
Send Edition Now option   195
Send Editions option   195
Server   248
Set Print Time dialog box   174
7 for Seven   367
7.0 PLUS Utilities   368-70
7th Heaven   371-73
Sharing command   31, 268
Sharing dialog box   260, 268-73
Sharing Setup dialog box   253
Show All command   178
Show Balloons command   33, 62
Show Borders command   200-201
Show disk info in header option   41-42
ShowShare   359-60
Shutdown dialog box   256
Snap option   195-96
Software compatibility
      See System 7 compatibility
Sound
      adding to System file   128
      managing   370, 374
      removing from System file   128
      system beep   22-23
Sound control panel   22-23
Sound Roundup   370
Speed Beep Pro   374
SpeedyFinder7   365-66
Staggered grid option   38-39
Startup drive   370
Startup Items folder   125, 142
Startup Manager   361-62
Stationer   370
Stationery Pads   70-71, 144-51, 370
      aliases   150
      comments   150
      creating   145-47
      defined   144
      editing   148-49, 151
      folders   150-51
      Get Info dialog box   147
      names   146-47
      opening   147-49
         Open command   151
      System 7 Savvy   139
Storage   302
Straight grid option   38-39
Subscribe To command   193
Subscribe To dialog box   193
Subscriber Options command   197-200
Subscriber Options dialog box   197-200

Subscribers
   defined   189
   editing   201-2
Suitcase   355
Suitcases
   fonts   355-56
   icons   156-57
   screen fonts   229-31
Super Comments   375
Super Seven Utilities   373-75
System enablers   396, 402-4
   problems   404
   versions for Macintosh models   403
System extensions
   See Extensions
System file   126-33
   access   126-28
   adding fonts   128
   adding sounds   128
   defined   4-5
   keyboard configurations   127-28
   removing fonts   128
   removing sounds   128
System File Cannot Be Changed
   dialog box   228
System Folder   113-33
   adding files   129-32
      Apple Installer   129
      application software   130
      manually   131-32
   configuring   389-91
   control panels   390
   deleting files   132
   extensions   123, 390
   modifying   128-29
   organization   115-25
   System 6   114-15
   transferring from System 6   389-91
System Picker   358-59

System resource
   monitoring   314-17, 372
System 7
   dialog boxes   153
   enhancing performance   394-95
   Finder desktop   29
   hardware requirements   378
   history   393-404
   installed with System 6   357-59
   installing   377-91
      See also Installation
   upgrading   392
   Version 7.1   395-98
      acquiring   397
      Hardware System Update   398
   versions   393-94
      choosing   399-402
      Performa series   398-99
System 7 compatibility   136-39
   checking software   381-85
   defined   137
   testing files   390-91
System 7 disk   345
System 7 installer   386-89
System 7 Pack   363-65
System 7 Savvy   137
   requirements for   137-39
System 7 Tuner   394-95
System 6
   desktop   28, 369
   dialog boxes   153
   installed with System 7   357-59
   MultiFinder   156, 161-62, 165-66
   replacing with System 7
      See Installation
   System Folder   114-15
   transferring folder to
      System 7   389-91
   using on networks   299-300
   using with File Sharing   299-300

System software
    components 4-7
    defined 2
    deleting old 385-86
    enablers
        See System enablers
    functions 2-4
    options at installation 387-89
    switching between versions 357-59
    tasks performed 7-8
    updates 377
    upgrades 377
    See also System 7; System 6
System Switcher 358

T

Templates
    See Stationery Pads
32-bit addressing 310-12
    crashes 312
    defined 311
    effect on RAM 312
    effect on virtual memory 312
    incompatibility 312
    solving incompatibility 328
    System 7 Savvy 138
Title bar pop-up menu 57-59
Transferring data between applications
    See Edition Manager
Trash
    aliasing 94
    emptying 64-66, 369
    Get Info dialog box 71-72
    positioning 67
    retrieving 66
    tips 66
    utilities 349-51
    warning before emptying 71-72
    See also Files, deleting
Trash Alias 375
Trash Chute 2.0 351
TrashAlias 1.1.1 354
TrashMan 350
TrashMaster 1.1 349
TrashPicker 1.0 350
TrueType fonts 234-40
    defined 234
    examples 236
    how they work 238-40
    printing 238-40
    vs. PostScript 235-37
TrueType scaling printers 240
Tune-Up 394-95
24-bit addressing 311

U

Unsharing files 274-75
User Options dialog box 296
User Preferences dialog box 262
Users & Groups control panel 258-59
Utilities 19-23, 345-75
    aliases 351-54
    Apple Menu 346-48
    collections 366-75
    extension managers 360-63
    File Sharing 359-60
    Finder 363-67
    font managers 354-57
    system software selectors 357-59
    Trash 349-51

V

Vector Plasma   373
View menu   44-48
    By Comment command   48
    By Date command   47
    By Icon command   44
    By Kind command   45-46
    By Label command   46
    By Size command   44-45
    By Small Icon command   44
    By Version command   47
Views, hierarchical
    See Hierarchical views
Views control panel   36-43
    accessing   36
    options   37
Virtual memory   306-10, 313
    advantages   306-7
    amounts provided   307
    defined   306
    determining size   308-10
    disabling   310
    disadvantages   307
    effect of 32-bit addressing   312
    enabling   308-9
    how it works   309-10
    requirements for using   307
Volumes
    access privileges   258-60, 268-73
      See also Access privileges
    accessing remotely
      See File Sharing; Networks
    aliasing   89-90
    designating owner   269-70
    disconnecting from remote   293-94
    finding   106
    finding information   67-73
    manipulating   272-73
    mounting automatically   290
    mounting shortcut   292-93
    owners   279
    selecting on networks   289-90

W

Wait!   370
Windows   11-13
    cleaning up   60-61
    closing   58-59
    defined   11
    display in active   44-48
    sizing   59

Z

Zap!   370
ZMakeAlias   354
Zooming   59

No-Risk Offer — 10 FREE HOURS OF TRIAL TIME

America's Most Exciting Online Service!

The Official America Online Membership Kit & Tour Guide puts the world at your fingertips — AT NO RISK! You'll find everything you need to take full advantage of this exciting online service, including:

◆ The America Online starter disk.

◆ 10 FREE hours of online time for new & current members — a **$60.00 value!**

◆ A readable, richly illustrated "traveling companion" to help you get the most from your time online.

With *The Official America Online Membership Kit & Tour Guide*, you can quickly access and download over 28,000 Mac software programs; get expert computing advice from top hardware and software companies; access stocks quotes, buy and sell stocks online and track your investments with an online portfolio management system. Plus international electronic mail, fax, US mail, message boards and more!

Novice and experienced online users alike will find *The Official America Online Membership Kit & Tour Guide* an exciting, value-packed alternative to the slower, command-structure services.

To order *The Official America Online Membership Kit & Tour Guide*, use the form in the back of this book or contact your local bookstore.

ISBN: 1-56604-012-4
Tom Lichty
402 pages plus disk $34.95

PUT SOME SPIN ON YOUR MAC!

Fun and increased productivity are at your fingertips with books that extend, enhance and excite your Mac. Ventana Press offers bestselling guides packed with games (games and more games!) plus a wealth of never-before-published tips, tricks, amusing novelties and hints to make your Mac even more enjoyable!

Whether you're a power user looking for new shortcuts or a beginner trying to make sense of it all, *Voodoo Mac* has something for everyone! Computer veteran Kay Nelson has compiled hundreds of invaluable tips, tricks, hints and shortcuts that simplify your Macintosh tasks and save time, including disk and drive magic, font and printing tips, alias alchemy and more!

Voodoo Mac
Kay Yarborough Nelson
ISBN: 1-56604-028-0
$21.95   340 pages

Ready, set, play! Your one-stop guide to fun and games on the Macintosh, *MacArcade* is the best deal going. Author Don Rittner has hand-picked the top 40 Mac shareware games, compiling them in this easy-to-use book/disk set. Plus, this unbeatable entertainment resource includes two high-density disks loaded with the best of the best—Rittner's top 10 games—ready to play!

MacArcade
Don Rittner
ISBN: 1-56604-038-8
$27.95   213 pages

To order these and other Ventana Press titles, use the form in the back of this book or contact your local bookstore or computer store. Full money-back guarantee!

For faster service, order toll-free 800/743-5369.
Ventana Press, P.O. Box 2468, Chapel Hill, NC 27515 (919) 942-0220; Fax: (919) 942-1140

ATTENTION AMERICA ONLINE USERS:
Hit keyword Mac500 for more information!

The Ultimate Mac Shareware Resource!

Prevost & Terrell
376 pages, 4 disks
$39.95

W hether you're a shareware veteran or skeptic, this book is required reading. Authors Ruffin Prevost, Rob Terrell and a team of impartial reviewers have carefully examined thousands of programs and handpicked the best. The only comprehensive guide to 500 of the best Mac shareware programs, *The Mac Shareware 500* is a four-disk, 376 page set offering users a program overview, tips for shareware sources, extensive operating instructions and much more.

The Mac Shareware 500 **also provides invaluable information on**

- ✹ The many different varieties of shareware, including an in-depth look at the politics and ethics of the shareware community.
- ✹ The best sources for acquiring shareware, whether you're buying direct from the author, receiving it through a user group or disk duplication service, or downloading it from your favorite online service.
- ✹ Checking your shareware for viruses, quickly and easily.
- ✹ Solving compatibility problems.

The book is packaged with three disks of the authors' top program picks from a variety of shareware categories, including business, games, clip art, fonts, utilities and more.

With the purchase of this book, you'll also receive five hours of free time on America Online whether you're a new or current member.

the Ventana Press

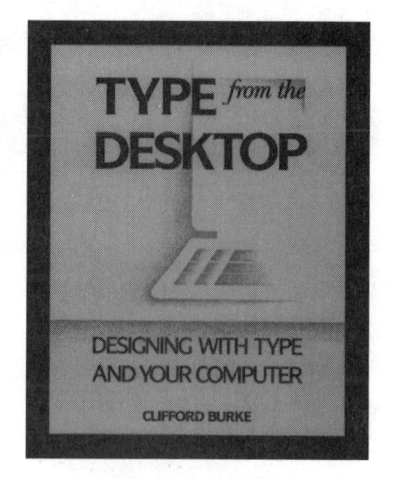

Desktop Design Series

Available from bookstores or Ventana Press. Immediate shipment guaranteed. Your money returned if not satisfied. To order or for more information contact:

Ventana Press, P.O. Box 2468, Chapel Hill, NC 27515
800/743-5369 (orders only)   919/942-0220   Fax 919/942-1140

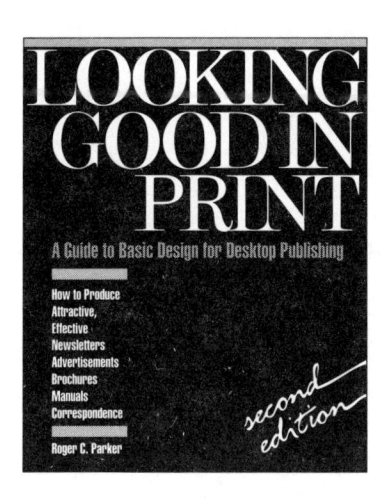

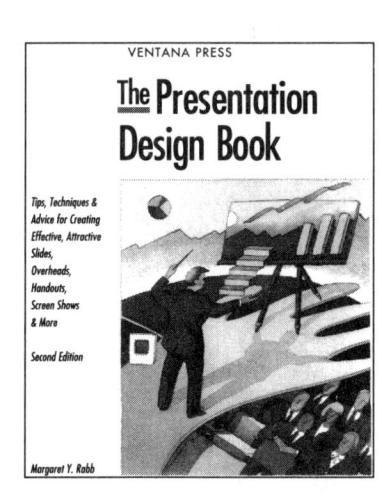

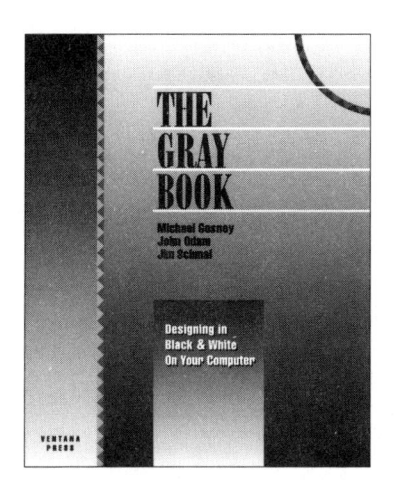

Newsletters From the Desktop
$23.95
306 pages, illustrated
ISBN: 0-940087-40-5

Now the millions of desktop publishers who produce newsletters can learn how to improve the design of their publications.

The Makeover Book: 101 Design Solutions for Desktop Publishing
$17.95
245 pages, illustrated
ISBN: 0-940087-20-0

"Before-and-after" desktop publishing examples demonstrate how basic design revisions can dramatically improve a document.

Type from the Desktop
$23.95
290 pages, illustrated
ISBN: 0-940087-45-6

Learn the basics of designing with type from a desktop publisher's perspective.

Looking Good in Print, Second Edition
$23.95
410 pages, Illustrated
ISBN: 0-940087-32-4

With over 200,000 copies in print, **Looking Good in Print** is looking even better. More makeovers, a new section on designing newsletters and a wealth of new design tips and techniques to broaden the design skills of the ever-growing number of desktop publishers.

The Presentation Design Book, Second Edition
$24.95
258 pages, illustrated
ISBN: 1-56604-014-0

How to design effective, attractive slides, overheads, graphs, diagrams, handouts and screen shows with your desktop computer.

The Gray Book Designing in Black and White on Your Computer
$22.95
208 pages, illustrated
ISBN: 0-940087-50-2

This "idea gallery" for desktop publishers offers a lavish variety of the most interesting black, white and gray graphics effects that can be achieved with laser printers, scanners and high-resolution output devices.

TO ORDER additional copies of *The System 7 Book, Second Edition* or any other Ventana Press book, please fill out this order form and return it to us for quick shipment.

	Quantity		Price		Total
The System 7 Book, Second Edition	_____	x	$24.95	=	$_____
The Official America Online Membership Kit & Tour Guide: Mac Edition	_____	x	$34.95	=	$_____
The Mac Shareware 500 Book/Disk Set	_____	x	$39.95	=	$_____
Voodoo Mac	_____	x	$21.95	=	$_____
Looking Good in Print	_____	x	$23.95	=	$_____
Type From the Desktop	_____	x	$23.95	=	$_____
The Presentation Design Book	_____	x	$24.95	=	$_____
The Gray Book	_____	x	$22.95	=	$_____
Newsletters From the Desktop	_____	x	$23.95	=	$_____
The Makeover Book	_____	x	$17.95	=	$_____
MacArcade	_____	x	$27.95	=	$_____

Shipping: Please add $4.50/first book for standard UPS, $1.35/book thereafter; $8.25/book UPS "two-day air," $2.25/book thereafter. For Canada, add $8.10/book. $_____

Send C.O.D. (add $4.50 to shipping charges) $_____
North Carolina residents add 6% sales tax $_____

                                                        Total $_____

Name _____ Co. _____

Address (No PO Box) _____

City _____ State _____ Zip _____

Daytime telephone _____

_____ VISA _____ MC Acc't # _____

Exp. Date _____ Interbank # _____

Signature _____

Please mail or fax to:
Ventana Press, PO Box 2468, Chapel Hill, NC 27515
800/743-5369 (orders only); 919/942-0220; FAX: 800/877-7955

TO ORDER additional copies of *The System 7 Book, Second Edition* or any other Ventana Press book, please fill out this order form and return it to us for quick shipment.

	Quantity		Price		Total
The System 7 Book, Second Edition	_____	x	$24.95	=	$_____
The Official America Online Membership Kit & Tour Guide: Mac Edition	_____	x	$34.95	=	$_____
The Mac Shareware 500 Book/Disk Set	_____	x	$39.95	=	$_____
Voodoo Mac	_____	x	$21.95	=	$_____
Looking Good in Print	_____	x	$23.95	=	$_____
Type From the Desktop	_____	x	$23.95	=	$_____
The Presentation Design Book	_____	x	$24.95	=	$_____
The Gray Book	_____	x	$22.95	=	$_____
Newsletters From the Desktop	_____	x	$23.95	=	$_____
The Makeover Book	_____	x	$17.95	=	$_____
MacArcade	_____	x	$27.95	=	$_____

Shipping: Please add $4.50/first book for standard UPS, $1.35/book thereafter; $8.25/book UPS "two-day air," $2.25/book thereafter. For Canada, add $8.10/book. $_____

Send C.O.D. (add $4.50 to shipping charges) $_____
North Carolina residents add 6% sales tax $_____

                  Total $_____

Name _____ Co. _____

Address (No PO Box) _____

City _____ State _____ Zip _____

Daytime telephone _____

_____ VISA _____ MC Acc't # _____

Exp. Date _____ Interbank # _____

Signature _____

Please mail or fax to:
Ventana Press, PO Box 2468, Chapel Hill, NC 27515
800/743-5369 (orders only); 919/942-0220; FAX: 800/877-7955

FINALLY! Mac News You Can Use From a Name You Can Trust!

If you keep up with magazines and trade publications about the Macintosh, you may have noticed how it's sometimes hard to tell the news from the snooze. But now you've got a source you can rely on. Because Ventana Press accepts no advertisements in our newsletters, we won't be swayed by the market propaganda. You'll get the straight dope on the things that matter to Mac users, compiled by the best writers in the business...our authors.

**2 Free Issues
The Ventana Mac Update**

In your two free issues of *The Ventana Mac Update*, you'll get the facts—and just the facts—on all the hot topics: the inside track on System 7, tips and tricks that will make anyone a power user, shareware bargains, and impartial hardware and software reviews.

If you purchased *The System 7 Book* directly from Ventana Press, you'll receive *The Ventana Mac Update* automatically. If you bought the book elsewhere, complete the form below and return it to Ventana Press, PO Box 2468, Chapel Hill, NC 27515. Fax 919/942-1140.

Order card for *The Ventana Mac Update*. Please send me two free updates on the latest news in the Macintosh community:

Name _____

Company _____

Address _____

City _____ State _____ Zip _____

Country _____ Telephone _____

To help you get the most from your system software...

we've compiled the best shareware & freeware utilities available for every version of System 7 into this value-packed companion disk! Customizing your system software is a snap with these time-saving productivity enhancers, including

- **System 7 Pack**   This great utility provides tons of handy Finder enhancements, including faster file copying, application linking, Command-key shortcuts, faster file name editing and quicker window opening.
- **AliasBOSS**   Alias management simplified—this helpful program makes it easy to create new aliases for groups of files, manage aliases you've already created and more!
- **Extensions Manager**   A great freeware program offering a host of powerful capabilities, including reordering startup items, creating and choosing extension groups and the ability to configure extension loading at start-up.
- **System Switcher**   This gem lets you designate which System Folder you want to use when you next restart, allowing you to switch seamlessly between System 6 and System 7, even on the same hard drive.
- **Trash Picker**   Allows you to specify if and when the trash should be emptied, including on startup or shutdown, at any timed intervals, or only when available disk space falls below a certain level.

Save money and time with these and many other invaluable fonts and utilities on *The System 7 Book Companion Disk*. To order, complete the order card below and return it with your payment:

Ventana Press, PO Box 2468, Chapel Hill, NC 27515
To order, call 800/743-5369
Other inquiries: 919/942-0220; Fax: 919/942-1140

YES, please send _____ copies of *The System 7 Book Companion Disk, Second Edition* at $9.95/disk. Please add $4.10 for regular UPS ground service; $7.00 for UPS "two-day" air. NC residents add 6% sales tax.
Prompt shipment guaranteed.

Name_____

Company_____

Address_____
             (no PO boxes, please)
City_____State_____Zip_____

Telephone_____

____Payment enclosed (check or money order; no cash, please)

____Charge my VISA/MC Acc't #_____

Expiration date_____ Interbank #_____

Signature_____